Principles of Minnesota Real Estate

Second Edition

Rick Larson

ROCKWELL PUBLISHING
COMPANY

TABLE OF CONTENTS

About the Author

Rick Larson began his career as a real estate salesperson in 1970 in a small, rural, family-owned real estate company. During his sales career, he sold nearly every type of real estate, including residential, agricultural, development, and commercial properties.

In 1977, Mr. Larson began training for a large national franchise organization. He personally trained nearly 1,000 new agents and 250 broker-franchisees.

In 1979, along with his partner, Joe Coyne, Mr. Larson created PROSOURCE Educational Services, one of the nation's largest real estate and insurance schools. Since its inception, more than 30,000 real estate and insurance agents and brokers have attended courses at PROSOURCE.

Mr. Larson has written articles for the *Minnesota Real Estate Journal*, the Minnesota Association of Realtors, the Minnesota Real Estate Advisory Task Force, and other groups. He is co-author of *Minnesota Real Estate,* 2nd Edition (Prentice Hall), and has authored 57 real estate licensing and continuing education courses.

Acknowledgments:

Joe Coyne, Todd Butzer, Dave Schneider, Jeanne Johnson, Janet Holt, Denton See, Lynn Folkens, Denny Anderson, Doug Ayers, Steve Dalluhn, Buck Larson, Tom Lundstedt, Archie Larson, Mary Adema, Carol Martin, Carl Zinn, Roald Marth, Barry Stranz, Lee Weiss, Jim Casey, and the entire administrative staff at PROSOURCE.

Chapter 1

NATURE, DESCRIPTION, AND USE OF REAL ESTATE

OUTLINE

I. Real Estate
   A. Land
   B. Improvements
   C. Rights
      1. air rights
      2. water rights
      3. mineral rights
      4. oil and gas rights
      5. support rights

II. Personal Property vs. Real Estate

III. The Law of Fixtures
   A. Fixtures defined
   B. Tests for fixtures
      1. attachment
      2. adaptation
      3. agreement
      4. relationship of the parties
   C. Exceptions
      1. trade fixtures
      2. emblements

IV. Land Description
   A. Metes and bounds
   B. Rectangular (government) survey
   C. Recorded plat
   D. Other methods of description

V. Government Land Use Controls
    A. Master development plan
        1. land survey
        2. economic survey
    B. Land use classifications
        1. residential
        2. commercial
        3. industrial (manufacturing)
        4. agricultural
        5. mixed use
    C. Land use restrictions
        1. building codes
        2. height limits
        3. setback, sideyard, and rearyard requirements
    D. Zoning changes and deviations
        1. amendments
        2. nonconforming uses
        3. variances
        4. conditional use permits

KEY TERMS

real estate   land
inverted pyramid   improvements
air rights   water rights
mineral rights   oil and gas rights
support rights   personal property
fixtures   attachment
adaptation   trade fixtures
metes and bounds   point of beginning
rectangular survey   principal meridian
base line   correction lines
guide meridians   ranges
township tiers   township
section   government lot
plat   datum
bench mark   zoning
master development plan   nonconforming use

variance   conditional use
building codes   economic survey
amendment   setback
sideyard   rearyard

CHAPTER OVERVIEW

What is real estate? This may seem like a simple question, but many lawsuits have been filed because people disagree about what real estate (or "real property") includes. If an item is considered part of the real estate, it transfers with the land when the land is sold. But if an item is considered personal property, the former owners can take it with them when they leave.

This chapter defines real estate, explains the difference between real estate and personal property, examines ways to determine whether an item would be considered part of the real estate, and explains how real estate is legally described. It also discusses government land use controls, which place limits on the owner's use of real estate.

REAL ESTATE

LAND

Obviously the term "real estate" includes the actual land. But real estate is more than just the surface of the earth.

Real estate includes land, improvements, and rights

A parcel of land can be viewed as an inverted pyramid, with its tip at the center of the globe and its base in the air above the earth's surface. A property owner owns not only the earth's surface but also has rights to things under the surface (such as minerals), and rights to use the airspace above the property.

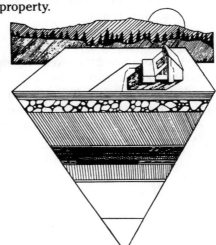

INVERTED PYRAMID

IMPROVEMENTS

Improvements: additions to property, either **of** or **to** the land, that increase its value, use, or enjoyment

Along with the land itself, real estate also includes improvements on the land. Improvements are additions to property that increase its value, use, or enjoyment. In other words, they "improve" the property.

There are two types of improvements: improvements **of** land and improvements **to** land. Examples of improvements of land include utility lines, streets, curbs, and sidewalks. Examples of improvements to land include houses, fences, garages, and other constructed items.

All improvements are part of the real estate

As a practical matter, it is not necessary to differentiate between improvements of land and improvements to land. All improvements are considered part of the real estate. But what about the kitchen appliances inside the house? Are they part of the real estate? How about the hot tub on the deck or the satellite dish in the back yard? If the property is sold can the seller take the satellite dish, or does the new buyer acquire it as part of the sale?

These and similar questions are ones that a real estate agent must know how to answer.

RIGHTS

Along with the land itself and improvements to the land, real estate also includes certain rights that accompany the land, such as the right to mine minerals beneath the surface, or the right to make use of water flowing past the property.

The following basic rights are described below:

- air rights,
- water rights,
- mineral rights,
- oil and gas rights, and
- support rights.

AIR RIGHTS

Air rights: the right to reasonable use of the air-space above land

In theory, using the inverted pyramid model, a landowner's rights extend to the center of the earth and to the upper limits of the sky. In fact, an owner's rights no longer extend to the upper limits of the sky. Through the Air Commerce Act of 1926 and the Civil Aeronautics Act of 1938, Congress gave the federal government complete control over the nation's airspace.

A landowner still has the right to use the lower reaches of airspace over the property, but may do nothing to interfere with normal air traffic.

> **Example:** A tall building lies directly beneath the path of aircraft flying into a nearby airport. The penthouse apartment includes a terrace area. The owner may not use the air above the terrace for any purpose that interferes with air traffic, such as launching high-altitude weather balloons.

This type of restriction is not considered a substantial interference with the owner's property rights. On the other hand, a property owner does still have certain rights in the airspace. If someone uses the airspace above the property in a way that causes substantial interference with the property owner's rights, an owner may be able to collect damages.

> **Example:** A military landing field is built near a chicken farm. Training flights take off and land at all hours of the day and night. The noise and vibrations from overflights are so severe that the chickens no longer lay eggs.
> The property is rocky and unsuitable for growing crops or grazing animals. It is no longer profitable as a chicken farm, but it is zoned agricultural, so the farmer cannot use it for any other purpose. The government may be required to pay compensation to the landowner for the diminished value of the land.

WATER RIGHTS

> A landowner whose property touches flowing water (a river or stream) is called a *riparian* owner. A landowner whose property touches non-flowing water (a pond or lake) is called a *littoral* owner.

All riparian or littoral owners may use the water that adjoins their property for swimming, boating, or other recreational purposes. They also have the right to take water for domestic uses such as drinking, washing, and watering a garden. They may use the water in any way that is "reasonable and beneficial"—that is, not wasteful. However, they may not divert the water for use on

Riparian or littoral rights: the right to reasonable and beneficial use of the water bordering or on the land

non-riparian or non-littoral land—land that does not adjoin or touch the stream or lake from which the water is taken.

> **Example:** Adams owns two lots, one adjoining the river and another across the road. The property across the road is a landlocked field. Adams pipes water from the river to irrigate the landlocked field. This use violates the rules of the riparian system.

A riparian or littoral owner is not allowed to use the water in a way that impairs the rights of other riparian or littoral owners. For example, an upstream owner on a river may not diminish the water flow in quantity, quality, or velocity. In a time of water shortage, all riparian or littoral owners must reduce their use. During a drought, a use that is ordinarily considered reasonable might be prohibited.

Appropriative Rights. Some states have modified riparian and littoral rights with the doctrine of prior appropriation. Especially in the arid western states, water rights are a very significant issue. There is often not enough water to go around, so the right to use water is regulated much more strictly. In these states, landowners whose property touches water still have a right to use the water for things that do not diminish it, such as boating and swimming. However, they may not use the water for other purposes without first obtaining a permit. Whether or not the water actually touches the property it will be used on is irrelevant, as long as the specific use is allowed in the permit.

Under the prior appropriation system, if several people have permits for the same body of water, the party who obtained a permit first can use as much water as the permit allows, even if that leaves too little water for the people who acquired permits later.

Minnesota does have a water appropriation statute, but it does not apply to the use of water for domestic purposes serving fewer than 25 persons. So most domestic use of water in Minnesota is still covered by the riparian and littoral system.

Minnesota allows appropriation of water only for large uses in special circumstances

UNDERGROUND WATER. Water rights also normally include the right to use underground water. In Minnesota, a landowner has the right to his or her share of the water beneath the property, along with neighboring property owners. In states that have a prior appropriation system, a property owner may be required to obtain a permit in order to drill a well or make use of any underground water.

NAVIGABLE WATERS. All navigable waterways in the United States are owned and controlled by the federal or state government. When land borders an ocean, sea, or navigable lake or river, the adjoining property owner only owns the land above the mean high water mark. The government owns all property below the mean high water mark and all property beneath the water.

The public may use all navigable waters

There is a public easement for right of way on all navigable waters. This means that the public has the right to use the waterways for transportation. The public also has the right to make reasonable use of the surface of the water (for swimming or boating, for example), unless specifically prohibited.

NON-NAVIGABLE WATERS. When a lake is non-navigable, it is called a meandering lake. The adjoining property owners own the submerged land. Ownership is generally divided by tracing lines from each property boundary to the center of the lake or stream. Each owner has title to the parcel of lake bed or stream bed adjoining his or her land, out to the middle of the body of water.

Land beneath non-navigable waters is owned out to the center-point of the lake or stream

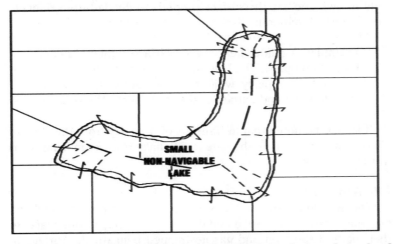

If a small lake is completely within the boundaries of one landowner's property, the landowner owns the entire lake bed.

ACCRETION AND RELICTION. Land beside a lake or river is gradually increased by **accretion** when waterborne silt is deposited on the shore. These deposits of sand or soil are called **alluvion** or **alluvium**. When land is added to by accretion, the landowner acquires title to the newly deposited soil.

Accretion: gradual addition to land beside a body of water

When a navigable body of water recedes gradually, the adjoining landowner acquires title to the newly exposed land. This is called **reliction** or **dereliction.**

SOLID MINERALS

Minerals are part of real property until extracted; then are personal property

Along with air and water rights, a landowner has subsurface rights, which include the right to minerals below the surface (gold, diamonds, silver, coal, iron, opals, copper, etc.). Minerals are considered part of the real property until they are extracted from the earth. Once removed from the earth, they become personal property. Ownership of solid minerals is simple to allocate: if the minerals are situated within the "inverted pyramid" beneath a particular parcel's boundaries, they belong to the owner of the parcel.

A property owner may sell mineral rights separately from the land.

This type of sale is sometimes called a horizontal division. The right to own and use the surface property is divided from rights to the subsurface minerals.

> **Example:** A landowner sells subsurface rights to a coal mining company. The landowner retains the right to use the surface property, while the coal company owns the right to mine and extract coal from beneath the surface.

It should be noted that in transfers of property from the State of Minnesota to individuals, the state traditionally reserves mineral rights in the property.

OIL AND GAS

Oil and gas rights: ownership rights to all oil and gas produced on property

The question of ownership is not so clear with respect to oil and gas, since they are not solid and do not always stay in one place. In their natural state, oil and gas lie trapped beneath the surface in porous layers of earth. However, once an oil or gas reservoir is tapped, the oil or gas begins to flow towards the point where the reservoir was pierced. This is because oil or gas deposits are under great pressure. When a well is drilled, it forms an area of lower pressure toward which the oil or gas migrates. Thus, a well drilled on one parcel of land could theoretically attract all of the oil or gas from surrounding properties.

> **A landowner has the right to drill for oil or gas and owns all of the oil or gas produced from wells on his property. The oil or gas becomes personal property once brought to the surface.**

But a landowner does not actually own the oil or gas until it is brought to the surface. This rule has the effect of stimulating oil and gas production, since the only way for a landowner to protect an interest in underlying oil or gas is to drill a well to keep the oil or gas from migrating to a neighbor's well.

Since most landowners don't have the necessary skill, experience, or equipment to drill for oil or gas themselves, they usually enter into lease agreements with oil or gas companies to drill the wells and extract the oil or gas.

SUPPORT RIGHTS

A landowner also has the right to the natural support provided by the land beside and beneath his or her property. For example, if a property owner has sold underlying mineral rights to a mining company, the mining company must take care not to dig its mines so close to the surface that the surface property caves in.

Support rights: the right to the natural support of the surrounding and underlying land

All of the rights described above are considered part of the real estate, although they may sometimes be severed from the property, as when mineral rights are sold separately from the surface rights. Some surface rights may also be severed from the property.

> **Example:** Johnson owns 80 acres of heavily timbered property. He does not want to sell the property, but he needs to make some money. He sells the timber rights to a local logging company. Johnson still owns the property, but the timber company owns the right to come in and cut down trees on the property. If Johnson sells the property, the new owner does not own the timber rights, because they have been sold to the timber company.

However, unless specifically severed, when real estate is sold or transferred, all of the corresponding rights are transferred along with the land.

PERSONAL PROPERTY vs. REAL ESTATE

Real property: the land, improvements, everything attached to the land, and every right that goes along with ownership

As you've seen, real estate (real property) includes land, improvements, and the rights that go along with land ownership. When a piece of real estate is sold, all of these things are usually included in the sale. They all become the property of the buyers. But anything on the property that is not legally considered part of the real estate is not included in the sale, and can be removed by the sellers.

> Anything that is not classified as part of the real estate is called *personal property*. An item of personal property may also be called a *chattel*.

Personal property: items that are generally movable, such as cars, furniture, and jewelry

Personal property is generally movable—that is, not attached to the land or improvements in any way. Items such as cars, furniture, dishes, books, and jewelry are all personal property. When a house is sold, the sellers usually take all of these with them when they move out.

Fixtures: items of personal property that have become attached to or associated with real estate

The distinction between real estate and personal property sounds like a simple one. However, some items that might ordinarily be considered personal property become attached to or associated with a piece of real estate in such a way that they are legally considered part of the real estate. These are called **fixtures**. It is sometimes difficult to decide whether a particular item is personal property or a fixture, and that leads to many disputes between buyers and sellers. (Can the sellers take the dishwasher with them? What about the hot tub or the satellite dish?) To help parties avoid this type of controversy, a real estate agent needs to understand the law of fixtures.

THE LAW OF FIXTURES

> Fixtures are items that started out as personal property, but are affixed to or associated with land or improvements in such a way that they are now legally part of the real estate.

Example: An owner decides to build a fence around his property. He orders a load of lumber which is delivered to the house. The pile of lumber is personal property. If the owner sells the house now, the lumber would be considered personal property that the seller could take with him when he leaves. However, if the lumber is used to build a fence on the property, it is considered an improvement or a fixture. The fence is attached to the property and is obviously meant to remain with the property.

> **The most significant factor in determining whether or not an item is a fixture is intent.**

What was the intent of the party who placed the item on the property? Was it meant to become part of the real estate or remain personal property?

There must be objective evidence of intent—it isn't enough for the owner to simply claim that he or she always intended to remove the item. In trying to determine true intent, several tests are used. These tests include:

- method of attachment,
- adaptation to the property,
- written agreement, and
- relationship of the parties.

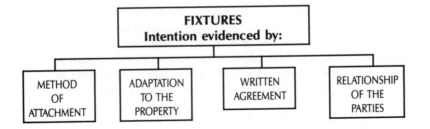

METHOD OF ATTACHMENT

The method of attachment test refers to how the item is attached to the property. If an item is permanently attached, it becomes part of the real estate. An item is considered permanently attached when it is:

- permanently resting on the land (like large buildings, such as houses and barns);
- affixed to the land by roots (as with trees and shrubs);
- embedded in the earth (like sewer lines or septic tanks); or
- attached by an enduring method (cement, plaster, nails, bolts, or screws).

> **When an item is permanently attached by any of these methods, it is considered an improvement or a fixture and is included as part of the real estate.**

Actual annexation: permanent attachment converts items to fixtures

However, an item can also be considered a fixture even when it isn't actually physically attached to the property. Attachment simply by the force of gravity may be sufficient, as in the case of a building without a foundation. An item may also be considered a fixture when it is enclosed within a room or building in such a way that it cannot be removed without dismantling it or tearing down part of the building. In any of these situations, there is said to be **actual annexation**.

Constructive annexation: non-attached items strongly connected with property are considered fixtures

Some completely movable items are so strongly connected with the property that they are considered fixtures, even though they are in no way actually attached. This is called the **doctrine of constructive annexation**. For example, keys to the house or the remote control for an electric garage door opener are considered fixtures.

The doctrine of constructive annexation also applies to items that have been temporarily removed for servicing and repair.

> **Example:** A sells his house to B. At the time of sale, the built-in dishwasher has been removed and is at a repair shop. A built-in dishwasher would normally be considered a fixture. Even though it is not actually in the house at the time of sale, the dishwasher is an item that should go with the house and would still be considered a fixture under the doctrine of constructive annexation.

ADAPTATION OF THE ITEM TO THE REALTY

> **If an item was specially designed or adapted for use in a particular building or is essential to the use of the building, it is probably a fixture.**

Adaptation to a building makes an item a fixture

Examples include items such as storm windows built for a particular building, or a window air conditioner installed in a wall slot.

Computers placed in a general purpose office building are usually considered personal property. However, in a recent lawsuit, components of a computer system housed in a specially built computer facility were held to be fixtures because they were specifically adapted to this particular building.

WRITTEN AGREEMENT

> **Regardless of any of the previously discussed considerations, if there is a written agreement between the parties stipulating how a particular item is to be treated, a court will respect and enforce the agreement.**

Written agreements determine which items are fixtures

When a seller wants to remove things that might be considered fixtures, he or she should inform the buyer, and include a statement in the purchase agreement specifying which items are excluded from the sale.

> **Example:** A house has a large entry hall with a beautiful chandelier hanging from the high ceiling. Prospective buyers looking at the house all admire the chandelier. But the chandelier came from the seller's grandmother, and seller intends to take it with her when she leaves. The seller includes a clause in the purchase agreement, specifically stating that the chandelier is not included as part of the sale.

In Minnesota, it is a common practice to list uncertain items in the purchase agreement. Any questionable items that are specifically included or not included in the sale would be added to the pre-printed purchase agreement form.

RELATIONSHIP OF THE PARTIES

When deciding whether an item is a fixture, the court will also consider the relationship of the parties. Are the parties seller and buyer, borrower and secured lender, or landlord and tenant?

Relationship of the parties is taken into account in fixture disputes

> **Between a seller and a buyer of real estate, the rules for determining what is a fixture are interpreted in favor of the buyer.**

> **Example:** An owner removes a plastic lamp from the entrance hall and replaces it with an expensive chandelier. When the owner sells the house, the chandelier will be considered a fixture that will transfer with the property when the house is sold (unless there is a specific written agreement stating that the chandelier is not included in the sale).

> **Between a borrower and a lender, the rules are interpreted in favor of the lender.**

Example: A borrower removes the lamp in the entrance hall and replaces it with an expensive chandelier. The borrower then defaults on his home loan and the lender forecloses the mortgage on the property. Since the rules are interpreted in favor of the lender, the chandelier is considered a fixture that is part of the real estate and is therefore covered by the lender's lien.

> **But between a landlord and a tenant, the rules are interpreted in favor of the tenant.**

A tenant who is simply renting an apartment probably does not intend to improve the property when he or she installs an item; it's simply for the tenant's own use. Any items installed by a tenant are most likely still personal property.

Example: A tenant removes the plastic lamp in the entrance hall and replaces it with an expensive chandelier. He places the plastic lamp on a closet shelf.

The chandelier would probably be considered personal property, rather than a fixture. When the tenant's lease is up and he moves out, he can remove the chandelier, return the plastic lamp, and take the chandelier with him when he moves.

Trade Fixtures. In a similar fashion, when a tenant installs items for the purpose of carrying on a trade or business, the tenant usually intends to remove the items at the termination of the lease. Such items are called trade fixtures.

Trade fixtures: items installed for the tenant's business: may be removed by the tenant

> **The accepted rule concerning trade fixtures is that they may be removed by the tenant.**

Example: A tenant who operates a beauty parlor installs shampoo basins, lighted mirrors, and adjustable chairs. When the tenant leaves, he may remove these items even though they may be affixed to the walls or floor by bolts and screws. However, the tenant is responsible for repairing any damage to the premises caused by the removal.

Sometimes a lease specifically requires that certain items remain with the property. For example, an owner may lease her property for use as a gas station. The lease between the parties specifically states that the tenant will provide the gas pumps, but the pumps will remain with the property when the tenant leaves. In this case, the written agreement overrides the general rule.

If a trade fixture is not removed by a tenant at the termination of the lease, it will be considered part of the real estate and the landlord will acquire ownership of the item.

EMBLEMENTS

Most plants (shrubs, trees, flowers, etc.) growing on the land are considered part of the real estate. However, a special situation arises concerning cultivated crops, also known as emblements. The actual crop that can be harvested, such as wheat, corn, or potatoes, is considered personal property. A problem may arise when property is sold after it has already been planted with annually cultivated crops.

Annually cultivated crops: property of the seller, who may re-enter to harvest

> **Annually cultivated crops are generally considered the property of the seller, unless otherwise agreed.**

In order to prevent conflict, a prudent real estate agent should make certain that a special provision is included in the purchase agreement that specifies ownership and disposition of the current crop.

If the crop was planted by a tenant farmer, the rules are interpreted in favor of the tenant. The tenant has the right to re-enter the land and harvest the crop, even if the lease has expired. This right is known as the **doctrine of emblements**.

LAND DESCRIPTION

In order to determine what is included with the real estate, it is essential to know where the boundaries of the property lie. A land description should identify a piece of property so that it can't be confused with any other property.

Land description in a deed must be precise

> **Minnesota law requires all deeds to contain an adequate description of the land being conveyed.**

An "adequate" description is one that allows a precise determination of what property is being referred to. An ambiguous or uncertain description is not legally acceptable.

Because a land description is an essential part of an agreement to transfer property, it is important for real estate agents to understand the basic elements of a valid description. There are three major types of land description commonly used today. These are:

- metes and bounds
- rectangular (or government) survey
- recorded plat

METES AND BOUNDS

Metes and bounds method: describes a property's boundaries with a series of compass directions and distances

The metes and bounds system is the oldest known method of surveying land. British colonists brought this system to America, and it was the primary method of describing property in the original 13 colonies. Under the metes and bounds system, a buyer and seller simply walked the perimeters of the property and established landmarks along the way (or a surveyor may have been hired to establish the landmarks). A landmark (often called a monument) might be a river, a certain tree, a pile of stones, or the neighbor's fence.

Landmark (monument): a fixed point used as a reference point in a metes and bounds description

The metes and bounds system is not the primary method of describing property in Minnesota, but a metes and bounds description is often still found on older property, and is sometimes used in addition to another method of description.

Point of Beginning. When a metes and bounds description is established, the boundaries of the property are identified by first referring to a certain landmark or monument as the starting point or point of beginning (POB). The landmark or monument might be a natural object such as a river or tree, or a man-made object such as a road or metal survey marker.

Point of beginning: a landmark used as a starting point

Once the point of beginning is established, the description then gives directions to enable you to trace the boundary of the tract all the way around. The direction or course is given in the form of a compass reading. The directions following the POB always proceed clockwise.

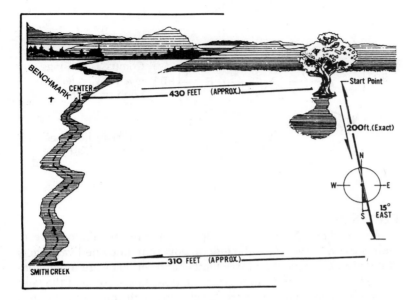

METES AND BOUNDS DESCRIPTION

A tract of land located in Ramsey County and described as follows: Beginning at the old oak tree, thence south 15° east, 200 feet, thence south 88° west, 310 feet more or less to the center line of Smith Creek, thence northwesterly along the center line of Smith Creek to a point directly east of Benchmark No. 318, thence north 88° east, 430 feet more or less to the point of beginning.

Older metes and bounds descriptions often used natural monuments such as "the old oak tree" or a pile of stones. But that created problems, since a tree can die or be chopped down, and stones can be moved. Modern metes and bounds descriptions often use government survey lines as reference points. At the point where the modern survey begins, a monument in the form of an iron pipe or a concrete or stone marker may be placed in the ground.

Compass Bearings. Directions in metes and bounds descriptions are given as compass bearings. A direction is described by reference to either north or south, whichever is closer. Thus, northwest is written as north 45° west, since it is a deviation of 45° to the west of north.

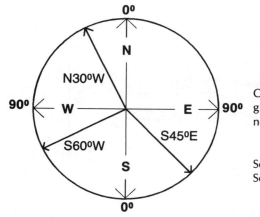

Compass bearings are given by reference to north or south

Southeast becomes South 45° East

RECTANGULAR SURVEY

Rectangular survey: a method of describing land by reference to a series of grids laid out over the United States

A second method of land description is the rectangular or government survey. In the 1780s the federal government owned vast tracts of undeveloped land. Land speculators and settlers were moving into the territories, and Congress was anxious to sell some of the land in order to raise money. It wasn't feasible to use the metes and bounds method for all of this property, so in 1784 the Continental Congress created the U.S. System of Public Land Surveys (USPLS). The purpose was to create a simple and reliable system for identifying public lands west of the Ohio and Mississippi rivers. The USPLS established the rectangular survey system in 1785. Thirty states, including Minnesota, use this system. Currently nearly 70% of the land area of the United States is described using the rectangular survey method.

Rather than using physical landmarks or monuments, the rectangular survey system is based on a series of imaginary lines running across the country. It then describes the land by reference to this series of grids. The grids are composed of two sets of lines, one set running north/south (lines of longitude) and the other east/west (lines of latitude). These grids may be confusing at first, and we recommend that you study the accompanying diagrams closely.

Principal meridian: the major north/south line in a rectangular survey grid

Base line: the major east/west line in a rectangular survey grid

MERIDIANS AND BASE LINES. Each grid has a principal meridian, which is the original north/south line established in that grid, and a base line, which is the original east/west line for that grid. There are 35 principal meridians across the country. Each principal meridian has its own name, and these are used to identify the different grids.

Principal Meridians and Baselines

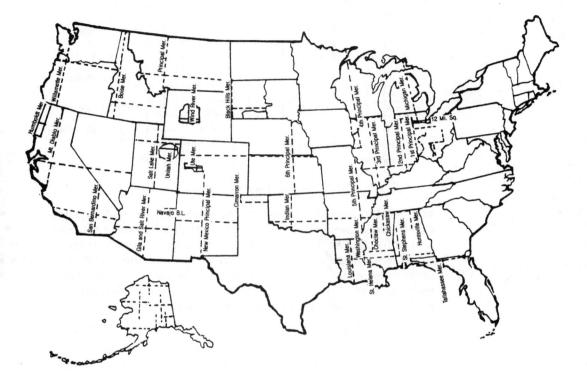

CORRECTIONS. Along with the principal meridians and base lines, there are additional east/west lines called correction lines, which run parallel to the base lines at intervals of 24 miles. Additional north/south lines called guide meridians run parallel to the principal meridian at 24-mile intervals. If you look at a globe of the earth, you can see that the lines of longitude come closer together as they near the north and south poles. Because of the curvature of the earth, all true north/south lines converge as they approach the poles. Therefore, each guide meridian only runs as far as the next horizontal correction line; then a new interval of 24 miles is measured and a new guide meridian is run. This way the guide meridians remain approximately the same distance apart and do not converge.

Correction lines and guide meridians: additional lines used to correct for the curvature of the earth in the rectangular survey method

East/west lines are
"Township lines,"
north/south lines are
"Range lines."

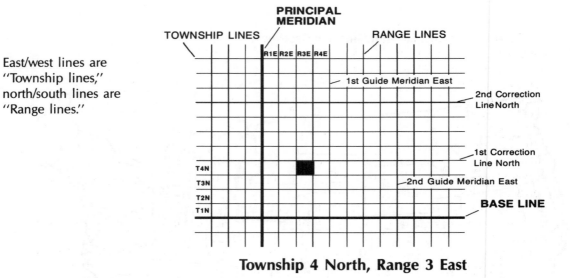

Township 4 North, Range 3 East

TOWNSHIPS. The intersection of lines form large 24 mile squares called tracts. These squares are further divided into smaller pieces of land by additional north/south lines running at six-mile intervals called range lines. The range lines divide the land into vertical columns called ranges. Additional east/west lines, called township lines, run at six-mile intervals from the correction lines. The township lines divide the land into horizontal rows called township tiers.

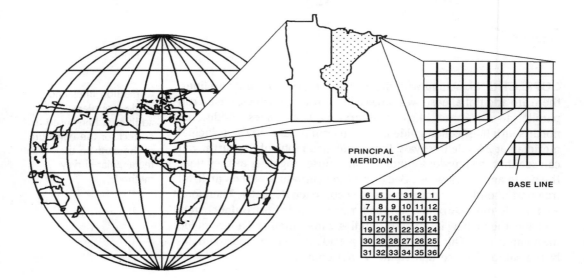

The square of land located at the intersection of a range and a township tier is called a township. A township is identified by its position in relation to the principal meridian and base line. For example, the township located in the fourth tier north of the base line and the third range east of the principal meridian is called "Township 4 North, Range 3 East" or T4N, R3E.

The grid systems are identical across the country, so it is necessary to include in a description the particular principal meridian that is being used as a reference point. Minnesota uses the Fourth and Fifth Principal Meridians. The Fourth Principal Meridian runs through the northeast corner of Minnesota. Since this principal meridian runs through only a small portion of the state, Minnesota also refers to the Fifth Principal Meridian. But the Fifth Principal Meridian does not actually run through the state, so the third guide meridian west of the Fifth Principal Meridian is used as a reference point. In Minnesota, the line of latitude that is the Standard Parallel North is used as a base line.

Township tiers: rows of land (running east/west) in a rectangular survey grid

Ranges: columns of land (running north/south) in a rectangular survey grid

Township: the parcel of land located at the intersection of a range and a township tier, which measures 6 miles by 6 miles

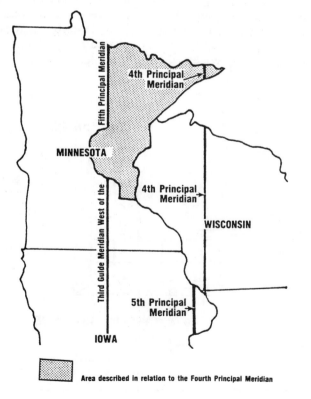

Area described in relation to the Fourth Principal Meridian

Since each principal meridian has its own base line, it is not necessary to refer to a specific base line. However, the description should mention the county and state where the land is situated so as to avoid any possible confusion.

Example: A description of a township might be T4N, R3E of the Fourth Principal Meridian, _____ County, state of Minnesota.

SECTIONS. Each township measures six miles square and contains 36 one-square-mile units called sections. The sections are always numbered in the same order, starting with number 1 in the top right-hand corner and ending with number 36 in the bottom right-hand corner. Each section contains 640 acres. Thus a half section is 320 acres, a quarter section is 160 acres, half of a quarter section is 80 acres, and a quarter of a quarter section is 40 acres. (See diagram.) The government survey system calls for disposal of the land in units equal to quarter-quarter sections containing 40 acres each. The procedure of splitting parcels into halves and quarters may be continued down to 2.5 acres. One acre equals 43,560 square feet.

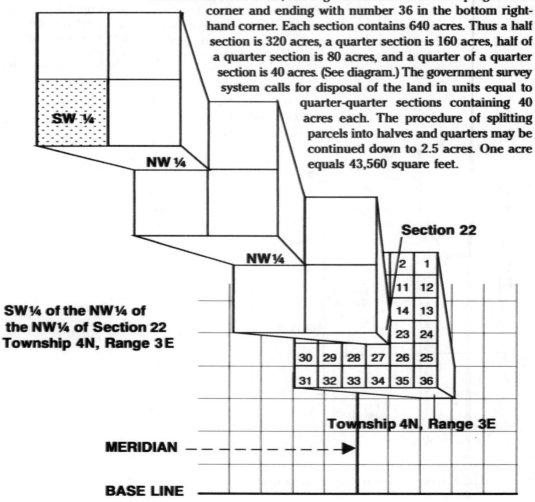

SW ¼

NW ¼

NW¼

Section 22

2	1
11	12
14	13
23	24

| 30 | 29 | 28 | 27 | 26 | 25 |
| 31 | 32 | 33 | 34 | 35 | 36 |

**SW¼ of the NW¼ of
the NW¼ of Section 22
Township 4N, Range 3E**

Township 4N, Range 3E

MERIDIAN

BASE LINE

GOVERNMENT LOTS. The rectangular survey method looks very straight and flawless in diagram examples. In reality, the sections are seldom perfect. Because of the curvature of the earth, the convergence of range lines, and human surveying errors, it is impossible to keep all sections exactly one mile square. Irregular portions of sections are specially numbered and called government lots. A government lot is simply a parcel of land of irregular shape or size that is referred to by a government lot number. The quarter sections along the north and west boundaries of a section are used to take up any excess or shortage in the section. Therefore, the quarter-quarter sections along the north and west boundaries of a township are often government lots. Natural obstacles such as a body of water or a rocky cliff may also make it impossible to survey a square mile section. A government lot may be established anywhere these problems occur.

> Government lot: a portion of a section that is given a special number because of its irregular shape or size

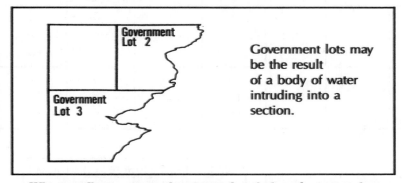

Government lots may be the result of a body of water intruding into a section.

When reading a rectangular survey description of property, it may be helpful to read it backwards, to determine the location and size of the property.

Example: The NW¼ of the NE¼ of Section 15, Township 4 South, Range 13 West of the Fourth Principal Meridian, _____ County, Minnesota.

To locate this property, first find the Fourth Principal Meridian. Then find the township by counting 13 range columns west of the principal meridian and four township tiers south of the base line. Once you have found the township, you can find section 15 because the sections are always numbered in the same order. Then divide section 15 into quarters since you are looking for property in the northeast quarter. Then divide the northeast quarter into quarters, and the property is the northwest quarter.

BASIC COMPONENTS OF
THE GOVERNMENT SURVEY SYSTEM

RANGE LINES

NOTE OFFSET AT CORRECTION LINE

T5N

6 MI. RANGE

STANDARD PARALLEL
(CORRECTION LINE)

R4W R3W R2W R1W R1E R2E R3E R4E

T4N

31 32 33 34 35 36

Township Lines

T3N

	1	6	5	4	3	2	1	6
	12	7	8	9	10	11	12	7
	13	18	17	16	15	14	13	18
	24	19	20	21	22	23	24	19
	25	30	29	28	27	26	25	30
	36	31	32	33	34	35	36	31

6 5 4 3 2 1

PRINCIPAL MERIDIAN

GUIDE MERIDIAN

24 MI

T2N

6 MI.

A TOWNSHIP

T1N

STANDARD PARALLEL
CORRECTION LINE

BASE LINE

24 MI.

T1S

A tract is
24 MI. X 24MI.
INCLUDES 16
TOWNSHIPS

IMPORTANT POINTS TO NOTE ON THIS DIAGRAM
1) TRACT = 24 × 24 MI. = 16 TOWNSHIPS
2) TOWNSHIP = 6 × 6 MI. = 36 SECTIONS
3) SECTION = 1 × 1 MI. = 640 ACRES
4) NOTE NUMBERING SEQUENCE OF SECTIONS

UNITS OF MEASUREMENT FOR LAND	
UNITS OF AREA	1 Tract = 24 mi. × 24 mi. (576 sq. mi.) = 16 townships 1 Township = 6 mi. × 6 mi. (36 sq. mi.) = 36 sections 1 Section* = 1 mi. × 1 mi. (1 sq. mi.) = 640 acres 1 Acre = 43,560 sq. ft. = 160 sq. rods 1 Square Acre = 208.71 ft × 208.71 ft.
UNITS OF LENGTH	1 Mile = 5,280 ft. = 320 rods = 80 chains 1 Rod = 16½ ft. 1 Chain = 66 ft. = 4 rods

* Note: To determine the area of partial sections, simply multiply the fraction
of the section by 640. For example,

1 half-section = ½ × 640 = 320 acres
1 quarter-section = ¼ × 640 = 160 acres
1 quarter-quarter section = ¼ × ¼ × 640 = 40 acres

RECORDED PLAT

The rectangular survey method of land description is best used on fairly large parcels of property. It tends to lose its effectiveness and become unwieldy as the parcel size decreases. Although more actual land area in the U.S. is described using the rectangular survey method, the recorded plat system is the most important land description method in terms of number of properties. It is the method used most frequently in metropolitan areas. Under this system, land developers subdivide land and assign lot numbers to identify individual sites within blocks. The land is described by reference to a subdivision plat. This plat is a survey map that shows the precise location and boundaries of individual properties. The plat map is recorded in the county where the land is located. This system of land description is sometimes called the lot and block, recorded map, or recorded survey system. Each plat is placed in a map book along with plats of other subdivisions in the county. The plat is then given a book and page reference number. To find the location and dimensions of a parcel of land, you would merely look in the map book at the county recorder's office. As an example, a recorded plat description might read as follows:

Recorded plat system: subdivided land is mapped and lot numbers are assigned to individual parcels; land is then described by reference to subdivision plat map which has been recorded

Lot 2, Block 4 of Tract 455, in the city of Minneapolis, county of Hennepin, state of Minnesota, as per map recorded in book 25, page 92, of maps, in the office of the recorder of said county.

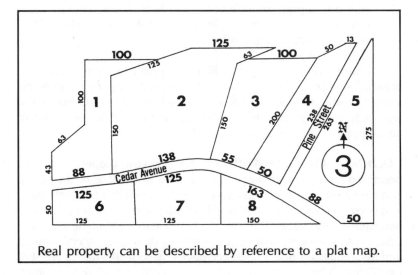

Real property can be described by reference to a plat map.

Once a plat map has been recorded, any reference to one of the numbered lots on the specified plat is a sufficient legal description of the lot. Since a detailed description of the lot is already on file in the recorder's office, that description may be incorporated into any legal document simply by reference to the particular plat map and lot number. Plat maps frequently contain other information in addition to a detailed description of the property boundaries. For example, they may include measurements of area, locations of various easements, right-of-way dimensions, location of survey markers, and records of conditions and restrictions applying to the land.

OTHER METHODS OF DESCRIPTION

There are other methods of describing land besides the three major systems discussed above. Any time an adequate description of property is already a matter of record (for example, one contained in a recorded deed), then a reference to the instrument containing the description is legally sufficient to describe the land. However, generalized descriptions such as "all my lands" or "Smith Farm" are not sufficient unless they allow an unambiguous determination of what property is being described.

> **Example:** A grant of "all my lands in St. Louis County" may be adequate because evidence can be introduced to prove exactly what lands the grantor owns in St. Louis County. However, a grant of "one of my lots in St. Louis County" is not adequate because it is impossible to determine which of several lots is being referred to.

A cautious real estate agent will always prefer to use the least ambiguous description possible, since a good legal description is insurance against future problems. It should be noted that street addresses are not acceptable descriptions in Minnesota and should be used only as an informal reference to the property.

VERTICAL LAND DESCRIPTION. Not all real property can be described simply by reference to a position on the face of the earth. Some types of property (such as a second-floor unit in a condominium) also need to be described in terms of elevation above the ground. These descriptions are made by reference to an established plane of elevation, called a datum. Most large cities have their own official datum, and frequently secondary reference points called bench marks are also established. A bench mark is a point whose position relative to a datum has been accurately measured. Surveyors can use the bench mark as a reference when it is more convenient than the datum. A bench mark may be a metal or concrete marker (often placed in a sidewalk or other stable position) that states the location relative to the datum.

> **Example:** A metal disk in the sidewalk at the corner of Oak and Elm Streets has the following words engraved on it: "Bench Mark No. 96, 17 feet above River City Datum."

Surveyors use the datum or a bench mark as a reference point in describing air lots.

> **Example:** A surveyor is plotting a condominium unit on the 16th floor of a new building on Elm Street. He first describes the property beneath the building. He then calculates that the 16th floor will be 230 feet above the sidewalk. He therefore shows in his survey that the floor of the unit on the 16th floor is 247 feet above the River City Datum as established by Bench Mark No. 96, because Bench Mark No. 96 is 17 feet above the datum.

GOVERNMENT LAND USE CONTROLS

Although a property owner has a large "bundle of rights" in his or her property, an owner's rights are limited by federal, state and local government regulations and controls. Government powers are superior to an individual's rights because government regulation of property and land use is necessary for the public good. It is important to recognize what types of controls the government may exercise over land use and to understand how these regulations affect certain properties and the rights of property owners.

Government land use controls take the form of comprehensive plans, zoning ordinances, building codes, subdivision regulations, and environmental legislation. These regulations may sometimes restrict or hamper the sale of property. A buyer planning to build a factory won't buy property located in an area that is zoned for residential use. A commercial buyer won't purchase an office building if it doesn't meet the fire code. In fact, it may even be illegal to transfer a building that doesn't meet certain code requirements. In any transaction, a real estate agent needs to know what government regulations are in force, and how they affect the property.

All real property is subject to government regulations and controls

PLANNING

During Colonial times, a landowner could do whatever he desired with his property. He could build a house or raise pigs or run a blacksmith shop, or he could even do all three on the same piece of property. But as the population grew and cities became crowded, people began to object to having a use like a pig farm right next to their house.

The first land use controls were zoning laws passed in New York City around 1916. Their purpose was to prevent business and industrial concerns from expanding into the fashionable residential areas. As urban populations grew, so did concerns about how the growth would affect a community. More and more cities began to pass zoning laws. Now, almost every city and town in the United States has some type of land use plan and zoning laws.

> **The purpose of current land use plans is to alleviate problems caused by the haphazard, unplanned growth of urban areas and to promote more rational development in the future.**

Minnesota law provides for the establishment of regional commissions to oversee development according to comprehensive plans drafted by individual cities.

LAND SURVEY. Before a land use plan can be developed, information has to be gathered about the area in question. One of the first steps in planning is to have a land survey made of the area. This survey should include mapping developed and undeveloped land, and showing the location of existing roads and utility lines.

ECONOMIC SURVEY. Along with a physical land survey of the area, an economic survey should be made. The economic survey analyzes the present and anticipated future economic needs of the area. This includes such things as current population and anticipated population growth, and a review of the retail, industrial, or agricultural facilities on which the area depends, and its expected future needs.

Master development plan: sets long-range development goals for the community

MASTER DEVELOPMENT PLAN. Once land and economic surveys have been made, it is time to develop a master plan (also called a comprehensive plan). To prepare a master plan, a city or regional planning commission is usually created. The planning commission is responsible for designing and adopting a long-term, general plan for all development within the city or county. The purpose of the plan is to outline the development goals of the community and to design an overall physical layout to achieve those goals. The plan must look at the current make-up of the community, and also consider its potential for the future.

The master plan must consider the entire region and provide for all necessary forms of land use. Of course the plan includes areas for housing. But there must also be industrial and commercial areas to provide jobs for the community. Along with working and going home to sleep, people need and want social, cultural, educational and recreational opportunities. A master plan should include areas that will provide for all these aspects of living.

> **Once the master plan has been adopted, development and land use regulations (such as zoning laws) must conform to the plan.**

For example, a wealthy suburban area may want to pass zoning laws that only allow single-family residences on quarter-acre lots. This would ensure that the community remained exclusive, expensive and purely residential. But suppose that in the master plan this community was considered one of the prime growth areas of the future. It designated the community for more diversified housing, and included retail areas to meet the needs of the growing population. Zoning this community for strictly residential quarter-acre lots would not be allowed under the master plan.

ZONING: LAND USE CLASSIFICATIONS

As its name suggests, a comprehensive or master development plan sets out the community's land use policies in general and sweeping terms. To carry out those policies, detailed zoning ordinances must be drafted. In most cases, these are enacted by the county or city council (usually with the planning commission's advice). Since zoning can have far-reaching effects, the council is required to hold public hearings before adopting new ordinances or changing current ordinances.

Zoning laws carry out policies of the master development plan

TYPICAL ZONING PROVISIONS

Zoning laws control the ways land may be used. They generally divide a community into areas (or zones) that are set aside for specific uses.

> **The purpose of zoning is to control and regulate growth and building in a way that is best for the general welfare.**

Zoning laws are meant to promote the health, morals, and safety of the inhabitants of the community.

Early zoning laws usually established only five land use categories:

- residential,
- commercial,
- industrial,
- agricultural, and
- mixed

Modern zoning regulations tend to be much more complicated. In addition to the five basic categories, numerous subcategories are used.

> **Example:** In Somewhere City, there are several types of residential zones. In zones designated R-1, only detached single-family houses are allowed. In R-2 zones, row houses and duplexes (as well as detached single-family houses) are permitted. R-3 zones also have apartments and condominiums, and any kind of housing (including mobile homes) is allowed in an R-4 zone.

An industrial zone might be divided into a section for light industry and a section for heavy industry. And sometimes a mixture of uses is allowed in a single zone, such as commercial and light industrial in the same zone, or multi-family residential and retail in the same zone. The purpose of placing certain uses in certain zones is to ensure that compatible uses are located in the same area.

While zoning laws serve the same purposes throughout the country, there is no uniformity of classifications. Each city or region may use a different type of code to classify the different zones. Real estate agents should become familiar with the classifications and the code system used in their area to designate different zones and categories.

When selling property, an agent should find out how the property is zoned, since this can have a significant effect on how the property can be used and who will want to buy it.

> **Example:** An attractive, Victorian-style house is for sale. A couple is interested in buying the house because they want to turn it into a restaurant. Can they? It may depend on the zoning category. If the area is zoned strictly for residential use, the house may not be used as a restaurant. A real estate agent should check the zoning laws to see if this type of use would be allowed.

Zoning classifications have a significant effect on property values

LAND USE RESTRICTIONS

Zoning laws regulate the overall use of the property, such as whether a house or an office building may be built. There are also laws that specify in detail how a building may be built: its size and placement on the property, the construction methods, and a wide variety of other considerations. Some of these issues are addressed in zoning ordiances, and some are dealt with in local regulations such as building codes.

BUILDING CODES

> **The purpose of building codes is to protect the public health and safety.**

Building codes are generally specialized; a city will have a fire code, a plumbing code, and so forth. These regulations set construction standards that must be met, as well as requirements for materials used in construction.

BUILDING PERMITS. Compliance with the building code is usually assured by requiring property owners to obtain a building permit before constructing or altering any building. Before a permit is granted, the building designs and plans are inspected to make sure that the proposed building meets the code requirements. Any substandard designs or other problems must be corrected before a building permit will be issued. Construction cannot begin without a permit. Once construction begins, a building inspector examines various

Building permit: insures compliance with various safety and construction codes

phases of the construction. If any problems are noted, they must be corrected before construction may continue.

Once the building is completed, it is inspected again. If it meets all the building code standards, a **certificate of occupancy** is issued. Without this certificate, the building cannot legally be occupied.

Certificate of occupancy: issued only after construction has successfully passed safety inspection; required before building can be occupied

A smart real estate agent or prospective buyer may want to check with the building department to verify that the building has been inspected and approved, and that a certificate of occupancy has been issued.

SETBACK, SIDEYARD AND REARYARD REQUIREMENTS

Height limits and setback requirements: regulate size of building and its location on the lot

Most communities also have ordinances that regulate the height, size, and shape of buildings, as well as their location on the lot. The location is controlled by setback, sideyard and rearyard requirements.

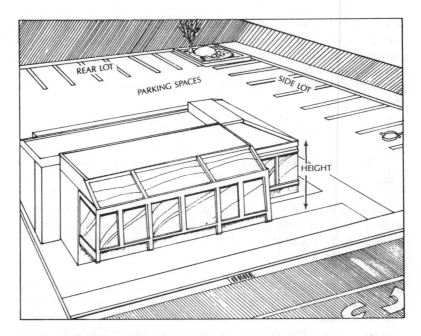

Zoning ordinances regulate a building's use, height, setback requirements, and off-street parking.

Some communities, rather than strictly prescribing the height limits and setback requirements for buildings, allow the use of the floor area ratio (FAR) method. FAR controls the ratio between the area of the building's floor space and the area of the lot it occupies. The FAR method allows flexibility in the shape and height of a building allowed on a lot.

Floor area ratio (FAR): a method to allow flexibility in the height and setback requirements

Example: A floor area ratio of two would permit 100% of the lot to be covered by a two-story building or 50% of the lot to be covered by a four-story building.

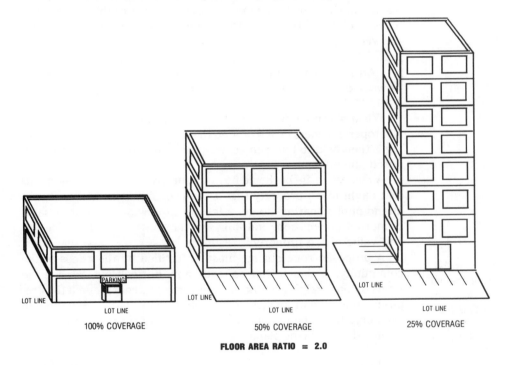

100% COVERAGE   50% COVERAGE   25% COVERAGE

LOT LINE   LOT LINE   LOT LINE

FLOOR AREA RATIO = 2.0

STATE REQUIREMENTS. In addition to local zoning ordinances, the state of Minnesota has also passed legislation that regulates lot size and setbacks in shoreland areas. The state Department of Natural Resources (DNR) works with cities and municipalities to prevent development that would have an adverse impact on the environment.

Minnesota law also provides for the establishment of regional commissions to oversee development according to the comprehensive plans drafted by individual cities. It is possible that these comprehensive plans will eventually supersede local zoning ordinances.

ZONING CHANGES AND DEVIATIONS

AMENDMENTS

Zoning ordinances can be amended. An amendment might reclassify one section of a zone to allow certain uses that were previously prohibited there—or to prohibit uses that were previously allowed.

> **An amendment may be initiated by an individual property owner or by the local government.**

When a zoning amendment is sought, notice must be given to all property owners in and around the area concerned. A public hearing is then held so that people may voice their opinions on the proposed amendment.

A real estate agent should be aware of any proposed amendments that might affect property that is for sale. The agent may want to attend public hearings to get a feel for how widely the proposal is supported or opposed, and how the changes would affect the use and value of the property.

Zoning changes must be justified by the needs of the community, must not harm rights of others, and must conform to the master development plan

A proposed zone change must be justified by the needs of the community. A change can be made only if it will not damage the rights of those relying on the current zoning category, and if the proposed amendment makes more sense than the current zoning category. Also, the amendment must not violate the community's master development plan.

When a new zoning designation is imposed on a neighborhood, some owners find that the way they've been using their property is no longer permitted, even though it was fine under the old law.

> **Example:** Burt opened a small bakery in an area zoned for mixed residential and commercial use. A few years later, the city council rezoned the neighborhood to residential only.

Burt's bakery is now a **nonconforming use**—it doesn't conform to the new zoning law. It would not be fair to order an owner to discontinue a nonconforming use immediately. That could create a lot of uncertainty: "If I open a business here, will I be ordered to shut it down six months from now if the zoning laws change?"

Nonconforming use: an existing use that does not conform to a new zoning law, but is allowed to continue

> **Zoning laws usually provide that existing nonconforming uses may continue.**

So Burt will still be able to operate his bakery, even though it does not meet the new zoning requirements. However, a nonconforming use is subject to a number of restrictions. These restrictions are intended to gradually phase out the nonconforming use.

For instance, as a general rule, a nonconforming use may not be enlarged or expanded. When the buildings involved in a nonconforming use become obsolete, the owners are usually not allowed to renovate them. Even maintenance and repairs may be restricted. The owners could make minor repairs, but major repairs that would extend the lifespan of the building might not be permitted. And ordinances generally provide that if a nonconforming building is destroyed by a hazard such as a fire or earthquake, it may not be rebuilt. Any new structure must comply with the current zoning regulations.

> **Example:** If Burt's bakery burned down, he could build a house on the property, but would not be allowed to rebuild the bakery.

Some ordinances also place a time limit on the nonconforming use. In other words, it will only be allowed to continue for a specific amount of time. As long as the time limit is reasonable, it will generally be upheld by the courts. A factor in determining reasonableness is the life expectancy of the nonconforming building. If the life expectancy of the bakery building is 30 years, the ordinance may require that the nonconforming use be discontinued in 30 years.

VARIANCES

> **Like a nonconforming use, a variance permits a property owner to vary from strict compliance with the zoning ordinance. Unlike a nonconforming use, a variance is not an established use, but is a new use, change, or addition that the owner wants to make on the property.**

Variance: permission to use property in a manner not allowed under existing zoning law; provides flexibility in hardship cases

Sometimes zoning laws interfere unfairly with the way in which a property owner wants to use the property. A variance is a built-in safety valve to provide flexibility in the laws where injury to the property owner would outweigh the benefit of strict zoning enforcement.

A common example of a variance would be allowing the construction of a house even if the topography of the lot makes it impossible to comply with the normal setback and sideyard requirements.

> **Example:** Judith's property is located in an area zoned for single-family residences that requires that all structures be set back at least 20 feet from the road. Judith's lot is an odd-shaped end lot, with a large, rocky outcrop on one side. Judith finds it impossible to build her house 20 feet from the road. She applies for and obtains a variance to build her house only 18 feet from the road.

Variances are usually granted where strict compliance with the zoning ordinance would cause undue hardship to the property owner. In the above example, strict compliance with the zoning ordinance would prevent Judith from building a house on her property.

A proposed variant use must not change the essential character of the area, or reduce the value of the surrounding properties. The fact that Judith's house is only 18 feet from the road instead of 20 is not going to significantly change the character of the neighborhood, or reduce the value of her neighbor's property.

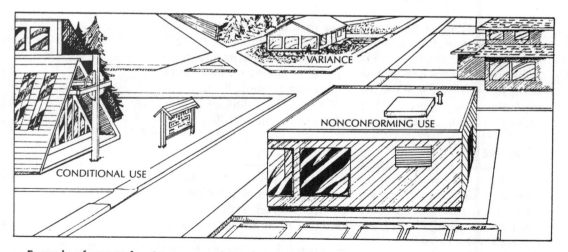

Example of nonconforming use, conditional use and variance

CONDITIONAL (SPECIAL) USE

Another common provision in zoning ordinances enables the zoning authority to issue special permits allowing certain uses in a neighborhood even though they are inconsistent with the zoning designation. These are referred to as conditional uses or special uses. Schools, hospitals, parks, churches, and cemeteries in neighborhoods that are otherwise strictly residential are often conditional uses.

Conditional use permit: special permission for an inconsistent use

> **A zoning ordinance usually has a specific list of conditional uses that may be allowed in a particular zone.**

The zoning authority controls the number and placement of these uses, and grants permits subject to conditions that limit their possible adverse effects on neighboring property. For example, the owner of a single-family residence may request a special use permit to operate a beauty salon in the basement. If permission is granted, it would typically include conditions such as parking restrictions, limited hours of operation, and sign restrictions which, if violated, could lead to revocation of the permit. Purchasers of property who wish to continue a special use should make their purchase contingent upon obtaining a new special use permit.

ENFORCEMENT OF ZONING ORDINANCES

> **A zoning ordinance usually provides that fines and other penalties can be imposed on a property owner who violates its rules.**

The owner may be required to tear down an illegal structure or stop an illegal use. However, most counties and cities don't have enough personnel to make routine checks on all the land uses in their jurisdiction. So unless someone files a complaint, a property owner may get away with a minor zoning violation.

The building permit system helps enforce zoning laws. If a permit application proposes a project inconsistent with the zoning, it will be turned down. Also, construction inspectors sometimes come across zoning violations and require them to be corrected.

CHAPTER SUMMARY

1. There are two types of property: real property and personal property. Real property is the land, anything affixed to the land, and rights and interests in the land.

2. Rights and interests in the land include air rights, water rights, mineral rights, oil and gas rights, and support rights. Improvements may be natural (growing) or man-made (fixtures). The tests for distinguishing fixtures from personal property are based on ascertaining the intent of the parties, and include the method of attachment, the adaptation of the item to the realty, the relationship of the parties, and any provisions in a written agreement.

3. All valid deeds must contain a legal description of the land being conveyed. There are three major types of legal description: recorded plat, metes and bounds, and government survey.

4. The metes and bounds method describes land by a series of courses and distances. It starts at a defined "point of beginning" and then describes the boundaries of the parcel until an enclosed tract of land has been described.

5. The government survey (or rectangular survey) describes land by reference to a series of grids. The original north/south lines of the grid are called "principal meridians," the original east/west lines of the grid are called "base lines." The overlapping lines create six mile square parcels called "townships." Each township is in turn made up of 36 sections. Each section is one square mile and contains 640 acres. Smaller parcels of land can be described by referring to portions of sections, e.g., the NW ¼ of the SW ¼ of Section 17.

6. The recorded plat method describes land by referring to a lot number on a plat map that has been filed with the county recorder. Because the plat map contains a detailed description of the land, simple reference to the plat map is sufficient.

7. The purpose of land use controls is to alleviate problems caused by haphazard, unplanned growth of urban areas, and to promote more rational development in the future. Zoning laws are also meant to protect the health, morals, and safety of the community's inhabitants.

8. The purpose of building codes is to protect the public health and safety. A building permit must be granted before construction can begin. Once a building is completed, it must be inspected. A certificate of occupancy will be issued if the building complies with the codes.

9. Zoning ordinances may be amended. A proposed change must be justified by the needs of the community.

10. A nonconforming use is a use that was already legally in place when a new zoning ordinance came into effect, but does not comply with the requirements of the new law. Although nonconforming uses are generally allowed to remain, they may be subject to certain restrictions.

11. A variance is a permit to build a structure or use property in a way that would not otherwise be allowed. Variances are usually granted when strict compliance with the zoning ordinance would cause undue hardship to the property owner.

12. A zoning authority can issue conditional use permits for uses that would ordinarily not be allowed in a zone. Permits are granted subject to conditions that limit the adverse effects of the use on the neighborhood.

CHAPTER 1—GLOSSARY REVIEW

A. fixtures
B. nonconforming use
C. government (rectangular) survey
D. personal property (chattels)
E. section

F. real estate
G. variance
H. lot, block and subdivision
I. metes and bounds
J. lien

1. All property other than real estate is known as _personal property (chattel)_

2. Land and its improvements and the rights to own or use them are collectively called _real estate_

3. When articles of personal property are permanently attached to the improvements, they become _fixtures_

4. A method of description that utilizes measures and directions to locate boundaries is _metes & bounds_

5. The recorded plat method of description is also referred to as _lot, block, & subdivision_

6. Permission to vary from strict compliance with zoning requirements may be obtained in the form of a _variance_

7. When a previously established use does not comply with the requirements of a new zoning ordinance, it may be allowed to continue as a _non-conforming use._

8. Townships, sections, and meridians are used in the _rectangular govt survey_ form of legal description.

9. A parcel of land measuring 1 mile × 1 mile and containing 640 acres is a _section._

43,560 ⌗ in acre
give you card

CHAPTER 1—REVIEW EXAM

1. The NW ¼ of Section 4 contains how many acres?

   a) 40
   b) 160
   c) 640
   d) 43,560

2. Contiguous lots are:

   a) lots with common boundaries.
   b) government lots.
   c) located only on cul-de-sacs.
   d) located only near lakes.

3. A township is:

   a) 36 miles square.
   b) 24 miles square.
   c) 6 miles square.
   d) 1 mile square.

4. A tract of land measuring 330 feet wide by 1,320 feet deep would contain:

   a) 1 acre.
   b) 10 acres.
   c) 20 acres.
   d) 40 acres.

5. The definition of real estate includes:

   a) buildings affixed to the land.
   b) airspace above the land.
   c) substances below the land.
   d) All of the above.

6. Which of the following is considered personal property?

   a) Drapery rods
   b) A freestanding refrigerator
   c) Built-in bookcases
   d) A ceiling fan

7. Peter Lincoln wants to sell his hobby farm, legally described as the S ½ of the NE ¼ of the NW ¼. Land in his area is selling for $1,200 per acre. What is the selling price?

   a) $36,000
   b) $6,000
   c) $12,000
   d) $24,000

8. What section is directly north of Section 22?

   a) Section 16
   b) Section 27
   c) Section 15
   d) Section 10

9. Dick Developer bought a 100-acre parcel to subdivide into 1-acre homesites. Which of the following legal descriptions would best achieve the developer's objectives?

   a) Government survey
   b) Monuments
   c) Subdivided plat
   d) Metes and bounds

10. Which of the following is NOT general-
    ly a use classification established by
    municipal zoning?

    a) Residential
    b) Mixed
    c) Commercial
    d) Architectural

11. The form of legal description most often
    used west of the Mississippi is:

    a) government survey.
    b) metes and bounds.
    c) informal reference.
    d) street address.

12. Real estate in Minnesota is bought and
    sold on the basis of which the following?

    a) Street address
    b) Legal description
    c) Plat size only
    d) Plat and parcel

CHAPTER 1—GLOSSARY REVIEW KEY

1. D
2. F
3. A
4. I
5. H

6. G
7. B
8. C
9. E

REVIEW EXAM KEY

1. b) A section contains 640 acres. A quarter section is 160 acres (640 ÷ 4 = 160).

2. a) Contiguous means "touching."

3. c) A township is 6 miles square. It contains 36 square miles.

4. b) 330 × 1,320 = 435,600 sq. ft.; 435,600 ÷ 43,560 = 10 acres.

5. d) Real estate includes items attached to the surface of the earth, plus airspace above and minerals below the surface.

6. b) Personal property is not permanently attached to real estate.

7. d) $\dfrac{640}{2 \times 4 \times 4} = 20$ acres

   20 × $1,200 = $24,000

8. c) The numbering system begins with Section 1 in the upper right (northeast) corner and zig-zags to Section 36 in the lower right (southeast) corner. The section directly north of Section 22 is Section 15.

9. c) The subdivided (recorded) plat is the simplest method by which large parcels are divided into smaller lots.

10. d) The most common zoning classifications are residential, commercial, industrial/manufacturing, agricultural, and mixed.

11. a) The government survey established sections, townships, and ranges in the western United States.

12. b) Real estate is described by accepted legal descriptions. The street address, plat size, and plat and parcel are examples of informal reference.

Rights and Interests in Land

Outline

I. Government Rights in Land
   A. Property taxes
   B. Eminent domain
   C. Police power
   D. Escheat

II. Estates in Land
   A. Freehold estates
      1. fee simple absolute
      2. fee simple defeasible
      3. life estate
   B. Leasehold estates
      1. estate for years
      2. estate at will
      3. estate at sufferance

III. Encumbrances
   A. Easements
      1. appurtenant
      2. in gross
   B. Deed restrictions (restrictive covenants)
   C. Liens
      1. government liens
      2. mechanics' liens
      3. mortgage liens
      4. judgment liens
      5. lien priority

IV. Encroachments

V. Licenses

KEY TERMS

police power	eminent domain
condemnation	ad valorem taxes
special assessment	escheat
freehold estate	fee simple absolute
fee simple defeasible	life estate
remainderman	reverter
life tenant	leasehold estate
estate for years	estate at will
estate at sufferance	encumbrance
easement	easement appurtenant
easement in gross	easement by necessity
prescriptive easement	deed restriction
lien	general lien
specific lien	government lien
mechanic's lien	lien notice
mortgage lien	judgment lien
encroachment	license

CHAPTER OVERVIEW

A person who has a property right or a claim against property is said to have an **interest** in the property. An interest might be an ownership right, a right to use the property, or a financial claim against the property. This chapter discusses government interests in property, individual possessory interests in property, and non-possessory interests in property.

GOVERNMENT RIGHTS IN LAND

Individual property rights are always subordinate to government rights

Ownership of property gives the owner certain rights. However, these individual rights are always subordinate to government rights. The previous chapter discussed the government's right to control or regulate land use through planning, zoning, and building codes. This chapter discusses additional, more specific powers that the government may exercise over privately owned property. These powers may require payment from the owner, or even result in a taking of the property from the owner.

PROPERTY TAXES

One of the most obvious examples of government rights in land is the government's right to tax the property. Taxing real property has long been a popular way of raising revenue for the government because land has a fixed location, is relatively indestructible and easy to assess, and is difficult to conceal.

> There are two types of taxes on real property: general property taxes (also called ad valorem taxes), and special assessments (also called special improvement taxes).

Buyers are always concerned about what the taxes are going to be on the property. It is especially important to learn whether there are any special assessments that the buyer will be required to pay, since these are an expense in addition to the general property taxes.

GENERAL PROPERTY TAXES. General property taxes are levied to support the general operation and services of government, such as police and fire protection. These taxes are called "ad valorem" (meaning "according to value") because the amount of the tax is calculated according to the value of the property being taxed. The higher the value of the property, the higher the taxes.

General property taxes: levied to support general governmental operations

Ad valorem taxes: those determined by the value of the property being taxed

Determining the Amount Needed. Each city or taxing community prepares a budget for the next year. This budget includes all of the items that tax money will pay for, such as police salaries, local welfare programs, public libraries, park maintenance, etc. In Minnesota, only counties have the authority to tax property, so each community turns over its budget to the county. The county then adds up the total amount needed, and may add additional county costs, such as county road maintenance.

The county then takes the total budget amount for the whole county and subtracts estimated revenue that will come from things like business licenses. The amount left over must be paid by property taxes.

Assessed Value. The next step in the tax process is to determine how much taxable property lies within the county. The county assessor's office has the duty to appraise each taxable piece of property.

Property value: determined by county assessor

> In Minnesota, real property is appraised at least every four years to determine its estimated fair market value.

Board of equalization: hears and decides appeals of value assessments

The assessed value of each piece of property is listed as of January 2nd of each year. A property owner who is dissatisfied with the assessment of his or her property may appeal to a county board of equalization. The board will either affirm or reduce the assessment.

It is important to note that certain special types of property are exempt from property taxation. These exempt properties include cemeteries, public hospitals, churches, and government-owned property.

Class tax rates: all real property taxed according to its category, e.g., agricultural, commercial, etc.

Class Tax Rates. Next, tax rates are applied to all assessed property. In Minnesota, all real property is categorized into classes. For example, residential property used as a homestead is class 1, agricultural land is class 2 and commercial property is class 3. Each class is then broken down into sub-classes. For instance, rural property used exclusively for growing timber is class 2b.

The significance of these categories is that a particular tax rate is assigned to each class. There are approximately 45 different categories, and each category may be taxed at a different rate. For example, low-income housing is class 4c. Class 4c property has a class tax rate of 2.4% of assessed value.

Tax extension rate: percentage of value to be paid in taxes

Tax Extension Rate. Once the budget has been determined, assessed values have been established, and class tax rates applied, each community can determine how much money it will need to meet its budget. It will then determine a tax extension rate (sometimes called a mill rate). This is the actual percentage that must be paid.

> **Example:** The total assessed value of all taxable property within a particular community is 500 million dollars ($500,000,000). When the class rate for each type of property is applied, the total amount is ten million dollars ($10,000,000). The total budget for this community is eight and a half million dollars ($8,500,000). In order to meet their budget, the community uses a tax extension rate of 85%.

Tax amount: assessed value × class tax rate × tax extension rate

The amount that each property owner must pay is determined by multiplying the assessed value by its class tax rate, then multiplying this amount by the tax extension rate.

> **Example:** Johnson owns property that is in a class which has a tax rate of 3%. The assessed value of his property is $50,000. Three percent of $50,000 is $1,500. The tax extension rate in his community is 85%. Eighty-five percent of $1,500 is $1,275. Johnson owes property taxes of $1,275.

This system may be a little confusing, but it is all figured out by the taxing authority. The individual owner simply gets a tax bill in the mail, stating how much he or she owes.

A buyer will want to know how much was required for taxes this year. This gives the buyer a rough idea of how much the taxes will be next year. What is significant to a buyer, and therefore to the real estate agent, is the assessed value of the property. The higher the assessed value of the property, the higher the taxes.

Another important point is how expensive a particular community is—in other words, what is the community's tax extension rate? If a community's budget is high in comparison to the value of property in the community, its tax extension rate will be high. At the time of this writing, tax extension rates varied by community from approximately 84% to 112%. The higher the tax extension rate, the more tax a property owner will have to pay.

Payment of Taxes. The fiscal tax year in Minnesota runs from January 1 through December 31. Once the tax amounts are determined, a tax bill is mailed to each property owner. Taxes may be paid in two installments, which are due on May 15 and October 15. Taxes become a perpetual lien on the property from January 2 in the year in which the taxes are due, until they are paid.

Taxes may be paid in two installments

> **Example:** The assessed value is determined as of January 2, 1992. The taxes are due and payable on May 15 and October 15, 1993.

When an owner receives a tax bill in the mail, it is actually for an amount based upon the assessed value last year, but due this year.

Failure to Pay. If a property owner does not pay the taxes when due, the property is in default and may be sold to the state, subject to redemption by the owner. Redemption is a right given to the owner that allows the owner to reclaim the property. The redemption period is five years for homestead property and is generally three years for other types of property. During this time period, the owner can redeem (reclaim) the property by paying back taxes, interest, costs and other penalties.

Delinquent taxpayers may redeem property within time limits; otherwise, public sale

If the owner has not redeemed the property by the end of the allowed time period, the owner will be removed from the property and the state will offer the property for public sale.

Special assessments:
levied to pay for specific
local improvements

SPECIAL ASSESSMENTS. The second type of real estate tax is the special assessment. Special assessments are different from general property taxes. They are levied for the cost of specific local improvements, such as streets and sewers. Only those pieces of property that benefit from the improvement are taxed, on the theory that the value of those properties will increase by the amount of the tax.

> **Example:** Property owners within the Thousand Oaks subdivision petitioned the city to have street lights installed. When the lights are installed, the properties within the Thousand Oaks subdivision must pay a special assessment to cover the cost of their new street lights.

Public improvement projects that result in special assessment liens are commonly funded by bonds issued and sold by the local agency making the improvement. Once bonds have been issued, the assessment becomes a lien on the benefitted properties, and is paid together with annual property taxes.

A problem may arise with a special assessment when property is sold after an improvement has been completed, but before the assessment is made. This is referred to as a **pending special assessment**.

> **Example:** Samuels owns property in the Thousand Oaks subdivision. The new street lights have already been installed, but Samuels has not yet received the special assessment bill. Samuels sells his property to Bernstein. Bernstein has no idea that the street lights are brand new, and that they were installed as a local improvement. Two months after moving into his new house, Bernstein receives a very large special assessment bill. Bernstein is not happy.

A real estate agent should ask about any special assessment liens on the property, and should also look for and inquire about any recent improvements or pending special assessments.

EMINENT DOMAIN

Property taxation affects nearly all property owners, and its purpose is readily understood. A less common and much misunderstood power of government is the power of eminent domain.

> **Under the U.S. Constitution, the government has the power to take private property for public use.**

This power is called **eminent domain**. When the government takes private property using this power, it is required to pay just compensation to the owner. This is usually the fair market value of the property.

Eminent domain can be exercised by the state, cities, counties, school districts, and other government entities. When private property is needed for public use, the government first offers to purchase the property it needs. If the owner rejects the offer, the government may seek to **condemn** the property. This is different than an action condemning property such as an old abandoned factory that has become a public hazard. When the government files a condemnation lawsuit under the power of eminent domain, it is because the government needs to make use of the property.

In a condemnation action, the court considers evidence concerning the fair market value of the property. Once the fair value is determined, the court directs the government to compensate the owner. Then the court will order the property condemned. The owner may appeal the decision, but once a final determination is made, the government may take the property in spite of any personal objections by the former owner.

Example: An area's rapidly growing population makes it essential to expand the road system. The new road expansion will run directly across Johnson's property. The government offers to purchase Johnson's property. Johnson stubbornly refuses, because he has lived in this house for 25 years and doesn't want to move, no matter what the price. The government files a condemnation suit under the power of eminent domain, seeking to condemn Johnson's property. The court determines the fair market value of the property, orders the property condemned, and orders the government to pay Johnson the determined value.

Eminent domain: the government's power to take property for public use upon payment of just compensation

POLICE POWER

Police power: the government's power to regulate property so long as it relates to public's safety and general welfare

Through the power of eminent domain, the government can take private property for a public use. Through its police power, the government can regulate how a private owner uses the property.

Police power is the state's power to adopt and enforce laws and regulations necessary for the public's health, safety, morals and general welfare.

When property is taken through eminent domain, the government must pay the property owner just compensation. When property is regulated under the police power, however, the government does not have to pay any compensation to the property owner.

A state's police power may be delegated to local governments. Police power allows state and local governments to regulate the way a person uses his or her property.

> **Example:** Zoning laws (discussed in Chapter 1) are an exercise of police power. If a zoning law designates an area as residential, then a property owner may not build a commercial building on the property.

Any exercise of the police power must meet certain constitutional limitations. In general, a regulation meets the constitutional requirements if the following four criteria are met:

1. it is reasonably related to the government's power to legislate for the protection of the public health, safety, morals or general welfare;
2. it applies in the same manner to all property owners who are similarly situated (it is not discriminatory);
3. it does not reduce the property value so much that it amounts to confiscation; and
4. it provides a benefit to the public by preventing harm that would be caused by the prohibited use of the property.

> **Example:** A local zoning ordinance provides that no buildings may be constructed closer to the river than 100 feet from the mean high water mark. The river has a tendency to flood every few years and the highest flood line in the past has been 90 feet from the mean high water mark.

This zoning ordinance is meant to protect the public's safety and general welfare. It applies to everyone who owns riverfront property. It does not reduce the property value so much that it amounts to confiscation, since riverfront property is valuable even without buildings. Plus, it does not completely forbid building, it simply establishes setback requirements. Finally, it provides a benefit to the public by preventing possible harm caused by flood damage if buildings were built too close to the river.

ESCHEAT

This chapter has discussed two ways in which the government may acquire property. If property taxes are not paid, the government may foreclose on the property. If the property is needed for a public use, it may be condemned under the power of eminent domain.

Another method by which the government sometimes acquires property is escheat. Our system of property ownership requires that all land be owned by someone. If there is no private owner, it is owned by the government. If property is abandoned, or if a person dies and leaves no heirs and no will stating how to dispose of his or her property, the property reverts to the state. This is called escheat.

Escheat: reversion of ownership of abandoned property to the state

ESTATES IN LAND

The first part of this chapter dealt with government interests in real property. This section discusses private interests in real property.

> **The word "estate" refers to an interest in land that is or may become possessory.**

Estate: a possessory interest in real property

In other words, someone has now, or may have in the future, the right to possess the property. Different types of estates are distinguished by their duration (for how long does the person have the right of possession?) and by their time of possession (does the person have the right to possess the property right now, or not until sometime in the future?).

The two main categories of estates are:

- freehold estates, and
- leasehold estates

There are also subcategories of estates within these two main groups. The type of estate is significant to a real estate agent. If an estate is being sold, the agent needs to know if the buyer's right to possession of the property will be limited in any way. Is there anything that could terminate the buyer's estate? Sometimes real estate agents are involved in leasing property. Because of this, it is also important for agents to understand the different types of leasehold estates.

FREEHOLD ESTATES

Freehold estate: an interest in property that is of indeterminate duration and possessory; owner holds (or will receive) title

The freehold estate got its name back in the Middle Ages. It originally referred to the holdings of a freeman under the English feudal system, and the name was carried on into the American colonies. When we say that a person "owns" property, we generally mean that he or she has a freehold estate.

> **There are three main characteristics of a freehold estate.**

First, the owner of a freehold estate holds a possessory interest in the property. This means that the owner has the right to possess the property. The second and most important characteristic of a freehold estate is that the owner's right of possession is of an indeterminate duration. This means that the length of time of ownership is unspecified and indefinite. There is no set or established time when ownership will end. Third, the owner of a freehold estate now holds or will in the future receive title to the property.

FREEHOLD ESTATE

- possessory
- indeterminate duration
- title

There are three subcategories of freehold estates:

- the fee simple absolute,
- the fee simple defeasible, and
- the life estate.

All of these meet the main requirements for freehold estates, but they also have additional identifying characteristics.

FEE SIMPLE ABSOLUTE. The fee simple absolute is the largest owner-ship interest possible. It is the highest and most complete form of ownership.

> **The owner of a fee simple absolute estate owns the whole "bundle of rights" that attach to the ownership of real property, including the right to use, lease, mortgage, improve or transfer the property.**

Fee simple absolute: the largest ownership interest possible; of potentially infinite duration and freely transferable

In a typical sale of residential property, the seller probably holds a fee simple absolute estate in the property.

A fee simple absolute estate is freely transferable. This means that the owner can sell, will, or even give away the property without anyone else's permission. This type of estate has no prescribed ter-mination date. Theoretically, a fee simple absolute estate can be owned in perpetuity (forever) by the owner or his heirs.

FEE SIMPLE ABSOLUTE

- possessory
- indeterminate duration
- title
- freely transferable and inheritable
- perpetual

FEE SIMPLE DEFEASIBLE. The second type of freehold estate is the fee simple defeasible. The word "defeasible" means capable of being defeated, annulled, or revoked.

> **A fee simple defeasible is an estate that may be defeated, an-nulled, or revoked upon the happening of a certain condition or event.**

Fee simple defeasible: a freehold estate that may terminate upon the happening of certain stated conditions

This type of estate is sometimes referred to as a determinable fee. The fee simple defeasible is qualified or limited by some condition placed on it by the person creating the estate. For instance, in transfer-ring an estate, the grantor may specify that the estate will continue only so long as a particular condition is met.

Example: Able conveys Blackacre to the First Christian Church and its heirs or assigns, so long as it is used for church purposes, but if no longer used for church purposes, it shall revert back to Able or his heirs.

In the example, the First Christian Church holds the same interest as the owner of a fee simple absolute, except that its interest is conditional and may terminate if the specified condition is not met.

The First Christian Church has the right to possess the property for an indeterminate duration, so long as the property is used for church purposes. The First Christian Church holds title to the property and can sell or transfer the property, but the sale or transfer is subject to the condition. If the new owner did not use the property for church purposes, the property would revert back to Able or his heirs.

FEE SIMPLE DEFEASIBLE

- possessory
- indeterminate duration (so long as the condition is met)
- title
- transferable and inheritable (subject to condition)

LIFE ESTATE. The third type of freehold estate is the life estate.

Life estate: a freehold estate that is measured by the life of one or more persons

> **A life estate is limited in duration to the life of a specified person.**

Example: Adam deeds property to his grandmother for her lifetime. Grandma has the right to possess and use the property for the rest of her life. She is the life tenant. The life estate terminates with her death.

Since the grantor (Adam) only gives an estate of limited duration (Grandma's lifetime) there must be an arrangement for the disposition of the estate upon Grandma's death.

Reversion. If the grantor retains the fee simple estate, upon the life tenant's death, the property will revert back to the grantor. The grantor holds what is called an estate in reversion. He or she is referred to as the **reverter**.

> **Example:** Adam transfers the property to his grandmother with a deed that states "to Elizabeth Simpson Collier for her lifetime. Upon her death, the property shall revert to Adam David Collier or his heirs."

Remainder. If the fee simple estate will go to someone other than the grantor, the future ownership is called an estate in remainder.

> **Example:** Adam gives a life estate to his grandmother, with the remainder to his daughter Jessica. The deed states: "to Elizabeth Simpson Collier for her lifetime. Upon her death, to Jessica Ann Collier or her heirs."

Jessica is called the **remainderman**; she has an estate in remainder.

The remainderman has a future possessory interest in the property.

Jessica does not have the right to possess the property right now, but she does have a right that will allow her to possess the property in the future. (A reverter's interest is also considered a future possessory interest.) Upon Grandma's death, the life estate terminates and Jessica receives a fee simple absolute estate.

Grandma is the life tenant (the holder of the life estate), and the duration of the life estate is measured by her lifetime. Grandma has the right to possess the property during her lifetime, and her right of possession is of indefinite duration (since no one knows exactly when she will die).

While she is alive, Grandma holds title to the property. She has the right to lease or even sell the property. But remember that she can only sell what she owns. If she sells the property, the buyer only receives the property for the rest of Grandma's life. If she leases the property, the lease is only good while Grandma is alive. When Grandma dies, the property automatically passes to Jessica. Jessica does not have to honor any lease that Grandma created.

Example: Grandma leases the property to Allison Bouvier for six months in the winter while she goes to Florida. After only three months in Florida, Grandma has a heart attack and dies. Allison's lease is no longer valid. The property automatically passes to Jessica.

A life tenant has certain duties created by the fact that there is someone with a future interest in the property.

A life tenant must not commit **waste**. This means that the life tenant must not engage in acts which will permanently damage the property, or harm the interests of the reversionary or remainder estate. The life tenant must allow for reasonable inspection of the property by the reverter or remainderman, who is permitted to check for possible waste.

Pur Autre Vie. A life estate may also be created based on the life of someone other than the holder of the life estate. This is called a life estate "pur autre vie" (for another's life). This type of estate is sometimes used to create security for ailing parents or disabled children who are unable to provide for themselves.

Example: Bob's mother is afflicted with Alzheimer's disease and is unable to care for herself. His sister Charlotte has been taking care of Mother. Bob deeds some property to Charlotte for the duration of Mother's lifetime. Upon Mother's death, the property is to revert to Bob. Charlotte has a life estate based on Mother's life. Charlotte owns and has the right to use and possess the property only until Mother dies. When Mother dies, the property automatically reverts to Bob.

In the example, Mother is the measuring life. The life estate lasts only as long as her lifetime. Charlotte is the holder of the life estate. She has the right to possess and use the property and is called the life tenant.

LIFE ESTATE

- possessory
- indeterminate duration (as long as the person who is the measuring life remains alive)
- title (but subject to rights of remainderman or reverter)
- lease or transfer (valid until the death of the person who is the measuring life)

Modern Practice. A real estate agent should be very cautious whenever handling a transaction that involves a life estate. The agent and all of the parties must remember that a life tenant may sell or lease the property, but upon the life tenant's death, the buyer or lessee loses his or her interest and the property passes to the reverter or remainderman.

In modern practice, life estates are seldom used because trusts can provide the same benefits with fewer potential problems. Plus, a trust has the additional safety factor of a trustee who looks out for the interests of the party who is to benefit by the trust.

However, life estates are still used in some situations. For example, property formerly owned by President Lyndon Johnson has been donated as a National Historical Site. However, President Johnson's wife, Ladybird, has a life estate in the property. She owns the property and has the right to possess and live on it for the remainder of her life. Upon her death, the property will become a National Historical Site.

LEASEHOLD ESTATES

A leasehold estate is a more limited interest in property than a freehold estate. The holder of a leasehold estate does not own the property, but merely has the right to possession of the property.

A leasehold estate is created by a contract called a lease. The parties to a lease are the landlord (lessor), who is the owner of the property, and the tenant (lessee), the party with the right of possession.

Leasehold estate: an estate created by a lease; the owner gives the tenant an exclusive right of possession

---

The lease grants the right of possession to the tenant for a specified period of time, with a reversion of the possessory rights to the landlord at the end of the rental period.

A lease is a contract; its provisions are interpreted under contract law. Understanding the different leasehold estates is important to any agent involved in leasing property. There are three types:

- the estate for years,
- the estate at will, and
- the estate at sufferance.

ESTATE FOR YEARS.

Estate for years: a leasehold estate of fixed duration

> **The estate for years is a tenancy for a fixed or specific time period.**

Its name is misleading in the sense that the duration does not have to be for a year or a period of years. It must only be for a fixed period of time.

Example: Bob rents a cabin in Northern Minnesota for a period from June first through September fifteenth.

Bob has an estate for years because the rental term is fixed. Since the rental term is fixed, the lease will terminate automatically on the expiration of the rental period. Neither the landlord nor the tenant is required to give notice to terminate the lease agreement. It simply ends at the specified time.

If either party wants to terminate the lease before the end of the term, they may do so only by mutual consent (both parties agree). Termination of a lease by mutual consent is called surrender.

Unless specifically prohibited by the lease, an estate for years is assignable by the tenant. This means the tenant may sublease or assign the interest in the lease to someone else. The lease agreement is not terminated, but is merely taken over by the new party.

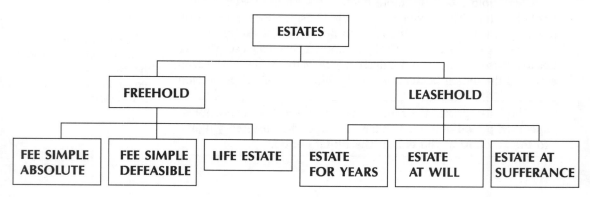

ESTATE AT WILL. A second type of leasehold estate is the estate at will.

Estate at will: a leasehold estate that exists indefinitely until notice is given

> An estate at will is a tenancy in which the tenant has the right to occupy and use the landlord's property for an indefinite period of time.

It is often created by a tenant taking possession of property without agreeing to a definite termination date.

> **Example:** Bianucci agrees to rent out the apartment over her garage to Reilly. She tells him that the rent is $400 per month. Reilly signs a lease agreeing to pay $400 rent on the first of each month, but they don't discuss how long he is planning to stay, and the lease does not specify a time period.

The most important characteristic of an estate at will is that it automatically renews itself. Each month Reilly pays rent, and the estate at will is automatically renewed for another month. That is why the estate at will is often referred to as a month-to-month lease. Unlike the estate for years, which automatically terminates, the estate at will automatically continues until one of the parties gives notice to terminate. Minnesota law requires a minimum of two weeks' or one rental interval's notice, whichever is more.

> **Example:** Reilly's estate at will continues automatically from month to month. If Reilly wants to leave, he must give Bianucci one full rental interval's notice. If Bianucci wants to end the rental, she must give Reilly one full rental interval's notice.

Failure to give proper notice will result in the automatic extension of the lease for an additional rental interval.

> **Example:** If Reilly moves out on April 1st, but he failed to give Bianucci notice that he was leaving, he will be liable for payment of April's rent and May's rent.

An estate at will may also be created after an estate for years has terminated.

Example: Melissa rents a house and signs a one-year lease. She pays rent on the first of every month. This is an estate for years, because it is for a fixed time period. When one year is up, Melissa does not sign a new lease, but she simply goes on paying rent on the first of every month, and the landlord accepts the money. Melissa now has an estate at will.

An estate at will may also arise when a lease has expired and the parties are in the process of negotiating the terms of the new lease.

Note that unlike an estate for years, which is not affected by the death of the landlord or tenant, the estate at will automatically terminates upon the death of the tenant.

ESTATE AT SUFFERANCE. An estate at sufferance is a situation created when the "tenant" originally took possession of the property lawfully but stays on without the owner's consent. This often occurs when the tenant originally had a valid lease, but holds over after the lease has expired, without the consent of the landlord.

Estate at sufferance: a situation created when a tenant who had a valid lease stays on without the owner's permission after the lease has expired

Example: Joe has a one-year lease to rent an apartment from Landlord Sam. At the end of the year, Sam does not want to renew the lease or keep renting to Joe, but Joe refuses to move out. Although Joe initially obtained possession of the property legally, under a valid lease, he is remaining without the landlord's consent.

> **An estate at sufferance is simply a way to distinguish between a tenant who lawfully entered into possession but holds over without consent, and a trespasser who never had permission to enter the land.**

Under an estate at sufferance, the tenant has no current right to possess the property. However, the landlord must follow the proper legal procedures for eviction (notice, a court hearing, and removal by a legal authority), as required by the Minnesota forcible entry and unlawful detainer statutes.

ENCUMBRANCES

When property is being sold or transferred, the new owner will want to know if there are any encumbrances on the property.

> **An encumbrance is any claim, right or interest in property held by someone other than the property owner or another who has the legal right to possess the property (such as a tenant).**

Encumbrance: a claim, right, or interest in another's property

Any non-possessory interest in property is an encumbrance or cloud on the title to the property.

An encumbrance can be financial, like mortgages or tax liens, or it may be non-financial, as with easements and deed restrictions.

EASEMENTS

> **An easement is a right held by one person to use another person's land for a particular purpose.**

Easement: a right to use another's land for a particular purpose

Easements affect the value and use of property, so real estate agents and prospective buyers should find out whether a property is subject to any easements.

> **Example:** Seller's five-acre property is subject to an easement owned by B&D Railroad. Railroad tracks run across the southeast corner of the property. Buyer wants to build a house on the property, but isn't thrilled about a railroad track going through his backyard. The value of the property is substantially reduced because of the railroad's easement.

Some of the most common easements are shared driveways, and easements for utilities such as telephone, sewer, and electric power lines. A standard title insurance report will list all recorded easements, but usually won't list any unrecorded easements. An agent should ask the seller about easements, and should also keep an eye out for indications that the property is used by other people besides the seller (the neighbors, for instance).

There are two types of easements: easements appurtenant and easements in gross.

Easement appurtenant: an easement that burdens one piece of land for the benefit of another piece of land

EASEMENTS APPURTENANT. An easement is said to burden a piece of land—it is an encumbrance or a burden on the property.

> **An appurtenant easement burdens one piece of land for the benefit of another piece of land.**

The land that is benefited by the easement is called the dominant tenement. The owner of the dominant tenement is called the dominant tenant. The land burdened by the easement is called the servient tenement, and the owner of the servient tenement is the servient tenant.

Probably the most common example of an easement appurtenant is a right-of-way easement providing access across one parcel of land to another.

Example: Morgan Albright owns a piece of property with a right-of-way easement to travel over neighbor Schindler's property to reach the road.

The Schindler property is the servient tenement because the easement runs across it. The Schindler property is burdened by the easement. The Albright property is the dominant tenement, because it benefits from the easement.

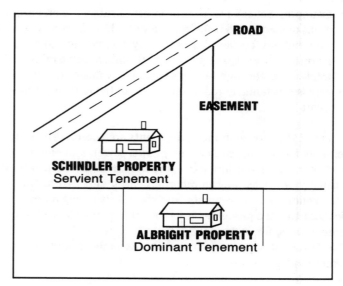

An appurtenant easement "runs" with the land. This means that if the land is transferred (sold, inherited, or given away), the easement is also transferred, even if the easement is not mentioned in the deed. An appurtenant easement cannot be sold separately from the property. Whoever owns the dominant property also owns the easement.

EASEMENTS IN GROSS.

> **An easement in gross belongs to an individual or a commercial entity. It does not run with the land.**

Easement in gross: an easement that belongs to an individual or entity, and does not run with the land

There is no dominant tenement involved with an easement in gross. There is only a servient tenement across which the easement runs.

> **Example:** Andy lives down the road from Carter. Carter grants Andy a personal easement to cross Carter's property and fish in the lake.

This is a personal easement in gross that will not pass with the land. If Andy dies the easement will be extinguished. Whoever inherits his property will not inherit the easement. A personal easement in gross cannot be sold or assigned. If Andy sells his property, the new owner does not have the right to cross Carter's property to fish in the lake. But most easements in gross are commercial rather than personal. The courts have held that unlike personal easements in gross, commercial easements in gross are freely assignable and transferable.

> **Example:** The Greentown Electric Company has an easement in gross to enter property to install and service its power lines. When Mega-Electric buys Greentown Electric, it also purchases the easement.

Note, however, that a commercial easement for a specific purpose usually cannot be sold for another purpose. For example, the electric company could not sell its easement for power lines to the local sewer district to run sewer lines through the easement.

When showing property to prospective buyers, a real estate agent should be able to explain all utility easements affecting the property.

An average residence may be subject to easements for the water company, the electric company, the gas company, a cable T.V. company, and the telephone company, just to name a few. All of these easements can have an impact on the value of the property.

> **Example:** If the electric company has an easement running through your backyard and installs unsightly power lines, this easement may substantially decrease the value of the property.
>
> If the local sewer district has an easement to run sewer lines under your property, which allows you to connect your plumbing to the sewer system, this may increase the value of the property.

CREATION OF EASEMENTS. It is fairly common for property to be affected by easements. When property is sold or transferred, the easements may be included. But how are easements originally created? There are several different methods of creation, including:

- express grant
- express reservation
- necessity
- dedication
- condemnation
- prescription, or
- recorded plat.

Express Grant. When an easement is created by express grant, the property owner expressly grants another person a specific right to use the property.

> **Example:** David sells the west half of his property to Martha. In the deed, he expressly grants Martha the right to use the private road located on his half of the property.

The creation of an easement by express grant must be in writing and must comply with all the legal requirements for a document conveying an interest in land. (See Chapter 3.)

Express Reservation. Creation of an easement by express reservation is similar to express grant, except that instead of giving away the easement, the landowner reserves it for himself, or for a third party.

> **Example:** David owns 80 acres abutting on a state highway and sells 40 acres containing all of the highway frontage to Martha. In the sale agreement and subsequent deed, he reserves to himself an easement across the 40 acres sold to Martha to provide access to his remaining 40 acres.

Necessity. If an easement is essential to a parcel of property, the court may find an easement by necessity.

> **For an easement to be created by necessity, the easement must be reasonably necessary for the enjoyment of the property, and there must have been a common grantor of the dominant and servient tenements.**

Easement by necessity: an easement which is essential to the use of property

In other words, one person (the common grantor) originally owned both halves of the property and then split it up.

If David in the example above had kept the 40 acres on the highway and sold the other 40 acres without specifically granting Martha a right of access, an easement would probably have been created by necessity, to give Martha access to the highway.

Dedication. A private landowner may grant the public an easement to use some portion of his or her property for a public purpose, such as a public walkway. This is called dedication.

> **The most common example of easements created by dedication occurs when a developer is trying to get approval for a new development or subdivision.**

The government may require the developer to dedicate certain portions of the development for public use, before granting approval. This usually includes amenities like sidewalks, recreation areas, or green areas.

Condemnation. The government may exercise its power of eminent domain and condemn private property for a public purpose.

> **The power to condemn property may also be granted to and exercised by private companies providing public services, such as railroads and power companies.**

In some cases, condemnation results in a transfer of title; in other cases, it merely results in the creation of an easement.

> **Example:** Because of population growth, the power company needs to run new power lines. The new lines would run across a portion of Halverson's property. The power company attempts to purchase an easement from Halverson but he refuses. The necessary property is condemned to create an easement for the power lines.

Prescriptive easement: an easement created by continuous, open use for 15 years

Prescription. A person can also acquire an easement simply by using the property as if the easement already existed. This is called an easement by prescription or prescriptive easement. Acquiring a prescriptive easement is similar to acquiring ownership of property through adverse possession. (See Chapter 3.) To claim a prescriptive easement, the party making the claim must have used the property in a way that was:

- open and notorious,
- hostile,
- reasonably continuous for at least 15 years, and
- under claim of right.

A use that is open and notorious means that the other party's use of the property is observable or apparent to the landowner, if the landowner pays attention to what is happening on the property. The use must also be hostile. Hostile simply means without the permission of the landowner. If the property is used with the owner's permission, an easement cannot be created by prescription.

> **In Minnesota, the party claiming the easement by prescription must have made use of the property for a period of 15 years or more.**

This use must be reasonably continuous. Continuous does not necessarily mean constant use, but only a continuous use that is normal for that property.

Example: Mrs. Green and Mr. Rose both own summer cottages on a cliff above the beach. There are steps to the beach cut into the rocky cliff between the properties. The steps are actually on Mrs. Green's property, but there is some confusion about the exact boundary line. Mr. Rose was told by the previous owner of his property that the steps were part of his property. Every summer for the last 15 years Mr. Rose has used these steps to get to the beach.

This is a continuous use even though Mr. Rose never uses the steps in winter. This is also a use under claim of right, since Mr. Rose believes that the steps are actually part of his property. A real estate agent should look for any use of the property by someone other than the owner. Such a use may be or could develop into an easement by prescription.

Note that there can be no prescriptive easements against government property. Even if all of the requirements listed above are met, a prescriptive easement cannot develop if the property is owned by the government.

Recorded Plat. If a landowner subdivides and sells his or her land according to a recorded plat, drainage, common areas, and utility easements would be shown on the plat. These easements are created simply by designating their location on the plat map and then recording the plat.

TERMINATING AN EASEMENT. Once an easement is created, it may exist indefinitely, or it may be terminated by actions of the parties, or by events beyond the control of the parties. An easement can be terminated by:

Easements usually exist indefinitely until terminated

- release
- merger, or
- abandonment.

Release. The holder of the easement may release his or her rights in the servient tenement at any time. This would be done with a written document, usually a quitclaim deed to the owner of the land subject to the easement.

Example: Carlucci has an access easement across Barton's property to reach the road. At the time the easement was created, Carlucci had no other access to the road. Several years later, the county built a new road that passed along the southern border of Carlucci's property. Carlucci no longer needs the road across Barton's property. Carlucci gives a quitclaim deed to Barton, releasing any claim he had on Barton's property. This terminates the easement.

Merger.   Since an easement is the right to make use of another's land, if the owner of the easement acquires ownership of the servient tenement, the need for the easement will no longer exist.

> **When the servient tenement and the dominant tenement are merged together under one ownership, the easement is terminated through merger.**

Example: Using the example above, suppose that Barton bought Carlucci's property before the new road was built. This would terminate the easement. When Barton owns both pieces of property, he has the right use the property any way he wants. He no longer needs an easement.

Abandonment.   An easement also may be terminated if the owner of the easement abandons it. Termination by abandonment requires proof that the owner intended to abandon the easement. This normally requires express acts by the owner indicating an intent to abandon it.

> **Mere non-use of the easement generally is not enough for abandonment.**

Example: Abernathy has an easement to cross Simpson's property to reach the lake. Abernathy breaks his leg, so he does not use the path all one summer. This is probably not enough for abandonment. But suppose Abernathy has not used the easement for five years and he plants a rose garden across the area where the path to Simpson's property used to be. He has abandoned the easement.

Easements are rights given to a particular person or entity to make use of another's property. They are a burden on the piece of property that is the servient tenement. They affect the property owner's use of the property, because the owner cannot interfere with the rights of the easement holder. Another type of encumbrance on property is the deed restriction. A deed restriction affects the property owner by placing restrictions on how the owner may use the property.

DEED RESTRICTIONS

Deed restrictions (including restrictive covenants, subdivision restrictions, and condominium bylaws) are privately created limitations on land use. These restrictions are placed on a landowner's use of the property by some previous owner.

Deed restrictions: limitations on land use placed on property by previous owner

> **Probably the most common example of private restrictions is the list of restrictions placed by a subdivider on lots within a new subdivision.**

Restrictive covenants may limit use of the property in a wide variety of ways. For example, they might restrict a lot to single-family residential use, require all structures on the property to be built of brick, or prohibit parking a recreational vehicle in the driveway. So long as the restrictions are not unconstitutional or in violation of some federal, state, or local law, or contrary to a judicial determination of public policy, they will normally be upheld and enforced by a court.

> **Example:** A subdivider imposes a restrictive covenant stating that no property within the subdivision may be sold to anyone who is black. This restriction would be unenforceable because it is unlawful discrimination.

> **It is up to the property owners to enforce restrictive covenants.**

If the character of a neighborhood changes because the residents failed to enforce the restrictions, they may be prevented from enforcing them later. In other words, even though a restriction is specifically listed in the deed, it is possible that the restriction is no longer enforceable.

> **Example:** Deed restrictions on property within the Whispering Pines subdivision state that no building additions may be made without approval of the architectural committee. However, the Whispering Pines subdivision is 30

years old and no architectural committee has even existed for the last 15 years. People within the subdivision have added family rooms, garages, and workrooms without any approval. This restriction is no longer enforceable, because the residents stopped enforcing the restriction.

LIENS

Lien: a financial encumbrance giving a creditor the right to sell the property and use the proceeds to pay off the debt

Easements and deed restrictions are both non-financial encumbrances on property. The other type of encumbrance is a financial encumbrance. A financial encumbrance is created when a lien is placed against the property.

> **A lien is a security interest in property. It is a charge against the property giving a creditor the right to sell the property (foreclose) and use the proceeds to pay the debt if the debtor fails to pay.**

The most common example is a mortgage.

Example: Joe buys a house for $100,000. He gets an $80,000 loan from the bank and gives the bank a mortgage for $80,000. The mortgage is a lien against the property. If Joe defaults on the mortgage, the bank has the right to sell the property and use the proceeds to pay off the mortgage.

A real estate agent should find out if there are any outstanding liens on the property. Liens are filed in the office of the county recorder in the county where the property is located.

The fact that there are liens on the property does not prevent its transfer or sale, but the transfer does not eliminate the liens. The new owner takes the property subject to the liens. It is extremely important for a buyer to know what liens are attached to the property before purchasing. In most cases, the buyer will require the seller to pay off any liens out of the sale proceeds.

There are many different types of liens, but all liens can be categorized as either general or specific.

Specific lien: attaches to a particular piece of property

Specific Liens. A specific lien is a lien that attaches only to a particular piece of property.

Example: A mortgage is a specific lien. It attaches only to the particular piece of property offered as security for the loan.

General Liens. A general lien is a lien that attaches to all of the debtor's property.

> **Example:** A judgment lien that arises after a court case is an example of a general lien. A judgment lien attaches to all property owned by the debtor.

All liens are either general or specific. But within these major categories, there are many different types of liens, such as:

- government liens,
- mechanics' or construction liens,
- mortgages, and
- judgment liens.

GOVERNMENT LIENS. Government liens include property tax liens, special assessment liens, and liens resulting from other taxes.

> **Property taxes and special assessments create specific liens against real property.**

The lien for general property taxes attaches to the taxed property on the first Monday in January in the year when payment is due. If the taxes are not paid, the state may foreclose and sell the property to collect the unpaid taxes.

A special assessment lien attaches to each of the properties that benefits from a local improvement. The amount of the lien is the owner's share of the cost of the improvement. As with general property taxes, if the property owner does not pay a special assessment, the property may be sold to collect the unpaid amount.

Other types of taxes, such as state and federal income taxes, can result in liens against real property. A federal income tax lien is a general lien against all of the taxpayer's property. The lien is not filed until payment of income taxes is delinquent.

MECHANICS' LIENS. A mechanic's lien (also called a construction lien) arises when someone provides labor, skill, equipment, or materials for improvements on the property. This includes people like contractors, subcontractors, surveyors, architects, engineers, painters, laborers, and plumbers. These liens are specific.

General lien: attaches to all of debtor's property

Government lien: for unpaid taxes or special assessments

Mechanic's lien: a lien filed by one supplying labor or materials for improvements on property

> **Mechanics' liens are authorized by Minnesota statute. Under the statute, a lien attaches when the first item of labor or material is furnished.**

Contractor lien notice: notifies property owners that a lien could be enforced against property if materials or labor are not paid for

Contractor Lien Notice. In Minnesota, contractors must provide property owners with a specific written notice informing the owners that a lien could be enforced against the property if those who provided materials or labor are not paid. This notice is normally included in the written contract between the parties. If there is no written contract, or if the contract does not include this notice, the contractor must give a written lien notice to the owner within **ten days** from the date of their agreement.

The required notice also warns the property owners that they could be responsible for money owed to subcontractors or others who provided labor or materials, even though the owners had no direct contract with them.

> **Example:** A property owner has a written agreement with a contractor to build a house on the property. The contractor hires several subcontractors (such as electricians, plumbers, and painters) to work on the house. The owner pays the contractor, but the contractor fails to pay the subcontractors. The subcontractors have liens against the property, even though the owner had no direct contract or agreement with them.

In the example, the owner could wind up paying double since he already paid the contractor and is also liable for the subcontractors' liens. To protect against this possible double payment, Minnesota law also requires that the written lien notice inform the owner that he or she is permitted to withhold from the contractor as much of the contract price as may be necessary to meet the demands of the other lien claimants (such as subcontractors). The owner may pay the subcontractors or laborers directly and then deduct that amount from the contract price paid to the contractor.

Subcontractor Lien Notice. Every person who contributes to the improvement of property in such a way that a lien could arise against the property, must give notice to the owner that such a lien could arise. This includes anyone who provides labor, skill, or materials. This notice must be given to the owner no later than 45 days after the lien claimant has first furnished labor or materials.

Example: On February 15, the owner signs a contract with a general contractor to build a house. The contract includes the required contractor lien notice. On April 12, work actually begins. A power shovel is used to begin excavation on the basement. The owner of the power shovel must give the owner the subcontractor lien notice within 45 days (by May 27).

Exceptions. The statute includes some exceptions, situations in which a lien notice does not have to be given. For example, the notice does not have to be given to an owner of a building with more than four units, or to owners of certain nonresidential property.

Enforcing the lien. In Minnesota, a mechanic's lien attaches when labor or materials are first provided, even though no documents have been filed.

> **To preserve and to be able to enforce the lien, the lien must be perfected by filing a lien statement in the county where the property is located.**

The lien statement must be filed within 120 days after the last item of labor or materials was furnished. If a lien statement is not filed by then, the lien terminates. A mechanic's lien must be enforced within one year by filing a foreclosure lawsuit. If no action is taken within a year, the lien is no longer enforceable.

Notice of non-responsibility. Whenever improvements are made to property, several people may be held responsible, such as the owner, a seller under a contract for deed, the landlord, or a tenant in possession. All of these people may be held to have authorized the improvements so as to subject their interest in the property to a mechanic's lien. An owner who has not authorized an improvement may protect himself or herself by posting a notice of non-responsibility. This notice simply states that the improvement is being made without the owner's authority.

Torrens recording. Although most documents affecting property in Minnesota are recorded in the county recorder's office, Minnesota also uses a property registration method called the Torrens system. (See Chapter 4.) If property is registered under the Torrens system, a mechanic's lien must be recorded on the certificate of title in order to be an encumbrance on the property.

Mortgage lien: voluntary
lien to secure repayment
of a loan

MORTGAGE LIENS. Perhaps the most common type of lien is the mortgage. A mortgage is a specific, voluntary lien created by a contract between the landowner (the borrower or mortgagor) and the creditor (the lender or mortgagee). The property owner gives the lender a lien against the property to secure repayment of a loan.

> **The essence of a mortgage is that the mortgagee (usually a bank or other institutional lender) can foreclose and force the sale of the property if the mortgagor fails to pay the debt.**

Mortgages are discussed in more detail in Chapter 7.

In some states, a deed of trust is used for the same purpose as a mortgage. There are three parties rather than the two found in a mortgage transaction. The borrower is called a trustor or grantor, the lender or creditor is called the beneficiary, and there is an independent third party (often an attorney or title insurance company) called the trustee. The deed of trust is not used in Minnesota.

Judgment lien: general lien
arising after a money
judgment in a lawsuit

JUDGMENT LIENS. Another fairly common type of lien is the judgment lien. Judgment liens are general liens. They arise after a lawsuit in which a money judgment is awarded. The winner of the lawsuit is called the judgment creditor. The judgment creditor is entitled to payment of the amount determined at trial. The loser is called the judgment debtor. If the judgment debtor does not pay, the judgment creditor may obtain a lien against the judgment debtor's property.

> **The lien attaches to all property owned by the debtor in the county where the judgment was entered.**

LIENS		
	General	**Specific**
Government liens (property taxes and special assessments)		X
Mechanics' liens		X
Mortgages		X
Judgment liens	X	

It also attaches to any property acquired by the debtor during the lien period. The lien period is the statutory time limit the judgment creditor has to take action on the lien. A notice of lien may also be filed in other counties in the state. This extends the lien to all of the property owned by the debtor in the other counties.

LIEN PRIORITY. It is not unusual for a piece of property to have several types of liens placed on it. One property may be encumbered by a mortgage, a mechanic's lien, and a tax lien. Often the total amount of the liens is more than the property will bring at a forced sale. Therefore, even after the property is sold, all of the liens cannot be paid in full.

Lien priority: the rules for distribution of proceeds from forced sale

In such a situation, the court must determine how the proceeds of the sale will be distributed. Rather than allocating the money among the lienholders in a pro-rata fashion, the normal rule is to pay the liens according to their priority. This means that the lien having highest priority is paid in full first. If any money is left over, the lien having second highest priority is paid, and so forth.

The general rule is that the priority of liens follows the order in which they were created.

In other words, the first lien to arise gets first priority for payment. However, there are some exceptions to this rule. Property tax and special assessment liens are superior to all other liens against the property. Therefore, property tax and special assessment liens have first priority even if there are other liens against the property that were created earlier. Also, a lien for general property taxes is superior to a lien for a special assessment, even if the special assessment lien was created first.

For priority purposes, the date used for mechanics' liens is the date work first started on the project. For other types of liens, the date used is the date the lien was filed and recorded.

Example: Certain property has the following liens against it:

- a judgment lien filed October 1st;
- a lien for a special assessment that attached November 10th;
- a mechanic's lien where work on the project started on September 30th, but the lien was not recorded until December 20th;
- a lien for general property taxes that attached January 1st.

When the property is sold at a foreclosure sale, the liens would be paid out of the sale proceeds in the following order:

1. general property tax lien
2. special assessment lien
3. mechanic's lien
4. judgment lien

ENCROACHMENTS

Encroachment: the unauthorized use of someone else's property

While an easement is a right granted to one party to use someone else's property, an encroachment is an unauthorized use of someone else's property.

> **Example:** When Carter built his new patio, it was built partially over the property line onto the neighbor's land.

Most encroachments are unintentional, the product of miscalculation or poor planning. An encroachment reduces the value, use, or enjoyment of the invaded property. When a dispute arises concerning an encroachment, a court can order an encroachment's removal, or if the cost of removal would be too high, it can award money damages instead.

> **Encroachments are not revealed by a title search. Accordingly, they are not covered by a standard title insurance policy. A physical inspection of the property may reveal an obvious encroachment, or a survey may reveal less obvious encroachments.**

Technically, an encroachment is not an encumbrance because it is not a right or interest held by the encroacher. However, if ignored for the 15-year statutory prescriptive period, the encroachment could ripen into an easement by prescription, or even title by adverse possession.

Real estate agents should check for encroachments by asking the seller and by inspecting the property to see if there are any visible encroachments. An agent may want to suggest that a survey be made if there are questions concerning boundary lines and possible encroachments.

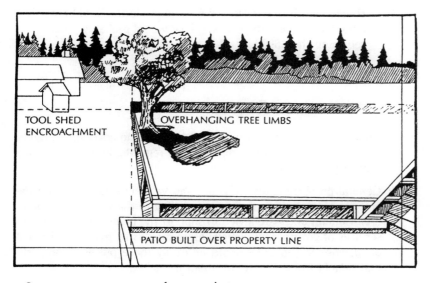

TOOL SHED
ENCROACHMENT

OVERHANGING TREE LIMBS

PATIO BUILT OVER PROPERTY LINE

Some common causes of encroachments

LICENSES

Like an easement, a license grants permission to enter another's property for a specific purpose. But a license does not create an interest in the property and is not an encumbrance against the title. It is simply a limited personal privilege to use the land.

A license is usually temporary or for a limited time period. For instance, a property owner might give someone permission to park in her driveway for two weeks. That would be considered a license.

A license can't be sold or assigned. If the licensee dies, the license terminates. A license may also be revoked or cancelled at any time by the person who issued the license.

> License: permission to enter another's property for a specific purpose; a limited personal privilege that does not create an interest in property

Example: Engles owns a large pasture right next to the freeway. For $500, Engles agreed to allow the XYZ Company to put up a billboard in one corner of the pasture. XYZ has a license to enter the pasture and put up the billboard.

Engles didn't ask what was going to be on the billboard. It turns out to be an ad for an X-rated movie theater, and Engles strongly disapproves. Engles tells XYZ to take the billboard down immediately. XYZ's license is revoked. Of course, Engles may have to pay damages to the XYZ Company for revoking the license. (That would probably mean returning the $500.)

CHAPTER SUMMARY

1. An individual's land use rights are subordinate to government rights. The government has the right to tax, regulate, and even to take private property for public use.

2. General property taxes are called "ad valorem" taxes because the amount of the tax is calculated according to the value of the property. General taxes are levied to support the general operation and services of government. Special assessments are levied for the cost of specific local improvements, and only those pieces of property that benefit from the improvement are taxed.

3. The power of eminent domain is the government's power to take private property for public use (condemn it). When private property is taken, the government must pay just compensation to the owner.

4. Police power is the power that allows state and local governments to regulate the way a person uses his or her property (such as through zoning laws or land use restrictions), for the protection of the public health, safety, and welfare.

5. If property is abandoned, or if a person dies and leaves no heirs and no will stating how to dispose of his or her property, the property will escheat to the state.

6. An estate is an interest in property that is or may become possessory. There are two types of fee simple estates, the fee simple absolute and the fee simple defeasible. The fee simple absolute is the highest and most complete form of ownership.

7. A life estate is an estate measured by someone's lifetime. The person who will receive the property when the life estate ends holds an estate in remainder or an estate in reversion.

8. A leasehold estate is a non-ownership, possessory interest in property. There are three types of leasehold estates: an estate for years, an estate at will, and an estate at sufferance.

9. An encumbrance is any right, claim, or interest in property held by someone other than the property owner or the one who has legal right of possession.

10. An easement is a non-financial encumbrance. Easements may be appurtenant or in gross. Easements may be created by express grant, express reservation, necessity, dedication, condemnation, prescription, or recorded plat.

11. Deed restrictions are privately created limitations on land use. The most common examples are restrictions placed on lots within a subdivision.

12. A lien is a financial encumbrance against property. Liens may be specific or general. The most common types of liens are government liens, mechanics' liens (construction liens), mortgages, and judgment liens.

13. An encroachment is an unauthorized use of someone else's property. Most encroachments are unintentional.

14. A license is similar to an easement; it grants permission to enter another's property for a specific purpose. However, a license does not create an interest in the property and is not an encumbrance against the title.

CHAPTER 2—GLOSSARY REVIEW

A. deed restrictions
B. in gross
C. mechanic's lien
D. appurtenant
E. police power
F. testate
G. intestate
H. life estate
I. eminent domain
J. lien
K. property taxation

L. easement
M. encroachment
N. judgment lien
O. statute of limitations
P. encumbrance
Q. fee simple estate
R. government lien
S. 120
T. ten
U. escheat

1. List three ways that government can acquire privately held land:
   1) _____ 2) _____ 3) _____

2. The broad right of the government to place reasonable restrictions on the use of privately held land is known as _police power_

3. When a person dies without a will, he is said to have died _intestate_

4. A right of use or enjoyment which one person has in the lands of another for a special purpose is called an _easement_

5. An impediment or cloud on title to real property is called an _encumbrance_

6. A tree that overhangs into a neighbor's yard is an example of _encroachment_

7. Private agreements that govern the use of land are called _survey account_
   deed restrictions → restrictive covenants

8. A hold or claim which one person has on the property of another to secure payment of a debt is a _lien_ .

9. A person who has not been paid for work performed on real property may file a _mechanics lien_

10. A party wall or shared driveway is an example of an easement _appurtenant_.
    ?

11. The right of an owner to occupy a parcel of real estate forever is called a _fee simple absolute_
    fee estate

12. The type of lien that takes priority over all others is the _____.

13. A contractor must give notice to the owner of his lien rights within _____ days of entering into an agreement.

IRS
mechanics - specific lien

CHAPTER 2—REVIEW EXAM

1. Real property taxes are computed based upon the:

    a) appraised value.
    b) market value.
    c) assessed value.
    d) income value.

2. The process by which the government exercises its right to take private lands for public use is:

    a) condemnation.
    b) escheat.
    c) foreclosure.
    d) eminent domain.

3. All of the following are government powers EXCEPT:

    a) deed restrictions.
    b) taxation.
    c) zoning.
    d) escheat.

4. The goverment has the power to take title to property through escheat when:

    I. an owner dies intestate and without heirs.
    II. an owner is delinquent on property taxes.

    a) I only
    b) II only
    c) Both I and II
    d) Neither I nor II

5. The term "estate" refers to:

    I. the amount of property owned by an individual.
    II. the collection of rights held in real estate.

    a) I only
    b) II only
    c) Both I and II
    d) Neither I nor II

6. When an individual or entity holds a claim against another's property, this is known as:

    a) a chattel.
    b) a life tenancy.
    c) an encumbrance.
    d) a license.

7. A claim against real property to secure repayment of a debt is:

    a) a deed restriction.
    b) an encroachment.
    c) an easement.
    d) a lien.

8. A private agreement governing the use of real property is:

    a) a deed restriction.
    b) a restrictive covenant.
    c) an encumbrance.
    d) All of the above

9. Which of the following would be used by a purchaser to protect against encroachments?

   a) Title insurance
   b) Abstract of title
   c) Survey
   d) Attorney's title opinion

10. Which of the following liens has top priority in the event of foreclosure?

   a) Mechanic's lien
   b) First mortgage
   c) Property taxes
   d) Court judgment

11. The right of a lessor to take possession after a lease has expired is known as the right of:

   a) recission.
   b) redemption.
   c) reversion.
   d) assignment.

12. The grantor of a life estate may retain:

   a) a leasehold estate.
   b) a qualified fee estate.
   c) rights of remainder.
   d) reversionary rights.

13. If A grants a life estate to B and specifies that title will be transferred to C upon death of B, all of the following are true EXCEPT:

   a) B is the life tenant
   b) C has a reversionary interest
   c) B owns the property
   d) C is the remainderman

14. A tenancy in which the lessee remains in possession of the property without the lessor's consent is a:

   a) tenancy for years.
   b) tenancy at sufferance.
   c) tenancy at will.
   d) periodic tenancy.

15. Which of the following estates does not terminate on the death of the holder of the estate?

   a) Life estate
   b) Estate for years
   c) Estate at will
   d) Estate at sufferance

16. All of the following are true of a fee simple absolute estate holder EXCEPT:

   a) His estate terminates upon death.
   b) He has the largest estate available in land.
   c) He has maximum control over the property.
   d) He can transfer his rights to others.

17. A married couple has been granted the right to occupy and use a 10-acre tract of land forever. Which of the following does the couple hold?

   a) A fee simple estate
   b) An estate for years
   c) A life estate
   d) A joint tenancy estate

18. In a life estate, the life tenant may do all of the following EXCEPT:

    a) will the property
    b) sell the property
    c) lease the property
    d) improve the property

19. All of the following could be encumbrances on real estate EXCEPT:

    a) a lien
    b) a lease
    c) a restrictive covenant
    d) a fixture

20. The estate that lasts so long as a condition is met is known as a:

    a) life estate.
    b) fee simple determinable.
    c) fee simple absolute.
    d) deed restriction.

21. The right of the government to establish zoning and land use laws is an exercise of which of the following?

    a) Police power
    b) Escheat
    c) Government survey
    d) Eminent domain

22. A contractor or subcontractor has how many days to perfect a mechanic's lien after last labor or material has been provided to the property?

    a) 10 days
    b) 45 days
    c) 90 days
    d) 120 days

23. An estate with a definite expiration date would be known as a:

    a) tenancy at will.
    b) fee simple absolute.
    c) tenancy at sufferance.
    d) tenancy for years.

24. All of the following would be considered to have an interest in land EXCEPT:

    a) a farmer who is leasing 20 acres
    b) a holder of an easement
    c) a hunter who has been given permission to hunt in a field
    d) a lender holding a mortgage lien

25. When the state acquires private property through condemnation for fair compensation, it has exercised which of the following government rights?

    a) Escheat
    b) Police power
    c) Taxing power
    d) Eminent domain

26. The process used by the government to take a property when the property taxes are in default is known as:

    a) condemnation
    b) police power enforcement
    c) foreclosure
    d) escheat

27. Mr. Smith has given Mrs. Jones permission to plant a garden on a corner of Mr. Smith's land. Which of the following does Mrs. Jones have?

    a) A license
    b) An easement appurtenant
    c) An encroachment
    d) An easement in gross

28. An encumbrance that might impair the title to a property is:

    a) mortgagable title
    b) deficit title
    c) a cloud on title
    d) marketable title

CHAPTER 2—GLOSSARY REVIEW KEY

1. I, K, U
2. E
3. G
4. L
5. P
6. M
7. A
8. J
9. C
10. D
11. Q
12. R
13. T

CHAPTER 2—REVIEW EXAM KEY

1. c) Assessed value × tax rate = property tax.

2. a) The process is condemnation; the right is eminent domain.

3. a) Deed restrictions are *private* restrictions on the use or sale of a property.

4. a) Property "escheats" to the government upon death of an intestate owner with no heirs.

5. b) An "estate" in land refers to the collection or bundle of rights in the property.

6. c) An encumbrance is a right in or claim against property held by someone other than the owner.

7. d) A lien secures payment of an indebtedness.

8. d) Deed restrictions and restrictive covenants are private agreements governing land use. They both create an encumbrance on title.

9. c) A survey would be used to point out zoning violations or encroachments.

10. c) Government liens for property taxes and special assessments always have top priority.

11. c) Reversion means to "go back". Upon lease expiration the right to occupy "goes back" to the lessor (landlord).

12. d) If a grantor retains reversionary rights in a life estate, upon the tenant's death ownership in fee simple reverts to the grantor.

13. b) A reversionary interest could only be held by A, the grantor.

14. b) A tenancy at sufferance is a holdover after the legal tenancy has expired.

15. b) An estate for years lasts until the predetermined termination date.

16. a) Fee simple absolute estates last "forever."

17. a) The right to occupy and use forever is a fee simple estate.

18. a) The life estate terminates upon the death of the life tenant. It cannot be willed.

19. d) A fixture *is* real estate. Liens, leases and restrictive covenants are encumbrances.

20. b) Fee simple determinable estates last "so long as" a condition is met (also called a determinable fee).

21. a) Police power is the government's right to enact and enforce laws governing land use.

22. d) The lien begins upon first improvement. It ends 120 days after completion unless it is "perfected."

23. d) A tenancy for years has a specific termination date.

24. c) Granting *permission* to use one's land
         creates a license. A license is NOT an
         interest in land.

25. d) Condemnation is the process by
         which the government exercises emi-
         nent domain.

26. c) The county forecloses on its proper-
         ty tax lien.

27. a) Permission to use someone's land is
         a license.

28. c) An encumbrance is a cloud on title.

Chapter 3

OWNERSHIP AND TITLE TRANSFER

OUTLINE

I. Sole Ownership
  A. Estate in severalty
  B. Syndication
      1. corporations
      2. real estate investment trusts
      3. partnerships

II. Multiple Ownership
  A. Tenancy in common
  B. Joint tenancy

III. Other Forms of Ownership
  A. Condominiums
  B. Timesharing
  C. Cooperatives

IV. Conveying Ownership
  A. Essential elements of a deed
      1. competent parties
      2. consideration
      3. words of conveyance
      4. legal description
      5. execution
      6. delivery and acceptance
  B. Types of deeds
      1. general warranty deed
      2. limited (special) warranty deed
      3. quitclaim deed
      4. sheriff's deed

V. Transfer After Death
   A. Testate
   B. Intestate

VI. Other Ways of Acquiring Rights
   A. Adverse possession
   B. Easement by prescription
   C. Easement by necessity

VII. Minnesota Homestead Rights
   A. Requirements
   B. Exceptions

VIII. Green Acres

IX. Alien Ownership

KEY TERMS

severalty
tenancy in common
right of survivorship
syndication
partnership
common area
bylaws
timeshare
proprietary lease
deed
minor
consideration
grant
attorney in fact
delivery
covenant of seizin
covenant of further assurance
warranty forever
quitclaim deed
will
intestate

co-ownership
joint tenancy
partition suit
corporation
condominium
limited common element
condominium association
cooperative
Subdivided Lands Act
bill of sale
competent
words of conveyance
power of attorney
execution
general warranty deed
covenant of quiet enjoyment
covenant against encumbrance
special (limited) warranty deed
sheriff's deed
testate
probate

devise

administrator

easement by prescription

homestead

alien

executor

adverse possession

easement by necessity

green acres

CHAPTER OVERVIEW

The previous chapters in this book discuss the different kinds of estates, interests, and rights in property. This chapter explains the various forms of ownership of real property. Real property may be owned in many different ways, and by different entities. For example, property may be owned by a single person, a married couple, a group of friends, a partnership, a city, a corporation, or the federal government. This chapter also explains the ways in which title can be transferred: by deed, or upon the owner's death, or through adverse possession.

SOLE OWNERSHIP

> **When title to real property is held by one person it is called sole ownership or an estate in severalty.**

Sole ownership: ownership by one person or entity

Real property may be owned in severalty by natural persons (human beings) or artificial persons (corporations, cities, states, etc.). When property is held by a business entity, it is usually held in severalty. There may be many people who are part of the business entity, but they are not joint owners. The property is actually held in severalty, in the name of the entity.

ESTATE IN SEVERALTY

The term "severalty" is derived from the word "sever," which means to keep separate or apart, so an estate in severalty is owned separately. The owner of an estate in severalty is free to dispose of the property at will (at any time, and in any way).

In Minnesota, a married individual may own real estate in severalty. However, statutes provide protection for the non-owning spouse by requiring that the spouse must agree to and sign any document(s) transferring ownership. This is true regardless of marital status at the time ownership was acquired.

> **Example:** Gina, a single woman, is the sole owner of a home. After marriage, Gina still holds an estate in severalty. However, her husband will be required to sign any ownership transfer documents.

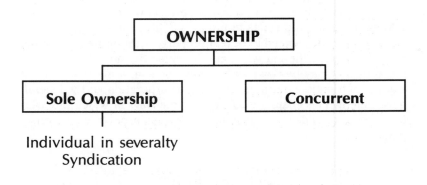

In Minnesota, real property owned by a married person cannot be sold or transferred without the signature of both spouses.

Thus the phrase "one to buy, two to sell" has become commonplace in real estate circles.

SYNDICATION

Syndicate: a group of people who have joined together to invest in real property; not a form of ownership

A syndicate is not really a form of ownership. It is simply a group of people who have joined together to engage in real property investments. A syndicate is not a recognized legal entity.

Like the word "company," the term "syndicate" can be used to refer to virtually any business organization. The XYZ Syndicate might be a corporation, a partnership, or a trust.

Business entities generally hold title to property in sole ownership. For example, when a corporation owns property, it usually holds title to the property in the name of the corporation. However, in some instances there is a different type of ownership. For example, individual partners may co-own property as joint tenants or tenants in common.

It is important for a real estate agent to understand some basic principles concerning how business associations can hold property, since the agent may be involved in the purchase or sale of property held by a business entity.

CORPORATIONS. The most sophisticated form of business association is the corporation. Corporations are composed of individuals who are empowered to conduct business as one person, the corporation.

> **The corporation is a separate entity from its stockholders. It is capable of perpetual existence and the death of stockholders does not affect its operation.**

A corporation is taxed separately from its shareholders. This "double taxation" is sometimes seen as a disadvantage of corporate ownership. The advantage of a corporation is that the stockholders' liability is limited.

Corporation: a separate entity with a perpetual existence; taxed separately from its shareholders

> **Example:** A corporation is sued. It loses the lawsuit and must pay damages. The stockholders are affected, because the price of their stock may go down. However, the stockholders are not individually liable for the amount of damages that must be paid.

The corporation, not the stockholders, owns the corporate property and controls the daily management functions. A corporation is run by its board of directors. When a corporation wants to buy or sell property all of the stockholders don't have to sign. The action must be authorized by a resolution of the board of directors. Someone within the corporation, such as the President or Chief Executive Officer, is generally given authority to act for the corporation. A title company will usually require proof of authorization by the board of directors before insuring a transaction.

> **Example:** A corporation is buying property. It is not necessary for every stockholder to sign the purchase agreement.

When a real estate agent is handling a sale for a corporation, the agent should know who is authorized to act for the corporation, and whose signature is required.

Real estate investment trust (REIT): an unincorporated group of at least 100 investors; taxed only on retained earnings

REAL ESTATE INVESTMENT TRUSTS (REITs). A real estate investment trust is established when a group of at least 100 investors form a trust and purchase certificates of ownership in the trust. The trust then invests in real estate and real estate mortgages and distributes any profits to the investors.

The trust is unincorporated, so it avoids corporate taxation. A trust is only taxed on its retained earnings. Most of its income is distributed to the stockholders to avoid any significant taxation to the trust. The profits distributed to the stockholders are taxed as ordinary income to the individual investors.

With an REIT, small investors can take advantage of big investment opportunities by pooling their resources.

> **Even though an REIT must have at least 100 investors, the entity has sole ownership of the property.**

PARTNERSHIPS. A partnership is a less complicated form of ownership than the corporation.

Partnership: an association of two or more persons joined to carry on a business for profit

> **A partnership is simply an association of two or more persons, who join together as co-owners to carry on a business for profit.**

There are two types of partnerships: general partnerships and limited partnerships. The duties and liabilities of partnerships are governed by the Uniform Partnership Act and the Uniform Limited Partnership Act, as adopted by Minnesota statute.

General Partnerships. The partners in a general partnership all share in the profits, debts, and management of the partnership. Each partner has an equal interest in and right to equal possession of the partnership property. The partners' interest in the profits, losses, and property is proportionate to their capital investment, unless otherwise agreed in a partnership agreement.

General partnership: all partners have equal share of management authority, assets and debts; property brought into partnership is partnership property, not individual property

The partnership may acquire property in the partnership's name. In general, all property brought into the partnership or acquired by the partnership is partnership property. The partnership property is subject to partnership obligations, but it is not open to the claims of the creditors of individual partners.

Each partner is both a principal for and an agent of the partnership for business purposes. So most acts of any individual partner, including the execution of legal documents, will be binding on the partnership. In other words, if one partner buys or sells property in the name of the partnership, the action is usually binding on the partnership. (See Chapter 9 for a general discussion of agency law.)

Limited Partnerships.

> A limited partnership is a partnership with one or more general partners and one or more limited partners. The general partners have unlimited partnership liability and an exclusive right to manage the partnership.

A limited partner's personal liability is limited to the amount of the limited partner's capital contribution. The limited partner has no voice in management. Profits and losses "pass through" the limited partnership to the limited partners in proportion to their ownership interest. In other words, a limited partner holding a 10% interest in the partnership would have income tax liability for 10% of the partnership's profits.

A limited partner has no ownership control over partnership property. The partnership property is controlled by the general partners just as in a general partnership. When a real estate agent is handling a transaction involving partnership property, the agent should make sure he or she is dealing with a general partner.

Joint Ventures. A joint venture is a partnership created for a single business transaction. It is not intended to be an ongoing business of indefinite duration. Joint ventures are generally governed by the same rules as partnerships.

> **Example:** A development corporation and a construction corporation form a joint venture to purchase and develop a 40-acre parcel of land. The developer and the builder would share in the costs of development and in the profits from lot sales.

SALE OF SYNDICATION INTERESTS. Ownership interests in a syndicate are examples of securities. These security interests (a share of stock in a corporation, for example) may be bought and sold separately from the entity itself. The sale of such securities is regulated federally by the Securities and Exchange Commission (SEC) and in Minnesota by the Commissioner of Commerce under the state "Blue Sky" laws. Under these regulations, registration of security interests may be required, and those who sell these interests for another and for a fee may be required to obtain a securities license.

Partners are both principals and agents of the partnership

Limited partner: liability limited to contribution; no voice in management

Joint venture: a partnership created for a single transaction

MULTIPLE OWNERSHIP

Multiple ownership:
when two or more
people simultaneously
share title to one piece
of property

Multiple ownership (also called concurrent ownership or co-ownership), exists when two or more people simultaneously share title to one piece of property. It is very important for a real estate agent to know if there is multiple ownership.

> **If the property is held by more than one owner, all owners must agree to the sale and sign any agreements.**

There are several forms of concurrent ownership, each with distinctive legal characteristics. The two most common forms of co-ownership are:

- tenancy in common, and
- joint tenancy.

The major difference between tenancy in common and joint tenancy lies in the disposition of an owner's interest in the property upon death. If a tenant in common dies, the deceased's interest goes to the deceased's heirs. If a joint tenant dies, the deceased's interest goes to the surviving co-owner(s). This feature is referred to as the right of survivorship.

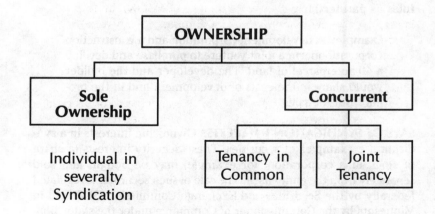

TENANCY IN COMMON

Tenancy in common is the most basic form of concurrent ownership. It is the residual category, which means that co-ownership that doesn't fit into any of the other categories is a tenancy in common by default.

> Unless the owners have an agreement to the contrary, Minnesota law presumes co-ownership is in the form of tenancy in common, with each owner holding an equal interest in the property.

Example: A deed transfers land to two unmarried individuals, but doesn't specify how they are taking title. They are presumed to take title as tenants in common, with each owner holding a 50% interest in the property.

In a tenancy in common, there is always an equal right of possession. However, each tenant in common may own an interest that is unequal but undivided. That is, there could be a 60/40 division of ownership between two tenants in common, but each would still have an equal right to possess all of the property. Regardless of the percentage of ownership, a tenant in common cannot be prevented from possessing the entire property and cannot be confined to any specific portion of the property.

Tenancy in common: co-ownership with equal rights of possession of the entire property

RIGHTS AND DUTIES OF TENANTS IN COMMON. In theory, there is no limit to how many tenants in common can share a property. There are also no restrictions on how they divide ownership. One tenant in common might own a ½ interest and 50 others might each own a $\frac{1}{100}$ interest.

> Unless specifically agreed otherwise, any income or proceeds generated by the property go to the individual tenants in proportion to their interest in the property.

Tenants in common share property income

Similarly, each tenant is required to share the property's expenses such as maintenance, insurance, taxes, mortgage payments, etc., in proportion to their ownership interests.

Example: Mike, Sean and Pat own property as tenants in common. Mike owns a ½ interest while Sean and Pat each own a ¼ interest. The property is a single family home that they rent to William for $800 per month. The expenses are divided proportionately, as is the income. Mike pays half of the expenses (such as property taxes) while Sean and Pat each only pay ¼. But Mike receives $400 of the rent, while Sean and Pat receive only $200 each.

Each tenant in common has the right to transfer or mortgage his or her interest in the property to another person, without the consent of the other tenant(s) in common. However, it takes all of the owners to transfer or mortgage the whole property.

Co-owner can transfer, will, or mortgage interest in property

Example: Continuing with the example above, Mike could sell his interest to Marie without even telling Sean or Pat. Marie would then own a ½ interest as a tenant in common with Sean and Pat. But Mike could not sell the whole property to Marie without the others. Sean and Pat would also have to agree to sell their interests, and all three tenants in common (Mike, Sean and Pat) would have to sign any agreements and sale documents.

This is important to buyers, sellers, and real estate agents. If someone is attempting to sell property that is held by more than one owner as tenants in common, an individual owner could only sell his or her interest in the property. In order to sell the whole parcel of property, all of the tenants in common must agree.

All owners are needed to transfer entire parcel

Since tenancy in common does not involve a right of survivorship, a tenant in common can will his or her interest in the property. When the tenant in common dies, his or her interest passes to the person named in the will. Or if a tenant in common dies without leaving a will, the deceased's interest passes to his or her heirs.

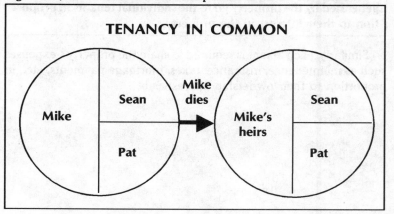

TENANCY IN COMMON

TERMINATION OF TENANCY IN COMMON. A tenancy in common can be terminated by agreement of all the tenants. They can agree to change to one of the other forms of ownership (such as joint tenancy), or they can agree to divide the property, so that each owns a portion in severalty. This division by agreement is called voluntary partition.

Termination of tenancy in common: by agreement or partition

A tenancy in common can also be terminated by the unilateral action of one of the tenants, without the others' consent. If Mike wants to end the tenancy in common, but Sean and Pat don't, Mike can file a partition action in court.

> **A partition suit is a legal action that divides the interests in the property.**

If possible, a court will actually divide the land, granting ownership in severalty to the separate parts. Often it is not possible to divide the property fairly, so the court orders the property to be sold and the proceeds are divided among the tenants in accordance with the fractional interests.

> **Example:** When Mr. Rundell died, he left his house to his seven children as tenants in common, with each child owning a $\frac{1}{7}$ interest in the property. The children cannot agree on what to do with the property. Some want to sell, some want to keep it and rent it out, some want to keep it and live in it. Since they cannot decide among themselves, one of the children files a partition action.
>
> It is impossible to divide a house up into seven different parts. So the court orders the house sold, with the proceeds divided evenly among the seven children.

In some cases, if practical, a judge may order part of the property sold and part of it physically divided.

> **Example:** Suppose that in the example above, the house is located on eight acres of land. The judge may order the house and the one acre of land surrounding the house sold, with the proceeds divided evenly, and then partition the remaining seven acres among the children, each receiving one acre.

A tenant in common in a partition suit may oppose a physical division of the property. He or she can present evidence (such as an appraisal) comparing the value of the divided property with the amount that a sale of the whole property would bring. If the divided property would be worth substantially less than the whole, the judge should order the property sold instead of physically divided.

JOINT TENANCY

Joint tenancy is the second type of co-ownership.

Joint tenancy: two or more people are joint and equal owners of real property and have a right of survivorship

> **A joint tenancy exists where two or more people are joint and equal owners of real property, and they have the right of survivorship.**

In the past, the common law required "four unities of title" to create a joint tenancy. These unities are the:

- unity of interest,
- unity of title,
- unity of time, and
- unity of possession.

The four unities simply meant that all joint tenants had to have acquired title from the same will or deed, at the same time, and all had to have an equal interest in and equal right to possession of the property. This requirement of the four unities has been abolished by statute in Minnesota. (It is still required in many other states.)

In Minnesota, a joint tenancy is created when a grant or devise of land is expressly declared to be in joint tenancy, regardless of whether all four unities exist. Each joint tenant has an equal interest in the property and an equal right to possess (occupy) the entire property. A particular joint tenant cannot be confined to any specific part of the property.

RIGHT OF SURVIVORSHIP. As long as joint tenants are alive, their relationship is similar to that of tenants in common. Each has the right to possess and use the entire property. The difference arises when one of the joint tenants dies.

> **When a joint tenant dies, his or her interest in the property passes automatically to the surviving joint tenant(s).**

The distinguishing feature of joint tenancy is this **right of survivorship**.

> **Example:** Mike, Pat, and Sean own property as joint tenants. Mike dies. Pat and Sean now own the entire property as joint tenants (including Mike's share). Mike's death simply reduced the number of owners from three to two.

Right of survivorship: when a joint tenant dies, interest automatically passes to surviving joint tenants

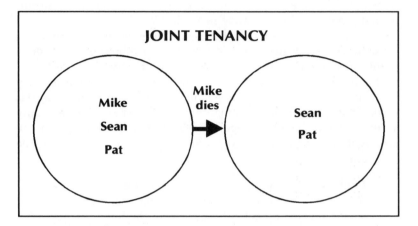

Since title passes directly to the other joint tenant(s) upon the death of one joint tenant, the deceased's interest may not be devised. (To devise is to give real property by will.) The heirs of the deceased joint tenant have no rights or interests in the joint tenancy property. A joint tenancy interest cannot be willed or inherited, because it no longer belongs to the joint tenant at the moment of death. As a result, joint tenancy property does not have to go through a lengthy probate process. This can spare the surviving joint tenants considerable expense and delay. The surviving owner(s) must simply record the death certificate and an executed affidavit of survivorship in order to eliminate the deceased's interest in the property.

Liens. Another result of the right of survivorship is that any liens against the deceased joint tenant's interest are extinguished upon his or her death. The surviving joint tenants take the interest free and clear of the deceased joint tenant's mortgage, judgment lien, or other debts. Because a lien against a joint tenant's interest is so easily lost, few creditors are willing to accept such an interest as security. A lien against the entire property—a mortgage signed by all the joint tenants, for example—is not lost if one or more of the joint tenants dies.

Liens against deceased joint tenant's interest are extinguished

TERMINATION OF JOINT TENANCY. Like a tenancy in common, a joint tenancy can be terminated by partition. The joint tenants may agree to divide up the property, or one of the joint tenants may file a partition suit against the other(s).

Joint tenancy may be terminated by agreement, by partition, or by severance

A joint tenancy may also be terminated by severance, which can occur in a number of different ways. Severance ends the joint tenancy and eliminates the right of survivorship, but unlike partition, it does not terminate the co-ownership. Instead, severance transforms a joint tenancy into a tenancy in common.

If all the joint tenants want to sever the joint tenancy, they can do so by signing an agreement to that effect. In Minnesota, this agreement does not have to be recorded to be effective.

Severance: transforms a joint tenancy into a tenancy in common; can occur without consent of other joint tenants

Each joint tenant also has the power to sever the joint tenancy without the consent of the other joint tenant(s). In Minnesota, this can be done by recording an instrument of severance in the county where the joint tenancy property is located. In some cases, the instrument of severance is simply a declaration of intent to sever the joint tenancy.

> **Example:** Mike and Pat own a house as joint tenants. Pat decides she wants to eliminate the right of survivorship, so she records a declaration severing the joint tenancy. Pat and Mike still own the house together, but they are tenants in common, not joint tenants.

In other cases, the instrument of severance is a deed transferring the joint tenant's interest to a third party.

> **Example:** Mike and Pat own some land as joint tenants. Pat sells her interest in the property to Jill. If Jill records her deed, that will sever the joint tenancy. Then Mike and Jill will each own a ½ interest, but they will be tenants in common, not joint tenants.

However, a transfer only severs the joint tenancy in regard to the transferred interest. When there are more than two joint tenants, the co-owners who did not transfer their interest remain joint tenants in relation to one another.

> **Example:** Mike, Pat, and Sean own some land as joint tenants. Pat sells her ⅓ interest to Jill, and Jill records her deed. That severs the joint tenancy as far as Pat's ⅓ interest is concerned, so Jill is not a joint tenant. Jill is a

tenant in common in relation to Mike and Sean. But Mike and Sean are still joint tenants in relation to each other.

If Jill were to die, her ⅓ interest would pass to her heirs, since the right of survivorship does not apply to her.

If instead Mike were to die, his ⅓ interest would belong to Sean, because the right of survivorship is still effective between Mike and Sean. Sean would then own a ⅔ interest and Jill would still own a ⅓ interest, and they would be tenants in common.

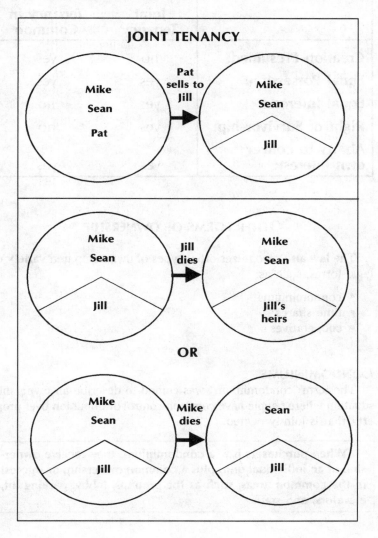

Severance can also occur without the consent of any of the joint tenants. A joint tenancy can be severed by court order. If a joint tenant goes bankrupt, the joint tenancy will often be severed in the court proceedings. And in Minnesota, when joint tenants are husband and wife, their divorce will sever the joint tenancy, unless the decree of dissolution expressly declares that they are still joint tenants.

COMMON FORMS OF JOINT OWNERSHIP		
	Joint Tenancy	Tenancy in Common
Creation Presumed:	no	yes
Equal Possession:	yes	yes
Equal Interests:	yes	no
Right of Survivorship:	yes	no
Ability to convey own interest:	yes	yes

OTHER FORMS OF OWNERSHIP

The law also recognizes other types of ownership in a variety of legal forms, such as:

- condominiums
- time shares
- cooperatives

CONDOMINIUMS

The term "condominium" was coined to describe an ownership situation where people have common control or dominion over property that is jointly owned.

Condominium: purchaser acquires ownership of an individual unit, plus an interest in the common areas

> When purchasers buy a condominium, they receive ownership of an individual unit, plus a common ownership or interest in the common areas, such as the grounds, lobby, parking lot, elevators, and stairs.

If a condominium is the owner's main residence, the owner may claim homestead rights in the condominium. Residential condominium ownership is popular in many urban and resort areas. Condominium ownership may also be used for commercial or business properties, such as office and professional buildings, medical clinics, shopping centers, or recreational developments.

CREATION. Condominiums are created in two ways. A developer may purchase land and obtain a construction loan for erecting a condominium project. Or an existing building (usually one with rental units) may be converted into condominiums. In Minnesota, when an existing building is converted into condominiums, the developer is required to give the existing tenants 120 days' notice prior to forcing them to vacate. The current tenants have an option to purchase the unit for 60 days from delivery of the notice.

THE DECLARATION.

> **Minnesota has adopted the Uniform Condominium Act, which regulates condominium sales and requires that a declaration be filed when a condominium is created.**

Uniform Condominium Act: regulates condominium sales and requires the filing of a declaration upon creation

This declaration must include certain information about the condominium, such as the legal description of the property. This description comprises the entire development, including the land and the buildings. It also includes a description of each individual unit.

The declaration also contains floor plans for the individual units, and descriptions of the common elements. It explains what percentage of interest each unit owner holds in the common areas, and what their percentage of expenses will be. Along with these percentages, it includes the number of votes each owner has in the condominium association.

The declaration must give the name of the condominium and describe the purpose for which the buildings are intended. In other words, are they meant to be residential apartments, commercial, or retail units? It also specifies all rights and liabilities of the unit owners, including any restrictions on use of the property.

Finally, the declaration includes a description of the "limited common elements." A limited common element is any common element or area of the property that is reserved for the use of one or more unit(s), to the exclusion of other units. Some examples of limited common elements are assigned parking spaces, storage units, and balconies.

UNIT OWNERS' ASSOCIATION. The declaration provides for the formation of a condominium owners' association. The association is made up of owners of the individual condominium units. Each unit owner is a member of the association.

Owners' Association: manages, controls, regulates, and maintains the common elements in a condominium

> **The main purpose of the association is to manage, control, regulate, and maintain the common elements in the condominium.**

The condominium association generally elects a board of directors. The board of directors is responsible for making decisions concerning maintenance, repair, and management of the condominium. The board of directors also enforces bylaws of the association. These bylaws are the rules and regulations that govern the condominium and the individual unit owners.

The association (usually through the board of directors) adopts rules, regulations, and budgets. It creates and amends bylaws. It also imposes and collects assessments.

The association is given the right to assess each unit for funds necessary for the maintenance, repair, or replacement of any of the common areas or facilities. Each unit is assessed an amount based on its assigned percentage. For example, if a unit owner has a 2% interest in the common areas, her portion of any maintenance costs would be 2% of the total. If individual owners don't pay the required assessments, a lien may be placed on the unit and eventually may be foreclosed.

Voting Power.

> **Normally, the voting power of each owner in the association is measured by percentage of interest.**

For instance, if a unit owner has a 3% interest in the common areas, her vote in the association would count as 3%. Some associations disregard the percentage of interest, and give every unit owner one vote.

TITLE AND TAXATION.

> **Each purchaser of a condominium unit receives a deed for his or her individual unit.**

The deed gives a legal description of the unit, and states what percentage of interest in the common areas the new owner is receiving.

Each condominium unit is assessed and taxed separately. The common areas are not taxed, since the assessed value of each unit includes the value of the percentage of interest in the common areas that go along with the unit.

The association maintains insurance on the common elements and the units. However, this insurance does not cover the interior of individual units. A unit owner who wants to be fully covered must purchase separate hazard and liability insurance for the interior of their unit.

Financing. Since individual condominium units are separately owned, they can be separately financed. An owner may mortgage or borrow against his own unit. If the owner defaults, the lender may foreclose against the individual unit. The rest of the owners in the building are not affected.

Disclosure and Rescission Rights.

> **Minnesota requires that certain disclosures be given to the purchaser no later than the date the purchase agreement is signed.**

It is common practice for these disclosures to be given to prospective purchasers when they first view the property. The disclosures include:

- a general description;
- a copy of the declaration, floor plans for the unit, bylaws, articles of incorporation, rules and regulations, and copies of leases and contracts charged to the association;
- the association's budget, including current and estimated future common expense assessments; and
- a description of insurance coverage.

A real estate agent should be aware that in Minnesota, purchasers of a condominium unit have the right to rescind (cancel) the agreement within 15 days after receiving these disclosures. If the agreement is rescinded, the purchasers receive a refund of their earnest money deposit. Upon rescission, it is as if there never was an agreement, so the broker is not entitled to any commission. However, if the purchaser was given the disclosure statement more than 15 days before signing the purchase agreement, the purchaser cannot rescind. This is why most real estate agents give prospective purchasers a copy of the required disclosures as soon as possible.

Sidenotes:

Condominium owners receive a deed for their individual unit, which is separately taxed

Purchasers must receive disclosure statement

Right to rescind purchase agreement within 15 days

TIMESHARING

Timesharing is a method of ownership similar to condominium ownership. But instead of purchasing an entire unit, buyers purchase a particular time period of use in a unit.

Timeshare: form of ownership where co-owners have exclusive right to possess property for specified times

> **In a timeshare arrangement, co-owners have the exclusive right to possess the property for specified time periods each year.**

Example: Alice has a timeshare interest in a condominium unit in Palm Springs. Alice's interest gives her the right to use the unit from December 1st through December 15th each year. She schedules her vacation during that period.

Bob, Carl, Diane, Elizabeth, and so on, have similar interests in the same unit, each for a different annual period. Each timeshare owner purchases his or her interest for a fraction of the total cost of the unit. A timeshare arrangement could be developed for any kind of housing, but it has been most commonly used for resort condominiums.

Timeshares in Minnesota are governed by the Subdivided Lands Act. This law is discussed in Chapter 10. A real estate agent should be aware that most sales of timeshare units must meet the disclosure requirements of the Subdivided Lands Act. Under the act, agents are required to hold an additional license, and timeshare purchasers have a right of rescission within five days after receiving a copy of the purchase agreement.

COOPERATIVES

Cooperative: title held by a nonprofit corporation; residents own shares and have proprietary leases

Like condominiums and timeshare arrangements, most cooperatives are residential buildings, although they may also be used for commercial or retail purposes.

> **Title to a cooperative building (and the surrounding land) is generally held by a corporation formed for that purpose.**

Instead of a corporation, a trust or partnership could hold title to the cooperative, but this is not as common as corporate ownership.

A person who wants to live in the building buys shares of stock in the corporation, instead of renting or buying a unit. The building's residents are the corporation's shareholders. Each shareholder is given a proprietary lease for their particular unit.

Example: A cooperative has a total of 33 units. There are one, two, and three-bedroom units. The units on the west side of the building have a view overlooking the lake, and are therefore valued higher than the units with no view. The units are assigned individual values running from 20 to 40 shares. The total value of the complex is 1,000 shares.

Johnson wants to acquire an interest in a one-bedroom unit with no view. His unit is valued at 20 shares. He must purchase 20 shares of stock in the cooperative corporation.

Davis wants to occupy a two-bedroom unit with a view of the lake. Her unit is valued at 35 shares. She must purchase 35 shares of stock in the corporation.

A proprietary lease has a longer term than most ordinary leases, and gives the shareholder considerably more rights than an ordinary tenant would have. The lease does not state a fixed rental amount for the term of the lease. Instead, each year an amount is determined that will be needed to pay the expenses of the building, the mortgage, insurance, operating expenses, and so on. Each leaseholder is then assessed an amount based on their percentage of ownership.

Example: In the example above, Johnson owns 20 shares, which is 2% of the total value of the complex. Davis owns 35 shares, which is 3½% of the total value of the complex. Johnson must pay 2% of the total operating expenses, while Davis must pay 3½%.

ASSOCIATION AND BYLAWS.

> **Cooperatives are generally run by a cooperative tenants' association. The association is managed by a board of trustees.**

Cooperatives are run by tenants' association, which is managed by a board of trustees

The trustees are stockholders and members of the association. They are elected by the members of the association.

The association usually passes bylaws for the governing of the cooperative. The association and the board of trustees manage the cooperative according to the guidelines set out in the bylaws. They generally have the right to assess the fees required for maintenance, repairs, and the general cost of effectively running the cooperative.

As with condominiums, members of a cooperative are assessed fees based on their share of the total value of the complex. The members must pay assessments and association fees. Members of the cooperative are also responsible for paying their share of the mortgage. If a member does not pay, the remaining members must make up the difference. They can then seek reimbursement from the member who did not pay. If the member still fails to pay, he or she can be terminated as a shareholder.

SUBDIVIDED LANDS ACT.   Sales of cooperative units are also covered by the Minnesota Subdivided Lands Act. This means that certain disclosure requirements must be met. As with timeshare units, the purchaser has a right of rescission, and agents are required to hold an additional license.

DIFFERENCES BETWEEN CONDOMINIUMS AND COOPERATIVES

There are some similarities between condominiums and cooperatives. In both instances, the individual owner has a right to possess a certain unit and has an interest in the common areas. However, there are also many differences.

Ownership.   One of the major differences is the fact that a condominium owner actually owns his or her individual unit and receives a deed for that unit. A cooperative owner merely has a lease for a specific unit. However, the owner of a cooperative acquires equity in the shares of the cooperative's stock. Like any property owner, if the market value of the property increases, the shareholder would reap the profits at the time of sale.

Condominium unit is owned; cooperative unit is leased

Mortgages.   In a cooperative, the corporation gives a single blanket mortgage on the entire building. In a condominium, there is no blanket mortgage on the entire building, but there may be separate mortgages on some or all of the individual units.

Separate mortgage for each condominium unit; one blanket mortgage for cooperative building

One of the major disadvantages of the cooperative is the financial interdependence of all of the shareholders. Because a blanket mortgage is used, one shareholder's financial instability could jeopardize the whole cooperative. There is a possibility that the entire building could be foreclosed and the lease extinguished, even though the owner was never delinquent in his or her own payments.

Taxes.   In a condominium, each unit owner receives an individual tax assessment and is responsible only for that amount. In a cooperative, a tax assessment is made on the entire building. Each owner is assessed an amount in proportion to the amount of stock owned. If an individual owner defaults on tax payments, the other shareholders must see that these taxes are paid or risk the entire building being sold at a tax sale.

Separate tax assessment for each condominium unit; one assessment for entire cooperative

Liens. An individual owner may have work done or services performed on a particular unit. In a condominium, a mechanic's lien only attaches to the unit where the work was done. In a cooperative, work done or materials ordered by one tenant could result in a mechanic's lien attaching to the entire building.

Mechanic's lien attaches to individual condominium unit, but to entire cooperative property

CONVEYING OWNERSHIP

Now that you have learned about the different rights and interests in property, and the different methods of ownership, it is time to learn how these interests can be sold or transferred.

> **When personal property is sold, a bill of sale is used.**

Bill of sale: document used to transfer ownership of personal property

This is significant to a real estate agent because if certain personal property is included in the sale of real estate, a bill of sale may be used.

> **Example:** Jacobs sells her house to Aldrich. Along with the sale of the real estate, Jacobs also sells Aldrich her living room furniture. A separate bill of sale will be used for the furniture.

When real estate is sold or transferred, a bill of sale is not used.

> **Conveying or transferring real estate is done with a deed.**

A deed is a document used by an owner of real estate (the grantor) to transfer all or part of an interest in the property to another party (the grantee). The act of conveying real estate ownership by deed is called a grant.

Deed: document used to transfer ownership of real property

ESSENTIAL ELEMENTS OF A DEED

To be valid, a deed must meet specific requirements and contain certain elements. A valid deed must:

- identify the parties,
- have a competent grantor,
- contain words of conveyance,
- contain a legal description of the property,
- state that consideration was given, if it is not a gift,
- be properly executed, and
- be delivered and accepted by the grantee.

IDENTIFIABLE PARTIES. To be valid, every deed must have an identifiable grantor and grantee.

Grantor: the person who transfers the property

> **The grantor is the person who conveys or transfers the property. The grantee is the person who newly acquires the property.**

Grantee: the person who acquires the property

If a mistake is made in the spelling of a party's name or if it is spelled differently in different parts of the deed, it will not invalidate the deed so long as it is clear who the party is meant to be.

> **Example:** In the body of the deed the name of the grantor is typed as "Pearse," but the signature at the bottom of the deed is spelled "Pearce."

The grantee or grantor may be a corporation or other legal entity (such as a partnership or trust), rather than a human being. These entities are adequate parties so long as they legally exist. In other words, they must meet the requirements for incorporation, or be licensed, or have the proper certificates on file so that they can be recognized as a legal entity.

COMPETENT GRANTOR. In addition to being clearly identifiable, the grantor must also be competent. Competent means of legal age and sound mind. Legal age in Minnesota is 18 years old. If the grantor is incompetent, the deed is voidable. To cancel a deed for lack of mental capacity, there must be clear and convincing evidence of the grantor's incompetency.

Competent: at lease 18 years old and of sound mind. A grantor must be competent for a deed to be valid

When a deed is made by a minor (someone under 18), the minor has the option of either ratifying or disaffirming the deed. A minor can only disaffirm a deed upon reaching the age of majority, or within a reasonable time thereafter. If action is not taken within a reasonable time, the right to disaffirm is lost.

> **Unlike the grantor, the grantee does not have to be competent.**

Property can be transferred to someone who is a minor or is insane. The only requirement is that the grantee be alive and identifiable.

> **Example:** Grandma Evans transfers the deed to her old farm to her favorite grandson Billy. Billy is only 17 at the time. Billy is an adequate grantee who can accept the

property. However, he is not competent as a grantor, because he is underage. If Billy wants to sell or transfer the property, he must do so through a guardian.

WORDS OF CONVEYANCE (GRANTING CLAUSE). The core of a deed is the granting clause. This is the portion of the deed containing the words that actually convey the property to the new owner.

The requirement of words of conveyance is easily satisfied.

Words of conveyance: the words that actually convey the property

> **No particular words are necessary, so long as the words express the intention to transfer ownership or an interest in the property.**

Usually one word such as "grant" or something similar is sufficient. However, some deeds (especially older ones) often contain several words of conveyance. Included in the granting clause is the **habendum clause**, which identifies the type of estate being transferred.

A typical granting clause, including the habendum clause, might read:

Habendum clause: identifies the type of estate being transferred

> *"Grantors . . . do hereby give, grant, bargain, sell, and convey unto the said grantees . . . to have and to hold forever . . .*

LEGAL DESCRIPTION. A deed must also contain a legal description of the property.

> **The most common methods of legal description are the metes and bounds method, the rectangular survey method, and the recorded plat method.**

Legal description: the most common methods are metes and bounds, rectangular survey, and recorded plat

Another acceptable type of description is simply a reference to another recorded document that describes the property using the metes and bounds, rectangular survey, or recorded plat system. (These methods of land description are explained in Chapter 1.)

It is important to note that a street address is not an adequate legal description, since it does not identify the exact boundaries of the property. Street addresses are also subject to change over time, which could create identification problems.

Consideration: what was given in exchange for the property

CONSIDERATION.

CONSIDERATION. A deed should state that consideration was given by the grantee to the grantor. The exact amount of consideration does not need to be given.

> In Minnesota, it is common to use the phrase, "For one dollar ($1.00) and other good and valuable consideration," or simply the phrase "for valuable consideration."

These phrases show that consideration was given, but allow the parties to maintain some privacy regarding the exact amount paid.

Sometimes property is given as a gift. In this case, the deed will often say something like "for love and affection."

Execution: a deed must be in writing and signed by the grantor

EXECUTION. A valid deed must be properly executed to satisfy the Statute of Frauds. This means that the deed must be in writing and be signed by the grantor.

> The Statute of Frauds requires any transfer of an interest in real property (with the exception of leases with a duration of one year or less), to be in writing and signed by the grantor.

The grantee's signature is not required. Usually the signature is made at the end of the document, but there is no requirement that the signature be in a certain place. However, it should be clear that the signature applies to the entire document.

If there is more than one grantor, all of the grantors must sign the deed. The signature of the grantor's spouse may also be required to release statutory marital interests in real property (such as a conveyance of homestead property). For this reason, it is a good idea to state the grantor's marital status in the deed and to obtain the spouse's signature if the grantor is married.

If the grantor is unable to write, the deed may be signed by a mark. A mark may be used if the grantor is illiterate and cannot write his or her own name, or if the grantor is handicapped or disabled. If the grantor signs by a mark, the name should be written or typed in near the mark, and the act of making the mark should be witnessed.

Some states require that all grantors' signatures be witnessed, but Minnesota only requires witnesses if the grantor is unable to sign his or her name.

Power of attorney. Sometimes a deed is signed by someone else instead of the actual grantor. This might happen, for instance, if the grantor is out of the country when the property is conveyed, and so cannot be there in person to sign the deed. When someone has the authority to sign for the grantor, they are said to have "power of attorney." The person who actually signs the document under the power of attorney is the "attorney in fact." To establish power of attorney, there must be a written document authorizing someone else to act as an agent on behalf of the grantor. The document granting the power of attorney is then recorded.

When the attorney in fact signs a deed or other document for the actual grantor, he or she usually signs the grantor's name and then places his or her name beneath it. A power of attorney may be revoked by the grantor at any time.

For a signature by power of attorney to be effective, the grantor must be alive on the date of delivery of the deed. The death of the grantor automatically revokes the power of attorney. Someone taking property by a deed signed under power of attorney should make sure that the power of attorney is still in effect.

Power of attorney: a recorded document authorizing a person (the attorney in fact) to act on someone else's behalf

DELIVERY AND ACCEPTANCE.

> **A deed does not transfer title until it is delivered by the grantor, with the intent to pass title, and is accepted by the grantee.**

Actual physical delivery of the deed is usually necessary. The grantor must intend to pass title and surrender control of the property. If the grantor retains any power to recall the deed, there is no valid delivery because there was no real donative intent. Delivery must take place during the grantor's lifetime. Just as a deed cannot be given to a dead grantee, it cannot be delivered by a dead grantor.

Delivery requires intent to pass title and surrender control of property

> **Example:** Margaret made out a deed transferring property to her niece Elizabeth. She then placed the deed in a safety deposit box. Upon Margaret's death, the deed was found. However, there was no effective transfer to Elizabeth because there was no delivery and acceptance. Margaret was dead before the deed was found, and a deed cannot be delivered by a dead grantor.

When a deed is delivered, it is also necessary that the grantee actually accept. If there is a dispute concerning acceptance, the courts try to find in favor of acceptance. But in some circumstances, the grantee may not want to accept, either for personal reasons, or because it would not be in his or her best interest.

Acceptance: the grantee must want to acquire the property

Example: Moynihan owns property worth $10,000 that he wants to deed to his son. However, the property has a tax lien on it of $9,000. The son does not want to accept the property because of the tax liability.

A VALID DEED

I hereby grant . . . . words of conveyance
Lot 1, Block 2,
    Greenacres addition . . . . . . description of property
to Enos Palmer . . . . identifiable grantee
for $1.00 and other
    valuable consideration . . . . consideration
(signed) Sam Quigley . . . . signature of identifiable
                    and competent grantor

OTHER ELEMENTS. Many deeds contain other elements that are not specifically required for the deed to be valid, but it may be helpful if they are included. For instance, almost all deeds are dated, but it is not a legal requirement that the deed contain the date of conveyance.

A deed should also state the nature of the interest the grantor is conveying (for example, a fee simple or life estate). When not specified, the grantor's entire interest is presumed to pass to the grantee. The nature of the respective interests of multiple grantees should also be specified. If not specified, courts will presume ownership as tenants in common with all grantees holding equal shares.

TYPES OF DEEDS

There are many different types of deeds. Unless specifically stated otherwise, all deeds transfer whatever rights were held by the grantor to the grantee. The difference between types of deeds is the extent of the promises concerning the property, given by the grantor to the grantee.

The four main types of deeds used in Minnesota are the:

- General Warranty Deed,
- Limited (Special) Warranty Deed,
- Quitclaim Deed, and
- Sheriff's Deed.

GENERAL WARRANTY DEED.

> The deed that provides the greatest protection to a purchaser of real estate is the general warranty deed. This type of deed is the one used most often in Minnesota.

General warranty deed: grantor makes five covenants against defects in title that arose before or during grantor's ownership

A real estate agent handling the sale of a residence will usually see a general warranty deed.

The grantor of a general warranty deed makes five basic covenants or promises. These covenants warrant against defects in the title that arose either before or during the grantor's period of ownership. The five covenants the grantor gives are the covenants:

- of seizin,
- of quiet enjoyment,
- against encumbrances,
- of further assurance, and
- of warranty forever.

These covenants, while no longer specified in warranty deed forms, are included by statute.

With the covenant of **seizin**, grantors promise that they have the interest they intend to convey, and the lawful right to convey that interest.

The covenant of **quiet enjoyment** promises the grantee the right to occupy and enjoy the premises without interference from anyone else claiming a right to the property.

The covenant **against encumbrances** promises that the property is free from all unspecified encumbrances. But remember that there may still be specific encumbrances mentioned in the deed, such as easements.

The covenant of **further assurance** makes the grantor responsible for any further acts necessary to make sure title is clear.

And finally, the **warranty forever** promises that the grantor is responsible and will bear the expense of defending the title if anyone asserts a rightful claim against it.

LIMITED (SPECIAL) WARRANTY DEED. The special warranty deed is very similar to the general warranty deed. However, it does not contain all five covenants found in the general warranty deed.

Form No. 1-M — WARRANTY DEED
Individual (s) to Individual (s)

Minnesota Uniform Conveyancing Blanks (1978)

Miller-Davis Co., Minneapolis

No delinquent taxes and transfer entered; Certificate
of Real Estate Value (   ) filed (   ) not required
Certificate of Real Estate Value No._____
_____ , 19 _____

_____
County Auditor

by_____
Deputy

STATE DEED TAX DUE HEREON: $ _____

Date:_____ , 19 _____

(reserved for recording data)

FOR VALUABLE CONSIDERATION, _____
_____ , Grantor (s),
(marital status)

hereby convey (s) and warrant (s) to _____
_____ , Grantee (s),
real property in _____ County, Minnesota, described as follows:

SAMPLE

(if more space is needed, continue on back)
together with all hereditaments and appurtenances belonging thereto, subject to the following exceptions:

Affix Deed Tax Stamp Here

_____

_____

_____

STATE OF MINNESOTA

COUNTY OF _____ } **ss.**

The foregoing instrument was acknowledged before me this _____ day of _____ , 19_____ ,
by _____ , Grantor (s).

NOTARIAL STAMP OR SEAL (OR OTHER TITLE OR RANK)

SIGNATURE OF PERSON TAKING ACKNOWLEDGMENT

Tax Statements for the real property described in this instrument should
be sent to (Include name and address of Grantee):

THIS INSTRUMENT WAS DRAFTED BY (NAME AND ADDRESS)

SAMPLE

This form available from Miller/Davis Forms, Minneapolis, MN (612) 332-5144

> **Typically, the grantor makes no promises regarding defects that existed before he or she acquired ownership of the property.**

The grantor only warrants that he or she has not encumbered the property or caused any defects in the title.

This type of deed is used most often by entities that do not have the power or authority to make further warranties (e.g., corporations). A real estate agent working with commercial properties will often see a special warranty deed.

QUITCLAIM DEED. A quitclaim deed contains no warranties of any sort. A quitclaim deed simply conveys whatever interest the grantor has when the deed is delivered.

The form of a quitclaim deed is similar to the other types of deeds, except that the words in the granting clause are different. The critical wording in a quitclaim deed usually states that the grantor:

"hereby conveys and quitclaims"

Note that a quitclaim deed does not use the term "grant" so it is clear that no warranties are even implied.

A quitclaim deed may convey nothing at all if the grantor had no real interest in the property at the time the deed was executed.

Example: Able and Baker are neighbors and good friends. They are uncertain where the exact boundary line is between their property. A fence runs between the properties 29 yards from Baker's house. Baker thinks his true property line is actually 30 yards from the house, but he isn't really concerned about the one yard difference.

Able and Baker both want to sell their property, but don't want the expense of hiring a surveyor. They agree that the fence will be the boundary line. Baker gives Able a quitclaim deed for one yard of property on the other side of the fence.

Years later, when a survey is done, it is found that the fence is right on the true boundary line. Baker's quitclaim deed didn't actually transfer any interest, since Baker did not really own one yard on the other side of the fence.

Sidenotes:

Limited warranty deed: contains some, but not all, warranties against defects in title

Quitclaim deed: a deed without warranties, most often used to cure technical defects in title

But if the grantor does have an interest in the property, a quitclaim deed will convey that interest as well as any other type of deed.

> A common reason for using a quitclaim deed is to remove clouds on title.

These are defects that normally result from technical flaws in an earlier conveyance, such as a misspelling of one of the parties' names or an error in the description of the estate. A quitclaim deed may also be used when the grantor is unsure of the validity of his or her title and wishes to avoid any warranties.

Example: A grantor holds title by virtue of an inheritance that is being challenged in probate court. If the grantor wants to transfer the property, he or she would prefer to use a quitclaim deed.

If an owner wants to use a quitclaim deed to transfer property, a real estate agent and the new buyer should be a little wary. Why does the owner want to use a quitclaim deed? Are there possible problems or doubts concerning ownership? Are there defects in the title? These questions should be answered before the sale takes place, so that the buyer does not experience unwelcome surprises in the future.

Sheriff's deed: deed given to buyer at foreclosure sale

SHERIFF'S DEED. A sheriff's deed is the type of deed given to someone who purchases property at a foreclosure sale. The deed should state the source of the sheriff's authority and the amount paid at the foreclosure sale. This type of deed conveys the title owned by the foreclosed party. It is similar to a quitclaim deed in that it contains no warranties from the former owner.

TRANSFER AFTER DEATH

A deed transfers property while the grantor is alive. A deed cannot be delivered by a dead grantor. However, property can be transferred after the grantor's death.

Will: document used to transfer ownership of property after death

> A deceased person's property is transferred according to the terms of a will, or if there is no will, according to Minnesota statutory rules.

Property that someone inherits, either by will or under the statutes, is often sold rather than kept for personal use. It is therefore helpful for a real estate agent to have a general understanding of how property is inherited or acquired by will.

TESTATE

A person who dies and leaves behind a valid will is said to have died testate. This simply means that there is a testament (a will) that states how the property should be distributed.

Testate: when a person dies leaving behind a valid will

Before discussing wills, it may be helpful to have an understanding of the general terminology used. The person making out the will is called the testator. A testator bequeaths personal property to legatees and devises real property to devisees. An amendment to a will is called a codicil. An executor is named in the will and is the person who carries out the directions in the will, under the supervision of the probate court. If an executor is not named in the will, the court will appoint an administrator to carry out the directions of the will. Probate is the process by which a deceased's assets are distributed.

WILL TERMINOLOGY

testator: one who makes a will
bequeath: transfer personal property by will
devise: transfer real property by will
codicil: an amendment to a will
executor or administrator: carries out the directions in the will or from the probate court
probate: procedure to distribute a deceased's assets

REQUIREMENTS. In general, a will must be:

1. in writing,
2. signed by a competent testator, and
3. the signature must be witnessed by two or more competent witnesses.

In Writing.

To transfer real estate, a will must be in writing.

Remember that under the Statute of Frauds, transfers of real estate must be in writing.

Normally all wills must be in writing. However, under certain circumstances, Minnesota will recognize an oral will (called a nuncupative will) to dispose of personal property. A **nuncupative will** is a will spoken by a person who is near death. The will must be spoken at the time of the testator's last sickness and must be witnessed. If the testator recovers, the will is no longer valid. After hearing a nuncupative will, the witness must promptly write down what was heard and submit it to probate. Remember that real estate can never be devised by an oral will.

Some states, although not Minnesota, recognize a holographic will. A holographic will is an unwitnessed will written entirely in the testator's own handwriting.

Signature. In Minnesota, any person of sound mind who is 18 years old or older may make a will leaving personal property and real estate. Just as the grantor of a deed must be competent, so must a person making out a will. If the person is found to have been incompetent at the time the will was executed, the will may be held invalid.

The requirements for signing a will are the same as for signing a deed. The testator should sign the will personally, but if unable to sign a full signature, the testator may use a mark or may grant power of attorney to someone else to sign the will under the direction of the testator.

Witnesses. After drawing up a will, the testator must sign the will in the presence of two witnesses. They then sign the will as witnesses. In order to validate the will, the witnesses must be able to testify that the testator signed or acknowledged the signature in their presence.

INTESTATE

A person who dies without leaving a will is said to die intestate.

Intestate: when a person dies without leaving behind a valid will

The law provides for the distribution of an intestate owner's property by a process called intestate succession.

The rules of intestate succession are created by Minnesota statutes in the Minnesota Probate Code.

In general, the property of someone who dies intestate is distributed as follows:

1. If there is a surviving spouse, but no surviving children, the surviving spouse gets everything.

2. If there is a surviving spouse and surviving children, the first $70,000 goes to the spouse plus one-half of the remaining balance. The other one-half of the remaining balance is divided equally between the children. Note that if a child has died before his or her parent, but there are grandchildren, the grandchildren take their parent's share.

Elective Share.

> **In Minnesota, rather than following the statutory rules for intestate succession as outlined above, a surviving spouse has a right to take an elective share.**

When a spouse takes an elective share, the spouse receives a life estate in the homestead property and the children have a remainder interest in fee simple. The surviving spouse is also entitled to one-third of the remaining property. The children divide the remaining two-thirds. (If there is only one child, the spouse and child each take one-half.)

3. If there is a surviving spouse and surviving children who are not issue of the surviving spouse (for example, children from a previous marriage), the surviving spouse gets one-half and the remaining one-half is divided between the children.

4. If there are surviving children, but no surviving spouse, the children share equally.

5. If there is no surviving spouse or children, everything goes to the decedent's parents.

6. If there is no surviving spouse, children, or parents, the estate is divided among the brothers and sisters of the decedent.

Intestate succession: the process by which an intestate owner's property is distributed

Elective share: spouse's alternative to the share he or she would receive by intestate succession

7. If there is no surviving spouse, children, parents, brothers and sisters, or their issue, to the next of kin.

8. If there are no surviving heirs, the property will escheat to the state. (Escheat is described in Chapter 2.)

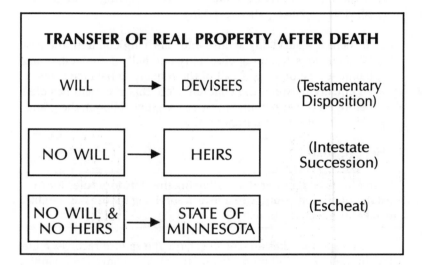

OTHER WAYS OF ACQUIRING RIGHTS

When you think of acquiring rights in property, you normally think of the property being transferred by deed or will. However, there are other ways of acquiring rights in property that are less common, but just as effective. Rights in property may be acquired through adverse possession, or by the formation of a prescriptive easement or easement by necessity.

ADVERSE POSSESSION

Adverse possession: obtaining title through open and continuous possession

> **Adverse possession is the process by which possession and use of property can mature into title.**

The idea behind adverse possession statutes is to encourage the fullest and most productive use of property.

REQUIREMENTS. There are several requirements that must be met when a claim of adverse possession is made. The specific requirements vary by state. In Minnesota, the adverse possession must be:

- actual, open and notorious,
- hostile,
- continuous,
- exclusive,
- for 15 years or more,
- under claim of right,
- with payment of taxes for 5 years.

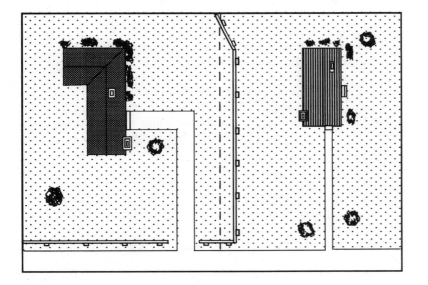

USE OF PROPERTY CAN MATURE INTO TITLE BY THE PROCESS OF ADVERSE POSSESSION

Actual, Open and Notorious. Possession of the property by the adverse possessor must be actual, open and notorious. This simply means that there must be actual possession of the property in a way that would put a reasonable owner on notice that the property was being threatened. You couldn't live in a hidden underground cave for fifteen years and then claim adverse possession of the property, since your possession was not obvious enough to give the real owner notice of your presence.

Hostile. Possession of the property must also be hostile. Hostility does not imply that the two parties hate each other. It simply means that the possession is of such a nature that a reasonable owner would normally object to this use of the land by someone else.

If the owner has given permission to someone else to use the property, the use can never develop into adverse possession. Use of the property must be open enough for the true owner to be aware of the use, and must be without permission.

Continuous. The requirement that adverse possession be continuous does not mean that the adverse possessor cannot ever leave the property. Continuous use simply means normal continuous use that a true owner would make of the property.

> **Example:** Johnson is the true owner of lakefront property. However, he is simply holding the property as an investment and has not even been out to look at it in over 20 years.
>
> Abott owns the property next to Johnson and believes that his boundary extends across part of Johnson's lot clear to the lake. Unfortunately, the boundary description of his property is in error. For 17 years Abott has used the beach almost every weekend all summer long. Abott seldom uses the property in winter because it is too cold.
>
> When a dispute arises as to ownership, and Abott learns that his boundary description is wrong, he claims the lakefront property as an adverse possessor. His use of the property is continuous enough to meet the requirement because it was normal use for this type of property.

Exclusive. To be adverse, possession of another's land must be exclusive. This means that the adverse possessor may not share possession with the true owner. Consider the example used above concerning the lakefront property. Suppose that Johnson also used the property. He works weekends, so he usually used the property during the week. Abott did not have exclusive use of the property.

Owners of vacant property or land held for future sale or development should make periodic inspections of their property to check for any signs of adverse possession. The mere posting of "no trespassing" signs may not be sufficient to prevent a claim of adverse possession.

Real estate agents and potential buyers should also check to see if there are any signs that someone besides the title owner is using the property.

Time Limit. An adverse possessor must also meet the statutory time limit required for a valid claim of adverse possession. This time period varies in different states.

> **In Minnesota the required time period is 15 years.**

An adverse possessor must have used the property for a period of at least 15 years to have a valid claim for adverse possession.

Claim of Right. Claim of right or color of title means that the adverse possessor has a good faith but mistaken belief that he or she is the owner of the land. An example of an adverse possessor with color of title is one who takes possession under an invalid deed.

An adverse possessor with color of title may acquire title to all the property described in the defective instrument (such as a deed), even if he or she occupies only part of the property.

Taxes.

> **Minnesota also requires that the adverse possessor pay taxes on the property for five consecutive years, except in the case of boundary disputes.**

When discussing adverse possession claims, some people imagine a stranger moving onto someone else's property and attempting to claim it as his own. In reality, most adverse possession claims are brought by neighbors, simply to clear up questionable title and settle boundary disputes.

Example: Halverson and Bernstein are neighbors. Halverson's deed states that his property runs 348 feet from the northern boundary, to a line of oak trees along the south end of the property. There are no longer any oak trees along the south end of the property, but there are four apple trees. For 30 years both Bernstein and Halverson have assumed that the apple trees marked the property boundary. Halverson landscaped, mowed grass, cultivated flowers, sprayed the trees, harvested the apples, and generally took care of all of the property up to and including the apple trees.

Bernstein is preparing to sell her property and has a survey made. No survey has been made of the property for almost 80 years. The new survey shows that Bernstein's true property line is actually three feet past the trees onto Halverson's side. Halverson files a claim for adverse possession of the three feet of property up to and including the apple trees.

Tacking. Tacking is the joining together of periods of adverse possession by different parties, to make one long time period. Most states, including Minnesota, allow the tacking of one person's term of possession to another's, if possession was acquired directly from the previous possessor.

Example: John was the true owner of property. Cathy thought she was the owner, but her deed was invalid. Cathy possessed the property for 7 years. She then sold the property to Philip, and gave him an invalid deed. Philip possessed the property for 10 years.

When Philip learned that his deed was invalid, he filed an action for adverse possession. He was allowed to tack together the two time periods. Cathy's 7 years of possession and Philip's 10 years of possession equal 17 years. This is enough to meet the 15-year requirement for adverse possession claims.

EXCEPTIONS. There are certain exceptions when a claim of adverse possession cannot arise. For example, it cannot be applied against infants or the mentally incompetent. If someone who is mentally incompetent owns property, the property cannot be claimed by another under adverse possession. If someone underage owns property, the 15-year time limit for adverse possession claims does not begin to run until the owner reaches the age of 21.

Public Lands.

Adverse possession cannot be claimed on public lands, such as any land owned by the United States or Minnesota State, or lands a city, county or other municipal district holds in a proprietary capacity, such as public school lands, or public parks, etc.

Torrens System. Land that is registered under the Torrens system is also not subject to adverse possession. (The Torrens system is discussed in Chapter 4.)

EASEMENT BY PRESCRIPTION

Another way that rights in property may be acquired is when someone claims an easement by prescription. An easement by prescription is similar to adverse possession. This type of easement is acquired by using the property as if an easement already existed. Like adverse possession, the use must be actual, open, notorious, hostile, and continuous for 15 years. (Easements by prescription are discussed in more detail in Chapter 2.)

Prescriptive easement: an easement created by continuous use

EASEMENT BY NECESSITY

An easement may also be acquired by necessity. If an easement is essential to a parcel of property, the court may find an easement by necessity. (Easements by necessity are also discussed in more detail in Chapter 2.)

HOMESTEAD RIGHTS

The preceding sections of this chapter have discussed ways property ownership may be conveyed or acquired. However, there are laws that allow an owner to keep some property that otherwise would be transferred against his or her wishes. These are commonly known as homestead laws.

Nearly every state has passed some type of homestead law to protect family residences from a forced sale by unpaid creditors.

Homestead law: state law that protects the family home from being sold to pay off debts

> The objective of homestead laws is to secure the family home from the reach of financial misfortune.

In adopting a homestead law, the legislature is saying that a person's obligation to support dependents by providing a home is as important as the payment of debts. Minnesota also provides favorable property tax treatment for homestead property.

REQUIREMENTS. A homestead is residential real estate that is occupied and used as a home by the owner. The homestead must be the owner's principal residence, so an owner can only have one homestead at a time. A homestead may be a single-family house, townhouse, duplex, condominium, cooperative, or even a mobile home. There are special provisions for agricultural homesteads.

Marital Status. Homestead rights can be established regardless of marital status. A homestead may be claimed by a married person or a single person. A homestead may be claimed by a married person when only one spouse is living on the property, due to separation, or if one spouse is a resident of a nursing home or care facility.

If one spouse dies, the homestead exemption still protects the surviving spouse and children if they continue to occupy the homestead property.

Limitations. In Minnesota the entire value of the homestead property is protected from creditors. There is no limitation on value. However, homestead property is limited to 160 acres in the country or one-half acre in town.

Exceptions. Under the homestead law, there is no protection against foreclosure of:

- property tax or special assessment liens,
- mechanics' liens,
- mortgage liens, or
- condominium association liens.

GREEN ACRES

Along with the protections under the Homestead Act, some homestead agricultural property receives additional special treatment. Minnesota has a special agricultural property tax statute. This law is commonly referred to as the "Green Acres" Act.

Green Acres Act: state law that gives special tax treatment to homestead agricultural property

> **The purpose of the law is to equalize the tax burden on agricultural property.**

Under the Green Acres Act, real estate consisting of ten acres or more, or a nursery or greenhouse, is entitled to special valuation and tax deferment if it is actively and exclusively devoted to agricultural use, and is homestead property. (There are also certain other rules under which the property may qualify even if not specifically homestead property).

The value of property that falls under this rule is determined solely with reference to its appropriate agricultural classification. The assessor does not consider any added values resulting from nonagricultural factors. In other words, the assessor does not value the property at its highest and best use, but at its current agicultural use. Property is considered to be in agricultural use if at least ⅓ of the total family income is derived therefrom, or the total income is $300 plus $10 per tillable acre, and the property is devoted to the production for sale of livestock, dairy animals, dairy products, poultry, fur bearing animals, horticultural and nursery stock, fruit, vegetables, forage, grains, bees, apiary products, slough, wasteland, or woodland.

An application for deferment of taxes and assessments under this rule must be filed by May 1 of the year prior to the year in which the taxes are payable. For example, an application would be made by May 1, 1992 for deferment of taxes payable in 1993.

ALIEN OWNERSHIP

Most property can freely be transferred to anyone the owner chooses to transfer it to. However, Minnesota has recently passed a statute that restricts ownership of agricultural land. This type of restriction on an owner's ability to sell or transfer property is quite unusual. It will be interesting to note whether this statute is changed or challenged in the future. For now, the statute is in force.

> **Under this statute, no one can acquire an interest in agricultural land in Minnesota except a citizen of the United States or a permanent resident alien.**

No corporation, partnership or other business entity may acquire an interest in agricultural land unless at least 80% of the stock is held by citizens or permanent resident aliens.

A permanent resident alien is described as someone lawfully admitted to the United States for permanent residence, who actually maintains a principal residence and lives here for at least six months out of the year.

EXCEPTIONS

This statute does not apply to land that is acquired by devise or inheritance. In other words, someone owning agricultural land in Minnesota may will the land to an alien. If someone owning agricultural land dies intestate, and the person who would inherit under Minnesota's intestacy statutes is not a U.S. citizen or permanent resident alien, the person will still inherit. It also does not apply to land acquired by process of law in the collection of debts, or through enforcement of a lien.

ENFORCEMENT

If there is reason to believe that someone is violating this act, the commissioner of agriculture will file an action in district court. If a violation is found, the court will order the owner to divest itself of the property. The owner has one year from the date of the order to sell or otherwise divest itself of the property. If not done within a year, the land is sold at public sale in the same way as a mortgage foreclosure.

CHAPTER SUMMARY

1. When title to real property is held by one person or entity it is called sole ownership.

2. Property may be owned solely by one individual or by a syndicate (a corporation, partnership, or real estate investment trust).

3. Multiple or concurrent ownership exists when two or more people simultaneously share ownership of one piece of property. The two most common forms of co-ownership are tenancy in common and joint tenancy.

4. In Minnesota, unless an agreement exists to the contrary, co-ownership is presumed to be a tenancy in common. With a tenancy in common, there is an equal right of possession, but each tenant may own an unequal interest. There is no right of survivorship.

5. With a joint tenancy, each tenant has an equal interest and an equal right of possession. Joint tenants have a right of survivorship. When a joint tenant dies, his or her interest in the property automatically passes to the surviving joint tenant(s).

6. The owner of a condominium owns an individual unit, plus an interest in the common areas. Minnesota has adopted the Uniform Condominium Act, which regulates condominium sales and requires that disclosures be given to prospective purchasers.

7. Buyers of a timeshare purchase a particular time period of use in a unit. Timeshares in Minnesota are governed by the Subdivided Lands Act.

8. Title to a cooperative is held by a corporation. Someone who wants to live in the cooperative buys shares of stock in the corporation. Each shareholder is then given a proprietary lease in a particular unit within the building.

9. A deed is a document used to transfer real estate. A valid deed must identify the parties, have a competent grantor, contain words of conveyance, contain a legal description of the property, state that consideration was given, be properly executed, and be delivered and accepted.

10. The four main types of deeds used in Minnesota are the general warranty deed, limited warranty deed, quitclaim deed, and sheriff's deed.

11. A general warranty deed makes five basic covenants. These are the covenants of seizin, of quiet enjoyment, against encumbrances, of further assurance, and of warranty forever.

12. A quitclaim deed conveys no warranties of any kind. It simply conveys whatever interest the grantor has when the deed is delivered.

13. Upon death, a person's property may be transferred by the terms of a will, or according to the Minnesota intestacy laws.

14. Property may also be acquired by adverse possession. In Minnesota, the adverse possession must be actual, open, notorious, hostile, continuous, exclusive, for 15 years or more, under claim of right, and with payment of taxes for 5 years.

15. The Minnesota homestead law protects homestead property (up to 160 acres in the country or one-half acre in town) from a forced sale by creditors. The homestead law does not protect against property tax or special assessment liens, mechanic's liens, mortgage liens, or condominium association liens.

4 things

CHAPTER 3—GLOSSARY REVIEW

A. seizin *grantor owns prop. has right to convey*
B. quiet enjoyment *no one will try to claim interest*
C. deed *conveys rights held by grantor*
D. lease *right lessee to possess land of lessor*
E. grantor and grantee *owner / buyer*
F. declaration
G. vendor
H. delivered and accepted
I. delivered and recorded
J. limited common elements
K. general warranty

L. special warranty
M. quitclaim deed
N. sheriff's deed
O. vendor and vendee
P. severalty
Q. joint tenancy
R. grantor
S. grantee
T. tenancy in common
U. proprietary lease

1. A written legal document by which ownership of real property is transferred from one party to another is a _deed_.
must be in writing

2. The two parties to a deed are the _grantor / grantee_

3. In order to convey title, a deed must be signed by the _grantor_

4. Title does not pass to the grantee until the deed is _delivered & accepted_

5. Assurance to the grantee that he will not be disturbed by someone else claiming an interest in the property is called the covenant of _quiet enjoyment_

6. The type of deed that is considered to be the best deed for a grantee is a _general warranty_ deed.

7. A deed that conveys whatever interest in the premises is held by the grantor at the time of conveyance and contains no covenants or warranties is called a _quitclaim_

8. Someone who buys property at a foreclosure sale takes title by means of a _sheriff's deed_
AKA. certificate of sale

9. Property owned by one person is said to be owned in _severalty_

10. A form of concurrent ownership in which each tenant owns individual fractional shares in the entire property and no right of survivorship exists is called _tenancy in common_

11. A form of concurrent ownership in which all owners have equal shares in the property and the right of survivorship exists is called _joint tenancy_

12. Mr. and Mrs. Jones were co-owners of Highside. Mr. Jones died and their son inherited his father's interest. The form of ownership that Mrs. Jones and her son now have is _tenancy in common_

13. A condominium is created by filing a _declaration_

14. In a condominium, patios and balconies would likely be specified as _limited_ _common elements_

15. The document that allows the use of a cooperative apartment is known as a _proprietary lease_

study in book

seizen
further assurance

CHAPTER 3—REVIEW EXAM

1. In a quitclaim deed, the grantor covenants:

   a) that title is marketable.
   b) nothing.
   c) that he owns the property and has the right to convey title.
   d) that he will defend any claims.

2. All of the following are acceptable legal descriptions EXCEPT:

   a) street address and house number.
   b) lot, block, and subdivision.
   c) metes and bounds.
   d) government survey.

3. The act of conveying title from one to another is known as a:

   a) devise.
   b) descent.
   c) vending.
   d) grant.

4. The term "execution" in regard to a deed refers to:

   a) notarization.
   b) recordation.
   c) delivery and acceptance.
   d) signature(s) of the grantor(s).

5. All of the following are covenants of a warranty deed EXCEPT the:

   a) covenant of seizin.
   b) covenant of further assurance.
   c) covenant of title insurance.
   d) covenant of quiet enjoyment.

6. The covenant affirming that the grantor holds title and has the right to convey to another is the:

   a) covenant of further assurance.
   b) covenant against encumbrances.
   c) covenant of quiet enjoyment.
   d) covenant of seizin.

7. Which would be a logical type of deed to use to clear a cloud on title?

   a) Quitclaim deed
   b) Special warranty deed
   c) Warranty deed
   d) Sheriff's deed

8. The purchaser of property at a foreclosure sale would take title with a:

   a) quitclaim deed.
   b) special warranty deed.
   c) warranty deed.
   d) sheriff's deed.

9. The probate process:

   a) settles disputes between co-owners of property.
   b) rules on warranty claims.
   c) passes title to the proper devisees.
   d) determines claims under adverse possession.

10. Which parties must sign a deed to make it valid?

    (a) Grantors only
    b) Grantees only
    c) Both grantors and grantees
    d) Vendors only

11. Ownership in severalty refers to:

    a) more than one owner.
    b) the right of survivorship.
    c) ownership between husband and wife.
    (d) ownership by one person or entity.

12. Which of the following is necessarily true of tenants in common?

    a) Each tenant has an equal undivided interest in the land.
    b) Each tenant rents his or her share of the land.
    c) Each tenant has the right of survivorship.
    (d) Each tenant must join in the conveyance of title to the property.

13. An unmarried couple living together wants to buy a house. If either one should die, they want the deceased's share to go to his or her heirs. The form of ownership they should have is:

    (a) tenancy in common.
    b) tenancy by the entirety.
    c) joint tenancy.
    d) an estate in severalty.

14. John and Jane are buying a duplex together and want to make sure that if one of them dies, the other will inherit the deceased's interest in the property. Which form of ownership should they use?

    a) Tenancy in common
    b) Tenancy in the entirety
    c) Tenancy in severalty
    (d) Joint tenancy

15. If joint tenants disagree over the use of property and a court grants their request to split the property equally between them, with each holding an estate in severalty, the court action is referred to as:

    a) recission.
    b) separation.
    (c) partition.
    d) restitution.

16. John and Susan, husband and wife, owned a duplex as joint tenants. John died and Susan filed the death certificate and affidavit of survivorship. A few years later Susan married Larry. Which of the following is true about the ownership of the duplex?

    a) Larry and Susan are tenants in common.
    b) Susan can sell the duplex without Larry's signature on the deed.
    (c) Susan owns the duplex in severalty.
    d) Susan and Larry are joint tenants.

17. Which of the following would release an owner's interest in a property?

   a) General warranty deed
   b) Limited warranty deed
   c) Quitclaim deed
   d) All of the above

18. Which of the following is not essential to the validity of a deed?

   a) Recording
   b) Competent parties
   c) Execution by the grantor
   d) Consideration

19. Penny Pound, owner of a condominium unit, does not pay her monthly association fee. What remedy is available to the association?

   a) File a lien and foreclose, if necessary.
   b) Change the lock on Ms. Pound's door until she pays.
   c) File a special assessment in the recorder's office.
   d) There is no remedy available for the association.

20. Which of the following may not buy farmland in Minnesota?

   a) A farmer who has lost his farm in the last 3 years.
   b) A veteran without full entitlement.
   c) Aliens and non-American corporations.
   d) All of the above.

21. Insurance purchased by a condominium association would probably cover all of the following EXCEPT:

   a) an injury incurred in the lobby.
   b) an accident near the swimming pool.
   c) water damage in the laundry room.
   d) damage to the carpeting in an individual unit.

22. When a husband and wife buy property together and do not specify a form of ownership they are considered to be:

   a) joint tenants.
   b) tenants in severalty.
   c) tenants in entirety.
   d) tenants in common.

23. Miss Maple owned a home in severalty. She died testate. Upon her death her interest in the home would transfer to:

   a) the remaining owners.
   b) whomever she named in her will.
   c) the state in which she died.
   d) the executor of her estate.

24. Joe and Penny were divorced while they owned a home together. The court awarded the home to Joe, who later sold it to Sue using a general warranty deed for the conveyance. Which of the following covenants would protect Sue against future claims by Penny?

   a) Covenant of seizin
   b) Covenant against encumbrance
   c) Covenant of quiet enjoyment
   d) None of the above

25. Conveyance occurs at the moment the deed is:

    (a) delivered and accepted.
    b) recorded.
    c) signed by the grantee.
    d) signed by the grantor.

26. One could have a fee simple interest in all of the following EXCEPT:

    a) a single family home.
    b) a duplex.
    c) farm land.
    (d) a cooperative.

27. Which of the following liens cannot be foreclosed on homestead property?

    a) Condominium association lien
    b) Mechanic's lien
    c) Mortgage lien
    (d) Judgment lien

28. The Green Acres statute provides special tax treatment to which of the following?

    (a) Agricultural land of 10 acres or more
    b) State wildlife areas
    c) A city park
    d) Areas regulated by the Department of Natural Resources

Chapter 3—GLOSSARY REVIEW KEY

1. C
2. E
3. R
4. H
5. B
6. K
7. M
8. N
9. P
10. T
11. Q
12. T
13. F
14. J
15. U

CHAPTER 3—REVIEW EXAM KEY

1. b) There are no covenants (promises) contained in the quitclaim deed.

2. a) Street address is an informal reference, not a legal description.

3. d) The act is a grant; the document is the deed.

4. d) Execution refers to signature or performance.

5. c) There are five covenants in a warranty deed: seizin, quiet enjoyment, against encumbrances, further assurance, and warranty forever.

6. d) The covenant of seizin affirms that the grantor owns and has the right to convey title.

7. a) The grantor in a quitclaim deed simply gives up all rights (if any) to the grantee. There is no implication of ownership.

8. d) Someone who buys property at a foreclosure sale takes title with a sheriff's deed.

9. c) Probate is the process by which a deceased's interests are transferred.

10. a) The grantors sign (execute) the deed.

11. d) Severalty refers to severed (sole) ownership.

12. d) While interests in a tenancy in common may be unequal, each owner must sign documents of title conveyance (deeds, contracts for deed).

13. a) In a tenancy in common, the deceased's interests go to the deceased's heirs. There is no right of survivorship.

14. d) In a joint tenancy, the deceased's interests go to the remaining co-owner(s). The right of survivorship exists.

15. c) A partition splits the property into more than one parcel with each parcel held in severalty. It defeats the co-ownership arrangement.

16. c) Susan holds an estate in severalty. Note, however, that her new husband (Larry) must sign if Susan wishes to sell the property.

17. d) Every deed releases the owner's interest in a property.

18. a) Deeds need not be recorded to be valid.

19. a) The condominium association has the right to collect assessments. Unpaid assessments create a forecloseable lien against the unit and common element interest.

20. c) By law, aliens and non-American corporations may not buy Minnesota farmland.

21. d) Association insurance covers damage or accidents in the common elements, not in the units.

22. d) All multiple ownership is tenancy in common unless otherwise specified.

23. b) Sole owners may will their property to others. In the absence of a will, the property will go to the deceased's heirs through the law of intestate succession.

24. c) The covenant of quiet enjoyment promises that the grantee will not be disturbed by anyone claiming an interest in the property.

25. a) Title transfers upon delivery and acceptance of the deed.

26. d) In a cooperative, the tenants hold shares of stock and proprietary leases. A tenant's interest is personalty rather than realty.

27. d) The Minnesota Homestead Protection Act protects the homestead from foreclosure of general liens such as a judgments.

28. a) The Green Acres law allows agricultural properties to be taxed based upon agricultural value rather than speculative value.

Chapter 4

RECORDATION, ABSTRACTS, TITLE INSURANCE, AND CLOSING

OUTLINE

I. Public Recording System
   A. Recording process
   B. Requirements for recording
      1. dated, executed, acknowledged
      2. property taxes current
      3. state deed tax
      4. mortgage registration tax

II. Marketable Title
   A. Abstract of title
   B. Title search

III. Title Insurance
   A. Title report
   B. Types of policies
      1. owner's policy
      2. mortgagee's policy
      3. combination policy
   C. Policy premium

IV. Quieting Title

V. Torrens System
   A. Registration proceedings
   B. How ownership is transferred

KEY TERMS

recording	executed
acknowledgment	state deed tax
mortgage registration tax	marketable title
abstract of title	title insurance
title report	owner's policy
mortgagee's policy	quieting title
Torrens system	

CHAPTER OVERVIEW

A real estate agent's job does not end when the parties sign the purchase agreement. Many matters must be taken care of before the sale is finalized and a commission paid to the agent. The service provided by the agent during the closing process is every bit as important as the agent's marketing efforts prior to the sale. Careful shepherding of the parties through closing will prevent unnecessary delays and gain the agent a reputation for professionalism.

PUBLIC RECORDING SYSTEM

The fact that someone offers to sell property is no assurance that the seller actually owns the property. The risk is that the seller is not telling the truth, or that unknown to the seller, the title is defective. To limit this risk, every state has recording laws.

> **The purpose of the recording system is to protect purchasers of land by providing a method to determine who owns what interest in a piece of property.**

Recording system: designed to help determine ownership of property

A real estate agent is not required to verify a seller's title and is not required to make a title search. However, it is always helpful to know as much as possible about the property. By using the recording system, you can find out useful information about the property, such as:

- who is listed as the present owner,
- the legal description of the property,

- if there are any mortgages or other recorded liens on the property, and
- if there are any recorded easements or restrictive covenants that affect the property.

> **Prospective purchasers, and the public at large, are presumed to have notice of any interest in property that is recorded.**

Recorded interests can be discovered simply by examining the record. A new purchaser then protects his or her own interest by recording the new deed.

> **The Minnesota recording system is of the *race/notice* type.**

Race/notice system: first to record wins as long as he/she has no notice of prior conveyances

This means that it is a race to record. Whoever records first wins, as long as he or she has no notice of any previous conveyances.

> **Example:** Connelly sells his property to O'Donnel and gives him a deed on June 10. O'Donnel fails to record his deed. Then, on August 15, Connelly sells the same property to McMurphy. McMurphy has no knowledge of the sale to O'Donnel. McMurphy records her deed on August 15, the same day she received it.

McMurphy would win an action to determine ownership of the property even though O'Donnel purchased the property first. McMurphy won the race by recording first, and she had no knowledge of the previous sale.

A subsequent purchaser who has notice of a previous conveyance can never win, even if he or she records first.

RECORDING PROCESS

There are many types of instruments that can and should be recorded. The most common are deeds, easements, covenants, certain long-term leases, mortgages, and powers of attorney to convey real estate. To record a document, it must be deposited in the public recorder's office.

Recording: filing a document at the County Recorder's Office

In Minnesota, each county has a public recorder's office, known as the County Recorder's Office or the Registrar of Titles Office. The person in charge is called the recorder or registrar. Recording a document is accomplished by filing the original or a certified copy at the public recorder's office in the county where the property is located. (Documents pertaining to certain federal land may be recorded at the Bureau of Land Management.)

Once given to the recorder, the document is copied and placed in the public record. It may be copied by transcription, or by any photographic or photomechanical process (photocopiers, microfilm, etc.) that produces a clear, legible and durable record. These copies are generally numbered in chronological order as they are recorded. After being recorded, the original document is returned to the person who left it for recording.

INDEXING. The recorder indexes deeds according to grantor and grantee. In some states, deeds are indexed according to tract as well.

Indexing: means of cataloging documents at the recorder's office

> **In Minnesota, tract indices are maintained by the public recorder in some counties, but they are not considered official.**

Grantor/grantee indices are the only official indices authorized by statute.

These indices serve as the basis for title searches. A search of the grantor index will determine if the seller has already conveyed the interest in question to another party. A search of the grantee index will show the source of the grantor's title, and trace the title back through a chain of title (successive grantors and grantees) that is long enough to ensure the validity of the grantor's title.

Reception Books. As required by Minnesota statute, each public recorder keeps two books, the grantor's and grantee's reception books. In general, the books are supposed to show:

1. Date of reception (year, day, hour and minute)
2. Grantor
3. Grantee
4. Where the property is situated
5. To whom the document is to be delivered after recording
6. Fees received
7. Book and page where the document is recorded and kind of instrument (deed, mortgage, lien, etc.)

However, each county has a slightly different layout in the grantor/grantee books. The reception books usually show each document in the order it is received. They are also used to account for each document number, and to help people find documents that have been accepted for filing but have not yet been indexed.

NOTICE. One of the purposes of recording deeds and other documents is to provide notice of the transaction. Notice is knowledge of information about the property. Every purchaser or mortgagee of land is charged with notice of all prior recorded documents.

Constructive Notice.

> **Constructive notice is notice that is imparted by operation of law as a result of recording.**

Constructive notice: notice imparted by operation of law

The courts do not permit someone to claim ignorance of a recorded document. Even if the person did not actually see the document, if it was in the public record, the person is deemed to have constructive notice of it.

> **Example:** Smith grants an easement across his property to Jones and Jones records the easement. Smith then sells his property to White. White claims that the easement is extinguished because he could not tell that it existed by looking at the property and Smith never told him about it.
>
> The easement is still valid and White is deemed to have constructive notice of it. Even though he had no actual notice, a check in the recorder's office would have shown a record of the easement.

Actual Notice.

> **When information is acquired personally by a party, he or she is said to have actual notice.**

Actual notice: notice acquired personally by inspection, being told, or some other means

Information or notice may be gained from the seller, from other parties, or from inspection of the property.

> **Example:** Abbot tells Simpson that he wants to sell his property. Simpson is interested. When Simpson goes to look at the property she notices that a large power transformer is located at the back of the property. Abbot tells Simpson that the power company has an easement. Simpson has actual notice of the power company's interest in the property.

In the grantor/grantee system of indexing, it is possible that a deed could be recorded in such a way that a title search would not discover it.

Example: Suppose Abbot gives a deed to Baker, who does not record his interest. Baker then conveys to Carter, who promptly records. If Abbot then makes another (illegal) conveyance of the same property to Dunlap, Dunlap will not be able to discover Carter's interest because Carter is not in Abbot's chain of title. There is a break in the chain of title between Abott and Carter because the connecting interest was never recorded by Baker.

The general rule in situations like this is that the subsequent purchaser (Dunlap) is not charged with constructive notice of the deed to Carter because it is not in the chain of title. A deed outside the chain of title is called a "wild deed."

Wild deed: deed outside the chain of title

REQUIREMENTS FOR RECORDING

Almost any document that affects title to land may be recorded, if it is in recordable form. This includes a deed, a mortgage, a contract, a judgment, or a lis pendens. (A lis pendens is a notice stating that there is a lawsuit pending which may affect title to certain property.)

> **Recordable form means that the document is properly dated and executed, contains the required signatures, is acknowledged, and contains a drafting statement.**

(The specifics of properly executing a deed are discussed in Chapter 3.)

ACKNOWLEDGED. All documents must be acknowledged before they can be recorded.

> **An acknowledgment is a formal declaration by the person signing, that it is a valid signature and was signed voluntarily.**

Acknowledgment: formal declaration by person signing that signature is valid and act was voluntary

An acknowledgment must be witnessed and certified by someone who is legally authorized to do so. In most cases, acknowledgments are certified by a notary public (notarized), but judges, recorder's office clerks, and certain other officials also have the authority to certify them. The purpose of an acknowledgment is to protect against forgeries.

TAXES. If the document is conveying property, it must show that state deed tax and any delinquent property taxes have been paid, and must include a certificate of real estate value. It must also include the name and address of the person who is to receive the tax statements and the name and address of the grantee.

State Deed Tax. Minnesota charges a tax on each deed or other instrument that transfers or conveys property. This is known as the state deed tax or transfer tax. This tax has to be paid before the deed may be recorded. (The details of state deed tax are discussed in Chapter 6.)

Mortgage Registration Tax. Minnesota also charges a mortgage registration tax on all new mortgages of real property. This tax must be paid before a mortgage may be recorded. (The details of the mortgage registration tax are also discussed in Chapter 6.)

MARKETABLE TITLE

As was mentioned above, the fact that someone offers to sell property is no assurance that the seller actually owns the property. It is also no assurance that title is free and clear of defects or claims by other parties. Title that is reasonably free from risk of litigation over possible defects is called marketable title. Marketable title is title that has no serious defects and is free from any undisclosed encumbrances. It is title that would be acceptable to a reasonably well-informed and prudent buyer.

> Marketable title: title that has no serious defects or undisclosed encumbrances

A seller is required to provide marketable title to the property at closing. If the seller cannot provide marketable title, the sale will usually not close.

ABSTRACT OF TITLE

The first step in determining whether title is marketable is to acquire an abstract.

> An abstract of title is a short account of what appears in the public records affecting the title of a particular parcel of property.

> Abstract of title: short account of what appears in the public record regarding a piece of property

It contains a chronological summary of all grants, conveyances, wills, transfers and judicial proceedings which in any way affected title, together with all liens and encumbrances of record, showing whether or not they have been released.

The abstract does not guarantee the validity of the title. It merely discloses items that are of public record. Keep in mind that an abstract does not reveal things like encroachments or forgeries, because these things do not appear on the public record.

ABSTRACT UPDATE. In Minnesota, the seller must furnish the buyer with an updated copy of the abstract. Upon examining the abstract, the buyer may raise objections to any liens or encumbrances that show up as affecting title. Questions about whether or not the title is marketable must be raised by the buyer prior to acceptance of the deed.

TITLE SEARCH. Once an abstract is obtained, it is usually submitted to the buyer's attorney to examine. The attorney traces the "chain of title." The chain of title is simply the history of ownership (title) of the property, along with any matters that affected title to the property (such as liens or encumbrances).

The attorney then renders a **title opinion**. This is simply the attorney's professional opinion of the current condition of the title. The title opinion generally states who the current owner is, and lists any outstanding liens, mortgages, restrictions, or encumbrances.

TITLE INSURANCE

Title insurance: policy that protects policy holder against defects in title

Despite the diligent efforts of abstracters and attorneys to give as accurate a picture of land ownership as possible, there is no guarantee that a finished abstract is completely accurate. People preparing abstracts are liable for mistakes due to their own negligence, but what if a recorded deed is a forgery, or was executed by someone who was legally incompetent? Given the complexity of real property law and the high cost of real estate, it is reasonable to expect that some landowners will want to take additional steps to ensure that their property interests are protected. One way of protecting an interest in property is by procuring a policy of title insurance.

TITLE REPORT

The procedure for obtaining title insurance involves two steps. First, a fee is paid to the title company to cover the cost of a title search. The title search involves an examination of the public records. This search may be done by an independent abstractor or attorney, or by an employee of the title company.

Many title companies have their own sets of records (called title plants) so they do not have to search the files in the recorder's office. Title companies typically do more research on property than an attorney. They will inspect public maps pertaining to the property, and will have a physical inspection done to determine parties in possession, to look for recent improvements to the property, and to find any apparent encroachments, survey problems, etc. While full survey coverage is not given, a limited survey coverage generally exists for the main dwelling.

After the title search is completed, the title company issues a report (preliminary title report) on the condition of the title. The report lists any problems found in the physical inspection and all defects and encumbrances of record. These items will be excluded from the policy coverage.

Title report: report issued by title company that discloses condition of title

> **In Minnesota, the general practice is for the seller to bring the abstract on the property up to date. It is then left up to the buyer to secure an attorney's opinion on the abstract or to purchase a title insurance policy.**

If a mortgage is given on the property, the lender may require that title insurance be purchased to protect the lender's interest.

COMMITMENT. When title insurance is purchased, the current information about the title is written up and becomes the "**commitment**" for title insurance. A commitment is different from an abstract in that an abstract lists all of the recorded events that affected title to the property. The commitment simply shows the condition of title at this moment. It does not list all prior events.

Part I of the commitment lists the current owners of the property and all current recorded problems or objections, such as a mortgage, easements, or property taxes.

Part II of the commitment lists any exceptions, things **not** covered by the policy.

The title insurance policy protects against all defects not listed as exceptions. This generally includes protection against:

- errors in the title examination,
- errors in the abstract,
- errors in the public records, and
- hidden defects such as forgery, incompetency or misrepresented marital status.

TYPES OF POLICIES

Owner's policy: protects owner against latent defects in the chain of title

OWNER'S POLICY. The extent of protection given by a title insurance policy varies according to the nature of the policy. An owner's policy is purchased for the full sale price, so it covers the buyer's equity in the property. Under an owner's policy (the standard coverage policy), the policy holder is protected against latent defects in the chain of title, such as forged deeds, incompetent grantors, and improperly delivered deeds.

> **This policy covers risks which are a matter of public record, forgery, impersonation and incapacity of any person who was a party to a transaction involving title to the property, the possibility that a deed of record was not delivered with intent to convey title, any loss which might arise from a federal estate tax lien which is valid without notice on death, and any expenses incurred in defending title.**

The landowner may obtain coverage of specific items which are not included in the standard policy by purchasing an endorsement to cover the particular item. Title insurance will not protect a landowner from losses due to governmental action such as condemnation or changes in zoning. The owner's policy is good for the full amount of coverage stated in the policy for as long as the owner owns the property.

ALTA: the American Land Title Association, an organization dedicated to standardizing title insurance policies

ALTA. Title insurance policies have been standardized to some extent through the efforts of the American Land Title Association (ALTA). ALTA is a nationwide organization of title companies which promulgates a series of uniform title policies and also promotes professional standards and ethics within the industry. The most commonly used ALTA policies are the ALTA Owner's Policy, which provides standard coverage for owners, and the ALTA Loan Policy, which provides extended coverage for lenders.

MORTGAGEE'S POLICY.

> **The mortgagee's (or lender's or extended coverage) policy provides protection against risks to the lender.**

OWNER'S POLICY

(ALTA Residential Form; one-to-four family residences only)

COVERED TITLE RISKS

This Policy covers the following title risks, if they affect your title on the Policy Date.

1. Someone else owns an interest in your title.
2. A document is not properly signed, sealed, acknowledged, or delivered.
3. Forgery, fraud, duress, incompetency, incapacity, or impersonation.
4. Defective recording of any document.
5. You do not have any legal right of access to and from the land.
6. There are restrictive covenants limiting your use of the land.
7. There is a lien on your title because of:
   - a mortgage or deed of trust
   - a judgment, tax, or special assessment
   - a charge by a homeowner's or condominium association
8. There are liens on your title arising now or later, for labor and material furnished before the Policy Date—unless you agreed to pay for the labor and material.
9. Others have rights arising out of leases, contracts, or options.
10. Someone else has an easement on your land.
11. Your title is unmarketable, which allows another person to refuse to perform a contract to purchase, to lease or to make a mortgage loan.
12. You are forced to remove your existing structure—other than a boundary wall or fence—because:
    - it extends on to adjoining land or on to any easement
    - it violates a restriction shown in Schedule B
    - it violates an existing zoning law.
13. You cannot use the land because use as a single-family residence violates a restriction shown in Schedule B or an existing zoning law.
14. Other defects, liens or encumbrances.

This is an excerpt from the ALTA Residential Form used by the Title Insurance Company of Minnesota. Reprinted with permission.

The mortgagee's policy is generally required by lenders so that the mortgage can be sold on the secondary market. It protects only for the amount owed on the mortgage loan. Thus, as the loan is paid off, the liability decreases.

Another important point is that the mortgagee's policy is assignable to subsequent holders of the same loan. In other words, if the mortgage is assigned to someone else, the mortgagee's insurance policy may also be assigned.

COMBINATION POLICY. A combination policy is a combination of an owner's policy and a mortgagee's policy. It protects the lender up to the current loan balance and protects the owner for the difference between the loan amount and the purchase price.

POLICY PREMIUM

In some parts of the country, the seller pays all costs of the title search and insurance. But in Minnesota, the common practice is for the seller to pay the cost of bringing the abstract up to date. The buyer is then responsible for the cost of an attorney's title opinion or the title insurance policy.

A single payment is usually made to cover the insurance premium. The insurance policy essentially remains in effect for as long as the owner owns the property. However, the owner's policy actually protects the insured forever. If the insured gives a warranty deed, and a defect is later uncovered, the policy will cover the insured's liability even if the insured no longer owns the property.

An old insurance policy cannot be transferred or assigned to the new owner of the property. However, policies are routinely "reissued" to the new owner for a lower premium if the previous owner's policy is available for updating.

QUIETING TITLE

Quiet title action: an action brought to remove a cloud on the title (clear up doubt about the validity of title)

> **A quiet title action is used to remove a cloud on the title. A cloud on the title occurs whenever doubt exists as to the validity of the grantor's title.**

The property is unmarketable so long as the cloud exists. To clear the cloud, the seller may have to bring a quiet title action to get a judicial ruling on the title. The court makes a binding determination of the various parties' interests in a particular piece of real estate.

Example: A seller has found a potential buyer for his property. A search of the recorded documents shows a gap in title. (A gap occurs when the recorded documents don't indicate who owned the property for a certain time period.)

The seller brings a quiet title action. The defendants in the action are all parties who have a potential interest in the land. (This includes whoever the mystery person is that held title during the gap, even though this person's name is unknown.)

The seller asks the court to declare his title valid, thereby "quieting title" to the land. If no defendants appear to challenge the seller's title, the court will grant the seller's request. The buyer can then rely on the court action and consummate the sale.

TORRENS SYSTEM

Along with the recording system described at the beginning of this chapter, Minnesota also uses a method of registering title called the **Torrens system**.

> Under the Torrens system, the owner may apply to the courts for registration of title.

Torrens system: method used in Minnesota to register title; registrar of titles prepares certificate of title

REGISTRATION PROCEEDING

The application for registration is generally filed with the court administrator and a copy is then filed with the county recorder (or registrar of title). A court hearing is held to determine title. Anyone named in the abstract and anyone else claiming a right or interest in the property may attend the hearing and present proof of their claim.

Based on the outcome of the hearing, a government-appointed registrar of titles prepares a **certificate of title** naming the legally recognized title holder and listing any legally recognized encumbrances, such as mortgages or easements. The registrar keeps the original certificate and an "Owner's Duplicate Certificate" is issued to the property owner.

TRANSFERRING OWNERSHIP

If the owner wants to sell or convey the property, the owner has an abstracter prepare a **registered property abstract** (RPA). This abstract summarizes the information on the certificate of title and reports any unpaid taxes or other liens on the property. The buyer generally has an attorney examine the RPA to see if the condition of title is acceptable, or purchases a title insurance policy. If the title is acceptable, the seller gives the buyer a deed and the owner's duplicate certificate of title.

The buyer takes these documents to the registrar of titles, who cancels the seller's certificate and files a new certificate in the name of the buyer. Any liens or other encumbrances that have not been removed are carried over onto the new certificate. Any new encumbrances, such as a new mortgage, are noted on the new certificate. The registrar keeps the original and the new owner receives a duplicate of the new certificate. It is important to note that, unlike title to abstract property which passes upon delivery of the deed, Torrens title passes upon issuance of the new certificate of title.

CHAPTER SUMMARY

1. Recording is designed to protect purchasers of property from the secret claims of other parties. Indexing lists recorded documents according to grantor and grantee.

2. Marketable title is title that is reasonably free from risk of litigation over possible defects.

3. In Minnesota, the seller usually provides an updated abstract of title. The buyer then requests a title search and has an attorney render a title opinion, or the buyer may choose to purchase title insurance.

4. When title insurance is purchased, the title insurance company agrees to reimburse the policy holder for losses caused by defects in the title and also agrees to handle the legal defense of claims based on covered defects. A title policy may cover the owner, the lender, or both.

5. Under the Torrens system, an owner applies for registration of title with the court. A court hearing is held to determine title. A certificate of title is then issued, naming the legally recognized title holder.

CHAPTER 4—GLOSSARY REVIEW

A. lis pendens
B. title search
C. title opinion
D. recording
E. marketable
F. delivery
G. title insurance

H. abstract of title
I. chain of title
J. free and clear
K. acceptance
L. quiet title
M. Torrens
N. owner's duplicate certificate

1. Priority of a recorded instrument is determined by the date of _recording_

2. When one has traced the ownership of a parcel of land to the beginning of its recorded history, the result is known as the _chain of title_

3. A recorded notice stating that a pending lawsuit may affect title to a particular property is called a _lis pendens_

4. A summary of all recorded documents affecting title to a given parcel of land is called an _abstract of title_

5. After an attorney examines title, he or she will render a _title opinion_

6. Protection against incomplete or defective records of the title to land can best be obtained by securing _title insurance_

7. Title that establishes ownership of the real property in a reasonably clear manner upon examination of the public records is called _marketable_ title.

8. A system of land title registration used in Minnesota is called the _Torrens_ system.

9. In a transfer of title to Torrens property, the grantee receives a deed and an _owners. duplicate certificate_

CHAPTER 4—REVIEW EXAM

1. A "chain of title" is:

   a) a form of land measurement.
   b) a form of title insurance.
   c) an encumbrance on title.
   d) a chain of conveyances and record-
      ed interests.

2. Which of the following allows the legal
   title to be actually registered with the
   court?

   a) A chain of title
   b) Torrens certificate of title
   c) Attorney's opinion
   d) Title insurance

3. Legal action taken on a title claimant's
   behalf to resolve all "clouds" on title is
   known as a:

   a) suit for damages.
   b) foreclosure suit.
   c) quiet title suit.
   d) partition suit.

4. Which of the following is (are) true concerning recording of documents?

   I. All real estate documents must be
      recorded to be valid.
   II. Recordation of real estate docu-
       ments gives constructive notice.

   a) I only
   b) II only
   c) Both I and II
   d) Neither I nor II

5. The function of the county recorder is to:

   a) appraise properties.
   b) guarantee marketable title.
   c) make sure all necessary documents
      are recorded.
   d) prepare a condensed history of title
      and interests.

6. A lender making a loan secured by a
   conventional mortgage will probably require the borrower to buy:

   a) a mortgagee's title insurance policy.
   b) a mortgagor's title insurance policy.
   c) an owner's title policy.
   d) FHA mortgage insurance.

7. Title insurance would protect against all
   of the following EXCEPT:

   a) a forged deed.
   b) encroachments.
   c) errors in the public record.
   d) errors in the abstract.

8. A property sold for $85,000 and the
   mortgage amount is $68,000. The mort-
   gagee's title insurance policy would be
   for:

   a) $17,000
   b) $85,000
   c) $68,000
   d) $153,000

9. In the sale of registered property, which of the following would an attorney examine to determine whether or not the title is marketable?

    a) An updated abstract
    b) The certificate of title
    c) The owner's duplicate certificate
    d) The registered property abstract

10. Which of the following is most likely to examine an abstract?

    a) The broker
    b) The attorney for the seller
    c) The mortgagee
    d) The attorney for the buyer

CHAPTER 4—GLOSSARY REVIEW KEY

1. D
2. I
3. A
4. H
5. C
6. G
7. E
8. M
9. N

CHAPTER 4—REVIEW EXAM KEY

1. d) The "chain of title" links the present owner to all previous owners.

2. b) In the Torrens system, title is registered with the courts. The courts issue a Torrens Certificate of Title, which is held by the registrar of titles.

3. c) Clouds are removed through a quiet title suit.

4. b) Not all documents have to be recorded to be valid (an unrecorded deed, for example, can transfer title to the grantee). Recording gives constructive notice and establishes priority.

5. c) The county recorder is like a librarian in that he or she records and organizes documents.

6. a) Lenders wishing to protect their interests will require the borrower to purchase a mortgagee's (lender's) title insurance policy.

7. b) Title insurance does not protect against claims involving surveys or encroachments.

8. c) The mortgagee's policy protects the lender up to the current mortgage balance.

9. d) Marketable title in the Torrens system is determined by reviewing the registered property abstract (RPA).

10. d) The buyer will hire an attorney or a title insurance company to examine the abstract.

Chapter 5

REAL ESTATE CONTRACTS

OUTLINE

I. How a Contract is Created
   A. Express (declared) contracts
      1. bilateral
      2. unilateral
   B. Implied contracts

II. Enforceability of Contracts
   A. Valid
   B. Void
   C. Voidable

III. Essentials of a Valid Contract
   A. Capacity
   B. Mutual agreement
      1. offer and acceptance
      2. counteroffer
      3. contractual intent
      4. no fraud or misrepresentation
      5. no mistake
      6. no duress
   C. Lawful objective
   D. Consideration
   E. In writing
      1. Statute of Frauds
      2. Minnesota Plain Language Act

IV. Performance and Discharge
   A. Executed vs. executory
   B. Assignment

    C. Novation

    D. Legally impossible

    E. Death

    F. Mutual rescission

V. Remedies for Breach

    A. Acceptance of partial performance

    B. Unilateral rescission

    C. Specific performance

    D. Money damages

    E. Liquidated damages

VI. Purchase Agreement

    A. Uniform Vendor and Purchaser Risk Act

VII. Option

VIII. Lease

    A. Types of leases

        1. gross/fixed

        2. net

        3. percentage

        4. land/ground

        5. graduated/step up

        6. escalator

        7. sandwich lease

    B. Termination of leases

    C. Minnesota Landlord-Tenant Act

IX. Contract for Deed

KEY TERMS

contract	forbearance
Statute of Frauds	mutual agreement
offer	counteroffer
acceptance	fraud
undue influence	duress
lawful objective	consideration
valid	void
voidable	rescission

cancellation
liquidated damages
purchase agreement
option
escalator lease
gross lease
percentage· lease
graduated lease
estate for years
constructive eviction
security deposit
contract for deed

novation
specific performance
unilateral
Uniform Vendor and Purchaser
  Risk Act
net lease
land/ground lease
sandwich lease
estate at will
Minnesota Landlord-Tenant Act
habitability
equitable redemption

CHAPTER OVERVIEW

Contracts are a significant and inescapable part of the real estate business. Listing agreements, purchase agreements, option agreements, and lease agreements are all contracts. It is important for real estate agents and brokers to be able to recognize and understand the various types of real estate contracts. This chapter describes real estate contracts and explains what legally constitutes a contract, how a contract can be terminated, what is considered a breach of contract, and what remedies are available when a breach occurs.

HOW A CONTRACT IS CREATED

Almost everyone has a basic understanding of what a contract is. Simply stated, a contract is "a legally binding agreement between two or more competent persons to do or not to do certain things for consideration." Since real estate agents work with many different types of contracts, and with many different clients, it is important to understand how contracts are created. A contract may be expressly created, or may be created by implication.

EXPRESS CONTRACT

An express (or declared) contract is one that has been put into words.

Express contract: has been put into words

It may be spoken or written. Each party to the contract has stated what he or she is willing to do and knows what is due from the other party. Most contracts are express agreements. If Alan says "Will you cut my hair for $10?" and Burt says "OK," they have an express contract. If a homeowner signs a listing agreement with a real estate broker, it is an express contract.

Some contracts are partly express and partly implied. In a restaurant, the prices are written on the menu. When you order a meal, it is understood that you agree to pay the price on the menu, although you don't actually say that to the waiter.

IMPLIED CONTRACT

> **An implied contract, or contract by implication, is created by the acts of the parties, not by express agreement.**

Implied contract: created by acts of the parties, not by express agreement

An implied contract has not been put into words, but the agreement is presumed to exist because of the parties' actions.

> **Example:** Sylvia has an account at the drug store near her home. One day when she's in a hurry, Sylvia runs into the store, grabs a bottle of aspirin, and waves it at the clerk. The clerk smiles and nods, and Sylvia rushes out of the store with the aspirin.

Their actions create an implied contract. After Sylvia leaves, the clerk charges the aspirin to Sylvia's account. When Sylvia gets the bill, she will be required to pay, even though she did not specifically tell the clerk that she wanted the aspirin charged to her account.

UNILATERAL OR BILATERAL. All contracts are either unilateral or bilateral. A unilateral contract exists where only one of the contracting parties is legally obligated to perform. The most common unilateral real estate contract is the option agreement.

Unilateral contract: only one party is obligated to perform

A contract is bilateral when each party makes a binding promise to the other. Most contracts are bilateral.

Bilateral contract: each party makes a binding promise to the other

> **Example:** A tells B, "I'll pay you $100 if you paint my fence this week." B says, "Sure, I'll start tomorrow." They have a bilateral contract, because B has promised to paint the fence, and A has promised to pay.
>
> But suppose that when A says, "I'll pay you $100 if you paint my fence this week," B doesn't commit herself. This

is a unilateral contract, since only A has made a promise. If B paints the fence this week, A is bound to pay her $100. But A can't require B to paint the fence, because B didn't promise to do it.

FORBEARANCE. Most contracts are agreements to do something. However, a contract could also be an agreement not to do something. This is called a forbearance.

Forbearance: an agreement not to do something

> **Example:** Grandma agrees to pay Julian's college tuition if Julian promises not to smoke or drink while he is in college. Julian's part of the agreement is a forbearance.

A common real estate example of forbearance occurs when a lender agrees not to foreclose if the borrower agrees to a new payment schedule.

ENFORCEABILITY OF CONTRACTS

A contract's legal status falls into one of three categories:

1. valid
2. void
3. voidable

LEGAL STATUS	LEGAL EFFECT	EXAMPLE
VALID	Binding and enforceable	An agreement with all the requirements for a valid contract
VOID	No contract at all	An agreement for which there is no consideration
VOIDABLE	Valid until rescinded by one party	A contract with a minor

VALID

Valid contract: meets all legal requirements for formation

> **A valid contract is an agreement that meets all the legal requirements for contract formation (as outlined later in this chapter).**

If one of the parties doesn't fulfill his or her side of the bargain, the other can sue to have the contract enforced.

If the contract contains all of the essential ingredients, the contents are proven in court, and it is free of any negative influences, it is a valid and binding agreement that the court can enforce.

VOID

When an agreement doesn't meet one or more of the requirements for valid contract formation, the agreement is considered legally void.

Void contract: fails to meet one or more requirements for formation; void contract is not binding

> **In the eyes of the law, a void contract is actually not a contract at all.**

It has no legal effect. It is not binding on the parties and it can't be enforced in court. If both parties fulfill their part of the agreement, fine. But if one breaches and the other sues, the judge will rule that no contract was formed, and will refuse to enforce the agreement. This most often occurs because one of the essential elements necessary to form a valid contract is completely lacking.

> **Example:** Broker signs a listing agreement with Seller. Seller had been declared mentally incompetent by a court prior to entering into the contract. Since Seller had no capacity to enter into a contract, the contract is void.

VOIDABLE

A voidable contract appears to be valid, but has a defect giving one or more of the parties the power to avoid performance or rescind the agreement.

Voidable contract: one or more parties have the power to rescind agreement; to disaffirm a contract, action must be taken

> **A voidable contract usually results when one of the parties has taken advantage of the other in some way.**

For example, contracts entered into as a result of fraud are normally voidable by the injured party (the person defrauded).

Voidable means that the injured party can choose whether or not to go through with the agreement. The injured party can expressly ratify the agreement and go ahead with the terms of the contract. Or the contract could be **disaffirmed**—that is, the injured party could ask a court to terminate it.

> **Example:** Boyack sells some property to Paggiore, after showing Paggiore a forged mineral survey stating that the property has a vein of iron ore running through it. When Paggiore finds out about the fraud, she may choose to go ahead with the sale and buy the property anyway, or she could sue to have the contract rescinded.

It is important to note that action must be taken to rescind or disaffirm a voidable contract.

Unlike a contract that is void from the outset, a voidable contract cannot simply be ignored. Failure to take action within a reasonable time may result in a court declaring the contract impliedly ratified.

Remember that a voidable contract is only voidable by the injured party. (The injured party is the one who is underage, or has been taken advantage of, or who was forced to sign under duress, etc.) The contract is still binding on the non-injured party.

> **Example:** Scott sells her property to Thompson. She is unaware that Thompson is only 17. Since Thompson is underage, the contract is voidable. Thompson may disaffirm the contract. However, if Thompson chooses to go ahead with the contract, Scott is bound. Scott does not have the right to disaffirm.

ESSENTIALS OF A VALID CONTRACT

For a contract to be valid, binding and enforceable, certain essential ingredients must be present. If they are not present, the contract may be void or voidable. When dealing with real estate contracts, it is important for the agent to recognize whether all of the essential elements are present. If not, there may be problems with enforcing the contract.

CONTRACTUAL CAPACITY

To make a valid contract, a person must have contractual capacity.

Capacity: parties must be at least 18 years old and mentally competent

> **This means that the person must be at least 18 years old, and must also be mentally competent.**

This requirement protects minors and the mentally ill, who might enter into contracts without really understanding the consequences.

AGE EIGHTEEN. Age 18 is sometimes referred to as the age of majority. Those under the age of 18 (minors) have limited contractual capability. The broad general rule is that if a minor signs a contract, it is voidable by the minor. That is, it can't be enforced against the minor. However, if the minor follows through with the contract, the other party remains bound.

> **Example:** Klayman sells a house to Elliot for $40,000. Unknown to Klayman, Elliot is only 17. When Elliot tells his parents about his purchase, they are furious. The downpayment is money that Elliot was supposed to be saving for college. If they can convince Elliot to do so, he can disaffirm the contract.
>
> However, if Elliot decides to keep the property, Klayman is bound by the contract. He cannot force Elliot to return the house when he finds out that Elliot is only 17.

The purpose of the "law of majority" is to prevent minors from entering into agreements they may be too young to understand. In some circumstances, the general rule may be limited by such factors as misrepresentation.

> **Example:** Suppose that Klayman thought Elliot looked kind of young, so he asked Elliot how old he was. Elliot lied and told him that he was 19, and showed him a forged driver's license showing his age as 19. Elliot would probably not be allowed to disaffirm this contract, because of his intentional misrepresentations.

It may also be important to note that an emancipated minor generally has capacity to contract. An emancipated minor is a person under 18 who:

- is or has been married;
- is on active duty in the armed forces; or
- has a declaration of emancipation from a court.

A contract with an emancipated minor is not voidable due to minority.

MENTAL COMPETENCE. A person who is entirely without understanding cannot make a valid contract. After a person has been declared mentally incompetent by a court (because of mental illness, mental retardation, or senility), any contract he or she enters into is void. If a person made a contract before the declaration of incompetence, but while of unsound mind, a court-appointed guardian can ask the court to have the contract set aside.

Mentally competent: not declared incompetent by a court and not temporarily and involuntarily incompetent

In a few cases, contracts entered into by a person who is temporarily incompetent (under the influence of alcohol or drugs, for example) may be voidable. Action to void this type of contract must be taken within a reasonable time after regaining mental competency. To void the contract, the person may be required to show that he or she was involuntarily intoxicated.

MUTUAL AGREEMENT

The next requirement for a binding contract is mutual agreement.

Mutual agreement ("meeting of the minds"): all parties agreed to the terms of the contract

> **Mutual agreement simply means that all of the parties have agreed to the terms of the contract. This mutual agreement is sometimes referred to as a "meeting of the minds."**

A mutual agreement exists when there is:

- an offer and acceptance,
- contractual intent, and
- no fraud, misrepresentation, mistake, duress, or undue influence.

OFFER AND ACCEPTANCE. The process of forming a contract begins when one person makes an offer to another. An offer shows the willingness of the person making it to enter into the contract under the stated terms. To be valid, an offer must:

1. be communicated,
2. express a willingness to contract, and
3. be definite and certain in its terms.

Offer: must be communicated, definite and certain, and express a willingness to contract

Acceptance: must be communicated in the agreed manner within the agreed time and before revocation of offer

> **The person making the offer (the offeror) must communicate the offer to the individual receiving the offer (the offeree). To bind the offeror, the offeree must communicate acceptance in the agreed-upon manner within the agreed-upon time (or before the offer is revoked).**

If the offer proposes a real estate contract, it must be in writing (except for a lease for a term of one year or less). If no time or manner of acceptance is stated in the offer, a reasonable time and manner will be implied.

Contractual intent must be clear

CONTRACTUAL INTENT. Whatever words make up the offer, they must clearly indicate that the offeror intends to enter a contract. An offer must have definite terms—it isn't binding if it is too vague. It should state at least such basic terms as the subject matter, the time for performance, and the price.

COUNTEROFFER.

Counteroffer is actually a new offer

> **A counteroffer, also called a qualified acceptance, is actually a rejection of the offer and a tender of a new offer.**

Instead of accepting all the terms of the offer or rejecting it outright, the offeree "accepts" with certain modifications. This will happen when some, but not all, of the terms of the original offer are unacceptable to the offeree. This qualified acceptance reverses the roles of the parties: the offeror becomes the offeree and can accept or reject the counteroffer. If he or she chooses to accept the counteroffer, the acceptance must be communicated to the person who made it—the original offeree. If the original offeror rejects the counteroffer, the offeree cannot go back and accept the original offer. The original offer was terminated.

> **Example:** Jacobson offers to buy Sarducci's property under the following conditions: purchase price of $215,000, closing date January 3, and downpayment of $35,000. Sarducci agrees to all the terms but the closing date, which she wants to be February 3. By changing one of the terms, Sarducci has rejected Jacobson's initial offer and made a counteroffer. Now it is up to Jacobson to either accept or reject Sarducci's counteroffer.

NEGATIVE FACTORS. Offer and acceptance are the expression of mutual consent to the terms of an agreement. But to create a binding contract, consent must be freely given. It is not freely given when it is the result of negative factors such as:

- fraud,
- misrepresentation,
- mistake,
- duress, or
- undue influence.

Consent must be freely given

If a buyer's offer or a seller's acceptance is influenced by any of these negative forces, the contract is voidable by the party who was victimized.

The victim may choose to go ahead with the contract or disaffirm it.

Fraud or Misrepresentation. Fraud is any form of deceit or misrepresentation by which one party tries to gain unfair advantage over another, and the other party relies on the fraudulent statement or action.

Victim of negative force(s) may either go ahead with contract or disaffirm it

---

To disaffirm a fraudulent contract, the victim must show that the fraud affected his or her decision to enter into the contract.

To disaffirm, victim must show decision to contract was affected by fraud

A misrepresentation is an untrue statement or a concealment of a material fact. A misrepresentation may be intentional (in which case it is fraud), or it may be unintentional. Most misrepresentations occur because of carelessness or negligence, rather than intentionally.

In Minnesota, there are 11 requirements for a charge of fraud or misrepresentation.

1. There must be a representation (a statement or a nondisclosure),
2. the representation must be false,
3. it must have to do with a past or present fact,
4. the fact must be material to the transaction,
5. the fact must be something one would be able to know,
6. the person making the representation must know that it is false, or make the representation with disregard for whether it is true or false,
7. the person making the representation must intend for someone else to rely on it,

8. someone is induced to act,
9. the actions are in reliance on the representation,
10. damages are suffered, and
11. the damage is attributable to the representation.

Agent may be liable for negligent as well as intentional misrepresentations

It is important to note that Minnesota does not require an intent to deceive or injure. An agent may be liable for negligent misrepresentations as well as for intentional misrepresentations. A negligent misrepresentation is a false statement made with disregard for whether it is true or not. It is made without sufficient information to justify the statement, or without taking proper steps to find out whether or not the statement is true. Brokers have been held liable for misrepresenting:

- defective sewers,
- leaky basements,
- the condition of the foundation,
- the condition of a heating apparatus,
- the existence of water, sewer, or gas connections,
- the condition of the septic system,
- the fact that the building was in violation of the building code,
- the fact that the broker had a personal interest in the property,
- the size of the lot, and many other things.

Mistake. Unlike the other negative factors that can make a contract voidable, mistake in a legal sense does not involve bad faith, misrepresentations, or villainy.

If both parties are mistaken about important fact or law, either may disaffirm contract

> **If both parties are mistaken about some fact or law that is important to their contract, either of them may disaffirm the contract.**

This is known as mutual mistake.

Example: Cynthia sells her property to Joe. Joe tells Cynthia that he plans to use the property for a retail store. Cynthia assures Joe that it is zoned commercial. Joe also believes that it is zoned commercial, since there are several commercial establishments in the next block. Unfortunately, they discover that recent zoning changes have been made. The dividing line is right in front of Cynthia's property. Her property is actually zoned strictly residential. The contract is probably voidable because of their mutual mistake.

If only one party to a contract is mistaken, it is known as a unilateral mistake.

One party is mistaken: contract is not voidable unless other party knew about mistake and did nothing to correct first party

> **A contract is not voidable because of a unilateral mistake unless the other party knew about the mistake and did nothing to correct it or to advise the first party of the mistake.**

Example: Cynthia sells her property to Joe. Joe plans to use the property for a retail store. However, he does not tell Cynthia his plans. He assumes the property is zoned commercial, but he doesn't check it out, and Cynthia never says anything about the zoning. When Joe discovers his mistake, it is unfortunate, but the contract is not voidable.

Duress or Menace.

> **Duress is compelling someone to do something—like sign a contract—against his or her will, with the use of force or constraint.**

A person who signs a contract because he or she is being unlawfully confined (that is, forced to stay in a place against his or her will) is said to have signed under duress. A contract is also signed under duress if the signer's spouse, child, or close relative is being unlawfully confined, or if their property is being unlawfully detained.

> **Menace is the threat of duress, or the threat of violent injury to a person, or to his or her spouse, child, or close relative.**

The threat of injury to a person's reputation (as in blackmail) is also menace. Any contract signed as a result of duress or menace is voidable by the victim.

Undue Influence. Undue influence is using one's influence to pressure a person or taking advantage of another's distress or weakness of mind to induce him or her to enter a contract.

Contracts entered into because of duress, menace, or undue influence are voidable by the victim

Example: Broker Bob has a 92-year-old grandmother who is in poor health and beginning to lose some of her mental capacity. Grandma decides to sell her house and move in with a daughter. Another broker would charge a commission of only 6 or 7%. But Broker Bob convinces Grandma that she should keep things in the family. He persuades Grandma to sign an exclusive listing agreement providing him with a 25% commission upon the sale of her house.

> **Contracts entered into because of undue influence are voidable by the victim.**

LAWFUL OBJECTIVE

Contracts for performance of illegal acts are void

Another requirement for a valid and enforceable contract is that the purpose of the contract must be lawful.

> **If one person promises to pay another for committing an illegal act, their contract is void and cannot be enforced by a court.**

Examples of contracts with unlawful objectives are contracts to pay interest rates in excess of the state's usury limit, or contracts relating to unlawful gambling. If a contract does not have a lawful objective, it is void.

A contract may contain some lawful provisions and some unlawful provisions. In these situations, it may be possible to sever the unlawful portions of the contract and enforce the lawful portions.

> **Example:** Smith and Jones enter into a contract to buy and sell an apartment house. A clause in the contract prohibits the buyer from renting any of the apartments to persons of a certain race. The contract to buy and sell the property would probably be enforceable, but the clause prohibiting rentals to members of a certain race would be void.

CONSIDERATION

Consideration: contract must involve exchange of something of value to the parties

Even when the parties have the capacity to contract, they have reached a mutual agreement, and there are no negative factors present, it is not a valid contract unless it is supported by consideration. Consideration is something of value exchanged by the parties. The exchange of consideration is what distinguishes a contractual promise from the promise of a gift. The promise may be to pay a certain amount, or do a particular act, or to not do a particular act (a forbearance).

The typical real estate sales contract contains a promise by the purchaser to pay a certain amount of money to the seller, and a promise by the seller to sell (to convey title to the purchaser). Both parties have given and received consideration.

> **As a general rule, the contract will be enforceable as long as the consideration has value, even though the consideration exchanged is not equal.**

Value does not have to be equal

Even though one party struck a bad bargain, it is still an enforceable contract.

> **Example:** Zanuck's house was appraised at $175,000. He's anxious to sell it very quickly because he thinks he may have to leave the country in a hurry. When Halverson offers $75,000 for the house, Zanuck accepts, and they execute a written contract.
>
> As it turns out, Zanuck won't have to leave the country. He wants to back out of the sale, but Halverson wants to go through with it. Although Zanuck's consideration is worth more than twice what Halverson is giving, their contract is binding.

Of course, when the consideration is grossly unequal, that may be a sign that there was fraud, undue influence, duress, or menace involved in the contract negotiations. But unless one of those negative factors is proven, the contract is enforceable.

However, in cases where the disparity in value is quite large a court may refuse to grant specific performance. In the previous example, a judge might rule that $75,000 is not legally adequate consideration. In that case, though Zanuck might have to pay Halverson damages for breach of contract, he would not be ordered to actually sell Halverson the house. (Specific performance is discussed later in this chapter.)

STATUTE OF FRAUDS. The Statute of Frauds is a law requiring certain types of contracts to be in writing and signed. As the name suggests, the Statute of Frauds is intended to prevent fradulent claims. The parties to an unwritten contract are likely to later disagree about exactly what each agreed to do. Putting a contract in writing helps

Statute of Frauds: requires certain contracts, such as those relating to real estate transactions, to be in writing

eliminate disputes, because the document is solid evidence of the existence of an agreement and its essential terms.

Only those types of contracts covered by the Statute of Frauds must be in writing to be enforceable. Other contracts may be oral.

> **In Minnesota, almost all contracts relating to real estate transactions are required to be in writing.**

This includes any agreement creating, granting, assigning, surrendering, or declaring an estate or interest in land.

Leases for one year or less do not have to be written

However, there is one exception to this rule. Leases for a term of one year or less are not required to be in writing.

A VALID REAL ESTATE CONTRACT

Competent Parties

Mutual Agreement

Lawful Objective

Consideration

In Writing

Minnesota law requires plain language in certain contracts

MINNESOTA PLAIN LANGUAGE ACT. Minnesota also has a statute requiring plain language in certain written contracts. There are some exceptions, but in general, consumer contracts must be written in a clear and coherent manner using words of common and everyday meaning.

This act requires that plain and simple language be used in **listing agreements** and **residential leases** of three years or less. The Minnesota Plain Language Act is enforced by the Attorney General.

PERFORMANCE AND DISCHARGE

Once an agreement has been reached, the problems are sometimes only beginning. The contract must still be carried out. The parties to the contract may perform as agreed, or be discharged from the duty to perform, or be charged with breach of contract for failing to perform.

EXECUTED OR EXECUTORY

An executed contract is one that has been fully performed—both parties have done what they promised to do. With respect to contracts, the terms "executed" and "performed" are synonymous.

An executory contract has not yet been fully performed. One or both of the parties have not begun to carry out their promises, or are in the process of carrying them out.

ASSIGNMENT

Most contracts are fully performed or executed by the original parties. However, sometimes one or more of the parties wants to sell or otherwise assign part of the contract to someone else. As a general rule, either party to a contract may make an assignment. But this right may be limited by the contract itself. The contract may specifically provide that one party can't assign without the other party's consent.

Assignment: the sale or transfer of contractual rights; some contracts prohibit assignment or require consent

> **Example:** Landlord and Tenant sign a two-year residential lease. The lease provides that Tenant cannot assign her rights and duties under the lease to anyone else without Landlord's permission.

Even without a provision prohibiting assignment, a contract for personal services cannot be assigned without consent. If I contract to have you play the piano at a party, you can't send your sister over instead.

Listing agreements are considered personal services contracts. So if a broker has a listing agreement, she cannot assign the agreement to another broker without the seller's consent.

Contracts for personal services (such as listing agreements) require consent before assignment

When an assignment is made, it is important to keep in mind that the assignor (the original party) isn't relieved of all liability under the contract. Suppose the assignee (the new party) doesn't carry out his contractual duties. The other party sues, but the assignee turns out to be judgment-proof (has no money or assets). The assignor is secondarily liable, and can be required to pay the other party if the assignee doesn't.

Assignor still has secondary liability

Example: Tenant 1 assigns the remainder of his lease to Tenant 2. Tenant 2 pays for a couple of months and then skips town. Landlord tries to go after Tenant 2 for the rest of the rent, but Tenant 2 can't be found. Tenant 1 is secondarily liable and can be required to make the remaining payments.

NOVATION

Novation: withdrawing party is released from liability

> **A novation is similar to an assignment; the difference between them concerns liability. When a contract is assigned, there is continuing liability on the part of the assignor (the original contract party). The novator, on the other hand, is released from liability.**

Example: Sellers sign a purchase agreement with the Franks. The Franks then decide they don't want the house. But they know that the Gibsons are looking for a house. They show the Gibsons the house and the Gibsons love it. They introduce Sellers to the Gibsons. Sellers find out that the Gibsons are actually in a much better financial position than the Franks. Sellers agree to release the Franks and accept the Gibsons as new purchasers under the same contract.

The Franks have novated. They are relieved of all liability connected with the contract.

Novations must comply with rules for contract formation

A novation can only be arranged with the original party's consent. A novation is essentially a new contract, so it must comply with all of the rules for contract formation, including the mutual consent requirement.

The term "novation" doesn't always refer to the substitution of a new party. It can also refer to the substitution of a new obligation in place of the original one. If the original parties tear up a two-year lease and execute a five-year lease, that's a novation.

LEGALLY IMPOSSIBLE

If the objective of a contract becomes legally impossible to carry out, the law will consider the contract discharged.

Example: Mark contracted to build a four-unit condominium on Harold's property, which was zoned for multifamily residential use. Immediately after Mark and Harold signed the contract, the neighborhood where the property is located was rezoned to allow only single-family homes. As a result of the rezoning, it is legally impossible for Mark and Harold to carry out their contract. The contract is void.

If object of contract becomes legally impossible, contract considered discharged

DEATH

A contract may sometimes terminate at the death of one of the parties. For example, a listing agreement terminates at the death of the listing broker.

But sometimes a death does not terminate the contract. For example, Tenant rents an apartment from Landlord and has a three-year lease. Two years into the lease, Landlord dies. This does not automatically terminate Tenant's lease. The new owner of the property would take the property subject to any existing leases.

MUTUAL RESCISSION

> **A rescission is occasionally referred to as a "contract to destroy a contract."**

Mutual rescission: an agreement to terminate a previous agreement

The buyer and seller sign an agreement that terminates their previous agreement and puts them as nearly as possible back in the positions they were in prior to entering the agreement. If any money or rights exchanged hands (such as a downpayment), they would be returned. If just one of the parties wants to rescind and circumstances justify such a unilateral rescission, a court might order the rescission. So a rescission can be by mutual agreement or by court order.

REMEDIES FOR BREACH

A breach of contract occurs when a party fails, without legal excuse, to perform any promise contained in the agreement. When a breach occurs, there are five possible remedies for the damaged party:

1. acceptance of partial performance
2. unilateral rescission

Breach of contract: a party fails, without legal excuse, to perform any promise in an agreement

3. specific performance
4. money damages
5. liquidated damages

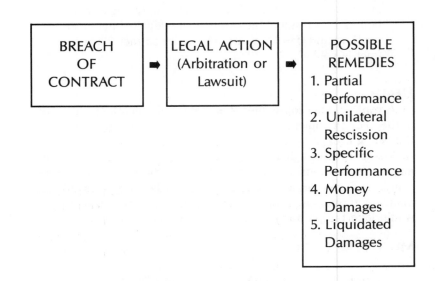

PARTIAL PERFORMANCE

Partial performance: a party may accept partial accomplishment of terms by other party

There is a partial performance when one of the parties has not completely accomplished all of the terms of the agreement, but has completed some (usually a majority) of the agreement. The other party may accept partial performance and simply consider the contract discharged because it is too difficult or not worth the trouble of pursuing other remedies.

UNILATERAL RESCISSION

Unilateral rescission: only one party asks for a rescission of a contract

Sometimes one party to a contract doesn't want to enforce the other party's promise. Instead, he or she just wants to undo the contract. In that case, he or she may ask a court to rescind the contract.

> When a contract is rescinded, each party returns any consideration the other has given.

All of their contractual obligations are terminated.

Rescission is available under a variety of circumstances. Whenever a voidable contract is disaffirmed—because of lack of capacity, fraud, undue influence, duress, menace, or mistake—the court will rescind it. When only one party is entitled to rescission, it is called a unilateral rescission.

SPECIFIC PERFORMANCE

Sometimes the nonbreaching party to a contract doesn't just want to be compensated for the harm that resulted from the other's breach. Instead, the nonbreaching party wants to make the other party do what he or she promised to do.

Specific performance: a court orders a party to do what the contract says

---

When a court orders a defaulting party to perform under the terms of the contract, it is called specific performance.

Specific performance is generally not granted when a damages (monetary) award will be just as effective. For example, a car dealer won't be ordered to sell you a particular car when you could get an identical one from another dealer. But if the object of a contract is one of a kind, then specific performance is an appropriate remedy. A damages award won't enable you to buy an identical one, because there isn't another just like it.

Specific performance is sometimes used in enforcing real estate contracts, because a piece of real property is generally unique. A damages award may not be sufficient compensation for breach of an agreement to transfer real property.

MONEY DAMAGES

A damages award (a sum of money intended to compensate the nonbreaching party) is the standard remedy in a contract dispute. If a seller breaches a contract, the buyer may choose to sue for money damages to compensate for the damage the breach caused.

Money damages: intended to compensate nonbreaching party

LIQUIDATED DAMAGES

The parties to a contract sometimes agree in advance what amount will serve as full compensation to be paid should one of the parties default. This lessens the possibility of expensive litigation. The parties agree in advance that if there is a breach, the damages will be set at a specific sum or calculated according to a specified formula. The nonbreaching party will accept the liquidated damages instead of suing for actual damages.

Liquidated damages: an agreed-upon amount serving as full compensation in case of breach. Must be a reasonable amount, not a penalty

> **As a general rule, a court will enforce a liquidated damages provision if the amount is reasonable and does not constitute a penalty, and the type of harm is such that it is difficult to ascertain or estimate the actual damages accurately.**

A contract to purchase real property often provides that the buyer's earnest money deposit will be treated as liquidated damages. If the buyer breaches the contract, the seller gets to keep the deposit.

PURCHASE AGREEMENT

> **In Minnesota, the purchase agreement (also known as an offer to purchase, contract of sale, or earnest money contract) is probably the most commonly used document in the sale of real property.**

The purchase agreement serves two functions:

Purchase agreement:

1. earnest money receipt,
2. buyer's offer, and
3. when signed by both parties, a contract of sale

- First, it is a receipt for the buyer's earnest money deposit made in conjunction with the buyer's firm offer to purchase.
- Second, it becomes the contract of sale after it is properly signed by the buyer and seller.

Once the agreement has been signed by all parties it becomes a binding contract (assuming that it includes all the elements of a valid contract, discussed above), and the terms cannot be modified without agreement by all parties.

A purchase agreement is a bilateral agreement. This means that both parties have made promises and are bound by the agreement. Essentially, the seller promises to sell, and the buyer promises to buy.

UNIFORM VENDOR AND PURCHASER RISK ACT

A purchase agreement in Minnesota is covered by the Uniform Vendor and Purchaser Risk Act.

Uniform Vendor and Purchaser Risk Act: protects buyer in event of destruction of property

> **Under this act, if the new buyer has not taken possession, and title has not passed, and there is a material destruction of the property, the seller cannot enforce the contract.**

The buyer is entitled to the return of any earnest money or other money that has already been paid. But if the damage is minor and repairable, the seller may repair the damages and then still enforce the contract.

> **Example:** Ruby sells her house to Jack. After the purchase agreement is signed, but before Jack receives title or takes possession, the house burns to the ground. Ruby cannot enforce the contract and make Jack go through with the sale. However, if only one room of the house had been damaged by the fire, and Ruby promptly repaired the damage, she might still be able to enforce the contract.

TYPICAL CLAUSES

Each purchase agreement differs, but there are some typical clauses and provisions that are found in most agreements. Most state the location and date of the agreement, the names of the parties involved, a description of the property, and the price offered. Typical agreements also include a provision stating the amount of any earnest money deposit and where the deposit will be held.

The agreement usually describes how title is going to be conveyed (for example by warranty deed), and the seller agrees to convey marketable title and provide an abstract. Most agreements generally include clauses providing for payment of any existing mortgage indebtedness against the property and for payment of property taxes, insurance, mortgage interest, etc., along with a list of any outstanding assessments on the property.

The agreement should provide a specific closing date. Along with the closing date, the agreement should also give a date of possession (the date the purchaser may actually take possession of the property). A list of closing expenses may be given designating which party is responsible for what costs. There are also usually clauses for additional conditions, such as items of personal property that are to be included as part of the sale; what happens in the event of destruction of the property prior to closing; the fact that the sale is conditional upon the buyer obtaining financing on certain terms; and what the parties' rights are in the event of default.

No. 1517A
MILLER/DAVIS Co.
Minneapolis, MN
DO NOT COPY
Subject to Copyright Laws

STANDARD
PURCHASE AGREEMENT

WHITE-Office Copy
YELLOW-Buyer's Copy
GREEN-Seller's Copy
PINK-Buyer's Receipt

1 _____ , Minnesota _____ , 19 ___

2 RECEIVED OF _____

3 the sum of _____ Dollars ($ _____

4 by _____ as earnest money to be deposited the next business day after acceptance in trust account of listing brok

5 (unless otherwise specified in writing) and in part payment for the purchase of the premises legally described as _____

6 _____

7 _____

8 located at (Street Address) _____

9 City of _____ , County of _____ , State of Minneso

10 including all plants, shrubs and trees, all storm windows and/or inserts, storm doors, screens, awnings, window shades, blinds, curtai

11 traverse-drapery rods, attached lighting fixtures with bulbs, plumbing fixtures, water heater, heating system, humidifier, central air conditionir

12 electronic air filter, automatic garage door opener with controls, water softener, cable television outlets and cabling, BUILT-INS to inclu

13 dishwasher, garbage disposal, trash compactor, oven(s), cooktop stove, microwave oven, hood-fan, intercom, installed carpeting, IF AM

14 located on the premises which are the property of Seller and also the following personal property: _____

15 _____

16 _____

17 all of which property Seller has this day sold to Buyer for the sum of: $ _____

18 _____ Dolla

19 _____

20 which Buyer agrees to pay in the following manner: Earnest money of $ _____ and

21 $ _____ cash on or before _____ , the date of closing, and the balan

22 of $ _____ by financing as follows: _____

23 _____

24 _____

25 _____

26 _____

27 _____

28 _____

29 _____

30 _____

31 *Attached are* _____ addendums which are made a part of this agreement.

32 **SUBJECT TO** performance by Buyer, Seller agrees to execute and deliver a _____ Warranty Dee

33 to be joined in by spouse, if any, conveying marketable title to the premises subject only to the following exceptions:

34 (1) Building and zoning laws, ordinances, State and Federal regulations. (2) Restrictions relating to use or improvement of the premises withc

35 effective forfeiture provision. (3) Reservation of any minerals or mineral rights to the State of Minnesota. (4) Utility and drainage easemer

36 which do not interfere with present improvements. (5) Rights of tenants, if any.

This form available from Miller/Davis Forms, Minneapolis, MN (612) 332-5144

REAL ESTATE TAXES Seller agrees to pay _____ / 12ths and Buyer agrees to pay _____ / 12ths of taxes due and payable in the year 19 ___ . Seller agrees to pay _____ / 12ths and Buyer agrees to pay _____ / 12ths of annual installment of special assessments due and payable in the year 19 ___ . _____ agrees to _____ on the date of closing all special assessments levied and pending. Buyer shall pay taxes due and payable in the year 19 ___ and any unpaid installments of special assessments payable therewith and thereafter. Seller warrants that taxes due and payable in the year 19 _____ will be _____ homestead classification. Neither Seller nor Seller's Agent makes any representation concerning the amount of future real estate taxes.

WARRANTIES Seller warrants that buildings, if any, are entirely within the boundary lines of the premises. Seller warrants that all appliances, heating and air conditioning, wiring and plumbing used and located on the premises are in proper working order on date of closing. Buyer has right to inspect premises prior to closing. Buyer shall satisfy himself/herself at his/her expense that all appliances, heating and air conditioning, wiring and plumbing are in proper working order before closing. Seller warrants that the premises are connected to: city sewer ☐ yes - ☐ no; city water ☐ yes - ☐ no. If the premises are destroyed or substantially damaged by fire or any other cause before the closing date, this agreement shall become null and void at Buyer's option, and the earnest money shall be refunded to Buyer.

POSSESSION Seller agrees to deliver possession not later than _____ closing. All interest, city water and sewer charges, electricity and natural gas charges, fuel oil and liquid petroleum gas shall be pro-rated between the parties as of _____ . Seller agrees to remove all debris and all personal property not included herein from the premises before possession date.

TITLE & EXAMINATION Seller shall, within a reasonable time after acceptance of this agreement, furnish an Abstract of Title, or a Registered Property Abstract, certified to date to include proper searches covering bankruptcies, State and Federal judgments and liens. Buyer shall be allowed 10 business days after receipt for examination of title and making any objections, which shall be made in writing or deemed waived. If any objection is so made, Seller shall be allowed 120 days to make title marketable. Pending correction of title, payments hereunder required shall be postponed, but upon correction of title and within 10 days after written notice to Buyer, the parties shall perform this agreement according to its terms. If title is not corrected within 120 days from the date of written objection, this agreement shall be null and void, at option of Buyer, neither party shall be liable for damages hereunder to the other, and earnest money shall be refunded to Buyer.

DEFAULT If title is marketable or is corrected within said time, and Buyer defaults in any of the agreements herein, Seller may terminate this agreement, and on such termination all payments made hereunder shall be retained by Seller and Agent, as their respective interests may appear, as liquidated damages, time being of the essence hereof. This provision shall not deprive either party of the right of enforcing the specific performance of this agreement, provided this agreement is not terminated and action to enforce specific performance is commenced within six months after such right of action arises. In the event Buyer defaults in his performance of the terms of this Agreement, and Notice of Cancellation is served upon the Buyer pursuant to MSA 559.21, the termination period shall be thirty (30) days as permitted by Subdivision 4 of MSA 559.21.

ACCEPTANCE Buyer understands and agrees that this sale is subject to acceptance by Seller in writing. Agent is not liable or responsible on account of this agreement, except to return or account for the earnest money.

AGENCY DISCLOSURE _____ stipulates he or she is representing the _____ in this transaction. The listing agent or broker stipulates he or she is representing the seller in this transaction.

I, the owner of the premises, accept this agreement and the sale hereby made.

I agree to purchase the premises for the price and on the terms and conditions set forth above.

SELLER _____   BUYER _____

SELLER _____   BUYER _____

Delivery of all papers and monies shall be made at the office of:

Company _____   Selling Agent _____

Address _____   City _____ Zip _____

THIS IS A LEGALLY BINDING CONTRACT. IF NOT UNDERSTOOD, SEEK COMPETENT ADVICE.

Many agreements provide that the buyer's deposit will serve as liquidated damages to the seller in the event of the buyer's default. Some agreements may include a clause stating that "time is of the essence." In other words, the time limits set by the contract must be met or the contract is voidable. If the agreement is accepted, it must be signed by both parties, and a copy given to each party. See the sample purchase agreement included in this chapter for examples of typical clauses normally found in a contract to purchase and sell real estate.

OPTION

An option agreement is essentially a contract to make a contract.

Option: a contract that creates a right to acquire property for a fixed price during a set period of time

> **It is an agreement that creates a right to buy, sell, or lease property for a fixed price during a set period of time.**

For example, a seller may grant an option, which essentially says that the seller promises to sell for a certain amount, if the buyer decides to buy.

Since an option agreement is a contract, it must have all the necessary elements of a contract: offer, acceptance, and consideration. The parties to an option agreement are the optionor (generally the seller) and the optionee (generally the buyer).

UNILATERAL CONTRACT An option agreement is a unilateral contract, an instrument that binds only one party and is accepted by performance.

> **Example:** Bob offers to sell Mike his house for $100,000 and tells Mike that he will keep the offer open for two weeks if Mike pays Bob $500. Mike pays the $500. Bob is the only person bound by the option agreement. Mike does not have to buy the house for $100,000, but Bob must keep the option open for two weeks.

> **Once the optionee accepts the option, the optionor is bound to keep the option open for the specified period of time.**

The optionee is not required to exercise his or her right to buy or lease the property. The optionee may exercise the option at his or her discretion. However, if the optionee decides to buy or lease, he or she should give written notice of acceptance to the optionor according to the terms of the agreement. If the optionee fails to exercise the option right within the specified time, the option automatically expires, and the optionor retains the option consideration.

Optionee not required to exercise right

CONSIDERATION. The option agreement must be supported by valuable consideration, which may take the form of cash, property, or a promissory note.

> **The consideration may be nominal in nature and no minimum amount is required. But the consideration must pass between the parties.**

A mere recitation of the consideration in the agreement will not be sufficient. The only exception is in a lease-option agreement—the provisions of the lease themselves will be sufficient consideration to support the option.

WRITING. The option contract must be in writing; oral agreements are unenforceable. Since the option anticipates that a sale may take place, the underlying terms of the sale (price, legal description, financing terms, etc.) should be correct and specified in detail in the option agreement.

CONTRACT RIGHT.

> **The executed option creates a contract right. It is not an interest in real property.**

Option contract: must be in writing, but is not an interest in real property

An option cannot be used as security for a mortgage. In an option agreement, the title does not pass and the optionee has no monetary rights against the title. The death of the optionor will not affect the rights of the optionee, who may still exercise the right to purchase or lease; the option contract is binding on the heirs and assignees of the optionor.

LEASE

Lease: a contract for exclusive possession in exchange for rent payment

A lease is a bilateral contract between a landlord and a tenant. Since a lease is a contract, it must contain all of the essential elements necessary for a contract to be valid. Usually the landlord promises to let the tenant occupy the premises, for which the tenant promises to pay rent.

Some real estate agents are involved in leasing property. An agent may also be involved in the sale of property that is already being leased. The agent should know that the sale of property by the landlord does not terminate a lease. The new owner purchases the property subject to any existing leases. A basic understanding of landlord-tenant law and the various types of leases is essential in the modern world of real estate.

TYPES OF LEASES

There are several different rent structures that can be set up in lease agreements. The major types of leases are:

- gross or fixed lease
- net lease
- percentage lease
- land or ground lease
- graduated or step-up lease
- escalator lease
- sandwich lease.

GROSS OR FIXED LEASE

Most residential leases are fixed leases.

Fixed lease: tenant pays a fixed amount; landlord pays expenses

Under a fixed lease, the tenant pays a set or fixed rent, and the landlord pays all additional expenses, such as maintenance and repairs, taxes, special assessments, and insurance. Most tenants (especially residential tenants) under a fixed lease still pay utility items such as electricity and water.

NET LEASE

Net lease: usually commercial; tenant pays all expenses

When a tenant pays rent plus all maintenance and operating expenses such as utilities, taxes, insurance, and repairs it is called a net lease. Many commercial leases are net leases.

PERCENTAGE LEASE

Some commercial leases provide for a percentage rent.

> **The rental amount is usually based on a percentage of the monthly or annual gross sales.**

Percentage lease: based on gross commercial sales

Percentage leases are common with retail stores, especially in large shopping centers.

There are many types of percentage leases. For instance, under a pure percentage lease, the entire rental amount is based on a percentage of gross sales. Under the most common type of percentage lease, a fixed minimum rental amount is required along with a percentage of gross sales, or a percentage of gross sales above a certain specified amount.

LAND OR GROUND LEASE

> **In a ground lease, the landowner leases vacant land to a tenant.**

Ground (land) lease: for long-term use of land

This type of lease is popular in large metropolitan areas and is usually long-term, to make the construction of a building desirable and profitable. Upon expiration of a ground lease, all improvements become property of the landowner.

GRADUATED OR STEP-UP LEASE

> **A graduated lease is similar to a fixed lease except that it includes periodic increases in the rental amount.**

Graduated lease: periodic increases are set

These increases are usually set at specific future dates and are often based on the cost-of-living index.

ESCALATOR LEASE

> **An escalator lease is also similar to a fixed lease except that increases in building operating expenses are passed on to the tenant.**

Escalator lease: increases in operating expenses paid by tenant

The fixed rent is based upon the landlord's estimate of operating expenses. At year-end, excess expenses will be billed to the tenant.

SANDWICH LEASE

A sandwich lease is not really a type of lease, but refers to a situation where more than one lease is established.

Sandwich lease: created when tenant constructs building and leases space, or subleases existing building

Example: A tenant leases a parcel of land under a ground lease, and builds a 20-story office building on it. Then the tenant leases office space to different tenants. This creates a "sandwich lease." The original tenant who constructed the building is both a tenant (as to the land) and a landlord (as to the building).

A sandwich lease is also created when a tenant subleases property to a subtenant.

> **In Minnesota, the term "sandwich lease" is often used to refer to the original lease between the landlord and the original tenant, after the first tenant has sublet to a second tenant.**

TERMINATION OF LEASES

Most leases terminate on the date specified in the lease agreement. Sometimes when a lease expires, or is near expiring, the parties decide to renew the lease. Upon renewal the terms of the lease may be renegotiated, new or different terms may be added or deleted, and the rent amount may be increased or decreased.

ESTATE FOR YEARS. The different types of estates were discussed in Chapter 2.

> **An estate for years is a tenancy for a fixed or specific time period.**

Estate for years: for a specific time period

Since the rental term is fixed, the lease terminates automatically on the expiration of the rental period. Neither the landlord nor the tenant has to give notice to terminate the lease. It simply ends at the specified time.

If either party wants to terminate the lease before the end of the lease period, they may do so only if the other party agrees. This is called mutual consent. The termination of a lease by mutual consent is a surrender.

ESTATE AT WILL. With an estate at will, the tenant has the right to occupy and use the landlord's property for an indefinite period of time. An estate at will automatically renews itself each time the tenant continues to pay rent. Since it is for an indefinite time period, it cannot automatically terminate. An estate at will continues until one of the parties gives notice of termination.

> **Minnesota law requires a minimum of two weeks' notice of termination, or one rental interval's notice, whichever is more.**

Estate at will: minimum of two weeks' or one rental interval's notice required to terminate

> **Example:** Tenant rents an apartment on a month-to-month basis. There is no set lease period. The estate at will is simply renewed each month when Tenant pays the rent. If either Landlord or Tenant wants to terminate, they must give one month's notice.

An estate at will automatically terminates upon the death of the tenant.

CONSTRUCTIVE EVICTION.

> **Constructive eviction is a wrongful eviction that occurs when the landlord causes or permits a substantial interference with the tenant's possession of the property.**

Constructive eviction: a landlord's substantial interference with tenant's possession

Constructive eviction happens when an act materially disturbs the tenant's use or enjoyment of the premises so that the tenant is forced to move out. When a tenant is constructively evicted, the lease is terminated.

> **Example:** Tenant rents a small studio apartment from Landlord in August. Landlord tells Tenant that the apartment is heated by radiant heat. Tenant notices an old fashioned radiator along one wall. When it turns cold, Tenant discovers that the radiator is broken and produces no heat. Landlord refuses to repair or supply any heat.
> Tenant has been constructively evicted because of lack of heat. Tenant can terminate the lease without liability for any further rent.

In the past, a tenant was required to actually move out before being entitled to claim constructive eviction. However, this rule has been somewhat relaxed. In this day of tight housing markets, high rent, and high deposit requirements, it is often hard or even impossible for a tenant to immediately find a new apartment to move into. Therefore, even though a tenant has not actually moved from the premises, the tenant may sometimes claim constructive eviction and sue for damages or an abatement of rent.

MINNESOTA LANDLORD-TENANT ACT

Landlord-Tenant Act: establishes responsibilities of landlords and tenants

Like most states, Minnesota has passed a Landlord-Tenant Act. This act sets out requirements that a landlord and tenant must follow.

> **The intent of the law is to strike a balance of responsibilities and liabilities between landlord and tenant.**

The law designates:

- how much notice of termination is required (as described above),
- rules concerning security deposits,
- habitability rights, and
- rights upon the destruction of the property or death of the landlord or tenant.

SECURITY DEPOSIT. Many landlords want their tenants to provide some sort of security to insure payment of rent and to protect the property against damage. The amount of security varies from lease to lease.

Security deposit: money paid to make sure tenant performs as promised in the lease

> **In Minnesota, a "security deposit" is defined as any deposit of money, the function of which is to secure the performance of a residential rental agreement. This does not include a deposit that is exclusively an advance payment of rent.**

For example, some landlords require a payment of the last month's rent at the time of signing the lease. This amount is still considered rent and is not part of the security deposit.

When the lease is terminated and the tenant moves out, the landlord may only retain as much of the security deposit as is necessary to pay for damage caused by the tenant. A security deposit may not be retained to pay for normal wear and tear resulting from ordinary use of the premises.

TIME LIMIT. If some (or all) of the security deposit remains after paying for any damage, it must be returned to the tenant.

> **The Minnesota Landlord-Tenant Act requires that the deposit must be returned to the tenant within 21 days of termination.**

Some states require that interest be paid on the tenant's security deposit. In Minnesota, a returned deposit must also include 5½% 4% simple interest.

When the deposit is returned, a letter should also be included explaining the reasons for not returning any portion of the deposit. If the deposit is unlawfully kept by the landlord, and not returned to the tenant, the landlord may be liable for the amount of the deposit, plus damages.

If the tenant does not leave a forwarding address or return to claim the deposit, the landlord is released from the duty to return the deposit.

If a tenant has caused severe damage and the cost to repair is greater than the amount of the security deposit, the landlord may bring an action against the former tenant for the amount exceeding the deposit. The fact that a security deposit was paid does not protect the tenant from liability for additional damages.

Deposit must be returned, with interest, unless needed to pay for damage

POSSESSION. A tenant has the right to **possess** the rented premises on the agreed upon date. Implied in every lease is a covenant to deliver possession to the tenant. If a tenant is prevented from gaining possession, it is a breach of this implied covenant and may excuse the tenant from paying some or all of the rent.

> **Example:** Tenant Tom signs a lease with Landlord Lori. The lease is to begin on August 1. But on August 1, when Tom tries to move in, the former tenant is still living on the premises. Even though the lease states that Tom will begin paying rent on August 1, he would probably not be required to begin paying rent until he is actually able to move in.

HABITABILITY. In all contracts for the renting of residential premises, there is also an implied warranty of habitability.

Habitability: landlord has a duty to keep premises fit for human habitation

> **The warranty of habitability places a duty on the landlord to keep the premises fit for human habitation at all times during the tenancy.**

Any clause in a lease where the tenant waives this right is against public policy and will not be enforced.

> **Example:** Landlord owns a decrepit old building. Rather than spend any money to fix it up, Landlord simply charges very low rent and tells the tenants that they just have to take what they get.
>
> The building does not meet the fire code, it has plumbing problems, and several of the apartments have no heat. Landlord cannot get away with this. Even though the tenants have essentially agreed to accept the problems in return for low rent, Landlord's actions are against public policy. He can be required to make certain essential repairs, and the tenants could be excused from paying rent until these repairs are made.

A breach of the warranty of habitability by the landlord may relieve the tenant from the obligation to pay rent until the premises are made habitable.

> **A breach of the implied warranty of habitability often results in constructive eviction (discussed above).**

Destruction of building may terminate lease

DESTRUCTION. If a lease is for part of a building, such as an office, apartment, or commercial space, the destruction of the building will frustrate the entire purpose of the lease and the tenant will be released from the duty to pay rent.

> **For most residential leases, the destruction of the building terminates the lease.**

But if the lease is for the land and any buildings thereon, or for the use of an entire building, the destruction of the building or part of the building does not necessarily terminate the lease. The tenant could still be required to pay rent to the end of the rental period. This situation usually only occurs in a commercial or agricultural lease.

A lease should contain provisions as to how the parties will handle destruction of the premises. Normally, a lease specifies who will maintain insurance on the property, and who is liable for rebuilding if a structure is destroyed by fire or other casualty. If there is no express stipulation, and the building is destroyed without fault, the loss generally falls on the landlord.

DEATH.

> **Death of a landlord does not automatically terminate a lease.**

The executor of the deceased landlord's estate or the person who inherited the property would receive the property subject to any existing leases. However, when the specific lease period is up, the new owner has no duty to renew. The new owner may also terminate an existing lease upon giving proper notice.

The death of a tenant who holds an estate at will automatically terminates the tenancy. However, if a tenant has an estate for years, the tenant's death does not automatically terminate the lease. The personal representative of the deceased tenant may terminate the lease by giving proper notice. The notice required would be whatever notice period is required by statute, such as two weeks, or one rental period (usually one month). If the lease is for a longer time period, the Landlord-Tenant Act provides that the personal representative may terminate the lease by giving two months' written notice.

CONTRACT FOR DEED

In Minnesota, another type of real estate contract that is frequently used is the contract for deed. A contract for deed is sometimes known as a land contract or installment land contract. The parties to the contract are the **vendor** (seller) and the **vendee** (buyer). Under a contract for deed, the vendee buys the property on an installment basis. Periodic payments towards the purchase price are made over a period of time, generally years.

Contract for deed: acquisition of property on an installment basis; vendor retains title until full price is paid

LEGAL EFFECT

> **During the time that payments are being made, the vendor retains legal title to the property. The deed is not conveyed to the vendee until the full purchase price is paid.**

However, the vendee has equitable title to the property. This means that the vendee has the right to possession, use, and quiet enjoyment of the property while paying off the purchase price.

Equitable title: vendee has right to possession, use, and quiet enjoyment while paying off purchase price

Both parties to the contract can assign their interests in the contract, unless there is a specific agreement prohibiting assignment. A contract for deed is made up of three elements:

1. a contract,
2. the immediate transfer of possession from vendor to vendee, and
3. the vendor's promise to transfer legal title upon full payment of the contract.

Example: Bertoldo agrees to buy Quincy's farm for $250,000, to be paid at the rate of $25,000 per year for ten years. Quincy allows Bertoldo to take possession of the farm and promises to convey legal title to the farm to Bertoldo when Bertoldo has paid the full purchase price. Bertoldo and Quincy have entered into a contract for deed.

RECORDING

> **A contract for deed should be recorded to protect the vendee's rights, and in Minnesota contracts for deed must be recorded.**

Recording: contract for deed must be recorded to protect vendee's interest

Since the vendor retains title to the property, the vendee is in a vulnerable position. It is possible that the vendee could make all of the required payments, only to find that there is a problem in delivering title because the vendor has died, become legally incompetent, or did not pay existing mortgages on the property. Recording puts the public on notice that the vendee has an equitable interest in the property and that his or her interest is superior to any subsequent encumbrances.

In Minnesota, the vendee must record the contract for deed no later than four months after execution.

REASONS FOR USING A CONTRACT FOR DEED

When a contract for deed is used, the seller is actually financing the buyer's purchase. It is essentially a security device. The seller extends credit to the buyer and holds title to the property as security for repayment of the debt.

> **The contract for deed is widely used in Minnesota for financing rural land sales. It is also an effective financing tool as a means of selling homes during periods of tight money.**

CONTRACT FOR DEED   Form No. 54-M   Minnesota Uniform Conveyancing Blanks (1978) Miller-Davis Co., Minneapolis
Individual Seller

No delinquent taxes and transfer entered;
Certificate of Real Estate Value
  (   )filed   (   )not required
————————————— , 19——— .

—————————————————
                  County Auditor

By —————————————————
                  Deputy

(reserved for mortgage registry tax payment data)

(reserved for recording data)

MORTGAGE REGISTRY TAX DUE HEREON:

$—————— —

Date: ————————————————— , 19——

THIS CONTRACT FOR DEED is made on the above date by —————————————

—————————————————————— , ——————————————
                                                (marital status)

Seller (whether one or more), and —————————————————————

—————————————————————— , Purchaser (whether one or more).

Seller and Purchaser agree to the following terms:

1. PROPERTY DESCRIPTION. Seller hereby sells, and Purchaser hereby buys, real property in
————————————————— County, Minnesota, described as follows:

together with all hereditaments and appurtenances belonging thereto (the Property).

2. TITLE. Seller warrants that title to the Property is, on the date of this contract, subject only to the following exceptions:
    (a) Covenants, conditions, restrictions, declarations and easements of record, if any;
    (b) Reservations of minerals or mineral rights by the State of Minnesota, if any;
    (c) Building, zoning and subdivision laws and regulations;
    (d) The lien of real estate taxes and installments of special assessments which are payable by Purchaser pursuant to paragraph 6 of this contract; and
    (e) The following liens or encumbrances:

3. DELIVERY OF DEED AND EVIDENCE OF TITLE. Upon Purchaser's prompt and full performance of this contract, Seller shall:
    (a) Execute, acknowledge and deliver to Purchaser a ————————————————— Deed, in recordable form, conveying marketable title to the Property to Purchaser, subject only to the following exceptions:
        (i) Those exceptions referred to in paragraph 2(a), (b), (c) and (d) of this contract;
        (ii) Liens, encumbrances, adverse claims or other matters which Purchaser has created, suffered or permitted to accrue after the date of this contract; and

This form available from Miller/Davis Forms, Minneapolis, MN (612) 332-5144

(iii) The following liens or encumbrances:

; and

(b) Deliver to Purchaser the abstract of title to the Property or, if the title is registered, the owner's duplicate certificate of title.

4. PURCHASE PRICE. Purchaser shall pay to Seller, at _____ , the sum of _____ ($_____) , as and for the purchase price for the Property, payable as follows:

5. PREPAYMENT. Unless otherwise provided in this contract, Purchaser shall have the right to fully or partially prepay this contract at any time without penalty. Any partial prepayment shall be applied first to payment of amounts then due under this contract, including unpaid accrued interest, and the balance shall be applied to the principal installments to be paid in the inverse order of their maturity. Partial prepayment shall not postpone the due date of the installments to be paid pursuant to this contract or change the amount of such installments.

6. REAL ESTATE TAXES AND ASSESSMENTS. Purchaser shall pay, before penalty accrues, all real estate taxes and installments of special assessments assessed against the Property which are due and payable in the year 19___ and in all subsequent years. Real estate taxes and installments of special assessments which are due and payable in the year in which this contract is dated shall be paid as follows:

Seller warrants that the real estate taxes and installments of special assessments which were due and payable in the years preceding the year in which this contract is dated are paid in full.

7. PROPERTY INSURANCE.
   (a) INSURED RISKS AND AMOUNT. Purchaser shall keep all buildings, improvements and fixtures now or later located on or a part of the Property insured against loss by fire, extended coverage perils, vandalism, malicious mischief and, if applicable, steam boiler explosion for at least the amount of _____ .
   If any of the buildings, improvements or fixtures are located in a federally designated flood prone area, and if flood insurance is available for that area, Purchaser shall procure and maintain flood insurance in amounts reasonably satisfactory to Seller.
   (b) OTHER TERMS. The insurance policy shall contain a loss payable clause in favor of Seller which provides that Seller's right to recover under the insurance shall not be impaired by any acts or omissions of Purchaser or Seller, and that Seller shall otherwise be afforded all rights and privileges customarily provided a mortgagee under the so-called standard mortgage clause.
   (c) NOTICE OF DAMAGE. In the event of damage to the Property by fire or other casualty, Purchaser shall promptly give notice of such damage to Seller and the insurance company.

8. DAMAGE TO THE PROPERTY.
   (a) APPLICATION OF INSURANCE PROCEEDS. If the Property is damaged by fire or other casualty, the insurance proceeds paid on account of such damage shall be applied to payment of the amounts payable by Purchaser under this contract, even if such amounts are not then due to be paid, unless Purchaser makes a permitted election described in the next paragraph. Such amounts shall be first applied to unpaid accrued interest and next to the installments to be paid as provided in this contract in the inverse order of their maturity. Such payment shall not postpone the due date of the installments to be paid pursuant to this contract or change the amount of such installments. The balance of insurance proceeds, if any, shall be the property of Purchaser.

(b) PURCHASER'S ELECTION TO REBUILD. If Purchaser is not in default under this contract, or after curing any such default, and if the mortgagees in any prior mortgages and sellers in any prior contracts for deed do not require otherwise, Purchaser may elect to have that portion of such insurance proceeds necessary to repair, replace or restore the damaged Property (the repair work) deposited in escrow with a bank or title insurance company qualified to do business in the State of Minnesota, or such other party as may be mutually agreeable to Seller and Purchaser. The election may only be made by written notice to Seller within sixty days after the damage occurs. Also, the election will only be permitted if the plans and specifications and contracts for the repair work are approved by Seller, which approval Seller shall not unreasonably withhold or delay. If such a permitted election is made by Purchaser, Seller and Purchaser shall jointly deposit, when paid, such insurance proceeds into such escrow. If such insurance proceeds are insufficient for the repair work, Purchaser shall, before the commencement of the repair work, deposit into such escrow sufficient additional money to insure the full payment for the repair work. Even if the insurance proceeds are unavailable or are insufficient to pay the cost of the repair work, Purchaser shall at all times be responsible to pay the full cost of the repair work. All escrowed funds shall be disbursed by the escrowee in accordance with generally accepted sound construction disbursement procedures. The costs incurred or to be incurred on account of such escrow shall be deposited by Purchaser into such escrow before the commencement of the repair work. Purchaser shall complete the repair work as soon as reasonably possible and in a good and workmanlike manner, and in any event the repair work shall be completed by Purchaser within one year after the damage occurs. If, following the completion of and payment for the repair work, there remain any undisbursed escrow funds, such funds shall be applied to payment of the amounts payable by Purchaser under this contract in accordance with paragraph 8 (a) above.

9. INJURY OR DAMAGE OCCURRING ON THE PROPERTY.
   (a) LIABILITY. Seller shall be free from liability and claims for damages by reason of injuries occurring on or after the date of this contract to any person or persons or property while on or about the Property. Purchaser shall defend and indemnify Seller from all liability, loss, costs and obligations, including reasonable attorneys' fees, on account of or arising out of any such injuries. However, Purchaser shall have no liability or obligation to Seller for such injuries which are caused by the negligence or intentional wrongful acts or omissions of Seller.
   (b) LIABILITY INSURANCE. Purchaser shall, at Purchaser's own expense, procure and maintain liability insurance against claims for bodily injury, death and property damage occurring on or about the Property in amounts reasonably satisfactory to Seller and naming Seller as an additional insured.

10. INSURANCE, GENERALLY. The insurance which Purchaser is required to procure and maintain pursuant to paragraphs 7 and 9 of this contract shall be issued by an insurance company or companies licensed to do business in the State of Minnesota and acceptable to Seller. The insurance shall be maintained by Purchaser at all times while any amount remains unpaid under this contract. The insurance policies shall provide for not less than ten days' written notice to Seller before cancellation, non-renewal, termination or change in coverage, and Purchaser shall deliver to Seller a duplicate original or certificate of such insurance policy or policies.

11. CONDEMNATION. If all or any part of the Property is taken in condemnation proceedings instituted under power of eminent domain or conveyed in lieu thereof under threat of condemnation, the money paid pursuant to such condemnation or conveyance in lieu thereof shall be applied to payment of the amounts payable by Purchaser under this contract, even if such amounts are not then due to be paid. Such amounts shall be applied first to unpaid accrued interest and next to the installments to be paid as provided in this contract in the inverse order of their maturity. Such payment shall not postpone the due date of the installments to be paid pursuant to this contract or change the amount of such installments. The balance, if any, shall be the property of Purchaser.

12. WASTE, REPAIR AND LIENS. Purchaser shall not remove or demolish any buildings, improvements or fixtures now or later located on or a part of the Property, nor shall Purchaser commit or allow waste of the Property. Purchaser shall maintain the Property in good condition and repair. Purchaser shall not create or permit to accrue liens or adverse claims against the Property which constitute a lien or claim against Seller's interest in the Property. Purchaser shall pay to Seller all amounts, costs and expenses, including reasonable attorneys' fees, incurred by Seller to remove any such liens or adverse claims.

13. DEED AND MORTGAGE REGISTRY TAXES. Seller shall, upon Purchaser's full performance of this contract, pay the deed tax due upon the recording or filing of the deed to be delivered by Seller to Purchaser. The mortgage registry tax due upon the recording or filing of this contract shall be paid by the party who records or files this contract; however, this provision shall not impair the right of Seller to collect from Purchaser the amount of such tax actually paid by Seller as provided in the applicable law governing default and service of notice of termination of this contract.

14. NOTICE OF ASSIGNMENT. If either Seller or Purchaser assigns their interest in the Property, a copy of such assignment shall promptly be furnished to the non-assigning party.

15. PROTECTION OF INTERESTS. If Purchaser fails to pay any sum of money required under the terms of this contract or fails to perform any of Purchaser's obligations as set forth in this contract, Seller may, at Seller's option, pay the same or cause the same to be performed, or both, and the amounts so paid by Seller and the cost of such performance shall be payable at once, with interest at the rate stated in paragraph 4 of this contract, as an additional amount due Seller under this contract.
   If there now exists, or if Seller hereafter creates, suffers or permits to accrue, any mortgage, contract for deed, lien or encumbrance against the Property which is not herein expressly assumed by Purchaser, and provided Purchaser is not in default under this contract, Seller shall timely pay all amounts due thereon, and if Seller fails to do so, Purchaser may, at Purchaser's option, pay any such delinquent amounts and deduct the amounts paid from the installment(s) next coming due under this contract.

16. DEFAULT. The time of performance by Purchaser of the terms of this contract is an essential part of this contract. Should Purchaser fail to timely perform any of the terms of this contract, Seller may, at Seller's option, elect to declare this contract cancelled and terminated by notice to Purchaser in accordance with applicable law. All right, title and interest acquired under this contract by Purchaser shall then cease and terminate, and all improvements made upon the Property and all payments made by Purchaser pursuant to this contract shall belong to Seller as liquidated damages for breach of this contract. Neither the extension of the time for payment of any sum of money to be paid hereunder nor any waiver by Seller of Seller's rights to declare this contract forfeited by reason of any breach shall in any manner affect Seller's right to cancel this contract because of defaults subsequently occurring, and no extension of time shall be valid unless agreed to in writing. After service of notice of default and failure to cure such default within the period allowed by law, Purchaser shall, upon demand, surrender possession of the Property to Seller, but Purchaser shall be entitled to possession of the Property until the expiration of such period.

17. BINDING EFFECT. The terms of this contract shall run with the land and bind the parties hereto and their successors in interest.

18. HEADINGS. Headings of the paragraphs of this contract are for convenience only and do not define, limit or construe the contents of such paragraphs.

19. ASSESSMENTS BY OWNERS' ASSOCIATION. If the Property is subject to a recorded declaration providing for assessments to be levied against the Property by any owners' association, which assessments may become a lien against the Property if not paid, then:

    (a) Purchaser shall promptly pay, when due, all assessments imposed by the owners' association or other governing body as required by the provisions of the declaration or other related documents; and

    (b) So long as the owners' association maintains a master or blanket policy of insurance against fire, extended coverage perils and such other hazards and in such amounts as are required by this contract, then:

        (i) Purchaser's obligation in this contract to maintain hazard insurance coverage on the Property is satisfied; and

        (ii) The provisions in paragraph 8 of this contract regarding application of insurance proceeds shall be superceded by the provisions of the declaration or other related documents; and

        (iii) In the event of a distribution of insurance proceeds in lieu of restoration or repair following an insured casualty loss to the Property, any such proceeds payable to Purchaser are hereby assigned and shall be paid to Seller for application to the sum secured by this contract, with the excess, if any, paid to Purchaser.

20. ADDITIONAL TERMS:

SAMPLE

SELLER(S)   PURCHASER(S)

_____   _____

_____   _____

_____   _____

_____   _____

State of Minnesota } ss.

County of _____

The foregoing instrument was acknowledged before me this ____ day of _____ , 19____ ,
by _____ .

NOTARIAL STAMP OR SEAL (OR OTHER TITLE OR RANK)

SIGNATURE OF NOTARY PUBLIC OR OTHER OFFICIAL

State of Minnesota } ss.

County of _____

The foregoing instrument was acknowledged before me this ____ day of _____ , 19____ ,
by _____ .

NOTARIAL STAMP OR SEAL (OR OTHER TITLE OR RANK)

SIGNATURE OF NOTARY PUBLIC OR OTHER OFFICIAL

Tax Statements for the real property described in this instrument should be sent to

THIS INSTRUMENT WAS DRAFTED BY (NAME AND ADDRESS)

FAILURE TO RECORD OR FILE THIS CONTRACT FOR DEED MAY GIVE OTHER PARTIES
PRIORITY OVER PURCHASER'S INTEREST IN THE PROPERTY.

If financing is not available from an institutional lender, a buyer can make a downpayment and enter into a contract for deed with the seller for the remainder of the purchase price. If loan money is later available from an institutional lender, the buyer/vendee could pay off the contract and receive title to the property.

By using the contract for deed, the parties obtain the same advantages of any type of seller financing. The buyer avoids the need to make a large downpayment. The seller offering a contract for deed can attract a wider range of potential buyers and obtain a higher price for the property.

DEFAULT. A seller may also prefer to sell under a contract for deed to avoid lengthy mortgage foreclosure proceedings in the event of default.

If the vendee defaults and does not make the payments as agreed, the vendor must serve notice of default on the vendee.

> **Once the notice of default has been served, the vendee has a certain time period in which the property may still be redeemed. This is called the *equitable redemption period*.**

Equitable redemption period: vendee may redeem the property by curing default within specified time

If the contract for deed was executed between May 1, 1980 and July 31, 1985, the vendee must make all payments current within the following time periods:

- 30 days if the vendee has paid 0% to 9% of the purchase price;

- 60 days if the vendee has paid 10% to 24% of the purchase price;

- 90 days if the vendee has paid 25% or more of the purchase price.

If the contract for deed was executed on or after August 1, 1985, the vendee must make all payments current within 60 days of receiving notice, regardless of the percentage of purchase price paid.

If the vendee does not cure the default during the time period provided, the contract is cancelled and the vendor retains title to the property. The vendee no longer has any interest in the property and has simply lost any money already paid on the contract.

Extension. The time period allowed for redemption may be extended by a court if the vendee is unemployed, under-employed, facing catastrophic medical expenses, or having economic problems regarding farming.

CHAPTER SUMMARY

1. A contract is a legally binding agreement between two or more competent parties to do or not to do certain things for consideration. An express contract is one that has been put into words, either spoken or written. An implied contract is created by the acts of the parties.

2. When an agreement doesn't meet one or more of the requirements for a valid contract, it is considered legally void. If the contract appears to be valid, but has a defect giving one or more of the parties the power to avoid performance or rescind the agreement, it is a voidable contract.

3. For a contract to be valid, the parties must be competent (be over 18 and mentally competent), there must be mutual agreement between the parties, contractual intent, a lawful objective, and consideration. The Statute of Frauds requires that a real estate contract must also be in writing.

4. To create a valid contract, consent must be freely given. It is not freely given when it is the result of fraud, misrepresentation, mistake, duress, or undue influence.

5. Unless specifically prohibited in the agreement, most contracts may be assigned or novated. However, a contract for personal services cannot be assigned without consent. Real estate listing agreements are considered personal services contracts, so they are not assignable without consent.

6. A breach of contract occurs when a party fails, without legal excuse, to perform any promise contained in the agreement. When a breach of contract occurs, the possible remedies for the damaged party are: acceptance of partial performance, unilateral rescission, specific performance, damages, or liquidated damages.

7. A purchase agreement is a receipt for the buyer's earnest money deposit. After being signed by the buyer and seller, it becomes the contract of sale. A purchase agreement in Minnesota is covered by the Uniform Vendor and Purchaser Risk Act.

8. An option agreement is a contract to make a contract. It is an agreement that creates a right to buy, sell, or lease property for a fixed price over a set period of time.

9. A landlord-tenant relationship is created by a contract called a lease. The major types of leases are: gross or fixed, net, percentage, land or ground, graduated or step-up, escalator, and sandwich.

10. The two main types of leasehold estates are the estate for years and the estate at will. An estate for years is a tenancy for a fixed period of time. An estate at will is for an indefinite time period, and it automatically renews itself each time the tenant pays rent.

11. Constructive eviction is a wrongful eviction that occurs when the landlord causes a substantial interference with the tenant's possession of the property or materially disturbs the tenant's use and enjoyment of the premises.

12. Minnesota has a Landlord-Tenant Act which sets out requirements that landlords and tenants must follow.

13. A security deposit is any deposit of money meant to secure the performance of a residential rental agreement. When a lease is terminated, if some or all of the security deposit remains after paying for any damages, it must be returned to the tenant within 21 days, plus 5.5% simple interest.

14. Contracts for deed are used extensively in Minnesota. With a contract for deed, the vendee buys the property on an installment basis. The vendee has equitable title and the right to possession. However, the vendor retains legal title until the property is completely paid for. All contracts for deed in Minnesota must be recorded within four months of execution.

15. The remedy for default on a contract for deed is known as cancellation. The vendor serves notice of the default, and the vendee must redeem (cure the default) within 60 days.

CHAPTER 5—GLOSSARY REVIEW

A. executory
B. fraud
C. bilateral
D. unilateral
E. void
F. lawful objective
G. mutual agreement
H. money
I. consideration

J. contract for deed
K. forbearance
L. voidable
M. binding and enforceable
N. legal and unenforceable
O. offeror
P. offeree
Q. option
R. lease

1. A contract based upon a promise exchanged for a promise is a _bilateral_ contract.

2. When only one party to the agreement makes a promise, the result is a _unilateral_ contract.

3. An agreement in a contract in which one or both parties agree not to act in a certain manner is known as a _forebearance_

4. A legally valid contract is _binding & enforceable_

5. A contract which has no force or effect in law is said to be _void_ .

6. _mutual agreement_ means that there is an offer and acceptance; there is no fraud, misrepresentation or mistake; and the assent is genuinely and freely given.

7. The party who makes an offer to another is known as the _offeror_.

8. Inducing someone to enter into a contract by intentionally deceiving them is called _fraud_.

9. Something of value given in exchange for something else of value is known as _consideration_

10. A document which gives a buyer the right to occupy the property and receive a deed at a later time, after payment of the full purchase price, is a _contract for deed_

CHAPTER 5—REVIEW EXAM

1. A contract that has not yet been fully performed is:

   a) unenforceable.
   b) voidable.
   c) executory.
   d) executed.

2. A contract which exchanges a promise for performance is:

   a) implied.
   b) unilateral.
   c) bilateral.
   d) executory.

3. All of the following are essential elements of a contract EXCEPT:

   a) mutual agreement
   b) lawful objective
   c) consideration
   d) rescission

4. An installment land contract (contract for deed) is best defined as:

   a) an agreement in which the vendee pays regular installments to the vendor, who retains legal title.
   b) a method of immediate title conveyance while the vendee pays for the property in installments.
   c) a contract for the purchase of land only.
   d) a contract in which the vendor "takes back" a mortgage in lieu of cash.

5. The electrical wiring in a house listed with Broker Jones is defective. Jones is aware of this and intentionally deceives a buyer concerning the matter. The buyer purchases the home and later suffers financial loss due to the faulty wiring. This is an example of:

   a) mistake of law.
   b) fraud.
   c) mistake of fact.
   d) novation.

6. Which of the following requires that real estate sales contracts be in writing?

   a) Caveat Emptor
   b) Truth in Lending
   c) Statute of Limitations
   d) Statute of Frauds

7. Which of the following statements regarding a purchase agreement is true?

   a) The contract is binding upon both parties.
   b) It may be oral.
   c) The contract terms must be identical to the terms in the listing agreement.
   d) The contract conveys title when signed by both parties.

8. A contract that conveys the right to quiet enjoyment and use of property but does not convey title is a:

   a) bill of sale.
   b) lease.
   c) quitclaim deed.
   d) dedication.

9. When a lessee transfers his rights to another person, it is an example of:

    (a) assignment.
    b) acknowledgment.
    c) prescription.
    d) adverse possession.

10. Which of the following is true regarding the Minnesota Landlord-Tenant Act?

    a) The landlord can terminate the lease if the unit is uninhabitable.
    b) The landlord must pay 5% interest on the damage deposit.
    c) The tenant must receive the damage deposit within 10 days after giving notice of termination.
    (d) The tenant is entitled to 5.5% interest on the security deposit.

11. Which of the following must be recorded in Minnesota?

    a) Mortgages
    b) Deeds
    (c) Contracts for deed
    d) Leases

12. The equitable redemption period on a contract for deed is which of the following?

    a) The time following the sale of the property at auction
    b) 5 months
    c) 12 months
    (d) 60 days

13. A seller may keep the buyer's earnest money as liquidated damages if:

    a) it is stated in the listing agreement.
    b) the seller and broker agree.
    (c) the buyer defaults and the purchase agreement stipulates liquidated damages as a remedy.
    d) the seller failed to perform an essential element of the contract.

14. A contract in which one party purchases the right to buy within a specified period is:

    a) a purchase agreement.
    b) a listing agreement.
    c) a lease.
    (d) an option.

15. Under the Uniform Vendor and Purchaser Risk Act, if a property is destroyed after the purchase agreement is signed but before the buyer has taken possession or title has been transferred, what are the buyer's rights?

    a) The buyer must proceed with the purchase.
    b) The buyer may cancel the agreement but the seller retains the earnest money.
    (c) The seller cannot enforce the contract and the buyer's deposit is returned.
    d) The buyer's insurance company must pay for the loss.

16. A contract between two parties that legally binds one party to perform but allows the other party to withdraw under certain conditions is:

    a) executed.
    b) void.
    c) voidable.
    d) bilateral.

17. Susie Smith signed a purchase agreement to buy Jake Jacob's home. Jake then decided not to sell his home. Susie sued him and ended up with the house. Which remedy did she choose?

    a) Unilateral rescission
    b) Mutual agreement
    c) Specific performance
    d) Damages

18. Joe Tenant signed an apartment lease with Larry Landlord with a 3-year term. Joe then sublet the apartment to Sarah Subtenant. As a result of the sublease, the original lease between Joe and Larry is called a:

    a) dual lease.
    b) joint lease.
    c) sandwich lease.
    d) percentage lease.

19. A contract with a minor is:

    a) voidable.
    b) void.
    c) unilateral.
    d) illegal.

20. A commercial lease in which the tenant company pays a base rent plus a portion of the tenant's income is a:

    a) net lease.
    b) ground lease.
    c) gross lease.
    d) percentage lease.

21. All of the following are means of discharging obligations under a contract EXCEPT:

    a) novation
    b) assignment
    c) death of an indispensable party
    d) liquidated damages

22. In order to be enforceable, a contract for deed must be signed by which of the following?

    a) Grantee and grantor
    b) Vendee
    c) Vendee and vendor
    d) Grantor

23. Susan bought a home from George on contract for deed. Susan later sold the home to Jim, who assumed the contract for deed. George then sold his vendor's interest to Helen. Who is the fee owner of the property?

    a) Susan
    b) George
    c) Jim
    d) Helen

24. The Plain Language Act requires:

   a) that all real estate contracts be in writing.
   b) that all contracts for deed be recorded.
   c) that all listing agreements be written in simple language.
   d) that all leases in excess of a year be in writing.

25. Which of the following documents transfers possession but not legal title?

   a) A purchase agreement
   b) A lease
   c) An option
   d) A deed

26. If a buyer defaults on a contract and the seller keeps the buyer's earnest money, the seller has elected which of the following remedies?

   a) Money damages
   b) Partial performance
   c) Rescission
   d) Liquidated damages

27. Susie just signed a contract for deed to buy Herman's land. Susie is which of the following?

   a) Grantor
   b) Grantee
   c) Vendor
   d) Vendee

28. To comply with the Statute of Frauds, certain contracts must be:

   a) written by an attorney.
   b) acknowledged.
   c) in writing and signed.
   d) accompanied by earnest money.

29. A commercial lease requiring that the tenant pay a share of the expenses is:

   a) a percentage lease.
   b) a net lease.
   c) a gross lease.
   d) a standard lease.

30. An oral lease is enforceable unless it is for a term of:

   a) more than one year.
   b) one month or more.
   c) six months or less.
   d) one year or less.

31. Larry Landlord has not paid the utility bills for his apartment building, so the heat, water and electricity are shut off. Because of this, the tenants have the right to terminate their leases. Which of the following legal concepts does this example illustrate?

   a) Constructive eviction
   b) Mutual rescission
   c) Illegal use of rent money
   d) Eminent domain

32. A court may extend the equitable redemption period of a contract for deed because:

    a) the vendor is underemployed.
    b) the vendee is underemployed.
    c) the vendor is 65 or older.
    d) the vendee is 65 or older.

CHAPTER 5—GLOSSARY REVIEW KEY

1. C
2. D
3. K
4. M
5. E
6. G
7. O
8. B
9. I
10. J

CHAPTER 5—REVIEW EXAM KEY

1. c) Prior to execution, the contract is executory.

2. b) A promise for a promise is bilateral; a promise for performance is unilateral.

3. d) Rescission is a remedy for breach.

4. a) The vendee has equitable title; the vendor retains legal title.

5. b) Fraud involves intentional deceit.

6. d) The Statute of Fraud requires all real estate contracts (except leases for one year or less) to be in writing.

7. a) The purchase agreement is binding upon both the buyer and seller.

8. b) The lessor (landlord) grants the right of possession to the lessee (tenant); the lessor retains title.

9. a) Transferring rights to another, with the original party remaining liable, is an assignment.

10. d) The deposit plus 5.5% interest must be returned within 21 days of lease termination.

11. c) While mortgages, deeds, and long-term leases should also be recorded, the contract for deed is required by law to be recorded.

12. d) The vendee has 60 days from receipt of the notice of default to cure the default.

13. c) When a buyer breaches the purchase agreement, the seller may keep the earnest money as liquidated damages if the purchase agreement provides for that remedy.

14. d) In an option, the optionee purchases the right to buy.

15. c) If the property is destroyed prior to closing, the seller cannot force the buyer to proceed with the contract.

16. c) In a voidable contract, one party but not the other is legally bound to perform.

17. c) Specific performance requires the defaulting party to perform according to the specific terms of the contract.

18. c) Joe is "sandwiched" between the landlord and the subtenant.

19. a) The contract is voidable because the minor could disaffirm it.

20. d) Percentage leases are used for retail properties.

21. d) Liquidated damages is a remedy for default.

22. c) The vendee and vendor sign the contract for deed. (The grantee and grantor are parties to a deed.)

23. d) Whoever holds the vendor's interest in a contract for deed has fee title.

24. c) The Plain Language Act applies to listing agreements and residential leases of three years or less.

25. b) A deed transfers both possession and legal title; the lease and contract for deed transfer possession but NOT legal title.

26. d) When the seller retains the earnest money when the buyer breaches, it is known as liquidated damages.

27. d) The vendor is the seller; the vendee is the buyer.

28. c) The Statute of Frauds requires real estate contracts (except leases of one year or less) to be in writing.

29. b) In a net lease, the tenant pays a base rent plus some or all of the operating expenses.

30. a) The Statute of Frauds requires a lease for more than one year to be in writing.

31. a) In a constructive eviction, the tenant terminates the lease due because the landlord has caused or permitted a substantial interference with the tenant's use and enjoyment of the property.

32. b) If the vendee is unemployed, underemployed, or struggling with medical bills or farming problems, the court could extend the equitable redemption period beyond 60 days.

Chapter 6

BASIC REAL ESTATE MATH

OUTLINE

I. Fractions, Decimals and Percents
   A. Converting fractions to decimals
   B. Percentages
   C. Appreciation and depreciation

II. Brokerage Math
   A. Fees and commissions
   B. Proration
   C. Net proceeds
   D. Area
   E. Tax problems

III. Mortgage Math
   A. Mortgage amount and loan to value ratio (LTV)
   B. Calculating points
   C. Payment factors
   D. Total interest on a loan
   E. Principal and interest per payment and principal
      balance remaining

KEY TERMS

area	base
height	interest
principal	square feet
fraction	decimal
numerator	denominator

square   rectangle
per annum   net income
capitalization   value
prorations   percentage
triangle   gross income
profit and loss   commission
per diem

CHAPTER OVERVIEW

Math is a fundamental tool used by real estate licensees in all aspects of their profession. A real estate licensee uses math to compute loan amounts, closing costs, commissions and the square footage of property and homes.

FRACTIONS, DECIMALS AND PERCENTS

Once you know how to work with fractions, decimals, and percentages, you know the basics required for most real estate math problems. For example, a broker's commission is usually a percentage of the sales price. So a broker needs to know how to figure out a percentage to determine the amount of the commission.

CONVERTING FRACTIONS TO DECIMALS

Most people find it much easier to work with decimals than fractions. Also, most hand calculators multiply and divide by decimals. Therefore, it is generally advisable to change fractions into decimals. In order to do so, divide the top number of the fraction (called the numerator) by the bottom number of the fraction (called the denominator).

Example: To change ¾ into a decimal, divide the top number, 3, by the bottom number, 4.

$$3 \div 4 = .75$$

Example: to change ⅔ into a decimal, divide the top number, 2, by the bottom number, 3.

$$2 \div 3 = .66667$$

Of course, if you are using a hand calculator, it will make the conversion for you. Divide 2 by 3 and your calculator will give you the answer with the decimal point in the right place.

To change mixed numbers into decimals, simply convert the fraction part into a decimal.

Example: To change 7⅝ into a decimal, leave the 7 and convert the fraction. Divide the top number, 5, by the bottom number, 8.

$$5 \div 8 = .625$$

The number 7⅝ when changed to a decimal becomes 7.625

To add by decimals or subtract by decimals, line the decimals up by decimal point.

Example: To add 3.75, 14.62, 1.245, 679.0, 1412.8, and 1.9, put the numbers in a column with the decimals lined up and add.

$$
\begin{array}{r}
3.75 \\
14.62 \\
1.245 \\
679.0 \\
1412.8 \\
+\ \ \ 1.9 \\
\hline
2113.315
\end{array}
$$

To multiply by decimals, do the multiplication, ignoring the decimal points. Then give the answer as many decimal places as the total number of decimal places in the multiplying numbers.

Example: Multiply 24.625 times 16.15. The two numbers contain a total of five decimal places (three in 24.625 and two in 16.15).

$$
\begin{array}{r}
24.625 \\
\times\ 16.15 \\
\hline
397.69375
\end{array}
$$

Just add up the decimal places in the numbers you are multiplying and put the decimal point the same number of places to the left.

Example: Multiply .2 × .4. There is a total of two decimal places.

$$\begin{array}{r} .2 \\ \times\ .4 \\ \hline .08 \end{array}$$

Note that in this case a zero must be added to move the decimal point two places left.

To divide by decimals, move the decimal point in the outside number all the way to the right, and then move the decimal point in the inside number the same number of places to the right.

Example: Divide 26.145 by 1.5.

$$1.5 \overline{)\ 26.145}$$

Move the decimal in 1.5 all the way to the right (one place) and move the decimal in the inside number the same number of places to the right.

$$1.5. \overline{)\ 26.1.45}$$
$$\rightarrow \qquad \rightarrow$$

$$\begin{array}{r} 17.43 \\ 15 \overline{)\ 261.45} \end{array}$$

Just as with addition and multiplication, the above steps are unnecessary if you use a hand calculator. If the numbers are punched in correctly, the calculator will automatically give you an answer with the decimal in the right place.

Note: Don't confuse a decimal with the comma (,) that separates hundreds and thousands, as in $1,243,756. When using a calculator always put in the decimal point but never the comma.

PERCENTAGES

When finding a percentage of a number, the "of" means to multiply. For example, when you need to find 6% of $100,000 you simply multiply 6% times $100,000. When working percentage problems, it is necessary to convert percentages to decimals and vice versa, so that the arithmetic in a percentage problem can be done in decimals.

To convert a percentage to a decimal, remove the percentage sign and move the decimal point two places to the left. This may require adding one or more zeros.

Example: *98% becomes .98*
5% becomes .05
32.5% becomes .325
17½% becomes .175

To convert a decimal to a percentage, do just the opposite. Move the decimal two places to the right and add a percentage sign.

Example: *.15 becomes 15%*
.08 becomes 8%
.095 becomes 9.5%

The conversion of percentages to and from decimals is necessary to work a wide variety of real estate math problems, including commission, interest, capitalization, and profit and loss problems.

Whenever something is expressed as a percentage of something else, it means you should multiply. The word "of" means "times" or multiply.

Example: What is seventy-five percent of $40,000?

First convert the percentage to a decimal: 75% becomes .75; "of" $40,000 means "times" $40,000.

.75 × 40,000 = 30,000

Seventy-five percent of $40,000 is $30,000.

APPRECIATION AND DEPRECIATION

In the real estate market, a home often appreciates or depreciates in value. The change in value is generally given as a percentage. The idea is to express the value of the property after appreciation or depreciation as a percentage of the property's previous value. If there is no appreciation or depreciation, the value remains exactly the same. If there is appreciation, the value has increased. If there is depreciation, the value has decreased. Remember, a percent "of" something means that percent "times" something. If there is appreciation, you add the amount of appreciation to the original value. If there is depreciation, you subtract the amount of depreciation from the original value to determine current value.

Example: Mr. Arcola's house has depreciated in value 5%. If he originally paid $85,000 for it, what is it currently worth?

Compute: 5% of $85,000
$85,000 × .05 = $4,250

Subtract the amount of depreciation from the original value
$85,000 − $4,250 = $80,750
Mr. Arcola's house is currently worth only $80,750.

Example: Ms. DeWill bought her house 10 years ago for $92,000. She recently sold it for $142,000. What was the percentage of appreciation?

$92,000 × % = $142,000
Change the problem to solve for the unknown %
$142,000 ÷ $92,000 = %
$142,000 ÷ $92,000 = 1.5435
Change the decimal to a percent *1.54 = 154%*
154% (the amount she sold it for) − *100%* (the original value) = *54%*
The amount of appreciation was 54%

PROFIT AND LOSS. Percentage problems are also used to determine how much profit (or loss) there was when property is sold. There is a profit if the property sells for more than the seller originally paid, or had invested in the property. There is a loss if the property sells for less than the seller paid, or had invested in the property.

Example: Mr. Panza sold his house this year for $144,000. He paid $160,000 for it two years ago. What was the percentage of loss?

$160,000 × % = $144,000

Change the problem around so that you are solving for the missing percentage:

$144,000 ÷ $160,000 = %
$144,000 ÷ $160,000 = .90
Change the decimal to a percentage *.90 = 90%*
$144,000 is only 90% of $160,000
100% (the original value) − *90%* (what he sold it for) =
10%.
The percentage of loss was 10%.

Example: Ms. Brown bought a house eight years ago for $50,000 and sold it this year for a 30% profit (30% more than she originally paid for it). What did she sell it for?

Compute: 30% of $50,000
$50,000 × .30 = $15,000
Add the amount of profit to the original value
$50,000 + $15,000 = $65,000
Ms. Brown sold the house for $65,000.

BROKERAGE MATH

The brokerage fee/sales commission is calculated on the sales price (not the listing price). Remember that the amount of the commission is always negotiable between the parties. Cooperating brokers are paid a portion of the total brokerage fee, and salespeople earn a portion of their broker's earnings. Salespeople can only be paid by their own broker.

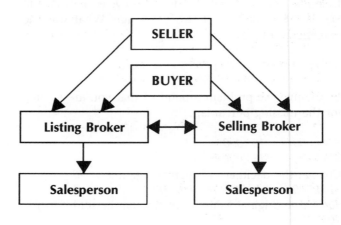

The sales commission or broker's fee is usually a certain percentage of the sales price that the parties have agreed on. The commission is calculated by multiplying the sales price times the agreed percent.

Commission:
sales price ×
agreed % = commission

FORMULA: *sales price × agreed % = commission*

> **Example:** Seller agrees to pay the broker a commission of 6.5%. The house sells for $167,500. How much is the broker's commission?
>
> *$167,500 × 6.5% = commission*
> Change the percent to a decimal (or use the % key on your calculator)
> *$167,500 × .065 = commission*
> *$167,500 × .065 = $10,887*
> The total commission amount is $10,887

A cooperating broker's fees are calculated by multiplying the total commission by the brokers' agreed on percentage.

Broker's earnings:
total commission ×
broker's % =
broker's earnings

FORMULA: *total commission × broker's % = broker's earnings*

Example: Using the same example given above, suppose that the house was listed by Broker A and sold by Broker B. Broker A splits fees 55% to the listing company and 45% to the selling company. How much did Broker A earn? How much did Broker B earn?

The total commission amount (using the problem above) was $10,887.

$10,887 × 55% = Broker A's earnings
$10,887 × .55 = $5,988
Broker A earned $5,988

$10,887 × 45% = Broker B's earnings
$10,887 × .45 = $4,899
Broker B earned $4,899

A salesperson's commission is calculated by multiplying the broker's earnings times the salesperson's percentage.

FORMULA:
broker's earnings × salesperson's % = salesperson's earnings

Example: Susan is a salesperson working for Broker Bob. Broker Bob is a cooperating broker, not the listing broker. Susan sold a home for $167,500. Broker Bob pays his salespeople 45%. How much did Susan earn on the sale?

The sales price was $167,500
The agreed commission to the listing broker was 6.5%

$167,500 × 6.5% = $10,887
As cooperating broker, Bob gets 45% of the commission
$10,887 × 45% = $4,899
Broker Bob pays his salespeople 45%
$4,899 × 45% = $2,205

Total Commission = $10,887
Listing Broker earns = $5,988
Cooperating Broker Bob earns = $2,694
Salesperson Susan earns = $2,205

Salesperson's earnings: broker's earnings × salesperson's % = salesperson's earnings

Using the same sales price, suppose that Broker Bob pays his salespeople ⅔. How much would Susan earn on the sale?

As cooperating broker, Bob received $4,899.

$4,899 × ⅔ = Susan's earnings
Change the fraction to a decimal
$4,899 × .67 = Susan's earnings
$4,899 × .67 = $3,282
Susan would earn $3,282
Bob would earn $1,617 ($4,899 − $3,282 = $1,617)

If you know the percentage agreed on as commission and the total commission amount paid, you may calculate the sales price.

FORMULA: *sales price × agreed % = total commission (total commission ÷ agreed % = sales price)*

Example: A broker was paid a 7% commission which amounted to $8,610. What was the sales price of the house?

sales price × 7% = $8,610
$8,610 ÷ .07 = sales price
$8,610 ÷ .07 = $123,000
The sales price of the house was $123,000

PRORATIONS

Proration is the allocation of one expense among two or more parties. Prorations are usually required at real estate closings, where the cost of such items as taxes and insurance are allocated between the buyer and the seller.

To work on a proration problem:

1) Find the annual or monthly amount of the expense.
2) Then find the daily rate of the expense (per diem). For real estate exams, it is usually sufficient to use 30-day months and 360-day years when converting monthly or annual rates to per diem rates. Thus, the daily rate equals 1/30th of the monthly rate or 1/360th of the annual rate. (However, it is becoming more and more common to use actual days in the month and 365-day

years, so be sure to check the method used when making proration calculations.)

3) Next, determine the number of days for which the person is responsible for the expense. Be sure to check whether the seller or the buyer is responsible for paying for the actual day of closing. (For the following problems, assume that the buyer is responsible for the day of closing.)

Making a graph showing when the taxes are due or have been paid, when the closing will take place, etc., may help you in visualizing who owes whom and the period of time they owe for.

Prorations: daily rate × number of days = amount owed

Example: Taxes on a property are $1,440, to be paid in arrears on December 31. If the closing is set for March 15, how much will the seller owe the buyer at closing?

	Closing	Taxes due
January 1	March 15	December 31
← Seller owes →	←	Buyer owes →

$1,440 ÷ 12 = $120 (taxes per month)
$120 ÷ 30 = $4 (daily rate)

Seller owes for all of January, all of February, and the first 14 days of March. *(30 + 30 + 14 = 74 days)*
74 × $4 = $296
Seller will owe buyer $296

If using exact days instead of a 30-day month, Seller would owe for 73 days. (31 + 28 + 14 = 73 days)
73 × $4 = $292

Example: On January 1, Mr. Kravitz paid an annual fire insurance premium of $230. If he sold his house on May 15, what prorated amount of the insurance premium would be returned to him?

$230 ÷ 12 = $19.17 (monthly)
$19.17 ÷ 30 = .64 (daily)

Seller owes for January, February, March, April, and 14 days in May *(30 + 30 + 30 + 30 + 14 = 134)*

134 × .64 = $85.76
Seller owed only $85.76
$230 − $85.76 = $144.24
Buyer must reimburse seller for $144.24

NET PROCEEDS

"Net" or "Net Proceeds" refers to the amount of money the seller will actually receive after all of the selling and closing expenses have been paid. The sales price minus all expenses equals the net proceeds.

Net proceeds:
sales price − expenses = net proceeds

FORMULA: *sales price − expenses = net proceeds*

Example: Constance sold her home for $121,000. The broker's commission was 6.5%; there is an existing mortgage of $82,000 which will be paid off; Constance owes $1,060 in property taxes; miscellaneous other costs amount to $1,679 (such as charges for an abstract, attorney's fees, a pest inspection, etc.). What is Constance's net proceed on the sale?

First, figure out all of the expenses (such as the broker's commission)
$121,000 × 6.5% = $7,865
Then, *add* all of the expenses.

$ 7,865	commission
82,000	existing mortgage
1,060	property taxes
1,679	misc.
92,604	TOTAL EXPENSES

Subtract the total expenses from the sales price.
$121,000 − $92,604 = $28,396

The amount of Constance's net proceeds is $28,396.

Using the above information, it is possible to calculate the percentage of net proceeds. The amount of net proceeds divided by the sales price equals the net proceeds percentage.

FORMULA: *net proceeds ÷ sales price = net proceeds %*

 Example: *$28,396 ÷ $121,000 = net proceeds percentage*

 $28,396 ÷ $121,000 = .2347
 $28,396 ÷ $121,000 = 23%
 Constance's net proceeds were 23% of the sales price

 In a similar way, if you know the net proceeds and the net proceeds percentage, you can calculate the amount of the sales price. Net proceeds divided by net proceeds percentage equals the sales price.

FORMULA: *net proceeds ÷ net proceeds % = sales price*

 Example: A seller receives $32,000 in net proceeds from the sale of a house. This represents 26% of the selling price. What was the selling price?

 $32,000 ÷ 26% = selling price
 $32,000 ÷ .26 = $123,077
 The selling price was $123,077

AREA PROBLEMS
SQUARES AND RECTANGLES. The formula for finding the area of squares and rectangles is: area equals base times height (or area equals length times width).

Area of rectangle:
area = base × height

$A = B \times H$

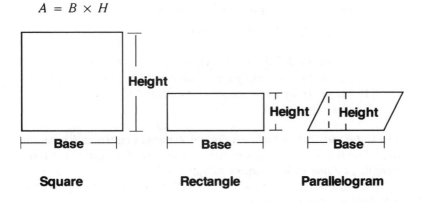

  Square   **Rectangle**   **Parallelogram**

Example: If a room measures 15 feet along one wall and 12 feet along the adjoining wall, how many square feet of carpet would be required to cover the floor?

Since the quantity A is unknown, multiply B times H for the answer.

$B \times H = A$

15 ft. × 12 ft. = 180 sq.ft.

180 square feet of carpet is needed to cover the floor.

Example: If carpet is on sale for $12 per square yard, how much would it cost to carpet the room in the above example?

First, determine how many square feet there are in a square yard, and then determine how many square yards there are in 180 square feet. A square yard is a square that is one yard on each side. There are three feet in a yard.

$B \times H = A$

3 ft. × 3 ft. = 9 sq.ft.

There are nine square feet in a square yard.

Now we'll divide 9 sq.ft. into 180 sq.ft. to see how many square yards there are in 180 square feet.

180 sq.ft. ÷ 9 sq.ft. = 20 sq.yd.

There are 20 square yards in the room. If carpet is selling for $12 per square yard, it will cost $12 × 20, or $240 to carpet the room.

Area of triangle:
area = ½ base × height

TRIANGLES. The formula for finding the area of a triangle is similar to finding the area of a square, except that instead of using base times height, you use ½ base times height.

FORMULA: *area = ½base × height*

$A = .5\,B \times H$

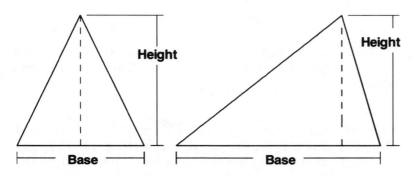

Example: If commercial building lots in a certain neighborhood are selling for approximately five dollars per square foot, for about how much should the pictured lot sell?

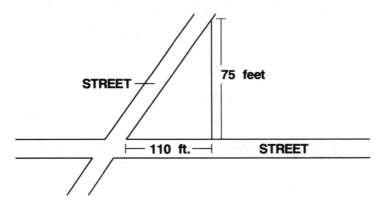

The quantity A is unknown; thus, multiply .5 B times H
.5 × 110 ft. × 75 ft.

The order of multiplication is not important. You can multiply 110 times 75 and then multiply that product by .5, or you can multiply .5 times 75 and then multiply the result by 110. The answer will be the same:

a) *110 × 75 = 8250*
   .5 × 8250 = 4125

b) *.5 × 110 = 55*
   55 × 75 = 4125

c) *.5 × 75 = 37.5*
   37.5 × 110 = 4125

The lot contains 4125 square feet. If similar lots are selling for about five dollars per square foot, this lot should sell for about five times 4125, or *$5 × 4125 = $20,625.*

ODD SHAPES. The best approach to finding the area of an odd-shaped figure is to divide it up into squares, rectangles and triangles. Find the areas of those figures and add them all up to reach the area of the odd-shaped lot, room, building or whatever else the problem requires.

> **Example:** If the pictured lot is leased on a 66-year lease for $3.00 per square foot per year, with rental payments made monthly, how much would the monthly rent be?

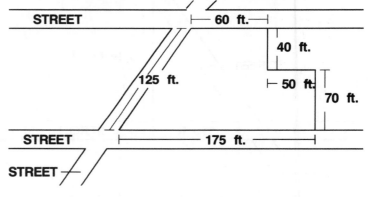

First, divide the lot up into rectangles and triangles.

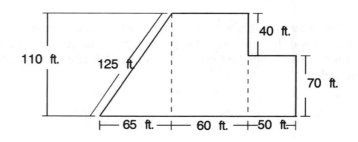

The next step is to find the areas of the following figures and add them together.

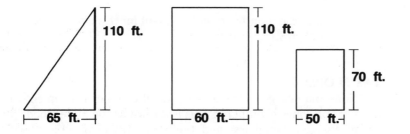

Triangle
$A = .5\ B \times H$
$A = .5 \times 65' \times 110'$
$.5 \times 65' \times 110' = 3575$ sq.ft.

Rectangle
$A = B \times H$
$A = 110' \times 60'$
$110' \times 60' = 6600$ sq.ft.

Rectangle
$A = B \times H$
$A = 50 \times 70$
50 ft. $\times\ 70$ ft. $= 3500$ sq.ft.

Add the three areas:

$$
\begin{array}{r}
3,575 \text{ sq.ft.} \\
6,600 \text{ sq.ft.} \\
+\ 3,500 \text{ sq.ft.} \\
\hline
13,675 \text{ sq.ft.}
\end{array}
$$

The lot contains 13,675 square feet. The annual rental at $3.00 per square foot per year would be:

$3 \times 13,675$ sq.ft. $= $41,025$ **per year**

The monthly rent payment would be one-twelfth of the annual rent:

$41,025 ÷ 12 = $3,418.75

Thus, the monthly rental payment for this odd-shaped lot is $3,418.75.

TAX PROBLEMS

Minnesota charges a tax on each deed or other instrument that transfers or conveys property. This is known as the State Deed Tax. If a mortgage is being assumed, the tax is only charged on the difference between the purchase price and the assumed mortgage. If no mortgage is being assumed, the tax is based on the total purchase price. The tax is $1.65 per $500 or fraction of that amount.

State Deed Tax: $1.65 per $500.00

Example: A home is being sold for $96,000. The buyer is assuming a $72,000 mortgage. The deed tax would be based on the difference between the assumed mortgage and the sales price.

$96,000 − $72,000 = $24,000
The deed tax is only charged on $24,000

The deed tax is $1.65 per $500, so first find out how many times 500 goes into $24,000

$24,000 ÷ 500 = 48
$1.65 × 48 = $79.20
The state deed tax on this sale would be $79.20

Example: A home is being sold for $106,000. The buyer is not assuming a mortgage, so the deed tax would be charged on the total purchase price.

$106,000 ÷ $500 = 212
$1.65 × 212 = $349.80
The state deed tax on this sale would be $349.80

In addition to the State Deed Tax, Minnesota also charges a Mortgage Registration Tax on all new mortgages of real property. This tax is 23 cents on each $100 of the new mortgage.

Mortgage Registration Tax: $0.23 per $100.00

Example: A buyer purchases a house and takes out a mortgage for $117,500. How much would the mortgage registration tax be?

The tax is 23 cents on each $100, so first determine how many times 100 goes into the mortgage amount.

$117,500 ÷ 100 = $1,175
$1,175 × .23 = $270.25
The mortgage registration tax on this sale would be $270.25

Tax calculations may also be necessary when figuring out the possible tax benefits to a transaction. For example, mortgage interest and real estate taxes may be deductible from taxable income. The total amount of deductions times a person's tax bracket equals the amount of tax savings.

Example: Last year an owner of a single family residence paid $1,300 in real property taxes and a total of $8,700 in mortgage payments ($7,800 interest and $900 principal reduction). How much can the owner deduct from taxable income? If the owner is in the 28% bracket, how much would he save on federal income tax?

The owner may deduct real property taxes and mortgage interest.

$1,300 + $7,800 = $9,100
The owner can deduct $9,100

The total amount of deductions times the tax bracket equals the amount of tax savings.

$9,100 × 28% = tax savings
$9,100 × .28 = $2,548
The owner would save $2,548

MORTGAGE MATH

MORTGAGE AMOUNT

When a buyer purchases a home, a large portion of the sales price is often financed with a mortgage. In order to determine the necessary mortgage amount, simply subtract the downpayment from the sales price.

Amount of mortgage:
sales price –
downpayment =
mortgage amount

FORMULA: *sales price – downpayment = mortgage amount*

> **Example:** Buyer is purchasing a home with a sales price of $98,500. He has agreed to pay a downpayment of 20%. What will be the amount of the mortgage?
>
> *$98,500 × 20% = downpayment*
> *$98,500 × .20 = $19,700*
> The downpayment is $19,700.
>
> To determine the mortgage amount, subtract the down-payment from the purchase price
>
> *$98,500 – $19,700 = $78,800*
> The amount of the mortgage will be $78,800

LOAN TO VALUE RATIO. The loan to value ratio (LTV) is the maximum percentage of the sales price (or value) that the lender will give as a loan. Conventional loans are often 80% of value. FHA and VA loans are often a higher percentage. In order to calculate the mortgage amount, multiply the sales price times the loan to value ratio.

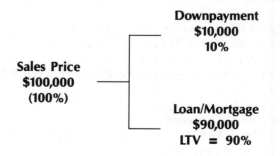

Sales Price
$100,000
(100%)

Downpayment
$10,000
10%

Loan/Mortgage
$90,000
LTV = 90%

FORMULA: *sales price × loan to value ratio = mortgage amount*

> **Example:** A lender's loan to value ratio is 75%. This means that the maximum percentage that the lender will give as a loan is 75% of the sales price. If the sales price of a home is $114,000, what is the mortgage amount?
>
> *$114,000 × 75% = mortgage amount*
> *$114,000 × .75 = $85,500*
> The maximum amount the lender will loan is $85,500

In a similar way, you can calculate the loan to value ratio if you know the sales price and mortgage amount.

FORMULA: *mortgage amount ÷ sales price = loan to value ratio*

Loan to value ratio: mortgage amount ÷ sales price = loan to value ratio

> **Example:** If the sales price of a house was $107,000 and the buyer got a mortgage for $96,400, what was the loan to value ratio?
>
> *$96,400 ÷ $107,000 = .90*
> The loan to value ratio was 90%

CALCULATING POINTS

The term "point" is a contraction of the larger term "percentage point." A point is one percentage point or one percent of a loan amount.

> **Example:** If a buyer got a loan for $85,000 and the lender charged six points, what is the dollar amount of the points?
>
> One point is one percent of the loan amount, so six points is 6% of the loan amount. In order to determine the dollar amount of the points, simply multiply the loan amount times the percentage points.
>
> *$85,000 × 6% = amount of points*
> *$85,000 × .06 = $5,100*
> The dollar amount of six points on this loan is $5,100

LOAN AMORTIZATION
MONTHLY PAYMENT FOR A $1,000 LOAN

YEARS	7%	7½%	8%	8½%	8¾%	9%	9¼%	9½%	9¾%	10%	10¼%	10½%
1.0	86.53	86.76	86.99	87.22	87.34	87.45	87.57	87.68	87.80	87.92	88.03	88.15
1.5	58.69	58.91	59.14	59.37	59.48	59.60	59.71	59.83	59.94	60.06	60.17	60.29
2.0	44.77	45.00	45.23	45.46	45.57	45.68	45.80	45.91	46.03	46.14	46.26	46.38
2.5	36.43	36.66	36.89	37.12	37.23	37.35	37.46	37.58	37.70	37.81	37.93	38.04
3.0	30.88	31.11	31.34	31.57	31.68	31.80	31.92	32.03	32.15	32.27	32.38	32.50
3.5	26.91	27.15	27.38	27.61	27.73	27.84	27.96	28.08	28.20	28.32	28.44	28.55
4.0	23.95	24.18	24.41	24.65	24.77	24.89	25.00	25.12	25.24	25.36	25.48	25.60
4.5	21.64	21.88	22.11	22.35	22.47	22.59	22.71	22.83	22.95	23.07	23.19	23.32
5.0	19.80	20.04	20.28	20.52	20.64	20.76	20.88	21.00	21.12	21.25	21.37	21.49
5.5	18.30	18.54	18.78	19.02	19.14	19.27	19.39	19.51	19.64	19.76	19.88	20.01
6.0	17.05	17.29	17.53	17.78	17.90	18.03	18.15	18.27	18.40	18.53	18.65	18.78
6.5	15.99	16.24	16.48	16.73	16.86	16.98	17.11	17.23	17.36	17.49	17.61	17.74
7.0	15.09	15.34	15.59	15.84	15.96	16.09	16.22	16.34	16.47	16.60	16.73	16.86
7.5	14.31	14.56	14.81	15.06	15.19	15.32	15.45	15.58	15.71	15.84	15.97	16.10
8.0	13.63	13.88	14.14	14.39	14.52	14.65	14.78	14.91	15.04	15.17	15.31	15.44
8.5	13.04	13.29	13.54	13.80	13.93	14.06	14.19	14.33	14.46	14.59	14.73	14.86
9.0	12.51	12.76	13.02	13.28	13.41	13.54	13.68	13.81	13.94	14.08	14.21	14.35
9.5	12.03	12.29	12.55	12.81	12.95	13.08	13.22	13.35	13.49	13.62	13.76	13.90
10.0	11.61	11.87	12.13	12.40	12.53	12.67	12.80	12.94	13.08	13.22	13.35	13.49
10.5	11.23	11.49	11.76	12.02	12.16	12.30	12.43	12.57	12.71	12.85	12.99	13.13
11.0	10.88	11.15	11.42	11.69	11.82	11.96	12.10	12.24	12.38	12.52	12.66	12.80
11.5	10.57	10.84	11.11	11.38	11.52	11.66	11.80	11.94	12.08	12.22	12.37	12.51
12.0	10.28	10.55	10.82	11.10	11.24	11.38	11.52	11.66	11.81	11.95	12.10	12.24
12.5	10.02	10.29	10.57	10.85	10.99	11.13	11.27	11.41	11.56	11.70	11.85	12.00
13.0	9.78	10.05	10.33	10.61	10.75	10.90	11.04	11.19	11.33	11.48	11.63	11.78
13.5	9.56	9.83	10.11	10.40	10.54	10.68	10.83	10.98	11.12	11.27	11.42	11.57
14.0	9.35	9.63	9.91	10.20	10.34	10.49	10.64	10.78	10.93	11.08	11.23	11.38
14.5	9.16	9.44	9.73	10.02	10.16	10.31	10.46	10.61	10.76	10.91	11.06	11.21
15.0	8.99	9.27	9.56	9.85	9.99	10.14	10.29	10.44	10.59	10.75	10.90	11.05
15.5	8.82	9.11	9.40	9.69	9.84	9.99	10.14	10.29	10.44	10.60	10.75	10.91
16.0	8.67	8.96	9.25	9.54	9.69	9.85	10.00	10.15	10.30	10.46	10.62	10.77
16.5	8.53	8.82	9.11	9.41	9.56	9.71	9.87	10.02	10.17	10.33	10.49	10.65
17.0	8.40	8.69	8.98	9.28	9.43	9.59	9.74	9.90	10.05	10.21	10.37	10.53
17.5	8.27	8.56	8.86	9.16	9.32	9.47	9.63	9.78	9.94	10.10	10.26	10.42
18.0	8.16	8.45	8.75	9.05	9.21	9.36	9.52	9.68	9.84	10.00	10.16	10.32
18.5	8.05	8.34	8.64	8.95	9.11	9.26	9.42	9.58	9.74	9.90	10.06	10.23
19.0	7.94	8.24	8.55	8.85	9.01	9.17	9.33	9.49	9.65	9.81	9.98	10.14
19.5	7.84	8.15	8.45	8.76	8.92	9.08	9.24	9.40	9.56	9.73	9.89	10.06
20.0	7.75	8.06	8.36	8.68	8.84	9.00	9.16	9.32	9.49	9.65	9.82	9.98
20.5	7.67	7.97	8.28	8.60	8.76	8.92	9.08	9.25	9.41	9.58	9.74	9.91
21.0	7.58	7.89	8.20	8.52	8.68	8.85	9.01	9.17	9.34	9.51	9.68	9.85
21.5	7.51	7.82	8.13	8.45	8.61	8.78	8.94	9.11	9.27	9.44	9.61	9.78
22.0	7.43	7.75	8.06	8.38	8.55	8.71	8.88	9.04	9.21	9.38	9.55	9.73
22.5	7.36	7.68	8.00	8.32	8.48	8.65	8.82	8.99	9.15	9.33	9.50	9.67
23.0	7.30	7.61	7.93	8.26	8.43	8.59	8.76	8.93	9.10	9.27	9.44	9.62
23.5	7.24	7.55	7.88	8.20	8.37	8.54	8.71	8.88	9.05	9.22	9.40	9.57
24.0	7.18	7.50	7.82	8.15	8.32	8.49	8.66	8.83	9.00	9.17	9.35	9.52
24.5	7.12	7.44	7.77	8.10	8.27	8.44	8.61	8.78	8.95	9.13	9.31	9.48
25.0	7.07	7.39	7.72	8.05	8.22	8.39	8.56	8.74	8.91	9.09	9.26	9.44
25.5	7.02	7.34	7.67	8.01	8.18	8.35	8.52	8.70	8.87	9.05	9.23	9.40
26.0	6.97	7.29	7.63	7.96	8.13	8.31	8.48	8.66	8.83	9.01	9.19	9.37
26.5	6.92	7.25	7.58	7.92	8.09	8.27	8.44	8.62	8.80	8.97	9.15	9.33
27.0	6.88	7.21	7.54	7.88	8.06	8.23	8.41	8.58	8.76	8.94	9.12	9.30
27.5	6.84	7.17	7.50	7.85	8.02	8.20	8.37	8.55	8.73	8.91	9.09	9.27
28.0	6.80	7.13	7.47	7.81	7.99	8.16	8.34	8.52	8.70	8.88	9.06	9.25
28.5	6.76	7.09	7.43	7.78	7.95	8.13	8.31	8.49	8.67	8.85	9.03	9.22
29.0	6.72	7.06	7.40	7.75	7.92	8.10	8.28	8.46	8.64	8.82	9.01	9.19
29.5	6.69	7.02	7.37	7.72	7.89	8.07	8.25	8.43	8.62	8.80	8.98	9.17
29.8	6.67	7.00	7.35	7.70	7.88	8.06	8.24	8.42	8.60	8.79	8.97	9.16
30.0	6.65	6.99	7.34	7.69	7.87	8.05	8.23	8.41	8.59	8.78	8.96	9.15
35.0	6.39	6.74	7.10	7.47	7.65	7.84	8.03	8.22	8.41	8.60	8.79	8.98
40.0	6.21	6.58	6.95	7.33	7.52	7.71,	7.91	8.10	8.30	8.49	8.69	8.89

PAYMENT FACTORS

A payment factor is the monthly payment of principal and interest required to fully amortize (pay off) a $1,000 loan at a specific interest rate over a specific term. The payment factor is used to determine how much monthly mortgage payments would be. Once it is determined how much the monthly payment would be on a $1,000 loan (using the table), simply multiply the amount by how many times $1,000 goes into the amount of the actual loan.

> **Example:** A buyer purchases a home for $130,000. He takes out a 30-year mortgage for $104,000 at an interest rate of 10.5%. How much will his monthly mortgage payments be?
>
> First, determine the payment factor on a 30-year loan at 10.5% interest.
> Using the above chart, find the correct interest rate in the top row. Then go down the left-hand column to the correct number of years. The payment factor is 9.15.
> Next, determine how many times 1000 will go into the amount of the actual loan.
>
> *$104,000 ÷ 1000 = 104*
> Multiply this number times the payment factor
> *104 × 9.15 = monthly payment*
> The buyer's monthly payments will be $951.60

TOTAL INTEREST ON A LOAN

Sometimes a purchaser may be interested in calculating the total amount of interest that will be paid over the life of a loan. To determine this amount, first calculate the total amount paid. The amount of the monthly payment times the number of payments equals the total amount paid. Take the total amount paid and subtract the principal (the amount of the loan) to determine the total interest paid.

> **Example:** Buyer purchased a house for $110,000. She took out a 30-year mortgage for $88,000 at 9½% interest. How much is her monthly payment? How much total interest will she have paid when the loan is finally paid off?

First, determine the payment factor using the above chart.

The payment factor for a 30-year loan at 9½% is 8.41.

$88,000 ÷ 1000 = 88
$8.41 × 88 = $740.08
Buyer's monthly payments are $740.08

Next, figure out how many payments she will make over the life of the loan.

12 months × 30 years = 360 months

Then, multiply the number of payments times the amount of the payment.

360 × $740.08 = total amount paid
360 × $740.08 = $266,428.80

Finally, subtract the principal (loan amount) from the total amount paid.

$266,428.80 − $88,000 = total interest paid
$266,428.80 − $88,000 = $178,428.80
The total amount of interest paid over the life of the loan will be $178,428.80

PRINCIPAL AND INTEREST PER PAYMENT AND PRINCIPAL BALANCE REMAINING

When a homeowner has a mortgage loan, he may want to discover how much of his monthly payment is interest and how much is principal. To calculate the interest portion of a monthly payment, first multiply the principal balance remaining by the interest rate. This will give you the annual interest. Then divide the annual interest by 12 to determine one month's interest.

Annual interest: principal balance × interest rate = annual interest

FORMULA: *principal balance × interest rate = annual interest*
annual interest ÷ 12 = 1 month's interest

Example: A homeowner is paying 11.5% interest on her mortgage. Her monthly payments are $725. The principal balance remaining on her loan is $67,500. How much of this month's payment will be applied to interest?

$67,500 × 11.5% = annual interest
$67,500 × .115 = $7,762.50
$7,762.50 ÷12 = $646.88
$646.88 of this month's payment will be applied to interest

Using the above information, you can also calculate what portion of the payment will be applied to reduce the principal. Simply subtract the interest portion of the payment from the total payment to determine the principal portion.

FORMULA: *total payment − interest portion = principal portion*

Example: Using the problem above, how much of the monthly payment will go towards principal?

$725 − $646.88 = $78.12

Out of the $725 monthly payment, $646.88 will be applied to interest and $78.12 will be applied to reduce the principal

Using the same figures, you can also calculate what the remaining principal balance is after this month's payment is made. To find the remaining balance, subtract the principal portion of the payment from the prior principal balance.

FORMULA: *prior principal balance − principal portion of payment = remaining principal balance*

Example: Using the problem above, the prior principal balance (the amount still owing on the loan) is $67,500. The principal portion of the payment was $78.12.

$67,500 − $78.12 = $67,421.88
The remaining principal balance is $67,421.88

FORMULAS

Converting Fractions to Decimals: *divide numerator (top number) by denominator (bottom number).*

Converting Percentages to Decimals: *move decimal point two places to the left.*

Brokerage math:
sales price × agreed % = total commission
total commission × broker's % = broker's earnings
broker's earnings × salesperson's % = salesperson's earnings
total commission ÷ agreed % = sales price

Prorations:
   1. find the annual or monthly amount
   2. find the daily rate
   3. determine the number of days owed
   4. multiply the daily rate times the number of days owed

Net Proceeds: *sales price − expenses = net proceeds*
net proceeds ÷ sales price = net proceeds %
net proceeds ÷ net proceeds % = sales price

Area Formula: *area = base × height*

Area Formula for Triangles: *area = ½ base × height*

State Deed Tax: *purchase price (or difference between purchase price and assumed mortgage) ÷ 500 = A*
A × $1.65 = state deed tax

Mortgage Registration Tax: *mortgage amount ÷ 100 = A*
A × .23 = mortgage registration tax

Mortgage Math:
sales price − downpayment = mortgage amount

Loan to Value Ratio:
sales price × loan to value ratio = mortgage amount
mortgage amount ÷ sales price = loan to value ratio

Calculating Points: *loan amount × percentage points = amount of points*

Payment Factors: *Determine payment factor by using amortization table*

Total Interest on a Loan: *loan amount ÷ 1000 = A*
A × payment factor = monthly payment
monthly payment × number of payments = total amount paid
total amount paid − loan amount = total interest paid

Principal and Interest and Remaining Balance:
principal balance × interest rate = annual interest
annual interest ÷ 12 = 1 month's interest
total payment − interest portion = principal portion
prior principal balance − principal portion of payment = remaining
principal balance

CHAPTER 6—REVIEW EXAM

1. Thompson bought a house 10 years ago for $93,000, and sold it this year for $126,000. What was his percentage of profit on the sale?

   a. 25%
   b. 30%
   c. 35%
   d. 40%

2. Seller agrees to pay Broker a commission of 7%. The house sells for $117,000. How much is Broker's commission?

   a. $1,671
   b. $8,190
   c. $7,512
   d. $11,700

3. Kelly is working as a salesperson. She sells a home for $122,000. The agreed upon commission was 6.5%. Kelly's broker pays her salespeople 45%. How much did Kelly earn on the sale?

   a. $3,568.50
   b. $4,250.87
   c. $7,930.00
   d. None of the above

4. The yearly taxes on a property are $1,296. The seller has paid the taxes in advance. At the closing date, the buyer owes the seller for 23 days of taxes. How much does the buyer owe the seller?

   a. $56.34
   b. $129
   c. $78.43
   d. $81.65

5. An owner sold a lot with a front footage of 90 feet and a depth of 250 feet for $2.25 a square foot. What was the selling price?

   a) $347.50
   b) $607.50
   c) $24,300
   d) $50,625

6. A building used for storage measures 100 feet by 220 feet. It rents for $0.32 per square foot per year. What is the rent over a year's time?

   a) $7,040
   b) $7,400
   c) $50,880
   d) $48,080

7. A rectangular property with 8,690 square yards has 318 front feet. What is the depth of the property?

   a) 245.94 feet
   b) 27.32 feet
   c) 27.32 yards
   d) 81.98 feet

8. The third quarter interest on a $7,600 loan at 8% interest is:

   a) $608
   b) $76
   c) $152
   d) None of the above

9. The outside dimensions of a two-story house measure 32.5 feet by 45.8 feet. The cost of construction of the first story was $31 per square foot and the cost of the second story was $22 per square foot. A detached garage measuring 21.6 feet by 20.8 feet cost $16 per square foot. What was the total cost of construction?

   a) $86,079
   b) $78,890
   c) $53,332
   d) $99,475

10. Thornton is buying a house for $112,000. He is assuming a mortgage of $78,000. The State Deed Tax is $1.65 per $500. How much State Deed Tax will Thornton have to pay?

    a. $1,287
    b. $369.60
    c. $112.20
    d. $257.40

11. Sanders is purchasing a home for $105,500. He is making a 20% downpayment, and will finance the rest with an 80% mortgage. What will be the amount of the mortgage?

    a. 92,000
    b. 84,400
    c. 88,600
    d. 94,200

12. Buyer purchases a home for $127,500. He takes out a 30-year mortgage for $102,000 at an interest rate of 11%. The payment factor is 9.53. What will his monthly payments be?

    a. $1,122
    b. $893.42
    c. $972.06
    d. $1,042.03

CHAPTER 6—REVIEW EXAM KEY

1. c) $93,000 × _____% = $126,000
   $126,000 ÷ $93,000 = _____%
   $126,000 ÷ $93,000 = 1.35
   Change the decimal to a percent = 135%
   Subtract the original value
   135% − 100% = 35%
   Thompson made a profit of 35%

2. b) Multiply the sales price times the agreed percentage to find the amount of the commission
   $117,000 × 7% = commission
   Change the percent to a decimal
   $117,000 × .07 = $8,190
   The broker's commission is $8,190

3. a) First determine the amount of the commission.
   $122,000 × 6.5% = commission
   $122,000 × .065 = $7,930
   Then determine 45% of the commission
   $7,930 × 45% = salesperson's earnings
   $7,930 × .45 = $3,568.50
   Kelly earned $3,568.50

4. d) First determine a per diem (per day) amount for the taxes.
   $1,296 ÷ 365 = daily rate
   $1,296 ÷ 365 = $3.55
   Then multiply the daily rate by the number of days owed
   $3.55 × 23 = $81.65
   The buyer owes the seller $81.65

5. d) The area of the lot is
   90 × 250 = 22,500 square feet.
   The sales price is
   22,500 × 2.25 = $50,625.

6. a) The area of the building is
   100 × 220 = 22,000 square feet.
   The annual rent is
   .32 × 22,000 =$7,040.00.

7. a) 8,690 square yards equals 78,210 square feet (9 × 8,690 =78,210). The area of a rectangle divided by its length gives the depth, and 78,210 divided by 318 is 245.94 feet, the depth of the lot.

8. c) 8% of $7,600 is $608.00
   (.08 × 7600 =608).
   One quarter of $608.00 is $152.00
   (.25 × 608 = 152).

9. a) Each floor of the house has an area equal to 32.5 × 45.8 or 1488.5 square feet. The cost of the first floor is 1488.5 × 31= $46,143.50. The cost of the second floor is 1488.5 × 22 = $32,747.00. The area of the garage is 21.6 × 20.8 449.28 square feet, so its cost is 449.28 × 16 = $7188.48. The total cost is therefore 46,143.50 + 32,747.00 + 7,188.48 = $86,078.98.

10.   c) Remember that State Deed Tax is only charged on the difference between the purchase price and the assumed mortgage, so subtract the assumed mortgage from the purchase price.
$112,000 − $78,000 = $34,000
Thornton only has to pay State Deed Tax on $34,000. The amount of the tax is $1.65 per $500, so divide $34,000 by $500.
$34,000 ÷ 500 = 68
68 × $1.65 = $112.20
Thornton will have to pay State Deed Tax of $112.20

11.   b) $105,500 × 80% = mortgage
Convert the percentage into a decimal
$105,555 × .80 = $84,400
The mortgage will be for $84,400

12.   c) The payment factor is based on monthly payments per $1,000 of loan. Therefore, you must first determine how many times 100 will go into the amount of the loan.
$102,000 ÷ 1000 = 102
Then multiply by the payment factor
102 × 9.53 = $972.06
Buyer's monthly payments will be $972.06

MORTGAGES AND LENDING PRACTICES

OUTLINE

I. Contract for Deed vs. Mortgage

II. Financing Documents
   A. Promissory note
   B. Mortgage

III. Mortgage Satisfaction or Assumption

IV. Mortgage Foreclosure
   A. Methods of foreclosure
      1. foreclosure by advertisement
      2. judicial foreclosure
   B. Deed in lieu of foreclosure

V. Methods of Principal and Interest Repayment
   A. Straight or term
   B. Amortized
   C. Partially amortized (balloon)
   D. Alternative repayment variations
      1. graduated payment
      2. adjustable rate (ARM)
      3. budget
      4. reverse annuity mortgage

VI. Conventional Loans
   A. Package
   B. Blanket
   C. Open-end

D. Purchase money
E. Insured

VII. Miscellaneous Mortgage Terms
A. Loan-to-value ratio
B. Equity
C. Subordination
D. Deed of trust

VIII. Minnesota Usury Law

KEY TERMS

contract for deed
state deed tax
promissory note
acceleration clause
mortgage satisfaction
power of sale clause
foreclosure
equitable redemption
judicial foreclosure
notice of default
deed in lieu of foreclosure
amortized loan
graduated payment mortgage
adjustable-rate mortgage (ARM)
conventional loan
blanket mortgage
purchase money mortgage
equity
deed of trust

mortgage
mortgage registration tax
prepayment provision
due-on-sale clause
assumption
default
statutory redemption
foreclosure by advertisement
deficiency judgment
sheriff's sale
straight note
partially amortized note
budget mortgage
reverse annuity mortgage
package mortgage
open-end mortgage
loan-to-value ratio
subordination
usury

CHAPTER OVERVIEW

No matter what the property is, or how great the sales agent, the buyer can't buy unless he or she can afford the purchase. For most people, there is no single transaction that involves more money than the purchase of a home. Because of the large amounts of money involved, most buyers are financially unable to pay cash for the property, so some type of financing must be arranged. The most common type of financing is the mortgage.

This chapter discusses mortgages, methods of loan repayment, and the process of foreclosure when the borrower defaults on a loan.

CONTRACT FOR DEED VERSUS MORTGAGE

> **The contract for deed and the mortgage are the two types of financing instruments used most frequently in Minnesota.**

Contracts for deed most often used for rural/agricultural property; mortgages most often used for urban residential property

The contract for deed is most often used for rural or agricultural property and mortgages are most often used for urban residential property.

CONTRACT FOR DEED. The contract for deed was discussed in detail in Chapter 5. A contract for deed is a type of seller financing. When a contract for deed is used, the buyer makes payments in installments. The seller retains title, but the buyer takes possession of the property. The buyer holds an equitable interest in the property. If the buyer defaults and does not redeem within the time limits, the contract may be cancelled and the seller will retake possession of the property. Since the seller retains title to the property until all payments have been made, the deed is not actually transferred to the buyer at the time of the sale. Therefore, there is no state deed tax on a sale under a contract for deed until all terms have been performed and title actually transfers. There is also no mortgage registration tax on a contract for deed.

Contract for deed: seller retains title until buyer pays in full; buyer takes possession

MORTGAGE. In contrast to the contract for deed, a mortgage is usually held by a bank or other lending institution.

> **With a mortgage, the buyer actually holds title to the property in addition to being entitled to possession and use of the property. The lender is merely given a lien on the property.**

Mortgage: buyer holds title to property; lender has a lien until repaid

When the mortgage is fully paid off, the lien is released.

If a mortgagor defaults on the mortgage, the property may be foreclosed. However, there is a statutory redemption period during which the mortgagor has the right to redeem the property. This statutory right is much longer than the simple right of equitable redemption that is given to the purchaser under a contract for deed.

Mortgagor has longer redemption period than contract purchaser

When property is sold and the deed (title) is actually transferred to the new owner, the seller must pay a state deed tax. When a mortgage is given on the property, the borrower must pay the mortgage registration tax.

CONTRACT FOR DEED	MORTGAGE
Buyer has possession, holds equitable title	Buyer has possession, holds legal title
Seller retains legal title	Lender is merely given a lien on the property
Cancellation if default	Foreclosure if default
Only equitable redemption, no statutory redemption	Equitable redemption and statutory redemption
No state deed tax	Seller pays state deed tax
No mortgage registration tax	Borrower pays mortgage registration tax

FINANCING DOCUMENTS

The two basic documents used in a standard mortgage loan are the promissory note and the mortgage itself. Both the promissory note and the mortgage are contracts and must meet all of the requirements for a valid contract.

PROMISSORY NOTE

> **A promissory note is a written promise to repay a debt.**

Promissory note: a written promise to pay a debt

One person (or entity) loans another money, and the other signs a promissory note, promising to repay the loan (plus interest, in most cases). The borrower who signs the note is called the maker, and the lender is called the payee.

PROMISSORY NOTE

_____, 19____   _____, Minnesota

_____
                        (property address)

In return for a loan that I have received, I promise to pay _____, plus interest,
to the order of the Lender. The Lender is _____.
The Lender, or anyone who takes the Note by transfer and is entitled to receive
payments under this Note, is called the "Note Holder".

Interest will be charged on unpaid principal at a yearly rate of _____%. My monthly
payments will be in the amount of $_____.

I will make my monthly payments on the _____ day of each month beginning on
_____. I will make these payments every month until all of the principal and
interest has been paid. If, on _____ (the maturity date), I still owe amounts under
this Note, I will pay those amounts in full on that date.

I have the right to make payments of principal at any time before they are due. I may
make a full prepayment or partial prepayment without paying any prepayment penalty.

If the full amount of any monthly payment has not been received within ____ days
after it is due, I will pay a late charge of ____% of my overdue payment.

Each payment will be applied first to interest then due, with the remainder applied
to the principal.

If I do not pay the full amount of each monthly payment on the date it is due, I will
be in default. If I am in default, the Note Holder may send me a written notice telling
me that if I do not pay the overdue amount by a certain date, the Note Holder may
require me to pay immediately the full amount of principal which has not been paid
and all the interest that I owe on that amount. That date must be at least 30 days
after the date on which the notice is delivered or mailed to me.

If I have been required to pay immediately in full as described above, the Note Holder
will have the right to be paid back by me for all of its expenses in enforcing this Note,
which may include reasonable attorneys' fees.

This Note is secured by a mortgage in favor of_____
_____ executed on the same date as this Note.

_____(Borrower)

This promissory note form is based on the FNMA/FHLMC Uniform Multi-state Fixed Rate Note for single-family
property, but has been considerably simplified.

The promissory note should:

1. be in writing,
2. identify the borrower and the lender (both of whom must have contractual capacity),
3. state the borrower's promise to repay a certain sum of money,
4. give the terms of repayment (including the interest rate),
5. be signed by the borrower,
6. be delivered by the borrower to the lender, and
7. be accepted by the lender.

Some states require that the borrower's signature be acknowledged or witnessed. This is not required in Minnesota.

BASIC PROVISIONS. In a real estate loan transaction, the promissory note should state that it is secured by a mortgage. The note should identify the mortgage by date or recording number.

> **The note and the mortgage are signed on the same date, and they are linked together. If the lender negotiates or assigns the note, the mortgage is automatically transferred along with the note.**

The mortgage can't be assigned unless the right to payment under the note is transferred too.

The note generally states the loan amount (the principal), the amount of the payments, and when and how the payments are to be made. It includes the maturity date, when the loan is to be fully paid off. The note also lists the interest rate, which may be either fixed or variable. If the rate is variable, the note should include how and when the rate and payment will change, and any limitations on the change. The note also typically includes an acceleration clause, which allows the lender to call the entire balance due (accelerate) in the event the borrower defaults in making the promised payments when due.

PREPAYMENT PROVISIONS. When a contract states a specific time for performance, the law requires it to be performed at the stated time—not after that time, and also not before that time. Suppose I'm going to buy your house, and we've agreed that closing will take place on January 6. If I tender the purchase price to you a week early, on December 30, you can refuse to accept it. The same rule applies to a loan agreement. If the promissory note obligates me to pay $789 on the 15th of each month, I don't have the right to pay more or pay sooner.

> **A promissory note may give the borrower the right to _prepay_—that is, make a larger payment than required, or pay off the entire loan before its maturity date.**

In fact, prepayment is permitted by the terms of most promissory notes. The note may simply state that the monthly payment is $789 "or more," or that the payments are due "on or before" the 15th of each month. Or the note may include a provision expressly stating that the borrower has the right to prepay.

Prepayment: no right to prepay unless expressly stated in note; fee may be charged

This is called the prepayment privilege. If a fee is charged for prepayment, the fee is called a prepayment penalty. All FHA and VA loans can be prepaid without penalty.

DEFAULT PROVISIONS. Many promissory notes have a late payment penalty. The penalty may be a per day fee; for example, $5 per day is added to the debt until the overdue payment is received. Or the penalty may be a percentage of the overdue payment; for example, a 5% penalty is added to the required monthly payment.

MORTGAGE

It is important to understand the relationship between the promissory note and the mortgage. A person borrowing money to buy real estate signs a promissory note in favor of the lender. The borrower then signs the mortgage.

> **The borrower, who is in fact _giving_ the mortgage, is known as the mortgagor. The lender, who is in fact _receiving_ the mortgage, is known as the mortgagee.**

Mortgagor: the borrower

Mortgagee: the lender

The mortgage is a contract that makes the real property collateral for the loan. It creates a lien on the property. If the borrower (mortgagor) doesn't repay as agreed in the promissory note, the mortgage gives the lender (mortgagee) the right to foreclose on the property.

Mortgage: a contract that makes real property collateral for a loan

A promissory note can be enforced whether or not it is accompanied by a mortgage. In the unlikely event a real estate loan is made without a security instrument like a mortgage, the payee/lender can file a lawsuit and obtain a judgment if the maker/borrower breaches the promise by failing to repay. But without a mortgage, the judgment may turn out to be uncollectible. For instance, the borrower

MORTGAGE

1. This Mortgage is given on _____, 19____. The mortgagor is _____ _____ ("Borrower"). This Mortgage is given to _____ _____("Lender").

2. Borrower owes Lender the principal sum of _____ dollars (_____). This debt is evidenced by Borrower's Note dated the same date as this Mortgage, which provides for monthly payments, with the full debt due and payable on _____, 19____, and for interest at the yearly rate of _____%.

3. This Mortgage secures to Lender the repayment of the debt evidenced by the Note, with interest, and all renewals, extensions and modifications, and the performance of Borrower's covenants and agreements under this Mortgage and the Note. For this purpose, Borrower does hereby mortgage, grant, and convey to lender, the following described Property located in _____ County, Minnesota:

Together with all the improvements, easements, rights, and appurtenances now or hereafter a part of the Property.

4. Borrower warrants and will defend the title to the Property against all claims and demands, subject to any encumbrances of record.

5. Upon full payment of all sums secured by this Mortgage, Lender shall discharge this Mortgage without charge to Borrower.

6. Until all sums secured by this Mortgage have been fully paid:
   a. Borrower will pay all taxes and assessments attributable to the Property which may attain priority over this Mortgage.
   b. Borrower will not demolish or remove any of the existing improvements on the Property without Lender's approval.
   c. Borrower will keep the improvements now existing or hereafter erected on the Property insured against loss by fire and any other hazards for which lender requires insurance.
   d. Borrower will not damage the Property, allow the Property to deteriorate, or commit waste. Lender or its agent may make reasonable entries upon and inspections of the Property.

7. If Borrower fails to abide by the terms of this Mortgage or defaults on the Note, Lender will have the option to require immediate payment in full of all sums secured by this Mortgage. Lender will give Borrower a notice specifying the default, the action required to cure the default, and a date by which the default must be cured.

8. If all or any part of the Property or any interest in it is sold or transferred without Lender's prior written consent, Lender may, at its option, require immediate payment in full of all sums secured by this Mortgage.

9. If any part of the Property is taken by condemnation (or conveyed in lieu of condemnation), the award or proceeds are hereby assigned and shall be paid to Lender.

By signing below, Borrower accepts and agrees to the terms and covenants contained in this Mortgage.

_____ (Borrower)   _____ (Date)

This mortgage form is based on the FNMA/FHLMC uniform single-family mortgage for Minnesota, but it has been considerably simplified.

may already have resold the property, so there's nothing left for a judgment lien to attach to.

> **Example:** John borrows $20,000 from his friend Sam. John gives Sam a promissory note. Sam knows that John owns some property that is worth at least $100,000, so he is not worried about John being able to repay. He assumes that he can always get his money out of the property.
>
> John defaults on the note and does not finish repaying Sam. When Sam tries to collect the money, he discovers that John has no bank accounts in this country, and he has sold all of his property. Sam will have a difficult time collecting any money.

By creating a lien on the property at the time of the loan, the mortgage ensures that the lender will be able to get at least some of its money back.

A mortgage should:

1. be in writing,
2. identify the parties (who must have contractual capacity),
3. identify the debt for which the mortgage acts as security and refer to the underlying promissory note,
4. give a full legal description of the mortgaged property,
5. be signed by the borrower,
6. be delivered by the borrower, and
7. be accepted by the lender.

ADDITIONAL PROVISIONS

Certain basic information should be included in every promissory note and mortgage. But most real estate loan agreements also include additional provisions governing default and transfer or encumbrance of the property.

These common additional terms generally provide extra protection for the lender. That's not surprising; when the parties work out the details of their agreement, the lender is ordinarily in a better bargaining position than the borrower. However, there are some limits on the protective provisions a lender can impose, especially on a loan secured by residential property.

ACCELERATION ON DEFAULT. Almost every real estate mortgage includes an acceleration clause.

Acceleration clause: gives lender right to demand immediate payment of entire loan amount upon default

> **This clause gives the lender the right to demand immediate payment of the entire loan amount upon the default of the borrower.**

It allows the lender to foreclose in the event the borrower defaults on any terms of the mortgage.

Acceleration is a lender's option, not an automatic event. The lender decides whether or not to accelerate, and when—after the borrower has missed one payment, or five or six. But the right to accelerate ends as soon as the borrower **cures** the default by tendering payment of the delinquent amounts, or taking whatever other action is necessary.

Cure: tendering payment of delinquent amounts or taking other required action

DUE-ON-SALE CLAUSE.

> **An alienation provision, or due-on-sale clause, calls for acceleration if the property is transferred.**

Due-on-sale clause (alienation provision): on sale, lender may demand immediate payment in full

Alienation clauses are routinely included in conventional loan agreements as a means of preventing sales by loan assumption or installment sales.

A lender can't include a provision in the loan agreement that totally prevents the borrower from selling or transferring the security property. That would be an **unreasonable restraint on alienation**. Transfer of property from one person to another is generally good for commerce, so the law protects an owner's right to freely transfer property.

However, lenders can use due-on-sale clauses to protect their interests. A due-on-sale clause provides that if the borrower sells or transfers any interest in the property without the lender's consent, the lender has the right to accelerate the loan and demand immediate payment in full.

MORTGAGE COVENANTS. A covenant is a promise to do or not do something. Mortgage covenants are promises the mortgagor (borrower) makes to the mortgagee (lender).

MORTGAGE COVENANTS

- **Covenant to pay property taxes.** If the borrower failed to pay the property taxes, the government could foreclose on its property tax lien, which has higher priority than the lender's mortgage lien. So the borrower promises to pay the taxes on time.

- **Covenant not to remove or demolish.** Destruction or removal of buildings or improvements on the mortgaged property could result in a loss in value that jeopardizes the lender's investment. Thus, the borrower promises not to remove or demolish buildings or other improvements without first securing the lender's permission.

- **Covenant to insure.** The borrower promises to carry adequate hazard insurance on the property to protect the lender from property damage due to fire or other perils.

- **Covenant of good repair.** If the property is not properly maintained, its value can decline, thus posing a risk to the lender. The borrower promises not to commit waste on the property or to otherwise permit its deterioration. The lender is allowed to make periodic inspections to be sure the borrower is keeping the property in good repair.

Mortgage covenant: a promise to do (or not do) something, e.g., pay taxes, take care of the property, etc.

If the mortgagor violates any of the mortgage covenants, the mortgagee is permitted to make use of the acceleration clause to demand the loan balance be paid in full at once.

MORTGAGE SATISFACTION OR ASSUMPTION

Once a mortgage is given on property, it must be satisfied by the mortgagor, or assumed by a new party. A mortgage is satisfied when it is paid in full. If the mortgage is assumed by a new party, the new party takes over the obligation of making the payments on the mortgage.

SATISFACTION

When a mortgage debt is paid in full, a "satisfaction of mortgage" is used to release the mortgage lien.

Mortgage satisfaction: document used to release lien when mortgage paid in full

The lender must deliver the satisfaction document to the borrower when full payment has been made. The mortgage will not be released as a lien of record until the satisfaction is recorded by the borrower.

ASSUMPTION

If a due-on-sale clause is not included in the mortgage, any real estate loan can be assumed.

Mortgage may be assumed if no due-on-sale clause

> **If a borrower sells the property to another who agrees to "assume and pay the mortgage according to its terms," the new borrower becomes primarily liable, and the original borrower retains a secondary liability in the event of default.**

Lender may permit novation

If the original borrower wishes to be relieved of any liability whatsoever, the lender may permit a substitution of liability, called novation, on approval of the new borrower's credit and financial status. Normally, the lender will expect to be compensated for the substitution in the form of an assumption fee or an upward adjustment in the existing interest rate, or both.

If a buyer purchases a property with an existing loan, but takes title "subject to" the loan instead of assuming it, he or she has no liability for payment to the lender. The seller remains primarily liable for the loan. Of course, the buyer is liable to the seller for payment.

MORTGAGE FORECLOSURE

Foreclosure: the right to force sale of property and have a debt paid out of the proceeds

The purpose of a mortgage is to give the lender the right to foreclose: to have the property sold and the debt paid out of the sale proceeds.

METHODS OF FORECLOSURE

Upon default, there are two methods under which a mortgage may be foreclosed.

> **Most mortgages in Minnesota include a *power of sale* clause. This is a clause which gives the lender the power to conduct a foreclosure and sell the mortgaged property without taking the matter to court.**

The power of sale method of foreclosure is sometimes referred to as **foreclosure by advertisement**. This is the most common method of foreclosure in Minnesota.

If a mortgage does not contain a power of sale clause, it must be foreclosed judicially. Even if the mortgage does contain a power of sale clause, the lender may still choose to foreclose judicially.

Power of sale clause: gives the lender power to sell property at a public auction without first going to court

FORECLOSURE BY ADVERTISEMENT.

> **When foreclosed under a power of sale clause, the property is advertised and then sold at a public auction held by the sheriff.**

Foreclosure by advertisement is nonjudicial

Notice that the property that is going to be sold must be advertised by published notice for six weeks prior to the sale. At least four weeks before the sale, a copy of the notice must be served on the person in possession of the property. If the property being foreclosed on is homestead property, the notice must be published and served on the person in possession at least eight weeks before the time appointed for the sale.

After the default, the borrower may still redeem the property up until the time of the sale. This is called the borrower's **equity of redemption**. The borrower redeems the property by paying all past-due installments and penalties. The loan is then reinstated and the property cannot be sold at a foreclosure auction.

Equity of redemption: a borrower's right to redeem property by paying past due amounts up until the time of sale

> **Statutory law in Minnesota also gives the borrower the right to redeem the property even after the auction. This is called *statutory redemption*.**

Statutory redemption: a borrower's right to redeem after a sheriff's auction; may last six or twelve months

Under the statute, the borrower may redeem the property for either six months or 12 months after the sale. The purchaser at the foreclosure sale is not entitled to possession of the property until the end of the statutory redemption period. A receiver may sometimes be appointed to manage the property until the end of the redemption period.

Deficiency Judgments. If the lender suspects that the sale would not cover the amount owing on the loan, it may want to seek a personal judgment against the debtor for the deficiency.

> **If the lender wants a deficiency judgment, the foreclosure must be a judicial foreclosure (through the courts).**

Nonjudicial foreclosure limits recovery to sale proceeds

If a lender forecloses nonjudicially, using a power of sale clause, its recovery is limited to the proceeds of the sale. The lender cannot bring any further action against the borrower, even if the sale proceeds do not cover the amount owing on the loan.

JUDICIAL FORECLOSURE. If a mortgage does not contain a power of sale clause, or if the lender wants to seek a deficiency judgment, the mortgage must be foreclosed judicially.

Judicial foreclosure: upon default, a lawsuit is filed by lender against borrower; required for obtaining a deficiency judgment

> **When a mortgage is foreclosed judicially, upon default, a lawsuit is filed by the lender against the borrower with the court in the county where the collateral property is located.**

When the complaint has been heard in court, in the absence of unusual circumstances, the judge will order the sale of the property to satisfy the debt. The court will appoint the sheriff or court commissioner to conduct the sale. The sale will take the form of an auction, and it is frequently referred to as a **sheriff's sale**.

The successful bidder at a sheriff's sale is awarded a sheriff's certificate of sale and will have the certificate recorded.

Judicial foreclosure involves "equitable redemption" period plus additional six- or twelve-month statutory redemption period

Between the date of the notice of default and the sheriff's sale, the borrower is entitled to redeem the property by curing the default. This is referred to as the period of **equitable redemption**. After the sale the borrower has an additional six months or 12 months to redeem the property, called the **statutory period of redemption**. (The time period is 12 months if the mortgage originated before July 1, 1967, or if the mortgage was more than ⅓ paid, or if the property contained more than 10 acres, or if the mortgagee is seeking a deficiency judgment.)

JUDICIAL FORECLOSURE

Complaint filed
Lis Pendens recorded
Court orders property sold
Notice of Sale published and posted
Sheriff's Sale
    (Period of Equitable Redemption ends)
    (Certificate of Sale issued and recorded)
Statutory Period of Redemption (six or 12 months)
Certificate of Sale becomes Sheriff's Deed

At the end of the redemption period, the recorded certificate of sale becomes a sheriff's deed, transferring the borrower's interest in the property to the person who was the successful bidder at the foreclosure sale. It is the redemption period which makes the mortgage very unappealing to many investors who, understandably, do not want to wait so long to gain title to the property. For this reason, bidders at mortgage foreclosure sales are uncommon and very often the lender acquires the rights to the property by bidding the amount owed.

After redemption period, the successful bidder takes title

> **The borrower is entitled to keep possession of the property during the redemption period. If the proceeds from the sale exceed the amount necessary to satisfy all valid liens against the property, the surplus belongs to the borrower.**

Required Notice. The lender's attorney normally records a lis pendens (notice of pending legal action), which will make the judgment of the court binding on all persons who acquire interests in or liens against the property while the foreclosure action is pending.

A notice of sale must be published and posted. To announce the sale, the judge orders a notice to be posted at the courthouse and published in a newspaper of general circulation in the county in which the property is located.

Junior Lienholders. A foreclosure sale destroys not only the borrower's interest in the property, but also the interests of any junior lienholders (those with subordinate liens).

Foreclosure sale destroys interest of junior lienholders

> **To protect junior lienholders, notice of the default and sale must be given to all junior lienholders who have recorded interests in the property.**

If the notices are not sent to a lienholder of record, that lienholder is not bound by the sale.

A junior lienholder can protect his or her interest by paying the delinquencies on the senior lien (curing the default) and adding the amount of these payments to the balance due on the junior lien, or by purchasing the property at the sale. The junior lienholder may then (if necessary) foreclose his or her own lien.

> **Example:** Smith borrows $10,000 from 1st Bank, secured by a first mortgage. Later, Smith borrows an additional $20,000 from 2nd Bank and gives 2nd Bank another mortgage (second mortgage). 1st Bank is the senior lienholder, and 2nd Bank is the junior lienholder.

If Smith defaults on 1st Bank's loan, 2nd Bank can pay off the amounts due and thus prevent 1st Bank from selling the property. The payment is added to the balance owed by Smith on 2nd Bank's loan.

As an alternative, junior lienholders may file a notice of intent to redeem. At the end of the borrower's statutory redemption period, junior lienholders are given five days in which they have the right to satisfy all prior indebtedness and thus take title to the property.

DEED IN LIEU OF FORECLOSURE

A borrower may be able to escape foreclosure by giving a deed in lieu of foreclosure.

Deed in lieu of foreclosure: borrower may choose to give deed to lender to avoid foreclosure

> **This simply means that the borrower gives the property deed to the lender, rather than going through the foreclosure process.**

This may help protect the borrower's credit and prevent the additional costs of foreclosure. The lender is not required to accept, but may be willing to accept a deed in lieu of foreclosure because it may save the lender time and expense.

Lenders may be hesitant to accept a deed in lieu of foreclosure because, unlike the foreclosure sale, this alternative does not wipe out junior liens. Thus, the lender may acquire title "subject to" other lien rights.

METHODS OF PAYING PRINCIPAL AND INTEREST

When a mortgage is given on property, the borrower is loaned a certain amount of money. This money must be paid back, usually with interest. There are several different methods of repayment and ways of calculating the interest on the loan.

Although a real estate salesperson is not a lender, it is helpful to understand the financing terms and methods. This is important for the salesperson's own understanding of the process, and also because many buyers will ask the salesperson questions about financing. Detailed financing questions should always be referred to a financial expert or a lending institution. But a salesperson may often be asked to simply explain a term or roughly describe the different options available.

STRAIGHT OR TERM

> **A straight or term loan is one in which only the interest is paid until the end of a predetermined period.**

The term of the note is usually short, such as three or five years. When the term is up, the full principal amount of the loan is due. In reality, most straight notes are not paid off at the end of the term. They are usually refinanced or renewed for a new time period. Of course, the terms of the note (such as the interest rate) are subject to change at the time of renewal.

> **Example:** Sylvio purchases some property and signs a straight note with the following terms. The loan amount is $80,000 with annual interest at 11.5%. Interest is payable every six months for a term of five years. At the end of the five years, the full principal amount of $80,000 will be due.
>
> When the five years has passed, if Sylvio does not have $80,000 to pay off the loan, he will probably refinance, either with the existing lender or a new lender.

A mortgage that secures a straight note is referred to as a straight-term mortgage, or simply a term mortgage.

FULLY AMORTIZED

Unlike the straight note, when a loan is fully amortized, the payments include both principal and interest.

> **A fully amortized loan is one that provides for complete repayment of the loan within an agreed period by means of regular payments that include a portion for principal and a portion for interest.**

As each payment is received, the appropriate amount of principal is deducted from the debt and the remainder of the payment, which represents the interest, is retained by the lender as earnings or profit. With each payment, the amount of the debt is reduced and the interest due with the next payment is recalculated based on the lower balance. The total payment remains the same throughout the term of the loan. With each new payment the loan balance is lowered, thereby reducing that portion of the payment attributed to interest and increasing that portion allocated to principal. An example is shown below.

PYMT. NO.	PRINCIPAL BALANCE	TOTAL PYMT.	INTEREST PORTION	PRINCIPAL PORTION	ENDING BALANCE
	Example: $90,000 loan @ 10¼%, 30-year term _(figures approximate)_				
1	$90,000.00	$806.49	$768.75	$37.74	$89,962.26
2	89,962.26	806.49	768.43	38.06	89,924.20
3	89,924.20	806.49	768.10	38.39	89,885.81
4	89,885.81	806.49	767.77	38.72	89,847.09
5	89,847.09	806.49	767.44	39.05	89,808.04

> **The long-term, fully amortized, fixed-rate real estate loan is the one borrowers are most familiar with and, in most cases, the type they would like to obtain when financing a home.**

This type of loan has obvious advantages for the borrower. Its repayment is spread out over a long time period (usually 30 years). This keeps the monthly payment at a manageable level, and the payment remains constant for the entire term of the debt. At the end of the period, the loan is entirely repaid.

PARTIALLY AMORTIZED (BALLOON)

Partially amortized loan: buyer makes series of interest and principal payments, and then pays final balance with one balloon payment

A partially amortized loan is similar to a fully amortized loan in that the loan calls for a series of payments that include a portion for interest and a portion that goes toward paying off the principal. However, the principal is not fully paid at the end of the loan term. A balloon payment must be made to pay off the remaining principal.

For instance, using the figures in the preceding example, a lender and a borrower might agree to calculate the loan payments as though the debt was going to be repaid over 30 years at 10¼% annual interest, but stipulate in the promissory note that the entire balance would be due and payable at the end of **five years**. The balance at the end of the fifth year would be $87,058.04, which would be the amount of the balloon payment.

> **The advantage to the borrower is that for the term of the loan, the monthly payments are dramatically lower than they would be if the debt were to be fully amortized over the five-year term. The disadvantage is the balloon payment that must be paid at the end of the term.**

Since the borrower is unlikely to have the cash available to make the balloon payment, he or she will probably refinance the loan.

ALTERNATIVE REPAYMENT PLANS

The long-term, fully amortized, fixed-rate loan was the preferred method of financing, especially for residential transactions, from the conclusion of the Great Depression in the late 1930's until the early 1980's. However, as property values and interest levels escalated to unprecedented levels by the end of the 1970's, new financing methods were devised to assure competitive yields for lenders and at the same time keep the loan payments at levels homebuyers could handle. Many exotic ideas were introduced, but two that have survived and are regularly used in today's marketplace are the adjustable rate mortgage (ARM) and the graduated payment mortgage (GPM).

GRADUATED PAYMENT. To help borrowers qualify for a loan, graduated payment plans call for lower payments in the early years of the loan.

Graduated payment loan: lower payments at the beginning, then increase gradually

> **Graduated payments are lower at the beginning and then increase for a period of five to seven years. After that, the payment amount remains the same for the rest of the loan term.**

The loan payments gradually increase in predetermined increments over the years as the borrower's income is expected to increase. Many graduated payment programs have been discontinued because of problems with high rates of default when the borrower's income did not increase as much as expected. However, a graduated repayment plan enjoys increased acceptance whenever interest rates on fixed-rate loans ascend to levels that are unacceptable to most borrowers.

ADJUSTABLE-RATE (ARM). An adjustable-rate mortgage (ARM) is a mortgage with an adjustable interest rate.

> **The lender periodically adjusts the interest rate so that it accurately reflects fluctuations in the cost of money. The rate is initially set by the cost of money at the time the loan is made.**

Adjustable-rate mortgage (ARM): interest rate adjusts at specific intervals

Once the rate has been set, it is tied to an index, such as the monthly average yield on three-year Treasury Bills. Future interest adjustments are based on the upward or downward movements of the index. When the interest rate changes, the loan payments also change to reflect a new amortization schedule.

ARM rates and payments change at specified periods, usually six months or one year. There are usually limits to the amount of rate and payment increases that can be imposed over the life of the loan. These limits are referred to as "rate caps" and "payment caps."

Adjustable-rate mortgages are popular when interest rates begin to climb, because the initial interest rate on an ARM is usually lower than on a loan with a fixed interest rate. Since the ARM shifts the risk of interest rate fluctuations to the borrower, lenders can afford to charge a lower initial rate for an ARM than they would for a fixed-rate loan.

BUDGET. A budget mortgage is a type of amortized mortgage.

Budget mortgage: payments include amounts for property taxes and insurance

> **Along with a portion of the payment going to interest and a portion to principal, the budget mortgage payment also includes amounts to cover property taxes and hazard insurance on the mortgaged property.**

Each monthly payment includes an amount that is 1/12th of the annual taxes and hazard insurance costs.

The money for taxes and insurance is placed in an escrow account (sometimes called a reserve account or impound account). When the taxes and insurance come due, the lender pays them out of this escrow account.

REVERSE ANNUITY MORTGAGE. With a regular mortgage, the lender pays you the loan amount in one lump sum. You then pay back this amount (plus interest) with regular payments. A reverse annuity mortgage is just the opposite. The lender pays you regular (usually monthly) payments. The lump sum loan amount plus interest is paid off when you die, or when the property is sold.

Reverse annuity mortgage: lender pays borrower a monthly sum plus a lump sum with interest at a future date

> **Reverse annuity mortgages have recently become popular with elderly, retired people.**

Example: Bertha is 83 years old. Her retirement income is not quite enough to live on. She does not have many other assets, but she does have a wonderful old house that is completely paid for. Bertha does not want to sell the house, because she wants to spend the rest of her life there.

Bertha gives a lender a reverse annuity mortgage. The lender pays her a lump sum every month. This amount supplements her monthly income and allows her to keep living in her house. When Bertha dies, her house will be sold. Out of the proceeds, the lender will be repaid the amount it loaned to Bertha, plus interest.

CONVENTIONAL LOANS

When property is purchased, and financing is needed, there are many different types of loans that can be made. There are conventional loans, and there is also government-sponsored financing.

Conventional loan: made by a conventional lender with no government agency involved

> A conventional loan is simply a loan made by a conventional lender, with no government agency involved.

It is helpful for a real estate agent to have a basic understanding of the different kinds of loans available and how they affect the borrower. The following chapter discusses goverment-sponsored financing programs. In this chapter, we will discuss various types of conventional loans and some common financing terminology.

PACKAGE MORTGAGE

Normally, when you think of a loan used to purchase real estate, you assume that only the real estate is used to secure the loan. However, occasionally a lender will allow personal property items to be included as part of the security for the loan. When the value of certain personal property items (such as a refrigerator or clothes washer and dryer) is added to the value of the real property, the maximum loan amount is increased.

Package mortgage: finances both real and personal property in the same loan

> By packaging real and personal property into one mortgage, the mortgagor is able to finance the personal property items over a longer period of time at the mortgage interest rate, which is generally lower than the rate charged in a personal property loan transaction.

If the mortgagor were to default on the mortgage, the personal property items would be included in any foreclosure proceeding.

A package mortgage has benefits and disadvantages. It allows the borrower to receive a larger loan, and to finance major purchases at the same rate as the mortgage. However, it also prevents the borrower from selling the personal property without the prior approval of the lender.

BLANKET MORTGAGE

Blanket mortgage: more than one piece of property serves as collateral

> **When a property owner offers more than one parcel of land as collateral for a loan, the mortgage given as secuity for the debt is called a blanket mortgage.**

This is the type of mortgage used in subdivision development.

Example: A developer purchases ten acres of land, making a 40% downpayment and financing the balance with a 60% loan. A mortgage is given to secure the debt. The developer then subdivides the land into twenty individual lots that will be offered for sale to the public. When the subdivision is complete, each of the twenty lots is subject to the lien of the original mortgage. Because one parcel has been divided into twenty, the mortgage is said to "blanket" all twenty lots.

The use of blanket mortgages is not limited to subdivisions. If a property owner offers two or more parcels of land to secure one loan (and this usually happens when the added value is necessary to support the loan amount requested) the mortgage given in return is a blanket lien. If the mortgagor were to default, a foreclosure of all properties subject to the lien would be the result.

Partial release: one or more pieces of property released from lien when blanket mortgage is partially repaid

No property subject to a blanket mortgage can be sold free of the lien of the mortgage without a release from the lender. Such a release is usually agreed upon in advance by means of a provision in the mortgage called a **partial release** clause. This clause stipulates that an individual lot will be released from the lien of the mortgage when a pre-agreed percentage of the loan has been repaid. In the example above, the partial release clause might state that a lot will be released when the mortgagor/developer has repaid 7% of the original debt. By this method the developer can sell a lot, repay the prescribed portion of the loan and deliver title, free of the mortgage lien, to the purchaser.

OPEN-END MORTGAGE

> An open-end mortgage allows the borrower to obtain further advances at a later date. The amount of any future advance is usually limited to the difference between the original loan amount and the current amount owing.

Open-end mortgage: allows a borrower to obtain additional advances in the future

Example: Garvey takes out a loan for $200,000. He has paid off a portion of the loan, and the amount currently owing is $150,000. If Garvey has an open-end mortgage, he can now obtain an additional advance of $50,000, without going through the process of obtaining a new loan and signing new documents.

Open-end mortgages usually include an an adjustable rate provision that allows the lender to raise or lower the interest rate according to the cost of money at the time the advance is requested. The open-end mortgage is most often used as a business tool by developers and farmers.

The alternative to the open-end mortgage is the **refinance**. When a property owner refinances an existing loan, he or she is obtaining a new loan. This means a credit investigation, a property appraisal, and a new promissory note and mortgage. Motives for refinancing usually involve either a desire to convert equity to cash or to reduce a burdensome monthly payment by taking advantage of the lower interest rates in an improved mortgage market.

Refinance: obtaining a new loan to pay off existing loan

One of the drawbacks to the refinance is that since a new mortgage is signed and recorded at the time of the refinance, its priority in relation to other liens is established at this later date. Liens recorded after the original mortgage but before the mortgage of the refinance would have a higher priority, thus increasing the lender's risk. Too much risk could cause the lender to refuse the loan.

PURCHASE MONEY MORTGAGE

When a borrower uses loan proceeds to buy real estate, and the purchased property serves as collateral for the loan, the loan is often called a purchase money mortgage. A purchase money mortgage is distinguished from a mortgage given on property that the borrower already owns, where the borrower uses the loan proceeds for repairs, improvements, or anything else besides buying the property itself.

Purchase money mortgage: proceeds are used to buy the collateral real estate

In Minnesota, the term "purchase money mortgage" is frequently used in a narrower sense, to refer to a mortgage that a buyer gives to a seller to secure payment of the purchase price of the property. This type of transaction is also called seller financing; the seller extends credit to the buyer, accepting a downpayment and a mortgage instead of immediate payment of the full purchase price. The mortgage is like any other mortgage, except that the mortgagee is the seller rather than an institutional lender.

INSURED CONVENTIONAL LOAN

A conventional loan is a loan made by a conventional lender. This means that no government financing is involved. If a loan is insured by the Federal Housing Administration (FHA) or guaranteed by the Veterans Administration (VA) or any other government agency (including state or city agencies), it is not a conventional loan.

When a conventional loan has a loan-to-value ratio over 80%, the borrower will usually be required to purchase private mortgage insurance. If the borrower defaults and the foreclosure sale proceeds are not enough to pay off the full amount owed to the lender, the insurance will protect the lender against loss. Since conventional loans are not subject to such strict government regulations as FHA and VA loans, insured conventional loans may have more flexible terms.

MISCELLANEOUS MORTGAGE TERMS

It is important for a real estate agent to be well informed and knowledgeable about all aspects of the real estate business. The more you know, the better able you are to help your clients. When discussing financing, it will be helpful to understand some of the following commonly used terms.

LOAN-TO-VALUE RATIO

Loan-to-value ratio: the ratio of the loan amount (principal) to the value (sales price or appraisal amount)

> **The loan-to-value ratio is the ratio of the loan amount (the principal) to the value of the property. The value of the property used for loan-to-value ratios is the sales price or the appraisal amount, whichever is less.**

Example: The property is worth $100,000, and the lender's maximum loan-to-value ratio is 80%. The maximum loan available is 80% of $100,000, or $80,000.

In the example above, if the appraised value was $100,000 but the purchase price was $90,000, the maximan loan amount would be based on the lower figure—the purchase price.

Example: $90,000
× 80%
$72,000

Most lenders feel that the more equity a borrower has in the property, the less likely the borrower is to default and lose the property through foreclosure. Therefore, the lower the loan-to-value ratio, the safer the loan is considered.

Example: The property is worth $100,000. The purchaser borrows $75,000. The loan-to-value ratio is only 75%. This is considered a safer loan than one with a loan-to-value ratio of 90%, because the buyer has more equity in the property ($25,000 instead of only $10,000).

The loan-to-value ratio on most conventional loans is usually 80% or less. A higher loan-to-value ratio will typically require some form of mortgage guarantee or default insurance.

EQUITY

Equity is the difference between the value of a piece of property and the charges against it.

Equity: the difference between the value of a piece of property and the charges against it

For example, if a property is worth $100,000 and the owner owes $80,000 towards the purchase price, her equity in the property is $20,000. If the property has a long-term mortgage, each payment decreases the debt and increases the owner's equity. An owner's equity will also increase if the property appreciates in value.

Market Value
- Total Debt
Equity

Example: Ten years ago, Thorpe purchased his house for $96,000. He borrowed $76,800 and gave the lender a mortgage. At that point, his equity in the property was

$19,200. Now Thorpe's house is worth $125,000. Thorpe has also reduced the principal debt to approximately $72,000. Thorpe's equity in the property is now $53,000. ($125,000 − $72,000 = $53,000)

SUBORDINATION

Lien priority is extremely important to every lender. The higher the lender's priority, the more likely that lender is to recover all (or most) of the debt if any lienholder forecloses.

> The priority of a mortgage depends on the date it was recorded. A mortgage has lower priority than any voluntary liens on the same property that were recorded earlier, and higher priority than any that were recorded later.

Subordination: acceptance of a lower lien priority

But a lender can agree to accept a lower priority position than the one established by the recording date. The lender may **subordinate** its mortgage to another mortgage that was (or will be) recorded later. The earlier mortgage that takes on a lower priority is called a **subordinated** mortgage. The later mortgage that is given a higher priority is called the **subordinating** mortgage.

Subordination is most common when a seller carries back a purchase money mortgage for part of the purchase price. The borrower/buyer intends to improve the security property, but to do so, he or she will have to obtain a construction loan. Construction lenders generally insist on having first lien position (the highest priority). As a result, the borrower won't be able to get the construction loan unless the seller is willing to subordinate the purchase loan.

A subordination clause can be included in the earlier mortgage, or a separate subordination agreement may be drawn up. The provision may subordinate the mortgage to a loan that has already been arranged, or to one that the borrower intends to apply for. Because subordination can have a drastic effect on the strength of a lender's security, any subordination provision must be drafted or carefully reviewed by a competent lawyer.

When the other loan hasn't been arranged yet, the provision should establish strict standards for the quality and purpose of the other loan. Otherwise, the borrower can subordinate the earlier mortgage to any kind of loan and do anything he or she wants with the money. That can make the subordinated lender's security worthless.

DEED OF TRUST

The deed of trust, also called a trust deed, is a type of security device not used in Minnesota, but very popular in many Western states. In some states, mortgages do not contain a power of sale clause and must be foreclosed judicially. In order to foreclose non-judicially, a deed of trust must be used.

The deed of trust is a three-party device. The parties to a trust deed are the trustor (borrower), the beneficiary (lender) and the trustee (neutral third party). The deed of trust conveys naked title to the trustee throughout the period of indebtedness. During this period, physical possession of the trust deed remains with the lender, although the borrower retains possession of the property.

When the debt is paid in full, the lender directs the trustee to reconvey the title to the borrower. The trustee releases the lien of the trust deed by signing and recording a deed of reconveyance. When a lender fails to release a borrower in a timely manner, the lender may be liable to the borrower in an action for damages.

FORECLOSURE. A power of sale clause is found in every deed of trust. Under this clause, a deed of trust is foreclosed just like a mortgage containing a power of sale clause, except that it is the trustee who is granted the power to sell the property upon default.

MINNESOTA USURY LAW

Usury is charging interest in excess of the rate allowed by law.

Usury: charging interest rates higher than allowed by law

Minnesota usury regulations and the usury rate are set by the commissioner of banking. The usury regulations apply to all real estate loans except:

- FHA/VA loans,
- loans to corporations, and
- loans in excess of $100,000.

CHAPTER SUMMARY

1. A contract for deed is a form of seller financing. The seller retains legal title, but the buyer has the right of possession. A mortgage is usually held by a bank or other lending institution. The borrower holds title to the property and the lender is merely given a lien against the property.

2. A promissory note is a written promise to repay a debt. A promissory note must contain all of the essential elements of a valid contract.

3. A mortgage is a contract that makes real property collateral for a loan. It creates a lien on the property. If the borrower doesn't repay as agreed in the promissory note, the mortgage gives the lender the right to foreclose on the property.

4. When a mortgage is paid in full, a "satisfaction of mortgage" is used to release the mortgage lien. Rather than paying off the mortgage, a borrower may sell the property to another who assumes the debt and agrees to pay the mortgage according to its terms.

5. Most mortgage foreclosures in Minnesota are done under a power of sale clause, which allows foreclosure by advertisement. The lender may conduct a foreclosure and sell the mortgaged property without taking the matter to court. If a mortgage does not contain a power of sale clause, or if the lender is seeking a deficiency judgment, the mortgage must be foreclosed judicially.

6. A straight or term note is a promissory note for a loan in which payments are made on the interest only. With an amortized note, payments include both principal and interest. If a note is fully amortized, the entire principal amount and all interest will be paid off within the agreed loan period.

7. With a standard loan, the interest rate and the amount of the payment remain the same throughout the term of the loan. However, there are several alternative financing plans such as graduated payment loans, adjustable-rate mortgages (ARMs), and reverse annuity mortgages.

8. There are several different types of loans available, including regular conventional loans, package loans, blanket mortgages, and open-end mortgages.

CHAPTER 7—GLOSSARY REVIEW

A. amortized loan
B. term loan
C. equitable redemption
D. statutory redemption
E. balloon
F. contract for deed
G. package mortgage
H. blanket mortgage

I. alienation clause
J. acceleration clause
K. equity
L. subordination
M. purchase money mortgage
N. adjustable-rate mortgage
O. graduated payment loan
P. defeasance clause

1. The right of a borrower to force a lender to return his property upon repayment of a defaulted loan plus costs after a foreclosure sale is known as _statutory redemption_

2. A mortgage pledging personal property as well as real property as security for a debt is a _package mortgage_

3. The clause that appears in both the note and the mortgage which allows a lender to demand immediate payment of the entire debt if default occurs is known as an _acceleration clause_

4. A loan that is repaid in one single lump sum at the end of the loan's life is called a "straight loan" or _term loan_

5. A loan in which payments are scheduled so the entire principal balance is repaid by the maturity date is known as an _amortized loan_

6. A final payment that is larger than preceding payments is known as a _balloon_ payment.

7. When more than one property is pledged as security for a single loan, the mortgage is known as a _blanket mortgage_

8. A mortgage given by the purchaser to the seller in partial payment for the property is known as a _____. _purchase money mortgage_

9. The difference between a property's market value and the debts against it is known as _equity_

10. A loan that allows a borrower to make smaller payments initially and to increase their size gradually over time is a _graduated payment loan_.

11. The clause that entitles a lender to accelerate the loan if it is assumed without the lender's approval is an _alienation clause_

CHAPTER 7—REVIEW EXAM

1. Which terms are closest in meaning?

   a) Mortgagor - lender
   b) Mortgagee - borrower
   c) Lender - mortgagee
   d) Borrower - lender

2. Subordination means:

   a) to pay off a loan sooner than required.
   b) to waive priority of claim to another lender.
   c) to sell a loan in the secondary mortgage market.
   d) renegotiating for a lower interest rate on a mortgage.

3. The instrument used to pledge real property as security for a loan is a:

   a) bill of sale.
   b) chattel agreement.
   c) Torrens certificate of title.
   d) mortgage.

4. The right of the mortgagor to reclaim his or her property after it has been foreclosed and sold is the:

   a) right of first refusal.
   b) equitable right of redemption.
   c) riparian right.
   d) statutory right of redemption.

5. A mortgagor who wished to give up title rather than face foreclosure would:

   a) record a notice of default.
   b) grant the mortgagee a deed in lieu of foreclosure.
   c) file a surplus money action.
   d) file a deficiency judgment.

6. A mortgagor pledges both real and personal property to secure a:

   a) blanket loan.
   b) budget loan.
   c) open-end loan.
   d) package loan.

7. A type of mortgage in which more than one property is used as security and that contains a "partial release" clause is a:

   a) blanket loan.
   b) package loan.
   c) purchase money mortgage.
   d) swing loan.

8. A loan which allows the borrower to later obtain additional funds by borrowing up to the amount of the original loan is a:

   a) wraparound loan.
   b) package loan.
   c) open-end loan.
   d) blanket loan.

9. When a buyer purchases a home using a purchase money mortgage, the seller:

   a) retains title.
   b) gets all cash.
   c) becomes the mortgagee.
   d) becomes the mortgagor.

10. An owner's equity in his or her property is best described as:

   a) the difference between market value and the amount owed.
   b) the difference between original purchase price and the amount owed.
   c) the current market value of the property.
   d) the total outstanding debt against the property.

11. John is in default on his mortgage. The original loan was $80,000. The current balance is $50,000. How long will John's statutory redemption period be?

   a) Six months
   b) 12 months
   c) As long as the lender allows
   d) 60 days

12. When a borrower wishes to obtain a loan in excess of 80% of the property value the lender is likely to require:

   a) owner's title insurance.
   b) homeowner's insurance.
   c) mortgage default insurance.
   d) certificate of hazard insurance.

13. The clause that appears in both the promissory note and mortgage and allows the lender to call the balance due and payable in full upon default is known as the:

   a) due-on-sale clause.
   b) satisfaction clause.
   c) acceleration clause.
   d) alienation clause.

14. The figure used by the lender in determining the maximum loan it will make is the:

   a) appraised value or purchase price, whichever is less.
   b) appraised value.
   c) purchase price.
   d) assessed value.

15. Charging an interest rate that exceeds the legal maximum ceiling is known as:

   a) defeasance.
   b) usury.
   c) subordination.
   d) a violation of Regulation Z.

16. Court-supervised foreclosure resulting from a lender's lawsuit is known as:

   a) cancellation.
   b) strict foreclosure.
   c) foreclosure by advertisement.
   d) judicial foreclosure.

17. The document that must be recorded to give notice that a mortgage has been paid in full is:

   a) the defeasance.
   b) the subordination agreement.
   c) the note.
   d) the statisfaction.

18. A form of financing in which the seller retains title but the buyer has right of possession is:

   a) a purchase money mortgage.
   b) an option.
   c) a contract for deed.
   d) a participation loan.

19. Herman gave a purchase money mortgage to Susan when he purchased her home. Herman is now in default. Which of the following is Susan's remedy?

   a) Cancellation of the note
   b) Foreclosure of the contract for deed
   c) Cancellation of the mortgage
   d) Foreclosure of the mortgage

20. Excess proceeds from the foreclosure public auction belong to:

   a) the mortgagee.
   b) the mortgagor.
   c) the auctioneer.
   d) the county's general fund.

21. The clause in a mortgage that requires the loan to be repaid when the property is sold is:

   a) the acceleration clause.
   b) the defeasance clause.
   c) the subordination clause.
   d) the alienation clause.

22. A young couple is interested in buying a home, but they have recently started new jobs. They expect their income to increase dramatically over the next few years. Which mortgage would be best for them?

   a) A reverse annuity mortgage
   b) A renegotiable-rate mortgage
   c) A graduated payment mortgage
   d) An adjustable-rate mortgage

23. A mortgage that is tied to an ecomonic index and may have interest rate or payment caps is:

   a) a renegotiable rate mortgage.
   b) a partially amortized mortgage.
   c) an adjustable-rate mortgage.
   d) a variable payment mortgage.

24. Which of the following is NOT true of a mortgage?

   a) The mortgagor holds a lien.
   b) The mortgagor has title.
   c) The promissory note is secured by the mortgage.
   d) The mortgage pledges the property as security.

25. Which of the following is most like a trust deed?

   a) Mortgage
   b) Contract for deed
   c) Warranty deed
   d) Quitclaim deed

26. First National Savings and Loan has begun foreclosure by action on a defaulted mortgage. The lender had to foreclose in this way because the mortgage did not include:

a) an acceleration clause.
b) an alienation clause.
c) a defeasance clause.
d) a power of sale clause.

27. The right of the mortgagor to cure the default and stop foreclosure proceedings is called:

a) statutory redemption.
b) deed in lieu of foreclosure.
c) redemption by action.
d) equitable redemption.

CHAPTER 7—GLOSSARY REVIEW KEY

1.	D		7.	H
2.	G		8.	M
3.	J		9.	K
4.	B		10.	O
5.	A		11.	I
6.	E			

CHAPTER 7—REVIEW EXAM KEY

1. c) The lender is the mortgagee; the borrower is the mortgagor.

2. b) In a subordination, the first mortgagee agrees to become the second mortgagee.

3. d) The document by which real property is pledged as security or collateral for a debt is the mortgage.

4. d) Statutory redemption occurs *after* the sale; equitable redemption occurs *before* the sale.

5. b) A deed in lieu of foreclosure stops the foreclosure process.

6. d) A package mortgage pledges both real estate and personal property.

7. a) A blanket mortgage covers two or more parcels of real estate.

8. c) An open-end loan is like a line of credit. The mortgagor may borrow up to a predetermined limit.

9. c) In a purchase money mortgage, the buyer (grantee) is the borrower (mortgagor) and the seller (grantor) is the lender (mortgagee).

10. a) Today's value minus today's debt equals today's equity.

11. b) It is 12 months in this case, because the balance has been reduced by more than one third of the original amount.

12. c) Conventional mortgages with a loan-to-value ratio of more than 80% typically require private mortgage default insurance.

13. c) The acceleration clause allows the lender to "call the note" upon default.

14. a) Loan-to-value ratio is based upon the purchase price or the appraised value, whichever is *less*.

15. b) A loan in which the rate exceeds the legal ceiling is said to be "usurious."

16. d) If the court supervises a lender's lawsuit, it is a judicial foreclosure (foreclosure by action).

17. d) The document is called a "satisfaction" or a "release."

18. c) The seller retains legal title under a contract for deed; the buyer obtains equitable title.

19. d) A purchase money mortgage is foreclosed in the same way as any other type of mortgage.

20.   b) The mortgagor receives excess proceeds. If the sale proceeds are insufficient to satisfy the debt, the lender may claim a deficiency judgment.

21.   d) The alienation clause is also known as the due-on-sale clause.

22.   c) The graduated payment mortgage allows the borrowers to make lower payments in the beginning and increase them as their earning power increases.

23.   c) An adjustable-rate mortgage (ARM) has a rate which is subject to change based upon a predetermined economic index.

24.   a) The mortgagor holds title; the mortgagee holds a lien.

25.   a) A trust deed (deed of trust) is a financing instrument used in many states (not in Minnesota, however).

26.   d) If the mortgage had included a power of sale clause, the lender could have foreclosed by advertisement.

27.   d) Equitable redemption is the right to redeem *before* the sale; statutory redemption is the right to redeem *after* the sale.

Chapter 8

INFLUENCES ON REAL ESTATE FINANCE

OUTLINE

I. Government Programs
   A. Federal Housing Administration (FHA) Insurance
   B. Veterans Administration (VA) Guaranty
   C. Farmer's Home Administration (FmHA)

II. Secondary Mortgage Market
   A. Federal National Mortgage Association (FNMA)
   B. Government National Mortgage Association (GNMA)
   C. Federal Home Loan Mortgage Corporation (FHLMC)

III. Discount Points

IV. Truth in Lending Act (Regulation Z)
   A. Disclosure requirements
   B. Advertising requirements

V. Real Estate Settlement Procedures Act (RESPA)

VI. Appraisal
   A. Value defined
       1. how value is created
       2. how value in exchange is created
   B. Principles of value
   C. Appraisal process
   D. Market data approach to value
       1. elements of comparison
       2. comparable sale must have been at arm's length

    E. Cost approach to value
        1. Replacement cost methods
        2. Depreciation
    F. Income approach to value
        1. contract rent vs. economic rent
        2. operating expenses
        3. capitalization
        4. gross rent multipliers
    G. Correlation and final estimate of value

KEY TERMS

FHA	HUD
MIP	escape clause
prepayment penalty	secondary financing
reserves	VA
VA guaranty amount	certificate of eligibility
certificate of reasonable value	assumption
funding fee	loan origination fee
discount points	FmHA
secondary mortgage market	primary mortgage market
FNMA	GNMA
FHLMC	Truth in Lending Act
finance charge	annual percentage rate
Regulation Z	RESPA
settlement statement	utility value
value in exchange	arm's length transaction
principle of substitution	highest and best use
supply and demand	principle of change
integration	cost approach
square foot method	unit-in-place method
quantity survey method	depreciation
deferred maintenance	equilibrium
disintegration	principle of contribution
principle of conformity	regression
progression	principle of anticipation
correlation	functional obsolescence
economic obsolescence	economic life
effective gross income	capitalization
gross rent multiplier	

CHAPTER OVERVIEW

Chapter 7 presented an overview of mortgages and conventional loans. This chapter looks at a variety of other aspects of real estate finance. It begins with a discussion of the government programs that provide alternatives to conventional loans—the FHA, VA, and FmHA programs. Next, it examines the role of the secondary mortgage market. It also explains some important federal regulations that residential lenders are required to comply with, the Truth in Lending Act and the Real Estate Settlement Procedures Act. The last section of the chapter focuses on appraisal, the expert valuation of real estate. A property's appraised value is an essential consideration in any lender's decision on whether or not to make a particular mortgage loan.

GOVERNMENT PROGRAMS

There are several government agencies that sponsor financing programs. These programs are geared towards middle- to low-income borrowers or special groups of people (such as veterans).

FEDERAL HOUSING ADMINISTRATION (FHA)

The Federal Housing Administration, or the FHA, was created by Congress in 1934 as part of the National Housing Act. The purpose of the act, and of the FHA, was to generate new jobs through increased construction activity, to exert a stabilizing influence on the mortgage market and to promote the financing, repair, improvement and sale of real estate nationwide.

FHA: the Federal Housing Administration; its primary function is to insure residential loans

> Today, the FHA is part of the Department of Housing and Urban Development (HUD); its primary function is to insure loans.

Approved lenders are insured against losses caused by borrower defaults on FHA-insured loans. The FHA does not build homes or make loans.

INSURER. The FHA is actually a giant federal insurance agency. Its insurance program is called the **Mutual Mortgage Insurance Plan**. Under the plan, lenders who have been approved by the FHA to make insured loans either submit applications from prospective borrowers to the local FHA office for approval or, if authorized by the FHA to do so, perform the underwriting functions themselves (e.g., review of appraisal, mortgage credit examination, etc.). Lenders who are authorized by the FHA to fully underwrite their own FHA loan applications are called direct endorsers.

As the insurer, the FHA incurs full liability for losses resulting from default and property foreclosure. In turn, the FHA regulates many of the conditions of the loan. FHA regulations have the force and effect of law; these regulations and FHA procedures and practices have done much to shape the face of the real estate lending industry today.

FHA loans have a number of features that distinguish them from conventional loans. The most significant differences are outlined below.

THE MIP.

MIP: the insurance premium paid to the FHA when taking out an FHA-insured loan

> **The feature that distinguishes FHA mortgage payments from conventional and VA mortgage payments is inclusion of the mutual mortgage insurance premium, more popularly referred to as the MMI or the mortgage insurance premium (MIP).**

For most FHA programs, the FHA mutual mortgage insurance premium is a one-time premium. It may be paid in cash at closing or financed over the term of the loan. The amount of the premium is 3.8% of the mortgage amount, regardless of whether it is paid in cash or financed. The premium will be refunded by HUD to the extent it is unearned when the loan is paid off early. In addition, an annual premium of 0.5% of the principal balance is charged to the borrower. This additional premium is charged for the first five, eight, or ten years of the loan, depending upon the loan-to-value ratio.

Example:

$100,000	Base loan amount
+ 3,800	Upfront MIP (3.8%)
$103,800	Loan with MIP
$100,000	Base loan amount
× .005	
$500	Annual premium
÷ 12	
$41.67	Monthly MIP

872.81   Monthly P&I at 9.5%
+ 41.67   Monthly MIP
$914.48   Monthly P&I and MIP

Regardless of the size of the downpayment, mortgage insurance is required on all FHA loans. (Conventional loans usually do not call for mortgage insurance unless the loan-to-value ratio exceeds 80%.)

HIGHER LOAN-TO-VALUE RATIO.

> **One important advantage of an FHA loan over a conventional loan is that downpayment requirements are substantially smaller.**

Downpayments for FHA loans are often less than 5%, compared to the 20% typically required for a conventional loan. However, because the FHA program is aimed at the low- to middle-income homebuyer, there is a statutory maximum loan amount. The maximum varies from one area to another, depending on the cost of housing in each area. In the highest cost areas in Minnesota, the maximum FHA loan amount is $107,600 for a single-family residence.

INTEREST RATES. The FHA does not set maximum interest rates for insured loans or limit the payment of loan discount points by the borrower. Interest rates on FHA-insured loans are freely negotiable, and therefore are determined by market trends in the financing industry. Since the interest rate is not limited, it is sometimes referred to as a "floating rate."

In addition, interest rates on FHA loans are exempt from the state usury regulations. So an interest rate that might be considered usurious on a conventional loan could be allowed on an FHA loan.

ESCAPE CLAUSE. Whenever a sales contract is signed by a purchaser prior to the receipt of an FHA appraisal, a buyer's escape clause must be included. This clause provides that the purchaser may terminate the contract if: 1) the agreed purchase price is significantly above the appraised value, or 2) the purchaser does not qualify for the loan financially.

ASSUMPTION. All FHA loans originated before December 15, 1989 can be assumed without lender approval if the property is sold again. Many conventional mortgages contain an **alienation** or **due-on-sale clause**, which grants the lender the right to demand that the loan be paid in full in the event of sale, or to approve the transfer and assumption of the loan by the new buyer. All FHA loans are assumable, but those originated on or after December 15, 1989, require lender approval of the new buyer who is assuming the loan.

NO PREPAYMENT PENALTY. Many conventional loans contain prepayment provisions that impose charges if the borrower pays off the loan within the first few years of its term. These charges can be quite substantial. FHA and VA loans do not contain prepayment penalties; they may be paid off at any time without additional charges. The borrower is required, however, to give a full 30-day notice of intent to prepay the loan. Failure to do so could result in as much as a two-month interest penalty.

SECONDARY FINANCING. The FHA minimum downpayment for a particular loan must be paid by the borrower in cash. The buyer may not use secondary financing from the seller or another lender to borrow any portion of the minimum downpayment.

FHA LOAN PROGRAMS

The FHA has several different programs. Here is a brief list of the ones most likely to interest typical homebuyers:

- **Section 203b**—Insures loans for the purchase or refinancing of single-family homes and residential duplexes, triplexes, and fourplexes. This is the standard FHA-insured loan, accounting for almost 75% of all FHA loans.

- **Section 203b(2)**—Insures loans for the purchase of single-family homes by veterans. (Not the same as a VA-guaranteed loan.)

- **Section 221d(2)**—Insures loans for the purchase or rehabilitation of low-income housing.

- **Section 234c**—Insures loans for the purchase or refinancing of condominium units.

- **Section 245**—Insurance for graduated payment mortgages (GPMs) and growth equity mortgages (GEMs).

- **Section 251**—Insurance for adjustable-rate mortgages (ARMs), used in conjunction with the 203b program or 234c program. The loan term must be 30 years.

FHA programs are generally open to all borrowers who intend to occupy the property being financed.

The FHA used to insure loans for investment property as well as owner-occupied property, but investor loans were eliminated from nearly all FHA programs in 1989. However, an investor loan that was made before the cutoff date can still be assumed.

VA-GUARANTEED LOANS

After World War II, Congress passed legislation to aid veterans returning to mainstream living. Part of this legislation was meant to help veterans buy homes by guaranteeing the repayment of a portion of first mortgages made to veterans. The guaranteed loan program is run by the Veterans Administration.

CHARACTERISTICS OF VA-GUARANTEED LOANS

The Veterans Administration guarantees repayment of certain residential loans made to eligible veterans. VA loans are available to help finance the purchase of single-family homes or multiple-family residences containing up to four units.

VA: the Veterans Administration; it guarantees loans made to eligible veterans

The VA guaranty protects the lender against loss on loans given to qualified veterans or their dependents. Only a portion of the loan is actually guaranteed by the VA. The maximum guaranty amount has been increased over the years, and is based on the amount of the loan.

NO DOWNPAYMENT.

Unlike most loans, a VA loan may be obtained with no downpayment. In other words, a loan-to-value ratio of 100% is allowed. The loan can be for 100% of the value of the property.

LOW INTEREST RATE. The interest rate on VA loans may not exceed the maximum allowable rate determined by the Veterans Administration. The maximum VA rate is normally below the prevailing market rate for conventional loans.

CERTIFICATES. Before a loan will be guaranteed by the VA, two certificates are required. The first is a **certificate of eligibility**, which establishes that the veteran is entitled to a VA loan. The second is a **certificate of reasonable value (CRV)**. The CRV establishes the value of the property. The amount of the loan that can be guaranteed is based on the CRV. If the property is selling for more than the appraised value, the veteran may choose to pay more. However, the amount guaranteed by the VA is based on the CRV. Anything above the CRV value must be paid directly by the veteran (for instance, as part of the downpayment).

> **Example:** John is a veteran who is eligible for a VA loan. The property has been appraised and a CRV issued in the amount of $110,000. Unfortunately, the property is priced at $115,000 and the seller refuses to take less. John really wants this property and decides to go ahead and pay $115,000. The extra $5,000 will have to come directly out of his pocket, or from secondary financing.

ESCAPE CLAUSE. Whenever a sales contract is signed by a purchaser prior to the receipt of a VA certificate of reasonable value, a buyer's escape clause must be included. This clause provides that the purchaser may terminate the contract if the agreed purchase price is significantly above the appraised value.

OWNER-OCCUPIED.

All VA-guaranteed loans must be for owner-occupied property. There are no investor loans guaranteed by the VA.

If the property is a single-family dwelling, the veteran must intend to occupy it as his or her residence. If the property is a multiple-family dwelling, the veteran must occupy one of the units.

PREPAYMENT AND ASSUMPTION. VA loans contain no prepayment penalties. Although VA loans are assumable, a complete credit check of the assumptor (the person assuming the loan) is required prior to the assumption of any VA loan made after March 1, 1988.

FUNDING FEE. VA loans have no mortgage insurance (neither private mortgage insurance nor FHA-style mutual mortgage insurance). However, a funding fee is charged.

The standard funding fee is 1.25% of the loan amount. Depending on the amount of the downpayment, there may be a reduced funding fee for purchase or construction loans. When the downpayment is 5% or more, but less than 10%, the funding fee is reduced to 0.75%. When a downpayment of 10% or more is paid, the funding fee is reduced to only 0.5%. All refinances require the standard funding fee of 1.25%.

LOAN ORIGINATION FEE. With VA loans, there is also a loan origination fee of 1%. The funding fee may be financed, but the 1% loan fee must be paid in cash at closing.

DISCOUNT POINTS. Any discount points are paid by the seller. The borrower is not allowed to pay discount points with a VA loan.

SECONDARY FINANCING. Secondary financing is permitted in conjunction with most VA loans, but the purchaser must qualify to make all mortgage payments, and full disclosure is required.

ELIGIBILITY

Eligibility for VA loans is based on the length of continuous active service in the U.S. armed forces. The minimum requirement varies depending upon when the veteran served.

90 days continuous active duty, any part of which occurred:

1. September 16, 1940 through July 25, 1947 (WWII)
2. June 27, 1950 through January 31, 1955 (Korea)
3. August 5, 1964 through May 7, 1975 (Vietnam)
4. August 2, 1990 through the end of the Persian Gulf War.*

181 days continuous active duty, any part of which occurred:

1. July 26, 1947 through June 26, 1950
2. February 1, 1955 through August 4, 1964
3. May 8, 1975 through September 7, 1980

24 months continuous active duty for veterans who enlisted after September 7, 1980, and before August 2, 1990, except:

1. individuals discharged for disability;
2. individuals discharged for hardship;
3. any case in which it is established that the person is suffering from a service-connected disability not the result of willful misconduct and not incurred during a period of unauthorized absence.

---

*The VA had not yet established a termination date when this book was printed.

Veterans who are discharged for hardship or for a nonservice-connected disability are eligible only if they have served a minimum of 181 days. There is no minimum active duty service requirement for veterans discharged for a service-connected disability.

Persons who have served six months active duty training only are not eligible. There is also no eligibility for persons who received a dishonorable discharge.

VA LOAN AMOUNTS

> There is no maximum VA loan amount, except for the requirement that the loan may not exceed the appraised value of the property (as determined by the CRV) or the sales price, whichever is less.

However, most (though not all) lenders require that the VA guaranty cover at least 25% of the loan. Under the current guaranty system, lenders are assured that between the VA guaranty and the proceeds from a foreclosure sale, there is little danger of losing money when a veteran borrower defaults. Thus as a practical matter, a vet with an entitlement of $36,000 will find it difficult to obtain a VA loan greater than $144,000 ($144,000 × 25% = $36,000).

Now that the maximum guaranty may go as high as $46,000, most lenders will make larger VA loans, but probably not over $184,000 ($184,000 × 25% = $46,000). Note that while the $184,000 maximum will be observed by the majority of lenders, there is no maximum set by the VA itself, and some lenders may be willing to make even larger VA loans.

VA allows secondary financing under certain conditions

If a downpayment is used in connection with a VA loan, VA regulations permit a buyer to finance part or all of the downpayment (secondary financing) if the following conditions are met:

1) the total of all financing does not exceed the reasonable value of the property;
2) the buyer's income is sufficient to qualify based on the payments required for both loans;
3) there are no more stringent conditions connected with the second mortgage than apply to the VA first mortgage (such as a prepayment penalty).

FARMER'S HOME ADMINISTRATION (FmHA)

The Farmer's Home Administration is a federal agency within the Department of Agriculture. It provides or assists in providing credit to farmers and others in rural areas where reasonable financing from private sources is not available.

FmHA has two types of loan programs. A loan may be made and serviced by a private lender but is guaranteed for a specified percentage by the FmHA. This is called a guaranteed loan. There are also insured loans that are originated and serviced directly by the FmHA. To be eligible for an FmHA loan, a borrower must be able to show that he or she could not obtain financing somewhere else. Discounts or points are not allowed with FmHA loans.

FmHA: Farmer's Home Administration; provides credit to farmers who cannot obtain financing from private sources

SECONDARY MORTGAGE MARKET

The **primary** or **local market** is the ground-level money market—the one that is most familiar to the public. It is the market where personal, automobile, business and mortgage loans are arranged between the borrower and the lender.

> The national or secondary market consists of private investors and government-sponsored agencies that buy and sell real estate mortgages.

Secondary market: the national real estate finance market, where investors buy and sell real estate loans

The government regulates the mortgage market through these agencies.

The amount of funds available in the primary market depends a great deal on the existence of the secondary market. An individual lender may have either an excess or a shortage of funds to loan out, depending on the conditions of the local economy. Buying and selling mortgages in the secondary market helps to balance out the excess or shortage by transferring funds from areas where there is an excess to areas where there is a shortage.

A real estate loan is essentially an investment, just like stocks or bonds. The lender commits its funds to making a loan in the expectation that the money will generate a return in the form of interest payments. Real estate loans can be bought and sold just like other investments. The value of the loan is influenced by the rate of return on the loan compared to the market rate of return, as well as the degree of risk associated with the loan (the likelihood of default).

FUNCTIONS OF THE SECONDARY MARKET

> **The secondary mortgage market serves two vital functions: it promotes investments in real estate by making funds available for real estate loans, and it provides a measure of stability in the primary market by moderating the adverse effects of real estate cycles.**

The effect the secondary market has on the primary market can be seen by taking a brief look at the flow of mortgage funds:

1. Mortgage funds are given to the homebuyer by a lending institution;
2. That mortgage is then sold by the lender to a secondary agency;
3. The secondary agency may in turn sell the mortgage to other investors in the form of mortgage-backed securities (a debt obligation with mortgages as collateral).

As mortgage-backed securities are sold by the secondary agency, more funds become available to that agency for the purchase of new mortgages from the primary market. As more mortgages are purchased from the primary market, more funds become available for lenders to pass on to borrowers. Were it not for the secondary market, a scarcity of money at the local level would be crippling; real estate activity would slow drastically and the entire community would suffer.

The secondary market is able to function as it does because of standardized underwriting criteria. Underwriting standards are used to qualify the borrower and the property, and include such items as loan-to-value ratios and income-to-expense ratios. Each mortgage issued by each individual lender must conform to the secondary market's **underwriting standards** or it will not be purchased on the secondary market. These standards assure a uniform quality control that inspires confidence in the purchasers of the mortgage-backed securities. The purchasers know that the mortgages backing the securities must be of a minimum quality, which lessens the risk of investing in properties that they cannot view or assess for themselves.

> **The existence of a secondary market has a stabilizing effect on local mortgage markets. It represents a medium for the exchange of funds and mortgages between investors from money surplus areas and those from money shortage areas.**

Because of the secondary market, investors are assured that even in times of inadequate funds, they can commit themselves to long-term real estate loans and still be able to liquidate them when necessary through the secondary market.

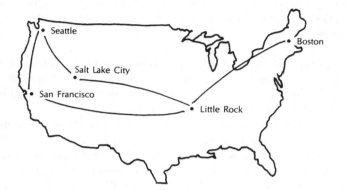

A shortage of money in one region of the country can be offset by transferring surplus monies from other regions.

The federal government has helped to create a permanent secondary mortgage market. While private investors (e.g., insurance companies and pension plans) make up a portion of the secondary market, the agencies created by the government are the major forces in the secondary market. These agencies are the:

- Federal National Mortgage Association (FNMA)
- Government National Mortgage Association (GNMA), and
- Federal Home Loan Mortgage Corporation (FHLMC).

FEDERAL NATIONAL MORTGAGE ASSOCIATION (FNMA)

The Federal National Mortgage Association, often referred to as "Fannie Mae," began as a federal agency in 1938, and its original purpose was to provide real estate lenders an element of liquidity by acting as a secondary market for their existing mortgage loans. This function is especially vital in tight money periods because by purchasing existing loans from real estate lenders, FNMA frees their money for reinvestment in the primary money market. The lenders continue to service the loans for a fee, which involves billing, collections, property tax follow-up work and foreclosure services, when necessary.

FNMA: the Federal National Mortgage Association; a leading secondary market agency that purchases loans from real estate lenders

Originally, FNMA purchased only FHA and VA loans; today it buys all types of mortgages.

In 1968, Congress enacted legislation that reorganized FNMA into a private corporation, and common stock for FNMA was offered over-the-counter for purchase by the general public. At the same time a new federal agency, the Government National Mortgage Association (GNMA), was created to assume FNMA's governmental responsibilities.

GOVERNMENT NATIONAL MORTGAGE ASSOCIATION (GNMA)

GNMA: the Government National Mortgage Association; a leading secondary market agency that purchases VA and FHA loans

GNMA, usually called "Ginnie Mae," was established in 1968, and is one of many federal agencies that are part of the Department of Housing and Urban Development (HUD).

GNMA mostly purchases FHA and VA loans. Its responsibilities also include the management and liquidation of certain older FNMA loans. It also purchases at the secondary market level many types of loans that are socially significant but are not necessarily attractive to private secondary market investors. These include, for example, loans for urban renewal projects and housing for the elderly, and special assistance programs such as the FHA Section 221d(2) loans.

GNMA's most prominent role is played through its **mortgage-backed securities program**, which is a comprehensive plan that enables qualified lenders to obtain additional funds for lending purposes by pledging blocks of their existing loans as collateral for securities issues. The mechanics of the program are beyond the scope of this text, but in essence it is government support for lenders who use the real estate loans they have made as collateral to raise money through the issuance of securities.

FEDERAL HOME LOAN MORTGAGE CORPORATION (FHLMC)

FHLMC: the Federal Home Loan Mortgage Corporation; a leading secondary market agency that purchases loans from savings and loans

Created through the Emergency Home Finance Act of 1970, the Federal Home Loan Mortgage Corporation, generally referred to as "Freddie Mac," buys mortgages in the secondary mortgage market from savings and loan associations and other institutional lenders.

The "credit crunch" of the late 1960's resulted in an outflow of funds from traditional savings institutions that was so severe that these institutions were barely earning enough to cover operating costs. There was no money available for real estate lending purposes.

The formation of the FHLMC created a reliable secondary market for savings and loans, enabling them to liquidate portions of their real estate loan holdings and to free money to make new real estate loans.

DISCOUNT POINTS

Discounts or discount points (often referred to simply as "points") have traditionally been associated with FHA and VA financing in residential loans. However, payment of points has become commonplace for conventional loans as well. The term "point" is a contraction of the larger term "percentage point." A point is one percentage point or one percent of a loan amount.

Example: On a $150,000 loan, one point would be $1,500; six points would be $9,000.

$150,000
x   .06
$9,000

Discount points are charged by lenders to increase their yield or return on a loan. If a lender can "discount" a loan, the interest rate charged the borrower does not have to be as high to meet minimum yield requirements.

Discount points: an amount charged by a lender to increase return on a loan

Depending on the circumstances, the points may be paid by either the buyer or the seller, except on VA loans, where the discount points must be paid by the seller.

Note that the discount is computed on the loan amount, not the sales price.

Example:

$100,000   sales price
$80,000   loan amount
6%   discount

$80,000
× 6%
$ 4,800   discount

Points paid by the seller are paid at closing by deducting the amount of the points from the amount of the loan proceeds. For instance, if the loan were for $80,000 and the lender required four points, 4% of the loan ($3,200) would be deducted from the amount actually advanced to the borrower (the loan would be discounted 4%). The remainder, $76,800, would be delivered to the borrower to finance the purchase. The borrower would sign a promissory note and mortgage agreeing to repay the entire $80,000 at the agreed rate of interest.

So, the lender advances only $76,800 but will be repaid $80,000 (plus interest). The buyer transfers the loan proceeds ($76,800) to the seller without making up the difference. In effect, the seller paid the lender $3,200 to induce the lender to make the loan with a lower than market interest rate. The $3,200 compensated the lender for the lower-yielding loan.

HOW MANY POINTS?

The question of how many points must be paid can only be answered with up-to-the minute information concerning yields required by lenders. The number of points required to increase the lender's yield by 1% is affected by many factors, including prevailing interest rates, the average time that loans are outstanding before being paid off, and the terms of the loan documents themselves.

> Currently the number of points to be paid is normally computed on the assumption that it takes six points to increase the lender's yield on a 30-year loan by 1%.

This is simply a "rule of thumb" that should be confirmed with the lender before a final quote can be made.

TRUTH IN LENDING ACT

The government regulates the entire lending industry by passing laws that are meant to protect the public. One such law is the Truth in Lending Act. This act is a federal law that requires lenders to disclose the complete cost of credit to consumer loan applicants. The act also regulates advertising of consumer loans. The purpose of the act is to promote the informed use of consumer credit by requiring disclosure of costs and terms.

Truth in Lending Act: federal law requiring lenders to make certain disclosures to borrowers on application for a loan

> The Truth in Lending Act applies only to loans from institutional lenders to consumers for non-business purposes.

Congress outlined the goals of the act, and delegated the responsibility of carrying them out to the Federal Reserve Board. The Federal Reserve Board's **Regulation Z** implements the Truth in Lending Act. Regulation Z sets out the detailed rules that lenders must comply with.

DISCLOSURE REQUIREMENTS

The primary disclosures that a lender or credit arranger must make to a loan applicant are the total finance charge and the annual percentage rate.

TOTAL FINANCE CHARGE. The total finance charge is the sum of all fees the lender charges a borrower in exchange for granting the loan. That includes the interest on the loan, plus charges like the loan origination fee, buyer's points, finder's fees, assumption fees, and service fees.

Title insurance costs, credit report charges, the appraisal fee, legal fees, and points paid by the seller are not included in the total finance charge.

ANNUAL PERCENTAGE RATE. The annual percentage rate (APR) states the relationship of the total finance charge to the amount of the loan, expressed as an annual percentage.

APR: the annual percentage rate; gives the relationship of the total finance charge to the amount of the loan

> **A loan's APR is higher than its annual interest rate, since it reflects all the other finance charges in addition to the interest.**

Example: A loan with an 11% annual interest rate might have an 11.25% APR.

The lender must give the loan applicant a clear, easily understandable disclosure statement. In addition to the total finance charge and the APR, the statement must disclose the total amount financed, the payment schedule, the total number of payments, the total amount of payments, and information regarding any balloon payment(s), late fees, or prepayment charges. In the case of a real estate loan, it must also state whether the loan may be assumed by someone who buys the secured property from the borrower.

Additional disclosures are required for adjustable-rate loans.

ADVERTISING REQUIREMENTS

The Truth in Lending Act strictly controls advertising of credit terms. Its advertising rules apply to anyone who advertises consumer credit, not just lenders and credit arrangers.

Example: A real estate broker advertising financing terms for a listed home has to comply with Regulation Z.

The cash price for a property and a loan's annual percentage rate can always be advertised. But if any other particular loan terms are stated in an ad, then full disclosure is required.

In other words, if any additional terms are included, all of the terms must be included.

Additional terms that would trigger full disclosure include down-payment, interest rate, monthly payments, or number of payments.

Example: If an ad says, "only $2,000 down," it will violate the Truth in Lending Act unless it goes on to reveal the APR and all the terms of repayment.

However, general statements such as "low down" or "easy terms" don't trigger the full disclosure requirement.

APPLICATION

The Truth in Lending Act applies to all real estate loans except:

- loans to corporations,
- loans made for business or commercial purposes, or
- owner financing (such as a contract for deed, or seller carrying a purchase money mortgage).

RESPA

Another federal law that regulates part of the real estate business is the Real Estate Settlement Procedures Act (RESPA). This act was passed in 1974 and is administered by HUD.

RESPA: the Real Estate Settlement Procedures Act; requires certain disclosures to loan applicants regarding closing costs

---

The purpose of RESPA is to regulate and standardize real estate settlement practices.

It requires that disclosures be made to loan applicants concerning closing costs. RESPA applies to most federally related loans. A loan is federally related if it meets all of the following criteria:

- it will be used to finance the purchase of real property,

Good Faith Estimate
of Real Estate Settlement Costs

Borrower(s) _____

Property Address _____

THIS FORM IS AN ESTIMATE OF ANTICIPATED COSTS YOU WILL BE REQUIRED TO PAY IN CASH AT TIME OF SETTLEMENT. IT MAY NOT INCLUDE ADDITIONAL UNANTICIPATED COSTS WHICH YOU MAY BE REQUIRED TO PAY AT SETTLEMENT.

    101 CONTRACT SALES PRICE $ _____
    202 Principal Amount of New Loan   — $ _____
         DOWN PAYMENT .... $ _____

ESTIMATED LOAN COSTS

    801 Loan Origination Fee _____ % $ _____
    802 Loan Discount to Borrower   _____
    803 Appraisal Fee   _____
    804 Credit Report   _____
    809 Tax Service Fee   _____
    902 Mortgage Insurance Premium   _____
   1101 Settlement or Closing Fee (Escrow)   _____
   1108 Title Insurance   _____
   1201 **Recording Fees:** Deed $ _____
         Deed of Trust/Mortgage   _____
         Releases   _____   _____
   1301 Survey   _____
   1302 Pest Inspection   _____
         _____   _____
         _____   _____
                                      TOTAL .... $ _____

ESTIMATED RESERVES AND ADJUSTMENTS

    901 Interest for 30 days @ $_____/day* $ _____
    903 Hazard Insurance Premium for _____ years to _____   _____
   1001 Hazard Insurance _____ months @ $_____ per month   _____
   1002 Mortgage Insurance
         _____ months @ $_____ per month   _____
   1004 County Property Taxes (Reserves)
         _____ months @ $_____ per month   _____
    107 County Property Taxes (Pro-Rates)
         _____ to _____   _____
         _____ to _____   _____
                                      TOTAL .... $ _____

ESTIMATED DUE AT CLOSING .... $ _____
         Less: 201 Deposit or Earnest Money $ _____   _____

ESTIMATED AMOUNT REQUIRED TO CLOSE .... $ _____

*This interest calculation represents the greatest amount of interest you could be required to pay at settlement unless you have applied for an FHA or VA loan. The actual amount could be more if the FHA/VA interest rate increases between the time you apply and the time of closing. The actual amount will also vary depending on the day of the month your loan is closed.

I acknowledge receipt of the "Settlement Costs Booklet".

_____
Borrower   Date

_____
Borrower   Date

ESTIMATED PAYMENT SCHEDULE

Principal and Interest $ _____
Reserve for Taxes   _____
Reserve for Insurance   _____
Reserve for PMI   _____
                                  _____
Total Estimated Payment $ _____

Prepared By	Date

RE 188 (Rev 7-86)

- it is secured by a first mortgage on residence property, and
- the lender is federally regulated, its accounts are federally insured, loans are made in connection with a federal program (such as FHA or VA) or will be sold to FNMA, GNMA, or FHLMC, or the lender makes more than $1 million per year in real estate loans.

In short, the act applies to almost all institutional lenders and to most residential loans.

REQUIREMENTS

The basic requirements under RESPA include:

1. The lender must give a copy of the booklet "Settlement Procedures and You" (written by HUD) to all loan applicants within three days of receiving a written loan application.
2. The lender must give the borrower a good faith estimate of settlement costs within three days after the loan application (a form called a "Good Faith Estimate of Real Estate Settlement Costs" is sometimes used).
3. The lender must itemize all loan settlement charges on a Uniform Settlement Statement.
4. No kickback or referral fees are permitted for referring customers to anyone for any transaction involving a federally related loan.
5. The amount of advance tax and insurance escrow payments that a lender can collect and place in an impound or reserve account is restricted.
6. The borrower has the right to inspect the actual Uniform Settlement Statement (HUD-1) form one business day prior to the day of closing.

APPRAISAL

Appraisal: an estimate or opinion of value at a specified time

An appraisal is an estimate or an opinion of value. The term "appraisal" also refers to the act of estimating value.

> An appraisal is usually a written statement, called an *appraisal report*, that sets forth the appraiser's opinion of the value of a piece of property as of a given date. A synonym for appraisal is *valuation*.

An appraiser may be asked to help a seller decide on a fair asking price, or a buyer may seek an opinion on how much to pay for the property. Most often, an appraisal is requested by a lender, when a buyer has applied for a loan. The lender uses the appraisal to decide whether the property is suitable security for a loan, and if so, what the maximum loan amount should be. Whoever employs the appraiser is the client. The appraiser is the agent. A principal/agent relationship exists and the laws of agency apply.

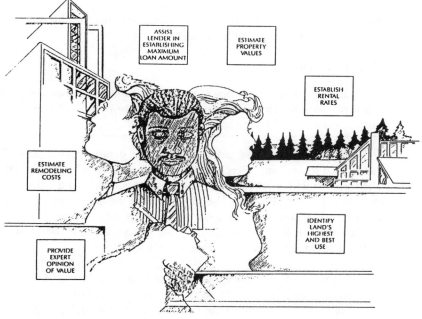

THE ROLE OF THE APPRAISER

In addition to helping determine a fair price or a maximum loan amount, an appraiser's services are regularly required for any one of the following reasons:

- to estimate the relative values of properties being exchanged;
- to provide an expert opinion of value for properties involved in the liquidation of estates, corporate mergers, corporate acquisitions or bankruptcies;
- to establish rental rates;

- to determine the amount of hazard insurance coverage necessary;
- to estimate remodeling costs or their contribution to value;
- to identify raw land's highest and best use;
- to estimate market value for taxation purposes;
- to help establish value in a condemnation proceeding.

Federal and state laws require Minnesota appraisers to be licensed or certified by the state. A real estate agent who does not hold an appraiser's license may perform a market analysis of property for a client in a real estate transaction. The analysis must not be referred to or treated as an appraisal, however.

VALUE DEFINED

> Value is a term with many meanings. The most common definition of value is "the present worth of future benefits." Value is usually measured in terms of money.

For appraisal purposes, value falls into two general classifications: **value in use** and **value in exchange**. A property might be worth one thing to its owner (use value) and quite another to a would-be purchaser (exchange value). Use value is often measured subjectively, whereas exchange value is determined more objectively.

Value in use: value to the owner/user

Value in use is also called utility, subjective value or emotional value. It is an item's value to its owner/user.

> **Example:** A large, expensive, one-bedroom home, designed, built and occupied by its owner would undoubtedly be worth more to the owner than to the buyer, who would look at the property objectively and expect more than one bedroom for the price.

Value in exchange: market value, the price the property would bring in a sale conducted under ideal market conditions

Exchange value, more commonly called market value, is the more significant of the two value classifications. Identifying the estimated market value of a property is the purpose of most appraisals, except where no resale market exists.

Market value is the highest price a property would bring if the sale were to take place under conditions ideal to both buyer and seller. These conditions include:

- an absence of abnormal pressure to act,
- exposure of the property to the open market for a reasonable period of time, and
- full knowledge of the property's merits and shortcomings.

> **The Federal Housing Administration offers a succinct explanation of market value: "The price which typical buyers would be warranted in paying for the property for long-term use or investment, if they were well informed, acted intelligently, voluntarily, and without necessity."**

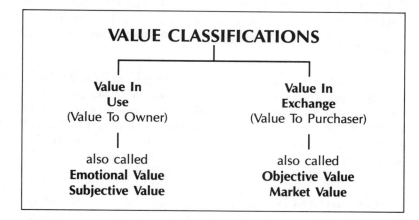

HOW VALUE IS CREATED

For an object to have value, it must contain two ingredients: **utility** and **scarcity**.

Utility refers to the ability to arouse desire for possession, and the power to give satisfaction. While this usually means an object must be useful, the terms utility and usefulness are not the same.

> **Example:** Warm clothing is useful but lacks utility for the individual in a tropical climate who seeks relief from the heat.

There must also be an element of scarcity. An object in excessive supply will lose value, regardless of its degree of utility.

Example: Food has a vital utility, but if more food is produced than can be consumed, the excess has no value.

HOW VALUE IN EXCHANGE IS CREATED

> **For an object to have a market value, the desire stimulated by its utility must be joined with the ability to buy it—purchasing power.**

Desire, coupled with purchasing power, translates into demand. But even with demand, there is no market value if the property is not freely transferable. Publicly owned properties, like libraries, universities and courthouses, are not transferable and have no market value.

Market value: what should be paid for a property in an arm's length transaction

MARKET VALUE VS. MARKET PRICE. Both the courts and lenders distinguish between market value and market price. Market price is the price paid for a property, regardless of whether the parties to the transaction were informed and acting free of pressures. Market value is what should be paid if a property is purchased and sold under the ideal circumstances previously described. A sale made under ideal conditions is called an arm's length transaction.

Market price: the price actually paid for a property, regardless of the conditions of the sale

FORCES INFLUENCING VALUE. There are major forces that influence our attitudes and behavior. Three of them interact to create, support, or erode property values:

- social ideals and standards,
- economic fluctuations, and
- government regulations.

Obsolete architectural styles, a change in attitude regarding family size, and the emergence of the two-car family are examples of social forces that affect (unfavorably) the value of homes with outmoded designs, too many bedrooms or one-car garages. Economic forces include employment levels, availability of money, interest rates, business trends or any other factors that affect the community's purchasing power. Government regulations, such as zoning ordinances, building restrictions or fire regulations, help shape the utility of land and serve to promote, stabilize or discourage demand for it.

PRINCIPLES OF VALUE

Over the years, by observing the actions of buyers, sellers and investors in the marketplace, appraisers have developed the principles of land utilization. Appraisers depend on the constancy of these principles to guide them when making decisions in the valuation process.

PRINCIPLE OF HIGHEST AND BEST USE

Highest and best use is among the most important of all considerations when trying to estimate the value of real property.

> **Highest and best use refers to the most profitable use: the use that will provide the greatest net return over a period of time.**

Highest and best use: the use that would produce the greatest net return over time

Net return usually refers to gross income minus expenses, but it cannot always be measured in terms of money. With residential properties, net return might manifest itself in the form of amenities, such as the pleasure and satisfaction derived from living on the property.

Estimating the highest and best use may be a simple matter of confirming that deed restrictions or an existing zoning ordinance limit the property to its present use. Often the present use of a property is its highest and best use. But change is constant and a warehouse site that was once profitable might now generate a greater net return as a parking lot.

Highest and Best Use
(Alternate Use Considerations)

Present Use Warehouse	Alternate Use 1 Parking Lot	Alternate Use 2 Service Station	Alternate Use 3 Triplex
Annual Net Income $19,280	**Estimated Annual Income** $16,800	**Estimated Annual Income** $20,500	**Estimated Annual Income** $14,300
Estimated Value $175,000	**Estimated Value** $151,000	**Estimated Value** $184,000	**Estimated Value** $132,000

The appraiser should consider potential uses for the land as though it were vacant, and for the land with its existing buildings, if any. By estimating the value of the land when put to alternate uses, the appraiser can decide whether the land is presently serving its highest and best use or if it could be put to a loftier use that would substantially increase its value.

PRINCIPLE OF CHANGE

Principle of change: property is in a constant state of change, through phases of integration, equilibrium, and disintegration

The appraiser must look at all property with the understanding that it is in a constant state of change.

> **It is the future, not the past, that is the primary consideration when estimating value.**

What is happening to the property? What is its future? How do prospective buyers view its potential? The appraiser's conclusions are dependent on his or her judgment, experience, astuteness and perceptiveness.

Equilibrium: a period of stability and little change.

Integration: period of development

Equilibrium: period of stability

Disintegration: period of decline

Related to the principle of change is the theory that property has a three-phase life cycle: **integration, equilibrium,** and **disintegration**.

Integration is also referred to as development. It represents the early stages of the cycle, when the property is being developed. Equilibrium is the period of stability, when the property undergoes little, if any change. Finally, disintegration is that declining period when the property's present economic usefulness is near an end and constant upkeep is necessary.

Every property has both a physical and an economic life and it is invariably the economic life—that period during which land and its improvements may be profitably utilized—that ends first. The appraiser must recognize and take into account the stage of the property's life cycle when estimating its present worth.

PRINCIPLE OF SUPPLY AND DEMAND

Supply and demand affect all marketable commodities. Supply refers to the number of properties available; demand refers to the number of properties that will be purchased. Values rise as demand increases and supply decreases, and diminish when the reverse is true.

Land supply, or lack of it, refers to the availability of land in a certain area which can serve a specific purpose.

Principle of supply and demand: values rise with increased demand and decreased supply; values fall with decreased demand and increased supply

> Land scarcity, by itself, does not create demand. The availability of financing, interest rates, wage levels, property tax levels, and population growth or shifts are all factors that influence the demand for real estate.

People who want real estate must also be able to afford it. The strongest desire must be coupled with purchasing power—the financial ability to buy the land.

PRINCIPLE OF SUBSTITUTION

This principle states that no one will pay more for a piece of property than they would have to pay for an equally desirable substitute property, provided there would be no unreasonable or costly delay in acquiring that substitute property. Substitution may be in terms of a property's use, design, or income. Explained another way, the principle of substitution holds that if two properties for sale or for lease are alike in every respect, the least expensive one will be in greater demand.

Principle of substitution: a buyer will not pay more for a property than it would cost to acquire an equally desirable substitute

PRINCIPLE OF CONFORMITY

> The maximum value of land is achieved when there is an acceptable degree of social and economic conformity in the area. Conformity should be reasonable, but not carried to an extreme.

From the standpoint of an appraiser, conformity takes several forms. With residences, it can mean similarities in the size and general structural quality of the homes in the area. Where there is inconsistency in this regard, there is value instability. A property's value is influenced to some degree by the surrounding properties. No property stands alone. The value of properties tend to move toward the surroundings. A home of noticeably lower quality than those around

Principle of conformity: maximum value is achieved with reasonable consistency in size and quality of structures, and socio-economic conformity

Progression: increase in value from surroundings

Regression: loss in value caused by surroundings

it will benefit from the surroundings through increased value (**principle of progression**). Conversely, a home of significantly higher quality than those around it will suffer in value because of the surroundings (**principle of regression**).

Retail stores grouped closely together, provided the use-density is in balance, is another example of conformity. Customers like to frequent shopping districts and are reluctant to shop at stores isolated from others. Being situated in a shopping district is desirable for a retailer as long as the competition does not become excessive.

PRINCIPLE OF CONTRIBUTION

Contribution refers to the value an improvement adds to the overall value of the property. Contribution is also referred to as increasing or decreasing returns. Some improvements will add more value than the expense of making them (**increasing returns**); others will cost more than they contribute to value (**decreasing returns**).

Principle of contribution: value added by a particular improvement

A remodeled basement ordinarily will not contribute its cost to the value of the home. On the other hand, the addition of a second bathroom, because of its functional worth, may increase a home's value by more than the cost of installing it.

PRINCIPLE OF ANTICIPATION

Principle of anticipation: present value is affected by expected future benefits or disadvantages of ownership

> **Value is created by the anticipated benefits of owning a property in the future. It is not past benefits, but future benefits, that arouse a desire to own.**

Anticipation can help or hurt value, depending on what informed buyers and sellers expect to happen to the property in the future. Normally, they expect property values to increase, because the supply is fixed and the demand continues to rise. However, in certain instances, buyers and sellers anticipate that values will decline, as when a large chunk of important retail property is to be condemned by the city for a street widening project.

PRINCIPLE OF COMPETITION

Principle of competition: the opportunity to make a profit stimulates and encourages competition

This principle states that the opportunity to make a profit stimulates and encourages competition. When the demand is high for a certain size, quality, style, and price of house, builders can make a healthy profit. As more and more builders attempt to meet the demand by building similar homes, the competition will drive the price and profits downward.

THE APPRAISAL PROCESS

Properly done, the appraisal process is orderly and systematic. The appraiser has the responsibility to form an opinion of value on which the client—buyer, seller, or lender—will undoubtedly base one or more important decisions. While there is no officially standardized procedure, appraisers generally carry out the appraisal process in the following manner.

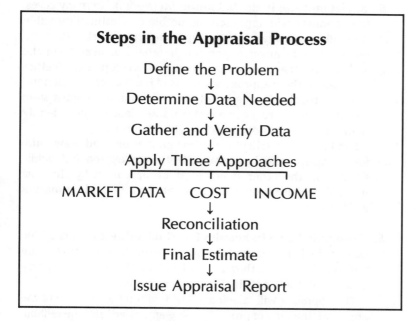

Steps in the Appraisal Process

Define the Problem
↓
Determine Data Needed
↓
Gather and Verify Data
↓
Apply Three Approaches

MARKET DATA   COST   INCOME
↓
Reconciliation
↓
Final Estimate
↓
Issue Appraisal Report

1. **Identify the Problem.** When the appraiser is hired, he or she is asked to solve a problem, to clarify the value of something. This involves identifying the property and establishing the purpose and function of the appraisal.

2. **Determine What Data Is Needed and Where It Can Be Found.** The data on which the value estimate will be based is divided into two categories: general and specific.

   General data has to do with matters external to the property being appraised. It includes population trends, prevailing economic circumstances, zoning, proximity of amenities (shopping, schools and public transportation), as well as the condition and quality of the neighborhood itself.

Specific data relates to the property being appraised. The appraiser will want to gather information about the title, the buildings and the site.

3. **Gather and Verify the General Data.**

4. **Gather and Verify the Specific Data.**

5. **Select and Apply the Valuation Method(s).** In many cases, the appraiser will approach the problem of estimating value three different ways: the cost approach, the market data approach, and the income approach. In other instances, he or she will use only the method that seems most appropriate. Whether one, two, or three approaches are used is a matter of judgment. If an approach to value is not used, the appraiser must state why it was not used (i.e., no rental market data for single-family home in all owner-occupied neighborhood.)

   Sometimes, a particular method cannot be used. Raw land, for example, cannot be appraised by the cost approach. A public library, on the other hand, must be appraised by the cost method because it does not generate income and no market exists for it.

6. **Reconcile Value Indicators for Final Value Estimate.** The figures yielded by each of the three approaches are called value indicators, meaning they give indications of what the property is worth but are not final estimates themselves.

   The appraiser will take into consideration the purpose of the appraisal, the type of property being appraised, and the reliability of the data gathered for each of the three approaches. He or she will place the greatest emphasis on the approach that seems to be the most reliable indication of value.

7. **Issue Appraisal Report.** The formal presentation of the value estimate and an explanation of what went into its determination are made in the appraisal report.

Market Data Approach to Value

The market data approach is the comparison of information on properties of a certain kind and class with characteristics of the property being appraised.

> Appraisers use this method whenever possible because intelligently selected market information is an excellent way to measure the actions of informed buyers and sellers in the marketplace.

Market approach: value is estimated by comparison with recently sold similar properties

Where there is an adequate number of recent sales of similar properties, the value indicated by the market data technique can be very reliable.

It is the appraiser's task to gather pertinent information about **comparable sales**, making feature-by-feature comparisons against the property under appraisal. The appraiser then translates his or her findings into an estimate of the market value of the **subject property**.

Comparable sales: similar properties recently sold

Subject property: property being appraised

The market data method is the most popular method for appraising single-family residences because there is usually an abundance of comparable data. Single-family residential sales account for the vast majority of real estate transactions nationwide.

The supporting appraisal methods—cost approach and income approach—will be used when there are not enough comparable sales to use the market data method. When appraising residences, an appraiser needs at least three reliable comparables to have enough data to form and support an opinion of value.

Elements of Comparison

> The appraiser gathers pertinent data on three or more properties that are comparable to the subject property. The test for whether a property is comparable or not involves checking the primary elements of comparison:
>
> - time of sale
> - location of the property, and
> - physical characteristics of the property

TIME. Generally, very recent sales are more reliable indications of market values than sales from the distant past. A rule of thumb is that the sale should have occurred within the previous year. Economic conditions change, and if the changes have been significant in the months or years since a comparable sale occurred, the appraiser may have to reject the comparable sale altogether. If the change has been a steady, but measurable, increase in property values in the area, the appraisal may be a simple matter of making adjustments for the appreciation that has generally affected values.

LOCATION. Prices for identical structures can vary from one neighborhood to the next. Usually, the closer in location the comparable property is to the subject property, the more likely its price will provide a meaningful guide to value. It is best if the comparable property and the subject property are in the same neighborhood.

If sales in the same area are not available, comparable property should be from competing areas. Certain elements should be similar, such as prestige, convenience, tax base, school districts, etc.

PHYSICAL CHARACTERISTICS. A comparison of physical characteristics includes the site and its buildings. Important site comparisons are frontage, depth, area, landscaping, and contour. Building characteristics consist of number of rooms, square footage, quality of construction, age, and functional utility. The most recent sales price of the subject property should not be taken into account, unless the sale was within the previous year.

COMPARABLE SALES MUST HAVE BEEN AT ARM'S LENGTH

Regardless of any other consideration such as time of sale or degree of structural similarity, if a comparable sale was not an arm's length transaction, the appraiser cannot rely on it as an indication of value.

Arm's length transaction: a sale where buyer and seller are informed, neither is under undue pressure, and the property is on the market for a reasonable length of time

> To qualify as an arm's length transaction, both seller and buyer must have been informed of the property's merits and flaws, neither can have been acting under unusual pressures or duress, and the property must have been tested in the marketplace for a reasonable period.

The appraiser must also consider seller and buyer motives when deciding whether to include or reject a comparable transaction. An owner might deliberately sell property for less than it is worth if there are tax advantages to be gained from doing so. An individual might pay more than market value for a lot adjoining her business property because she must have it for parking. Or a sale between relatives might be influenced more by love than a concern for market value. Many of the circumstances which would make a sale ineligible as an arm's length transaction would be revealed by interviews with the principals to the transaction or the agent of record.

The terms of the sale also do much to influence value today. More and more buyers have demonstrated a willingness to pay more for a property if the financing terms are attractive.

COST APPROACH TO VALUE

The cost approach to value involves estimating the cost to reproduce or replace existing buildings, then subtracting depreciation, then adding the estimated value of the site on which they rest.

One rationale for the use of the cost method is that it tends to identify the ceiling of the market value because buyers will not pay more for property than it would cost to replace it (principle of substitution). This approach is particularly useful in estimating the value of unique or special properties where comparable sales do not exist.

Cost approach: value is estimated by estimating cost to replace improvements, less depreciation, plus value of site

REPLACEMENT COST vs. REPRODUCTION COST

The terms replacement and reproduction are frequently used interchangeably, but technically there is a difference. Replacement cost is the estimated cost to construct, at current prices, a building with utility equivalent to the building being appraised, using modern materials and current standards, design, and layout. Reproduction cost, in contrast, is the estimated cost to construct, at current prices, an exact duplicate, or replica, of the building being appraised, using the same materials, construction standards, design, layout, and quality of workmanship.

Reproduction cost refers to replication, whereas replacement cost means a suitable replacement, not a replica. In most cases the appraiser is estimating the replacement cost of a building. This is especially true when appraising older properties. The cost of constructing an exact duplicate of a 50-year-old house, including original materials and quality of workmanship, would be prohibitive and greatly disproportionate to the actual market value of the house. Ordinarily, a reproduction cost estimate will result in an accurate estimate of a property's actual market value only when the property being appraised is new or nearly new. Under these circumstances, construction materials and comparable craftsmanship are readily available at competitive costs, and the problem of estimating accrued depreciation is minimal. For the balance of this chapter, any reference to cost means replacement rather than reproduction cost.

REPLACEMENT COST METHODS

There are three ways to estimate the replacement cost of a building: the square foot method, the unit-in-place method and the quantity survey method.

Square foot method: replacement cost estimate based on cost per square foot to build comparable structure

SQUARE FOOT. The square foot method involves multiplying the cost per square foot of a recently built comparable structure by the number of square feet in the subject property.

> **Because it involves comparing costs, it is sometimes called the** *comparative cost method*. **It is the method most often used by appraisers.**

The comparable building is unlikely to be exactly the same as the building being appraised because there will be variations in design, shape, and grade of construction that will moderately or substantially affect the square foot costs. The appraiser must make refinements in his or her estimates to reflect the cost variations. When a comparable new building is not available, the appraiser relies on current manuals for basic construction costs.

The number of square feet in a building is determined by calculating outside measurements, and multiplying width by depth.

Unit-in-place method: replacement cost estimate based on cost of components in building

UNIT-IN-PLACE. The unit-in-place method involves a series of estimates of the cost to replace specific component parts of the building such as floors, roof, plumbing, foundation and the like. The estimates use cost measurements such as the square foot and cubic foot when defining replacement costs of the various components. For example, one of the estimates might be a certain number of dollars per 100 square feet of roofing. Another component estimate would be a certain amount per cubic foot or cubic yard of concrete for an installed foundation.

> **By this method, the appraiser estimates separately the cost to replace all of the structure's component parts, adding them together in the end to find the replacement cost of the structure itself. All estimates include the cost of materials, labor, and profit.**

The unit-in-place method is more detailed and likely to be more accurate than the square foot method. Like the square foot method, it relies on cost manuals for component cost figures.

QUANTITY SURVEY. Sometimes referred to as the price take-off method, a quantity survey involves a detailed estimate of the quantities and prices of construction materials as well as the costs of installation (labor), which are added to the indirect costs (building permit, survey, builder's overhead, and profit) for what is generally regarded as the most accurate replacement cost estimate.

Quantity survey: replacement cost estimate based on detailed costs of materials and labor, plus indirect costs

> **Because it is time-consuming and very complex, the method is generally used by experienced contractors and price estimators. Appraisers seldom use this method.**

DEPRECIATION

Depreciation is the difference between the value of the existing improvements and the cost of replacing them. It represents a loss in value due to any cause, including age, neglect, undesirable features within the property or negative influences from without. In estimating total depreciation, there is no depreciation on the land.

Depreciation: loss in value from any cause

> **When appraising a used property, the value is determined by estimating the replacement cost, deducting the depreciation and adding the value of the land.**

In the absence of extraordinary circumstances, a used building is not worth as much as a new one. The difference is the depreciation.

Depreciation takes three forms: physical deterioration, functional obsolescence, and economic obsolescence.

PHYSICAL DETERIORATION. Also called **deferred maintenance**, this form of value loss is evidenced by wear and tear, decay, cracks, and structural defects. It is usually the most obvious form of depreciation. The extent of physical deterioration is measured by the cost to correct it. Accordingly, it is the simplest kind of depreciation to spot and estimate. Physical deterioration is curable or incurable (see below).

Physical deterioration: loss in value from deferred maintenance

FUNCTIONAL OBSOLESCENCE.

Functional obsolescence: loss in value from functional inadequacies on the property itself

> **This is a loss in value due to functional inadequacies such as poor floor plan, unappealing design, outdated fixtures, or too few bathrooms in relation to the number of bedrooms.**

The appraiser will classify functional obsolescence as either curable or incurable. Whether it takes the form of physical deterioration or functional obsolescence, curable depreciation is not so extensive that the cost of correcting it cannot be recovered in the sales price. Incurable depreciation is either impossible to correct or so expensive that it is not practical. It would make little sense, for example, to install an elevator in a three-story apartment house at a cost of $75,000 if, in the opinion of the appraiser, it would not add at least that amount to the value of the property. If it would not, the functional obsolescence caused by the absence of an elevator would be seen as incurable.

Example: In today's market, a house with four bedrooms and just one bath loses value due to functional obsolescence.

ECONOMIC OBSOLESCENCE.

Economic obsolescence: loss in value from causes occurring outside the property itself

> **Also known as *locational obsolescence,* economic obsolescence represents value losses from causes outside the property. It is a kind of depreciation resulting from the action of forces beyond a property owner's control.**

As a result, it is always incurable. Zoning changes, neighborhood deterioration, adverse changes in traffic patterns (such as a new freeway rerouting traffic away from a motel), or exposure to nuisances (like the noise from airplanes as they land and take off near a home) are examples of factors that can create economic obsolescence.

Properties near an airport may lose value to economic obsolescence, a negative external force in the form of low-flying aircraft.

Estimating depreciation accurately is the most difficult phase of the cost approach. In many cases, the depreciation estimates are highly subjective, and they are never any more reliable than the judgment and skill of the appraiser making them.

INCOME APPROACH TO VALUE

The income method of appraising is based on the idea that there is a relationship between an income property's earnings potential and its market value to an investor. The example below shows how the earnings potential is estimated:

10-UNIT APARTMENT BUILDING

Potential Annual Gross Income	$66,000
Less	
Bad Debt/Vacancy Factor (5%)	3,300
Effective Gross Income	62,700
Less	
Fixed Expenses	12,200
Maintenance Expenses	17,200
Reserves for Replacement	7,200
NET INCOME	$26,100

> When the fixed expenses, maintenance expenses, and replacement reserves have been deducted, the result is net income. It is this figure that is capitalized to determine the property's value.

CAPITALIZATION

Capitalization: converting estimated future net income into an estimate of present value by use of capitalization rate

The process of converting net income produced by an investment property into a meaningful value is called capitalization. The mathematical procedure is expressed as follows:

Annual Net Income (I) = **Capitalization Rate (R) × Value (V)**

Capitalization Rate (R) = **I ÷ V**

Value (V) = **I ÷ R**

The **capitalization rate** is the rate of return an investor receives or requires in connection with income producing property.

Ordinarily, income producing property is purchased for investment purposes. The investor seeks a certain rate of return on the capital invested in the property. When the desired return is selected, the equation shown above is used to determine how much an investor can pay for a property which is generating a known income and still realize the desired return.

Example:

1) property's annual net income = $10,000
2) investor's desired return = 12%
3) $10,000 ÷ 12% = $83,333

In the example, the investor can pay up to $83,333 for a property earning $10,000 net and realize the desired yield of 12%.

GROSS RENT MULTIPLIERS

Gross rent multiplier: a number which, when multiplied by the gross rent, gives a rough estimate of value

An alternative to capitalization that focuses on *gross* rents or income is called the **gross rent multiplier** (GRM) method.

In the gross rent multiplier method, the appraiser examines the relationship between sales prices in the area and gross incomes. By dividing each property's sales price by its annual gross rents, the appraiser will derive the gross rent multiplier.

Example:

Property 1)	$100,000	Price
	÷ $10,000	Gross rent
	10	GRM

Property 2)	$120,000	Price
	÷ $12,000	Gross rent
	10	GRM

Property 3)	$200,000	Price
	÷ $20,000	Gross rent
	10	GRM

The gross rent multiplier in this area is 10. If the subject property has a gross annual income of $15,000, the value will be $150,000 ($15,000 × 10 = $150,000).

The gross rent multiplier method can be used with other types of properties, but ordinarily it is not. It is applied almost exclusively to residential rental units.

> **Its principal weakness is that it is based on gross income figures and does not take into account vacancies or operating expenses.**

If two three-bedroom homes have the same income, the gross rent multiplier method would indicate they are worth the same. But if one is old and has higher maintenance costs, its value is actually less. At best, gross rent multipliers provide the appraiser with a rough approximation of value.

RECONCILIATION AND FINAL ESTIMATE OF VALUE

Throughout the appraisal process, the appraiser is searching for facts on which he or she will base the ultimate conclusions. In many cases, the facts are self-evident and require nothing beyond simple verification. In other instances, they are unclear, barely discernible as facts, and require expert interpretation.

Reconciliation: assembly and interpretation of factors affecting value to reach final estimate of value

In appraisal terms, **reconciliation** (also called **correlation**) refers to assembly and interpretation of numerous factors that operate independently, or merge, to influence values. Nowhere in the appraisal process does the appraiser's experience and judgment play a more critical role.

> The final value estimate is not the average of the indications of value delivered by the three appraisal methods—cost, income, and market data.

Rather, it is the figure that represents the appraiser's expert opinion of value after all tangible and intangible criteria have been identified, analyzed, and measured for the impact they will have individually and collectively on a property's value.

Once the final estimate of value is determined, it is put into the form of an appraisal report. The two most common types are:

- **Narrative.** A thorough, detailed, written presentation of the facts and reasoning behind an appraiser's estimate of value.
- **Form.** Brief standard form used by agencies, such as the FHA, and by lending institutions, such as banks and savings and loans. This is the most common type of appraisal report.

Whichever method is used, the appraiser has the responsibility to complete the correlation process and explain his or her reasons for the final value.

CHAPTER SUMMARY

1. The Federal Housing Administration (FHA) is part of the Department of Housing and Urban Development (HUD). It is a giant federal insurance agency. Approved lenders are insured against losses caused by borrower defaults on FHA-insured loans.

2. The Veterans Administration (VA) guarantees repayment of certain residential loans made to eligible veterans. Eligibility for VA loans is based on the length of service in the U.S. armed forces.

3. The Farmer's Home Administration (FmHA) is a federal agency that assists in providing credit to farmers and others in rural areas where reasonable financing from private sources is not available.

4. The primary or local market is the ground-level money market—the one that is most familiar to the public. The secondary or national market consists of private investors and government-sponsored agencies that buy and sell real estate mortgages. Buying and selling mortgages in the secondary market helps to balance out any money surpluses or shortages by transferring funds from areas where there is a surplus to areas where there is a shortage.

5. Government-sponsored agencies are the major forces in the secondary market. These agencies are the Federal National Mortgage Association (FNMA), Government National Mortgage Association (GNMA), and Federal Home Loan Mortgage Corporation (FHLMC).

6. A discount point is one percent of a loan amount. Discount points are charged by lenders to increase their yield or return on a loan. Points are paid at closing by deducting the amount of the points from the loan funds actually given to the borrower.

7. The Truth in Lending Act is a federal law that requires lenders to disclose the complete cost of credit to consumer loan applicants. A lender must disclose the total finance charge and the annual percentage rate.

8. The purpose of the Real Estate Settlement Procedures Act (RESPA) is to regulate and standardize real estate settlement practices. The law requires that certain disclosures be made to loan applicants concerning closing costs.

9. An appraisal is an estimate or opinion of value. The most common definition of value is "the present worth of future benefits." For appraisal purposes, value is generally measured in terms of money. To be valuable, an item must have utility, scarcity, demand, and transferability.

10. Appraisers have developed several "principles of value" to guide them in the valuation process. These include the principle of highest and best use, the principle of change, the principle of supply and demand, the principle of substitution, the principle of conformity, the principle of contribution, the principle of anticipation, and the principle of competition.

11. The appraisal process has several steps. The first step is to identify the problem. The appraiser then must determine what data is needed and where to find it (this includes general and specific data). Next the data must be gathered and verified. Valuation methods are then applied. The three methods are market data, cost, and income. The value indicators derived from using one or more of the three valuation methods are correlated into a final estimate which is written up in the appraisal report.

12. The market data method (the method most often used for appraising residential property) is based on comparing the values of similar properties. The cost method takes into account the cost of building a similar property. The income method uses the net income produced by a property (capitalization) or the gross income produced (gross rent multiplier) to estimate its value.

CHAPTER 8—GLOSSARY REVIEW

A. certificate of reasonable value
B. market data approach
C. cost approach
D. mortgage amount
E. interest rate
F. annual percentage rate
G. certificate of eligibility
H. capitalization
I. gross rent multiplier
J. replacement cost
K. reproduction cost

L. physical deterioration
M. functional obsolescence
N. economic obsolescence
O. FHA
P. FNMA
Q. GNMA
R. FHLMC
S. VA
T. FmHA
U. Regulation Z
V. RESPA

1. A uniform measure of the cost of credit that includes interest and finance charges is known as the _annual percentage rate APR_

2. The process of converting a future income stream into an expression of present value is called _Capitalization_

3. The document that shows the Veterans Administration valuation of a property for loan purposes is a _Certificate of reasonable value_

4. The cost of exact duplication of improvements with the same or very similar materials is called _reproduction costs_.

5. The cost of replacing improvements with others of similar quality but which are not an exact replica is known as _replacement costs_.

6. Loss in value due to causes external to the property is _economic obselescence_.

7. An agency of the government that insures mortgage loans is the _FHA_.

8. A method of valuing a property by comparing the subject property to similar properties that have recently sold is the _market data approach_.

9. An agency of the federal government that guarantees loans made to veterans is the _VA_.

10. The law requiring disclosure of a loan's annual percentage rate is _Regulation Z_

11. The federal act that applies to closings and requires a uniform settlement statement and good faith estimate is _RESPA Real Estate Settlement Procedure Act_.

12. The agency that insures, guarantees, and originates loans is the _FmHA_.

13. Points charged by lenders are computed as a percentage of the _mortgage amount_.

CHAPTER 8—REVIEW EXAM

1. The purpose of Regulation Z is to:

   a) regulate the amount of interest charged by lenders.
   b) established uniform usury laws.
   c) protect the lender against default.
   d) protect the borrower from hidden costs.

2. FHA insurance is designed to protect:

   a) the mortgagor from financial loss due to catastrophe.
   b) the lender.
   c) the seller.
   d) the broker.

3. ~~Discount points on VA loans are always:~~

   inaccurate

   ~~I. computed on the mortgage amount~~
   II. paid by the seller

   ~~a) I only~~
   ~~b) II only~~
   ~~c) Both I and II~~
   ~~d) Neither I nor~~ II

4. A 100% loan-to-value ratio is a feature of:

   a) FHA-insured loans.
   b) VA-guaranteed loans.
   c) conventional loans.
   d) conventional guaranteed loans.

5. The primary reason for discounting mortgages is to:

   a) increase the yield to the investor.
   b) qualify for mortgage insurance.
   c) reduce the sales price.
   d) meet federal lending requirements.

6. In appraising a 12-year-old, single-family home in a residential neighborhood, which approach would be most applicable?

   a) Market data approach
   b) Cost approach
   c) Income approach
   d) Gross rent multiplier method

7. If the cap rate increases, the value of the property:

   a) increases.
   b) decreases.
   c) stays the same.
   d) None of the above

8. A property has a value of $130,000 and cap rate of 7%. What would its value be if the cap rate were 10%?

   a) $143,000
   b) $117,000
   c) $91,000
   d) Need more information

9. A 5-bedroom home with one bath is an example of:

a) functional obsolescence.
b) physical deterioration.
c) economic obsolescence.
d) gross rent adjustment.

10. All of the following are examples of obsolescence EXCEPT:

a) neighborhood blight.
b) impractical floor plan.
c) two-story home with one bath located in the basement.
d) leaky basement.

11. Reproduction cost is defined as:

a) the present cost of rebuilding with the same or highly similar materials.
b) replacing an improvement with another having the same utility.
c) the cost utilizing caplitalization rate and value.
d) None of the above

12. Which of the following would be most likely to make an FHA-insured loan?

a) Federal National Mortgage Association
b) Federal Housing Administration
c) Federal Home Loan Bank
d) A qualified lending institution

13. Which of the following loans would not be regulated by Regulation Z?

a) An FHA loan to a married couple
b) A purchase money mortgage
c) A conventional loan
d) A VA loan to a qualified veteran

14. The agency that insures, guarantees, and grants loans is known as:

a) BHA
b) FmHA
c) VA
d) FHLMC

15. An appraiser would be most likely to use the cost approach on:

a) a single-family home.
b) a duplex.
c) a church.
d) a townhouse.

16. Income capitalization is most likely to be associated with appraisal of:

a) a condominium project.
b) a single-family home.
c) an apartment building.
d) a townhouse.

17. A lender who wishes to increase the yield of a mortgage will usually:

a) insure the loan.
b) sell the loan to Fannie Mae.
c) charge discount points.
d) lower the interest rate.

18. According to RESPA, when someone applies for a government-insured mortgage, the lender must give the applicant:

a) the annual percentage rate.
b) a good faith estimate of closing costs.
c) a narrative report.
d) copies of the listing agreement.

19. In the market data approach, adjustments to comparables would be made for all of the following EXCEPT:

   a) number of baths.
   b) square footage.
   c) financing terms.
   d) original cost.

20. Which of the following purposes is served by the capitalization approach?

   a) Estimate present value based on current or expected income.
   b) Estimate future value based on current gross income.
   c) Estimate present value by multiplying net income by rent multiplier.
   d) Estimate operating expenses based on highest and best use.

21. A property produces an income of $10,000 per year. Management expenses are $700 annually. Monthly heating costs are $92. If the property is valued at $80,000, what is the owner's approximate overall capitalization rate?

   a) 14%
   b) 10%
   c) 8%
   d) 7%

22. Which of the following ads would trigger full disclosure under Regulation Z?

   a) "Low downpayment"
   b) "Below market interest rate"
   c) "Interest rate of 9%"
   d) "$80,000 sales price"

23. The function of the FHLMC, FNMA and GNMA is to:

   a) grant new loans.
   b) purchase existing mortgages.
   c) purchase contracts for deed.
   d) discount fee simples.

24. A building valued at $195,000 has a gross income of $27,000 and expenses of 45%. What is its cap rate?

   a) 45%
   b) 13.8%
   c) 7.6%
   d) 6.2%

CHAPTER 8—GLOSSARY REVIEW KEY

1. F
2. H
3. A
4. K
5. J
6. N
7. O

8. B
9. S
10. U
11. V
12. T
13. D

CHAPTER 8—REVIEW EXAM KEY

1. d) Regulation Z, which implements the Truth in Lending Act, requires lenders to disclose finance charges and the annual percentage rate (APR).

2. b) The lender's unpaid balance is insured by FHA.

3. c) All points are computed on the mortgage amount. Discount points on a VA loan must be paid by the seller.

4. b) The VA-guaranteed loan is the only loan featuring a 100% loan-to-value ratio.

5. a) By charging a discount, the lender's yield is increased without increasing the borrower's interest rate.

6. a) The market data approach is the most important one for the appraisal of single-family residences.

7. b) There is an inverse relationship between the capitalization (cap) rate and the property value.

8. c) $130,000 × 7% = $9,100 (I)
    $9,100 ÷ 10% = $91,000.

9. a) Inadequate design or equipment causes functional obsolescence.

10. d) A leaky basement is an example of physical deterioration.

11. a) Reproduction cost is the cost of building a replica.

12. d) Approved lending institutions provide the funds for FHA-insured loans.

13. b) In Minnesota, a purchase money mortgage is a transaction between individuals (the seller and the buyer). Since no lending institution is involved, the transaction is not subject to Regulation Z.

14. b) FmHA (Farmer's Home Administration) is the only agency that insures, guarantees, and grants loans.

15. c) The cost approach is most often used for unique or special-purpose properties (churches, schools, etc.).

16. c) Income capitalization (the income approach) is used to evaluate income-producing properties (apartments, shopping centers, office buildings, etc.).

17. c) Discount points increase the lender's yield.

18. b) RESPA requires the lender to give a loan applicant a good faith estimate of closing costs and the booklet "Settlement Costs and You" at the time of mortgage application.

19. d) The appraiser does not consider what the original cost of the property was.

20. a) Capitalization is the process by which present value is estimated based upon expected income.

21. b)
$$\begin{array}{ll}
\$10,000 & \\
-700 & \text{management} \\
\underline{-1,104} & \text{heating } (92 \times 12) \\
\$8,196 & \text{net operating income} \\
\underline{\div 80,000} & \\
.1025 & 10.25\%
\end{array}$$

22. c) Under Regulation Z, only the price and/or APR may be stated in an ad without requiring full disclosure.

23. b) These secondary mortgage market agencies purchase mortgages from primary lenders.

24. c)
$$\begin{array}{l}
27,000 \\
\underline{\times \ 55\%} \\
14,850 \\
\underline{\div 195,000} \\
.076 \quad 7.6\%
\end{array}$$

THE OWNER/BROKER RELATIONSHIP

OUTLINE

I. Agency
   A. Parties
      1. principal
      2. agent
      3. third parties
   B. Law of agency
      1. liability to third parties
      2. imputed knowledge
      3. agent's fiduciary duties
         a. care and skill
         b. obedience, good faith, and loyalty
   C. Creating an agency
   D. Types of agency
   E. Dual agency

II. Listing Agreements
   A. Essential elements
   B. Types of listings
      1. exclusive right to sell
      2. exclusive agency
      3. open
      4. multiple
      5. net
   C. Compensation

III. Termination of Agency Relationships

IV. Broker's Financial Responsibilities
   A. Trust accounts
   B. Closing statements

V. Civil Rights and Fair Housing
   A. Federal anti-discrimination legislation
      1. Civil Rights Act of 1866
         a. constitutionality
         b. enforcement
      2. Federal Fair Housing Act of 1968
         a. application
         b. prohibited acts
         c. exemptions
         d. enforcement and penalties
      3. fair lending laws
   B. Minnesota Human Rights Act
      1. protected classifications
      2. prohibitions
      3. exceptions
      4. enforcement and penalties

KEY TERMS

agent
third party
primary broker
negligence
special agent
universal agent
listing agreement
protection period
exclusive right to sell
open listing
net listing
renunciation
trust funds
commingling
credit
Civil Rights Act of 1866
injunctive relief
panic selling
steering

principal
subagent
fiduciary
ratification
general agent
dual agency
override clause
protective list
exclusive agency
multiple listing
operation of law
revocation
trust account
closing statement
debit
Federal Fair Housing Act
blockbusting
redlining
Minnesota Human Rights Act

CHAPTER OVERVIEW

"Real estate agent" is a common term, but few people stop to think about what the word "agent" means. Agency is a special legal relationship in which one person acts for another. The first part of this chapter explains the rules that govern agency relationships, and how they affect real estate agents and their clients. Next, this chapter examines the elements of a listing agreement, the contract that creates an agency relationship between a real estate broker and a seller. Some of the financial responsibilities that a broker takes on in a real estate transaction are also discussed. The final section of the chapter provides an overview of the federal and state anti-discrimination laws that govern real estate transactions.

PARTIES TO AN AGENCY RELATIONSHIP

There are essentially two parties to an agency relationship: the principal and the agent. Someone outside the agency relationship, who deals with the principal through the agent, is referred to as a third party.

PRINCIPAL

> **A principal is anyone who authorizes another person (the agent) to represent him or her in dealing with other people (third parties).**

Principal: a person who authorizes another to act for him or her

In a typical real estate transaction, the principal is a property owner who wants to sell the property. The principal employs the services of a real estate broker, who is the agent. The broker/agent tries to find a buyer, and negotiates with prospective buyers on the principal's behalf.

In some transactions, a buyer is represented by a real estate broker. The buyer hires the broker to locate suitable property and negotiate the purchase. In that case, the buyer is that broker's principal. The principal is whoever has hired the agent to act on his or her behalf.

AGENT

> **An agent is anyone who is authorized to represent or act for someone else.**

Agent: a person authorized to represent another

As explained above, a real estate broker hired to represent a seller or a buyer is that person's agent. The broker is authorized to negotiate a sale or purchase on behalf of the principal.

In ordinary usage, a real estate salesperson is often called a real estate agent. In strict legal terms, however, the salesperson is not actually the agent of the seller or the buyer. Minnesota's real estate license law does not allow a salesperson to act independently of a broker. (See Chapter 10.) A salesperson must be licensed under a particular broker; that broker is called the salesperson's primary broker. In the eyes of the law, the salesperson is the agent of his or her primary broker. The broker (rather than the salesperson) is the agent of the seller or buyer. The salesperson is, in effect, "the agent of an agent." The agent of an agent is sometimes called a **subagent**.

Subagent: a person authorized to act on behalf of an agent; the agent of an agent

> **Example:** Walter Swift wants to sell his house. He lists the property with Don Chan, a licensed real estate broker. Chan is the primary broker for Veronica Gordon, a licensed real estate salesperson. Chan tells Gordon to handle Swift's listing, so Gordon advertises the property and shows it to prospective buyers. Eventually, Gordon negotiates the sale of the house to the Eckbergs.
>
> Swift, the seller, is Chan's principal. Chan is Swift's agent. Gordon is Chan's agent and Swift's subagent. Those are their legal relationships, even though Swift would probably refer to Gordon as "my real estate agent" in conversation.

THIRD PARTIES

Anyone outside the agency relationship who deals with the principal through the agent is called a **third party**. In the example just given, the Eckbergs (the buyers) are third parties. There is no agency relationship between Gordon or Chan and the Eckbergs.

In some cases, a third party has an agent of his or her own. Suppose the Eckbergs had hired a real estate broker named Jones to find a home for them. In that agency relationship, the Eckbergs would be the principals, Jones would be their agent, and Swift (the seller) would be considered a third party.

THE LAW OF AGENCY

Establishing an agency relationship has a number of important legal consequences. The principal can be held liable for the agent's actions in some cases, and the agent has certain legal duties toward the principal.

LIABILITY TO THIRD PARTIES

> **In establishing an agency relationship, the principal authorizes the agent to perform certain actions. When the agent performs these authorized actions, they are binding on the principal.**

For instance, if an agent is authorized to enter into a contract on behalf of the principal, the agent's signature on the contract binds the principal to the terms of the contract, even though the principal never personally signs the contract.

If a third party is harmed by an agent's actions, the principal may be held liable (as if the principal had performed the actions him or herself). If the principal authorized the agent to appoint a subagent, the principal may also be held liable for the subagent's actions.

> **Example:** To continue with the example used earlier, suppose Gordon (the salesperson/subagent) lied to the Eckbergs about the condition of Swift's house, to persuade them to buy it. After they move in, the Eckbergs discover some serious problems and realize that the house is worth much less than they paid for it.
>
> The Eckbergs sue Chan and Gordon for fraud. The judge decides that the Eckbergs are entitled to $65,000 in damages. A judgment for $65,000 is entered against both defendants. Chan, the broker, is held liable even though he did not lie to the Eckbergs himself or instruct his agent to lie to them. He is legally responsible to third parties for the actions of his agent.

IMPUTED KNOWLEDGE

Another important point of agency law is that the knowledge of the agent may be imputed to the principal. In other words, if a third party gives the agent some information, the principal could be held to have legal notice of that information. That's true even if the agent never actually gets around to telling the principal. So if a seller told the agent of a prospective buyer about a problem with the property, the buyer may be held to have known about the problem, even though her agent never passed the information along to her.

FIDUCIARY DUTIES

Fiduciary relationship: a legal relationship founded on trust and confidence

> **The relationship between an agent and a principal is described as a fiduciary relationship. A fiduciary is someone who acts for the benefit of another in a relationship founded on trust and confidence.**

The law holds a fiduciary to high standards of conduct, to prevent the fiduciary from disappointing or exploiting the other party's trust. The other party has a legal right to rely on the fiduciary.

The responsibilities that an agent owes the principal are called the agent's fiduciary duties. The agent's basic fiduciary duties are the duty to use reasonable care and skill, and the duties of obedience, accountability, and loyalty.

CARE AND SKILL. In acting for the principal, an agent is required to use reasonable care and skill. If an agent makes a mistake through carelessness or incompetence, that's a breach of his or her fiduciary duties. The principal can sue the agent to recover damages for any harm that results from the agent's mistake. (The legal term for a breach of duty caused by carelessness or incompetence is **negligence**. Negligence is contrasted with an intentional breach of duty.)

An agent is expected to use the degree of care and the level of skill that others competently engaged in the same business ordinarily use. When a court evaluates the performance of a real estate agent, the agent will be compared to competent real estate agents rather than to the general public. If competent real estate agents usually follow a certain practice, an agent who did not follow it could be held liable for negligence.

OBEDIENCE, ACCOUNTABILITY, AND LOYALTY. An agent owes the principal obedience, accountability, and loyalty. The agent must faithfully carry out the principal's instructions, and can be held liable for any failure to obey them.

> **The duty of loyalty requires an agent to put the principal's interests above all others, including the agent's own interests.**

If the principal reveals **confidential information** to the agent, the agent must not reveal it to anyone else, or take advantage of it for his or her own benefit.

> **Example:** The seller listed the property for $86,000, but he confided to his real estate broker that he'd be willing to accept $80,000. The broker needs her commission in a hurry, so she wants to close a sale immediately. She tells a prospective buyer to offer $80,000. That's a breach of the broker's fiduciary duties to the seller. If the seller discovers the broker's breach, he can sue her.

Also, because of the duties of loyalty and good faith, an agent must not conceal **material information** from the principal. Any fact that could influence the principal's judgment in the transaction should be brought to his or her attention. A real estate agent representing a seller should be especially careful to inform the principal of:

Material information: any fact that could influence the principal's judgment in a transaction

- the true value of the property, and anything that could be done to increase its value;
- any negative information about a prospective buyer's financial condition;
- any relationship between a prospective buyer and the agent.

When there is a relationship between the buyer and the agent—if the buyer is one of the agent's family members, business associates, or friends, or a business that the agent owns an interest in—it could create a **conflict of interest**. The agent's loyalty could be divided between the principal and the buyer. The principal might prefer to find a different buyer, or even a different agent. But as long as the agent tells the principal about his or her relationship to the buyer, the law does not require the agent to withdraw from the transaction.

AGENT'S FIDUCIARY DUTIES TO THE PRINCIPAL

Care and skill
Obedience
Accountability
Loyalty

C.O.A.L.

PENALTIES FOR BREACH OF DUTY. As you've seen, a principal can sue an agent for breach of fiduciary duty. When a seller sues his or her real estate agent, the court often orders the agent to pay back the commission the seller paid. The agent may also be required to pay additional damages to compensate the seller. On top of those financial penalties, the agent's breach of duty can lead to the suspension or revocation of his or her real estate license. (See Chapter 10.)

CREATING AN AGENCY RELATIONSHIP

The agent's fiduciary duties and the principal's liability for the agent's actions arise automatically when an agency relationship is established. So it is very important to understand the different ways that agency relationships are created.

WRITTEN AGREEMENTS.

> An agency relationship is most often created by an express, written contract between the parties.

When a seller hires a real estate broker, for example, the agency relationship is created by the **listing agreement**. In Minnesota, the listing agreement must be in writing and signed. (Listing agreements are discussed in detail later in this chapter.) A power of attorney is another type of document used to create an agency.

ORAL AGREEMENTS. An agency relationship can also be created orally, by a spoken agreement that never gets put into writing. An agency relationship can be created by oral agreement between a salesperson and a real estate broker. Minnesota law, however, requires a broker to obtain a written listing in order to offer an owner's property for sale.

> **Without a written listing, the broker does not have a right to sue the seller for the commission if the seller refuses to pay.**

TYPES OF AGENCY

An agency contract (such as a listing agreement) should specify the scope of the agent's authority: what actions he or she is authorized to carry out in order to accomplish the principal's goals.

> **If the agent exceeds the limits of the authority granted by the principal, the principal usually cannot be held liable for the agent's unauthorized acts.**

Agents are classified according to the amount of authority the principal has conferred on them. There are three basic types of agents:

- special agents,
- general agents, and
- universal agents.

SPECIAL AGENT. A special agent has limited authority to do a specific thing or conduct a specific transaction. Real estate brokers are usually special agents. Their authority is limited to a single transaction, such as the sale of a particular property.

Note that an ordinary listing agreement does not authorize the real estate broker to sign a binding contract on the seller's behalf, or to convey the property. The listing simply authorizes the broker to locate potential buyers and negotiate with them.

GENERAL AGENT. A general agent is authorized to handle all matters for the principal in a specified area. For example, a property manager is a general agent if he or she has authority to market and maintain the property, hire and fire maintenance personnel, enter lease agreements on the owner's behalf, and take full responsibility for managing the property. Also, a licensed salesperson is considered to be a general agent of the employing broker.

UNIVERSAL AGENT. A universal agent is authorized to do everything that can be done by a lawfully designated representative. This type of agent has the greatest possible degree of authority. A court-appointed guardian, charged with the care of someone who is no longer competent to manage his or her own affairs, is a universal agent.

DUAL AGENCY

A real estate agent who represents both the buyer and the seller in a transaction is a **dual agent**.

Dual agent: a real estate agent who represents both the buyer and the seller

> **Although dual agency is controversial, it is legal as long as both parties consent to it.**

A dual agent owes fiduciary duties to both buyer and seller. As a result, if either party discloses confidential information to the agent, the agent must not reveal it to the other party.

Critics of dual agency point out that there is an inherent conflict of interest in the arrangement. A seller is looking for the highest price, while the buyer is looking for the lowest price. It is difficult, if not impossible, to adequately represent these two opposing interests at the same time.

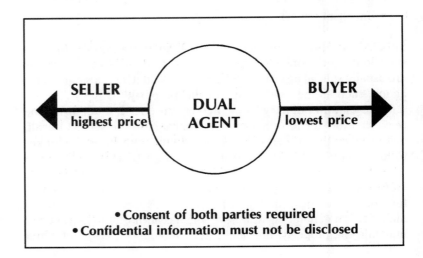

Dual agency also gives the agent an opportunity to manipulate one client in favor of the other. This is particularly likely to occur when the agent has an ongoing relationship with one party (a friend, relative, or established client) but not the other. Dual agency is inappropriate in this type of situation.

LISTING AGREEMENTS

A listing agreement is an employment contract between a seller and a real estate broker, appointing the broker as the seller's special agent for the purpose of finding a buyer. Because a listing agreement is a personal services contract, it can only be assigned to another broker with the client's (the seller's) consent.

Listing agreement: an employment contract between a broker and a seller

ESSENTIAL ELEMENTS

Since a listing agreement is a contract, it has to incorporate all of the elements required for a valid, enforceable contract (see Chapter 5). The parties must have contractual capacity, there must be mutual agreement and consideration, and the purpose of the contract must be lawful. In addition to those basic elements that any contract needs, Minnesota has some special requirements for listing agreements.

IN WRITING.

> **In Minnesota, a real estate broker is required by law to have a written, signed listing agreement before advertising the property for sale or lease.**

The broker is not even supposed to place a "For Sale" sign on the property until the listing agreement has been signed.

In spite of that law, sometimes a broker will start working for a seller under an oral agreement. The broker intends to get the listing in writing later on, but never does. Without a written contract, the broker cannot sue the seller for a commission—even if the broker has clearly earned the commission according to the terms of the oral agreement. Yet the broker can still be held liable to the seller for a breach of fiduciary duties. Working without a written listing is risky, as well as unlawful.

DESCRIPTION OF THE PROPERTY.

A listing agreement must identify the property to be sold or leased. The street address is useful, but it may not be enough to identify the property with certainty. It's a good practice to attach a legal description of the property to the contract as an exhibit. Any pages attached to a contract should be dated and initialed by the parties, to show that the attachments are intended to be part of the agreement.

PRICE AND TERMS. A listing agreement is required to state the price and terms of sale that the client is willing to accept. The client can refuse any offer that doesn't meet these terms without being liable for a commission. It is therefore very important for the price and terms to be set forth clearly and fully in the listing. (Any personal property that will be included in the sale should be specified, since that affects the price.) Of course, if the broker presents an offer that doesn't meet the listing terms and the client accepts it anyway, the client owes the broker the commission.

EARNING THE COMMISSION. Minnesota law requires a listing agreement to clearly state under what conditions the broker will be entitled to a commission. According to the terms of some listing agreements, the broker is entitled to the commission even if the transaction never closes, as long as the client and a ready, willing, and able buyer have agreed on the essential terms of a sale. But the seller can add a provision to the listing agreement making liability for the commission depend on the sale actually closing, or on some other particular event or condition.

If the contract between the buyer and seller is conditional (contingent on the results of an inspection, for example), the seller ordinarily doesn't owe the broker a commission unless the condition is either fulfilled or waived by the parties.

Most listing agreements make the client liable for a commission if he or she withdraws the property from sale or does anything to make it unmarketable.

COMMISSION AMOUNT. A provision stating the amount (or rate) of the broker's commission is another key part of every listing agreement.

There are no legal limits on real estate commissions—maximum or minimum. However, it is illegal for a real estate brokers' organization or brokers from competing firms to agree to charge a particular commission rate. That's price fixing, a violation of the antitrust laws. The possible penalties include treble damages (three times the amount of the actual damages) and a $50,000 fine.

So the broker's commission is negotiated with each client individually. Because the commission amount or rate is negotiable as a matter of law, it must not be preprinted on the listing agreement form. The figure has to be filled in for each transaction.

To emphasize that the commission is negotiable, Minnesota law requires that the following notice be included in every listing agreement. It must be printed in boldface type, and placed immediately before the provision relating to the broker's compensation.

NOTICE: THE COMMISSION RATE FOR THE SALE, LEASE, RENTAL, OR MANAGEMENT OF REAL PROPERTY SHALL BE DETERMINED BETWEEN EACH INDIVIDUAL BROKER AND ITS CLIENT.

This is known as the "negotiable commission" clause.

EXPIRATION DATE. In Minnesota, a listing agreement is unenforceable unless it contains a specific expiration date.

MINNESOTA LISTING AGREEMENTS

- In writing
- Price & terms
- Amount/method of compensation
- Negotiable commission clause
- Expiration date
- No holdover clause
- Protection period no more than six months

NO AUTOMATIC RENEWAL. A holdover clause (sometimes called an automatic extension clause) provides that the listing will renew itself indefinitely unless it is specifically cancelled by the seller. In Minnesota, it is illegal to include a holdover clause in a listing agreement, even if the seller is willing to have one. If the listing is to be renewed, the renewal must be negotiated and expressly agreed upon between the seller and the broker.

Holdover clause: states that listing will renew itself unless cancelled by seller; illegal in Minnesota

OVERRIDE CLAUSE AND PROTECTIVE LIST. Exclusive listing forms usually include an override clause (also known as an extender clause,

Override clause: provides that the broker is entitled to a commission if the property is sold to any person the broker negotiated with during the listing term

safety clause, or carryover clause). An override clause makes the client liable for a commission during a specified period after the listing expires, if the property is sold to someone the agent dealt with during the listing term. The period specified in an override clause is called the protection period, because the broker's interests are protected.

> **An override clause makes it more difficult for a buyer and seller to conspire to deprive the broker of a commission by waiting until the listing expires before signing a purchase agreement.**

In Minnesota, a protection period cannot last for more than six months.

An override clause is only enforceable if the broker provides the seller with a list of the prospective buyers he or she dealt with during the listing period. This list of names, known as a protective list, must be given to the seller within 72 hours after the listing expires. If no list is provided, the broker is presumed to have waived any right to a commission for a sale made after the listing's expiration date.

The broker must be prepared to prove that everyone on the protective list responded to an advertisement, contacted the broker or his/her agents, or was actually shown the property by the broker (or a salesperson) during the listing term. It isn't enough if the broker merely mailed out an advertisement during the listing term, but the buyer did not respond until after the term had expired.

> **Example:** The seller listed his property with the broker in September. The listing agreement would expire on December 1, but an override clause provided for a three-month protection period. The broker prepared an advertising letter describing the seller's property and mailed it on November 8 to twenty people who were likely to buy property of that type.
>
> One of those twenty people was Mr. Maplewood. Maplewood received the letter on November 9, but he didn't get around to responding until December 6, after the broker's listing had expired. Eventually, Maplewood bought the property directly from the seller.
>
> The broker gave the seller a protective list the day after the listing expired, and Maplewood's name was on the list. Even so, the broker is not entitled to a commission, because Maplewood did not inspect the property until after the listing period had ended.

Often a seller relists the property with a different broker immediately after the first listing agreement expires. In some cases, because of an override clause in the first listing, the seller ends up owing both the former broker and the new broker a commission. To protect sellers against this problem, most Minnesota listing forms state that the seller will not owe the broker a commission after the listing has expired, if the seller is obligated to pay a commission under a new listing agreement. However, if the listing agreement does not include that type of provision, Minnesota law requires the former broker to include a special notice in the protective list. The notice warns the seller that he or she could become liable for two commissions.

TYPES OF LISTING AGREEMENTS

There are three basic types of listing agreements:

- exclusive right to sell listings,
- exclusive agency listings, and
- open listings.

> **The distinctions between these three types of listings determine the conditions under which the seller will owe the broker a commission, and whether the seller has a right to list the property with more than one broker.**

EXCLUSIVE RIGHT TO SELL.   Under an exclusive right to sell listing, the seller must pay the broker's commission no matter who finds the buyer—even if the seller does. This is the type of listing used most often in the real estate industry, because of the protection it affords the broker.

Exclusive right to sell: broker gets commission no matter who sells property

> **Example:** The seller and the broker sign an exclusive right to sell listing agreement. The seller ends up selling the house to her next-door neighbor's cousin. The broker did not show the house to the cousin, and all of the negotiations took place directly between the seller and the neighbor's cousin. The seller is still required to pay the commission to the broker.

EXCLUSIVE AGENCY.   In an exclusive agency listing, the principal appoints one broker as the exclusive agent to procure a purchaser. The seller is then obligated to pay the broker a commission if the

Exclusive agency: broker gets commission unless owner sells property

property is sold by that broker or anyone else, except for the seller. The seller retains the right to sell the property him or herself, without having to pay the broker's commission.

> **Example:** Reconsider the example given above. Suppose the seller had signed an exclusive agency listing instead of an exclusive right to sell listing. When the seller negotiated the sale to her neighbor's cousin by herself, she would not owe the listing broker a commission.
>
> However, if any other broker assisted the seller in arranging the sale to the neighbor's cousin, the seller would still be required to pay the listing broker.

Both types of exclusive listings are considered to be bilateral personal service contracts. That is, the broker promises to exert best efforts to perform, and the seller promises to pay upon performance.

OPEN LISTING. An open listing is a non-exclusive listing. It allows the seller to contract with many brokers at the same time. The seller is liable for a commission only to the broker who is the **procuring cause** of the sale: the broker whose efforts bring the seller together with a ready, willing, and able buyer. The sale of the property cancels all other open listing agreements. To be the procuring cause, a broker must be primarily responsible for the parties' agreement, or the broker's actions must have started a chain of events that resulted in an agreement. If the seller found the buyer by him or herself, the seller does not have to pay a commission to any of the brokers with open listings.

Open listing: only procuring cause entitled to commission

The open listing is considered to be a unilateral contract because the broker is not making a promise to exert best efforts. The only promise is the seller's promise to pay if the broker performs.

Sometimes two brokers with open listings contribute to a particular sale, and they agree to divide the commission. But in some cases, brokers end up quarreling over which of them was the procuring cause. That's one of the chief disadvantages of an open listing.

The Code of Ethics of the National Association of REALTORS® encourages the use of exclusive listings (either exclusive agency or exclusive right to sell) rather than open listings. Exclusive listings reduce the potential for disputes among competing brokers. And at least in theory, exclusive listings result in better service for sellers

Minnesota Association of Realtors®
Exclusive Listing Contract

This contract involves the property at: _____

_____ (property)

"I" means: _____

"You" means: _____

_____ (the real estate broker).

LISTING

I give you the exclusive right to sell the property for the price of $ _____. I will require the

following terms: _____ .

_____ .

This contract starts _____ ,19 _____ and ends 11:59 p.m. on _____ ,

19 _____ . In exchange, you agree to list the property for sale. You may place a "For Sale" sign and a lock

box with keys on the property.

MY DUTIES

I will cooperate with you in selling the property. I will promptly tell you about all inquiries I receive about the property. I agree to provide and pay for any inspections and reports if required by the city or state. I agree to provide homeowners association documents if required. I will give the buyer an updated abstract of title, owner's duplicate certificate of title and registered property abstract, or title insurance to the property. I have the full legal right to sell the property. I will sign all closing documents (including a warranty deed or contract for a warranty deed) necessary to transfer to the Buyer full and unquestioned ownership of the property.

NOTICE

THE COMMISSION RATE FOR THE SALE, LEASE, RENTAL OR MANAGEMENT OF REAL PROPERTY SHALL BE DETERMINED BETWEEN EACH INDIVIDUAL REAL ESTATE BROKER AND ITS CLIENT.

YOUR COMMISSION

I will pay you as your commission _____ % of the selling price upon the happening of any of the following events:

(a) At the closing of the sale if I sell or agree to sell the property before this contract ends, even if I or another broker sells the property without your assistance;

(b) If you present a Buyer who is willing and able to buy the property at the price and terms required in this contract, but I refuse to sell;

(c) If I sell or agree to sell the property before this contract ends, but I refuse to close the sale; or

(d) If within _____ days after the end of this contract, I sell or agree to sell the property to anyone who:
(1) During this contract made inquiry of me about the property and I did not tell you about the inquiry; or
(2) During this contract made an affirmative showing of interest in the property or was physically shown the property by you and whose name is on a written list you gave me within 72 hours after the end of this contract.

I understand that I do not have to pay your commission if I sign another valid listing contract after the expiration of this Contract, under which I am obligated to pay a commission to another licensed real estate broker.

NOTICES ABOUT MY REAL ESTATE

As of this date, I have not received notices from any municipality, government agency, or homeowners association about the property that I have not told you about, and I agree to promptly tell you of any notices of that type that I receive.

FORFEITURE OF EARNEST MONEY

If a buyer of the property defaults and as a result forfeits the earnest money, you will get _____ % and I will

get _____ % of the earnest money.

ACCEPTED BY: ACCEPTED BY:

_____   _____
Real Estate Company   Owner

By _____   _____
       Agent   Owner

Date signed: _____ 19 _____   Address: _____

                                         _____

                                         Phone: _____

                                         Date signed: _____ ,19 _____

Rev. 6/84

Reprinted with permission from the Minnesota Association of Realtors®

than open listings. Because an exclusive listing gives the broker a more secure claim to a commission, he or she is likely to work harder to bring about a sale.

LISTING AGREEMENTS

| **Exclusive Right to Sell** (no matter who) | **Exclusive Agency** (anyone except the seller) | **Open** (procuring cause) |

Multiple listing service (MLS): an association of brokers who agree to share listings in order to achieve maximum exposure

MULTIPLE LISTING. A multiple listing is not a particular type of listing agreement; it is simply a listing (of whatever type) that the broker has submitted to a multiple listing service (MLS). An MLS is an association of brokers who have agreed to share exclusive listings, to maximize their exposure to the public and get them sold more quickly.

When property that one broker has an exclusive listing for is sold through the efforts of another broker in the MLS, the listing broker shares the commission with that other broker. In this type of situation, the other broker is often referred to either as a **cooperating broker** or as the **selling broker**. It's important to realize that the selling broker is a subagent of the seller (an agent of the listing broker). Many buyers mistakenly think that the selling broker is their agent, and only the listing broker is the seller's agent. But unless the buyer specifically has an agency contract with the selling broker, both brokers are representing the seller's interests.

NET LISTING. Like a multiple listing, a net listing is not really a distinct type of listing. A net listing fits into one of the three basic categories (exclusive right to sell, exclusive agency, or open listing), but the broker's commission is determined in a special way.

Net listing: a listing in which the broker's commission is the portion of the sales price over the seller's net amount

> **With a net listing, the seller stipulates a net amount of money he or she wants to derive from the sale of the property. If the property is sold, the broker's commission is the portion of the sales price over and above the seller's net amount.**

Example: A seller signs an exclusive right to sell listing with a broker. The seller wants to receive $145,000 from the sale. The listing agreement provides that this will be the seller's net (after the commission is deducted), and the broker will accept however much is left over as his commission. The broker sells the property for $158,000. The broker's commission is $13,000. ($158,000 − $145,000 = $13,000)

Although net listings are not illegal in Minnesota, they are strongly discouraged. The net listing arrangement lends itself readily to fraud by the broker. To give sellers with net listing agreements some protection, Minnesota law requires the broker to reveal the amount of his or her commission to the seller before the seller signs the contract with the buyer. Failure to reveal that information may result in suspension or revocation of the broker's license (see Chapter 10).

COMPENSATION AND FEE SPLITS

No matter what type of listing agreement is used, the only person a seller may pay for assistance in finding a buyer and negotiating the sale of the property is a licensed real estate broker. If an unlicensed person performs those services, it is illegal for the seller to compensate that person (with money or gifts of any sort). The same rule applies to buyers, landlords, and tenants as well as sellers: only a licensed real estate broker can be paid for assistance in negotiating a sale, purchase, or lease.

Also, none of the parties to a real estate transaction may pay a real estate salesperson directly.

> **The seller or other principal pays the salesperson's primary broker, and the broker pays the salesperson. It is illegal for a salesperson to accept compensation from anyone other than his or her primary broker.**

Brokers may only share their commissions with their own salespeople or with other licensed brokers (for example, an associate broker who works for the listing broker, or a cooperating broker from a different firm). It's legal for a Minnesota broker to split a fee with a broker from another state, as long as the other broker is properly licensed in his or her state. It is also legal to share commissions with the parties to the transaction.

TERMINATION OF AGENCY RELATIONSHIPS

Once an agency relationship has been created (by signing a listing agreement, for example), the agent owes fiduciary duties to the principal. Those responsibilities continue until the agency relationship is terminated.

An agency relationship may be terminated by:

- accomplishment of purpose,
- expiration of the agency term,
- operation of law,
- mutual agreement, or
- revocation by the principal.

Accomplishment of Purpose. Probably the most common way for an agency relationship to end is through accomplishment of the purpose of the agency. When the agent has accomplished what he or she was hired to do, the agency relationship terminates automatically.

> **Example:** A homeowner hires a real estate broker to sell her house. Once the property is sold and all of the details have been taken care of, the agency relationship ends.

Expiration of Term. An agency relationship also ends when the specified term of the agency agreement runs out. For example, when the expiration date stated in a listing agreement arrives, the listing broker is no longer the seller's agent, even if they haven't found a buyer yet.

Operation of Law. The law provides that agency relationships automatically terminate upon the occurrence of certain events. These events include:

1. the death or mental incapacity of either party,
2. the bankruptcy of either party,
3. destruction or condemnation of the property, or
4. loss of the broker's license.

Example: A homeowner hires a broker to sell his house. They sign an exclusive right to sell listing agreement with a term of six months. Only two months into the term of the agreement, the seller's house burns down. The broker's agency terminates automatically, by operation of law.

Mutual Agreement. Agency is a consensual relationship, which means that it is based on the consent of both parties. If both the principal and the agent want to end the agency, they can agree to terminate it at any time. When an agency is ended by mutual consent, neither party is liable to the other for damages.

Revocation. A principal may revoke the grant of agency powers at any time—in other words, fire the agent. If the agency agreement was open-ended, the revocation usually will not be considered a breach of contract.

> **On the other hand, if the agreement had a specific termination date (as every listing agreement in Minnesota must), the revocation may be a breach of contract.**

The principal can be held liable for any damages suffered by the agent because of the breach.

Example: Dan Mallett is planning to sell his house. He signs an exclusive right to sell listing agreement with broker George Westheimer. A few weeks later, Mallett starts dating a real estate salesperson who convinces him to change the listing to her broker. Mallett tells Westheimer his agency is revoked because he's giving the listing to a different broker.

At this point, Westheimer is no longer authorized to represent Mallett. Mallett had the right to revoke Westheimer's agency, but he is also liable for the consequences. If Mallett sells his property during what would have been Westheimer's listing term, a court would probably order him to pay Westheimer the full commission amount. (Also note that Mallett's new agent may be in trouble. It's a violation of the real estate license law to encourage someone to breach a contract. See Chapter 10.)

TERMINATION OF AGENCY

Acts of the Parties	Operation of Law
1. Accomplishment of purpose	1. Death or mental incapacity
2. Expiration of agency term	2. Bankruptcy
3. Mutual agreement	3. Property destroyed
4. Principal revokes	4. Agent loses license

BROKER'S FINANCIAL RESPONSIBILITIES

An agent is often called upon to receive, hold, or spend money that belongs to the principal or a third party. Handling another person's money is a tremendous responsibility, because there is considerable potential for wrongdoing and for mistakes with serious consequences.

Real estate brokers have financial responsibilities in connection with almost every transaction. Minnesota has strict laws that brokers must follow when handling money on a client's behalf and when dealing with the financial aspects of closing a sale.

TRUST FUNDS

Trust funds are money or other things of value received by a broker or salesperson on behalf of a client or any other person in a real estate transaction. This includes earnest money deposits, downpayments, rents, tax and insurance escrow payments, and damage deposits.

> **Improper handling of trust funds is probably the most common reason for revocation or suspension of a real estate license.**

TRUST ACCOUNT. A broker is required to maintain an interest-bearing account for the deposit of trust funds. The trust account may be at a bank, savings and loan association, or other financial institution. It can be a savings account or checking account, but it must pay the highest current passbook savings account rate of interest.

The broker has to keep detailed records for the trust account, showing every deposit and disbursement. A separate trust fund record for each real estate transaction is required. The trust account interest must be paid to Minnesota's Housing Trust Fund, unless the parties to a particular transaction agree in writing that the interest will be used in some other way.

PROHIBITED ACTIONS. The primary purpose of a trust account is to keep the trust funds separate from the broker's own money.

> **When a broker mixes trust funds together with his or her own money, it's called commingling. Commingling is illegal; it's both a breach of fiduciary duty and a serious violation of Minnesota's license law.**

Commingling: when a broker mixes personal funds with trust funds

There is one limited exception to the rule against commingling: a broker can keep some of his or her own money in the trust account to cover bank service charges or comply with minimum balance requirements. The sum of money to be used for those purposes can be any amount, but it must be specifically identified in the account records.

When there are any changes in the status of a broker's trust account (for example, if the broker opens a trust account at a new bank), the broker is required to notify the Commissioner of Commerce. A broker may not close a trust account without giving written notice to the Commissioner ten days in advance.

CLOSING STATEMENTS

A closing statement (also called a settlement statement) sets out the financial aspects of a real estate transaction. The statement itemizes the closing costs—every expense each party will be required to pay for to close the transaction. It also shows the total amount of cash the buyer will have to pay and the net cash proceeds that will go to the seller at closing.

Closing statement: itemizes the financial aspects of a real estate transaction

In Minnesota, real estate agents have two specific duties regarding closing costs. First, an agent is required to warn the buyer and the seller early on that they may have to pay certain closing costs. The agent must let the buyer know this before the buyer signs an offer to purchase, and must tell the seller before presenting an offer. Without this warning, some first-time buyers might believe the price they've offered will be their total expenditure, and some inexperienced sellers might regard the offered price as their net proceeds.

Second, Minnesota law makes it the listing broker's responsibility to ensure that both the seller and the buyer receive detailed closing statements. Each party should be given the statement at the time of closing, so that it reflects the actual receipts and disbursements in the transaction, not just estimates.

If the transaction is subject to the Real Estate Settlement Procedures Act (see Chapter 8), a Uniform Settlement Statement form (HUD-1) is used. A sample Uniform Settlement Statement is shown on the following pages. If RESPA does not apply, any one of several different forms may be used.

ALLOCATING EXPENSES.

Debit: an amount that one of the parties owes

Credit: an amount owed to one of the parties

> **Preparing a settlement statement involves determining what debits and credits apply in a given transaction and allocating them to the right parties. A debit is a sum that one of the parties owes; a credit is a sum owed to one of the parties.**

The division of expenses is usually determined by provisions in the purchase agreement or another written agreement between the parties. The allocation may also be influenced by local custom, as long as the custom does not conflict with the parties' written agreement.

> **Example:** A buyer usually pays the mortgage registration tax. Following that custom, the tax would be charged to the buyer at closing. When the Horgans arranged to buy the Minervinos' house, however, the Minervinos agreed in the purchase agreement to pay the mortgage registration tax. As a result, the custom will be disregarded and the tax will be charged to the sellers.

Of course, both local custom and agreements between the parties must not run contrary to local, state, or federal law. For instance, Veterans Administration regulations (which have the effect of law) prohibit buyers seeking VA-guaranteed financing from paying any portion of the loan discount points. If it is a VA loan, any discount points must be paid by the seller. The parties cannot agree to have the buyer pay the discount points instead.

The closing cost allocations described below are typical, but are not necessarily followed in every transaction.

A. Settlement Statement

U.S. Department of Housing
and Urban Development

OMB No. 2502-0265 (Exp. 12-31-86)

B. Type of Loan

1. ☐ FHA 2. ☐ FmHa 3. ☐ Conv. Unins.
4. ☐ VA 5. ☐ Conv. Ins.

6. File Number	7. Loan Number	8. Mortgage Insurance Case Number

C. Note: This form is furnished to give you a statement of actual settlement costs. Amounts paid to and by the settlement agent are shown. Items marked "(p.o.c.)" were paid outside the closing; they are shown here for informational purposes and are not included in the totals.

D. Name and Address of Borrower	E. Name and Address of Seller	F. Name and Address of Lender

G. Property Location	H. Settlement Agent	
	Place of Settlement	I. Settlement Date

J. Summary of Borrower's Transaction		K. Summary of Seller's Transaction	
100. Gross Amount Due From Borrower		**400. Gross Amount Due to Seller**	
101. Contract sales price		401. Contract sales price	
102. Personal property		402. Personal property	
103. Settlement charges to borrower (line 1400)		403.	
104.		404.	
105.		405.	
Adjustments for items paid by seller in advance		*Adjustments for items paid by seller in advance*	
106. City/town taxes to		406. City/town taxes to	
107. County taxes to		407. County taxes to	
108. Assessments to		408. Assessments to	
109.		409.	
110.		410.	
111.		411.	
112.		412.	
120. Gross Amount Due From Borrower		**420. Gross Amount Due to Seller**	
200. Amounts Paid By Or In Behalf Of Borrower		**500. Reductions In Amount Due To Seller**	
201. Deposit or earnest money		501. Excess deposit (see instructions)	
202. Principal amount of new loan(s)		502. Settlement charges to seller (line 1400)	
203. Existing loan(s) taken subject to		503. Existing loan(s) taken subject to	
204.		504. Payoff of first mortgage loan	
205.		505. Payoff of second mortgage loan	
206.		506.	
207.		507.	
208.		508.	
209.		509.	
Adjustments for items unpaid by seller		*Adjustment for items unpaid by seller*	
210. City/town taxes to		510. City/town taxes to	
211. County taxes to		511. County taxes to	
212. Assessments to		512. Assessments to	
213.		513.	
214.		514.	
215.		515.	
216.		516.	
217.		517.	
218.		518.	
219.		519.	
220. Total Paid By/For Borrower		**520. Total Reduction Amount Due Seller**	
300. Cash At Settlement From/To Borrower		**600. Cash At Settlement To/From Seller**	
301. Gross Amount due from borrower (line 120)		601. Gross amount due to seller (line 420)	
302. Less amounts paid by/for borrower (line 220)	( )	602. Less reductions in amt. due seller (line 520)	( )
303. Cash ☐ From ☐ To Borrower		**603. Cash** ☐ To ☐ From Seller	

SUBSTITUTE FORM 1099 SELLER STATEMENT

The information contained in Blocks E, G, H and I and on Line 401 (or, if Line 401 is asterisked, Lines 403 and 404) is important tax information and is being furnished to the Internal Revenue Service. If you are required to file a return, a negligence penalty or other sanction will be imposed on you if this item is required to be reported and the Internal Revenue Service determines that it has not been reported.

L. Settlement Charges

			Paid From Borrower's Funds at Settlement	Paid From Seller's Funds at Settlement
700. Total Sales/Broker's Commission based on price $ @ % =				
Division of Commission (line 700) as follows:				
701. $	to			
702. $	to			
703. Commission paid at Settlement				
704.				
800. Items Payable In Connection With Loan				
801. Loan Origination Fee	%			
802. Loan Discount	%			
803. Appraisal Fee	to			
804. Credit Report	to			
805. Lender's Inspection Fee				
806. Mortgage Insurance Application Fee to				
807. Assumption Fee				
808.				
809.				
810.				
811.				
900. Items Required By Lender To Be Paid In Advance				
901. Interest from to @$ /day				
902. Mortgage Insurance Premium for	months to			
903. Hazard Insurance Premium for	years to			
904.	years to			
905.				
1000. Reserves Deposited With Lender				
1001. Hazard insurance	months @$	per month		
1002. Mortgage insurance	months @$	per month		
1003. City property taxes	months @$	per month		
1004. County property taxes	months @$	per month		
1005. Annual assessments	months @$	per month		
1006.	months @$	per month		
1007.	months @$	per month		
1008.	months @$	per month		
1100. Title Charges				
1101. Settlement or closing fee	to			
1102. Abstract or title search	to			
1103. Title examination	to			
1104. Title insurance binder	to			
1105. Document preparation	to			
1106. Notary fees	to			
1107. Attorney's fees	to			
(includes above items numbers:	)			
1108. Title insurance	to			
(includes above items numbers:	)			
1109. Lender's coverage	$			
1110. Owner's coverage	$			
1111.				
1112.				
1113.				
1200. Government Recording and Transfer Charges				
1201. Recording fees: Deed $; Mortgage $; Reseases $				
1202. City/county tax/stamps: Deed$; Mortgage $				
1203. State tax/stamps: Deed $; Mortgage $				
1204.				
1205.				
1300. Additional Settlement Charges				
1301. Survey	to			
1302. Pest inspection	to			
1303.				
1304.				
1305.				
1400. Total Settlement Charges (enter on lines 103, Section J and 502, Section K)				

SELLER INSTRUCTIONS

If this real estate was your principal residence, file Form 2119, Sale or Exchange of Principal Residence, for any gain, with your tax return; for other transactions, complete the applicable parts of form 4797, form 6252 and/or Schedule D (Form 1040).

The Undersigned Acknowledges Receipt of This Settlement Statement and Agrees to the Correctness Thereof.

_____   _____
Buyer   Seller

SELLER'S CREDITS.

> On a closing statement, anything that increases the amount of money the seller will receive at closing is listed as a credit for the seller.

The seller's major credit, of course, is the purchase price. In addition to this, the seller may be entitled to credits for prorated taxes and insurance premiums, and the balance of any impound accounts in connection with existing loans. If the property is income property, there may be a credit for prorated rents.

SELLER'S DEBITS.

> Anything that decreases the amount the seller will receive at closing appears as a debit to the seller on the closing statement.

The seller's major cost at closing is ordinarily the payoff of any existing loans. The seller may also be charged a prepayment penalty in connection with the payoff, and will be responsible for the interest due for the month of closing.

The seller is usually responsible for payment of the broker's sales commission, his or her own attorney's fees, and a portion of the closing fee, notary fees, and recording fees. Depending on local custom or agreement between the parties, the seller may also be responsible for the abstract of title, a truth-in-housing inspection (and any necessary repairs), and discount points for the buyer's loan. If the property taxes are in arrears, the seller will also owe the prorated taxes due up to the date of closing. These would all be shown as debits to the seller on the closing statement.

If the seller finances the buyer's purchase (for example, by accepting a mortgage or contract for deed for part of the price), the amount of the seller financing will also appear as a debit to the seller on the closing statement.

BUYER'S CREDITS.

> Anything that decreases the amount of money the buyer will actually be required to pay at the time of closing shows up as a credit to the buyer on a closing statement.

For example, the buyer is credited for the amount of the earnest money deposit and for any deposit given to the lender to cover the initial loan costs such as the appraisal and credit report. Even though these deposits are expenses for the buyer, they are treated as buyer's credits on the closing statement because the buyer has already paid them, before closing.

The buyer may also be entitled to a credit for any prorated amounts such as property taxes or rents. And, as explained below, the buyer's financing will also appear as a credit for the buyer on the closing statement.

BUYER'S DEBITS.

> **A debit to the buyer is anything that increases the amount of money the buyer must bring to the closing.**

Obviously, the main cost for the buyer will be the purchase price, which appears as a debit to the buyer (and a credit to the seller) on the closing statement. In most transactions the purchase price will be offset by some form of financing, such as an institutional loan or seller financing. New loans or assumptions of existing loans are listed as credits for the buyer. The difference between the sales price and the financing is the downpayment.

After the purchase price, the buyer's largest debit at closing is typically the loan origination fee (often simply called the loan fee). This is a percentage of the loan amount charged by the lender to cover the administrative costs of making the loan. The FHA and VA limit the loan fee to one percent of the loan amount. Conventional lenders usually charge more (1-3%). To calculate the loan fee, simply multiply the loan amount (not the purchase price) by the percentage charged.

A loan assumption fee may be charged if the buyer is assuming an existing loan. FHA and VA assumption fees are minimal, but some conventional loan assumption fees are quite substantial, the equivalent of a loan origination fee.

In any transaction that does not involve a VA loan, the buyer may be responsible for paying all or some of the discount points to the lender. If the buyer pays points, they should be shown as a debit on the buyer's statement. Several other loan costs are customarily charged to the buyer in a real estate sale. These include the appraisal fee, credit report fee, amounts to be deposited into a reserve account for taxes and insurance, lender's title insurance premium, and prepaid interest. These will appear as debits on the buyer's closing statement.

The appraisal fee and credit report fee are usually set at a flat rate, which may vary depending on the location of the property and the person or firm preparing the report. Residential appraisals usually cost a few hundred dollars and credit reports are normally less than $100. The title insurance fee depends on the amount of the loan and may be obtained from the title company or a rate chart.

Reserve accounts (also called impound accounts) are trust accounts maintained by the lender to pay property taxes and insurance premiums. The borrower may pay a portion of these expenses each month along with the principal and interest payment. When taxes or insurance premiums become due, the lender pays them out of the reserve account. When the loan is originated, the lender may ask the borrower to deposit an initial amount into the reserve account. This is usually enough to cover two to six months' worth of tax and insurance payments.

Prepaid interest (also called interim interest) is the amount of interest due on the loan during the first month of the loan term. Interest on a mortgage is normally paid in arrears. That is, the interest for a given month is paid at the end of the month. When a new loan is made, however, the interest is paid in advance for the month of closing.

> **Example:** Closing occurs on June 15. Interest for the period June 15 through June 30 is paid at closing. The first regular payment on the loan is then due on August 1, and it covers the interest due for the month of July.

To calculate the amount of interim interest due, multiply the daily interest rate (1/360th of the annual rate) by the number of days between the closing date and the end of the month, and then multiply the result by the amount of the loan.

Other items typically charged to the buyer include the buyer's own attorney's fees, notary fees, recording fees, and a share of the closing fee.

Depending on the status of the property taxes, the buyer may owe an amount to the seller. If the property taxes have been paid for a period after the closing date, the buyer will have to reimburse the seller. If taxes are in arrears, the seller owes the amount in arrears.

Example: Assume that the closing date is June 15, and the seller has already paid taxes through the end of June. The buyer would owe the seller an amount equal to the tax for the last half of June. If the closing date were not until July 15, the seller would owe the amount of tax due from the end of June until July 15.

In calculating the amount of tax payable it is necessary to know the daily rate of the tax and the number of days for which each party is responsible. The expense can then be prorated (allocated) between the parties. The process of **proration** is also used to allocate such items as interest on assumed loans, premiums on assumed insurance policies, and rents for income property. (See the proration discussion in Chapter 6.)

CIVIL RIGHTS AND FAIR HOUSING

Fair housing laws apply to sellers, buyers, landlords, tenants, and real estate agents

Discrimination in real estate transactions is prohibited by a number of federal and Minnesota state laws. Property owners and real estate agents are required to comply with these laws, and in some cases compliance can affect the owner/broker relationship. This section of the chapter explains the requirements of these anti-discrimination laws and the consequences of violating them.

FEDERAL LAWS

The eradication of discrimination began on the federal level with the 13th and 14th Amendments to the Constitution. These amendments, passed after the Civil War, abolished slavery and guaranteed equal protection under the law.

Federal laws prohibiting discrimination include the Civil Rights Act of 1866, Title VIII of the Civil Rights Act of 1968 (usually referred to as the Federal Fair Housing Act), the Equal Credit Opportunity Act, and the Home Mortgage Disclosure Act. For the most part, these laws are based on the 13th and 14th Amendments.

CIVIL RIGHTS ACT OF 1866. Suppose Mr. and Mrs. Jones try to buy a home in a subdivision. Their offer is refused because they are black. What can Mr. and Mrs. Jones do? What can the agent who is representing the Joneses do? What kind of liability, if any, would the agent representing the sellers have?

The Civil Rights Act of 1866 prohibits discrimination on the basis of race or ancestry in any property transaction in the United States. The act states, ". . . all citizens of the United States shall have the same right, in every state and territory as is enjoyed by white citizens thereof to inherit, purchase, lease, sell, hold and convey real and personal property."

> The **1866 Act contains no exceptions and applies to all property, whether real or personal, residential or commercial, improved or unimproved. (But remember, this act only applies to discrimination based on race or ancestry.)**

Constitutionality. The constitutionality of the 1866 Act was challenged in a landmark case decided by the U.S. Supreme Court just a few weeks after Congress passed the 1968 Civil Rights Act.

> Mr. and Mrs. Joseph Jones tried to buy a home, or to have one built for them, in a subdivision being developed by the Mayer Company near St. Louis. When their offer was refused, they brought suit against the Mayer Company based on the 1866 Civil Rights Act, claiming the refusal was evidence of racial discrimination. The court ruled in favor of the Joneses and held that the 1866 Act was constitutional. *Jones v. Alfred H. Mayer Co.*, 392 U.S. 409 (1968).

This court decision established three important ideas:

1) The 1866 Act prohibits all racial discrimination in the sale and rental of property, whether through private or state action (action by a government or government official), because the right to buy or lease property can be impaired as effectively by those who place property on the market as by state or local governments.
2) The act is constitutional under the 13th Amendment to the U.S. Constitution. This amendment abolished slavery and also gave Congress the power to enforce the amendment through appropriate legislation.

   The 1866 Civil Rights Act is "appropriate legislation." The 13th Amendment was intended to eliminate not only slavery but also the various conditions and aspects associated with slavery, often referred to as "badges of slavery." One of these "badges" was the inability to own or exchange property. Therefore, it

The Civil Rights Act of 1866 prohibits discrimination on the basis of race or ancestry in property transactions

was proper for Congress to eliminate this badge of slavery through legislation authorized by the 13th Amendment.

3) The provisions of the 1866 Act are independent of and not superseded by the 1968 Fair Housing Act. The Court noted that the 1866 Act is not a comprehensive fair housing law. It does not address discrimination on grounds other than race or ancestry; it does not deal with discrimination in services or facilities connected with housing, financing, advertising, or brokerage services; and it does not provide for any federal agency to assist aggrieved parties or for intervention by the Attorney General. The 1866 Act is a general statute, enforceable only by private parties bringing their own private lawsuits.

By contrast, the Fair Housing Act of 1968 is a detailed housing law covering a great variety of discriminatory practices and enforceable by the complete range of federal authorities.

Enforcement. Suppose you are a real estate agent representing a buyer whose offer is rejected because of race. What remedies does he or she have? The injured party can bring a lawsuit against the seller. Anyone who is unlawfully discriminated against under the 1866 Act may bring a lawsuit in federal district court. The act does not specify a time limit for filing an action, so the lawsuit must be filed within the time limit specified by state law for similar claims. In Minnesota, this time limit is 180 days after the discriminatory act occurred.

Court remedies for racial discrimination: injunction, actual damages, and punitive damages

If the buyer (or other plaintiff) wins the discrimination suit, the following remedies are available:

- injunctive relief,
- actual damages, and
- punitive damages.

Injunctive relief is a court order requiring the defendant to do or refrain from doing a particular act. For example, the court might order the owner to sell the house to the plaintiff.

Actual damages are money awards that compensate the party for the damages caused by the discrimination. This may include out-of-pocket expenses (such as rent or transportation payments) or awards for emotional distress. In some cases, awards for actual damages can total thousands of dollars, and, in exceptional cases, even hundreds of thousands of dollars.

Punitive damages are intended to punish the wrongdoer and discourage others from engaging in similar behavior. There is no limit on the amount of punitive damages that may be awarded for claims brought under the 1866 Act. In some cases, punitive damage awards have exceeded $100,000.

CIVIL RIGHTS ACT OF 1866
Prohibits Discrimination Based on: **Race or Ancestry**
Exceptions: **None**

FEDERAL FAIR HOUSING ACT. Another federal law prohibiting discrimination is Title VIII of the Civil Rights Act of 1968 (referred to as the Federal Fair Housing Act), which states: "It is the policy of the United States to provide, within constitutional limitations, for fair housing throughout the United States."

The act prohibits discrimination based on *race, color, religion, sex, national origin, handicap* or *familial status* (families with children) in the sale or lease of residential property or vacant land intended to be used for residential purposes. The law also prohibits discrimination in advertising, lending, real estate brokerage, and certain other services in connection with residential transactions.

The Federal Fair Housing Act prohibits discrimination based on race, color, religion, sex, national origin, handicap, or familial status in residential transactions

Application. Most sales, rentals, and exchanges of residential property are covered by the Fair Housing Act. Unless specifically exempt, the law covers transactions involving:

1) any building or structure, or portion of a building or structure, which is occupied as, or designed or intended to be occupied as, a residence; and,
2) vacant land which is offered for sale or lease for the construction of any building(s) or portion(s) of building(s) to be used for residential purposes.

Prohibited Acts. Under the Federal Fair Housing Act, the following acts are unlawful if based upon race, color, religion, sex, national origin, handicap, or familial status:

1) refusing to rent or sell residential property after receiving a bona fide offer;

2) refusing to negotiate for the sale or rental of residential property;
3) any action that would make residential property unavailable or deny it to any person (under this general clause, actions such as **steering** and **redlining** are prohibited, as well as many other discriminatory practices and marketing methods);
4) discriminating in the terms or conditions of any sale or rental of residential property or in providing any services or facilities in connection with such property;
5) discriminatory advertising or any other notice which indicates a limitation or preference or intent to make any limitation, preference or discrimination;
6) making any representation that property is not available for inspection, sale or rent when it is in fact available;
7) inducing or attempting to induce, for profit, any person to sell or rent property based on representations regarding entry into the neighborhood of persons of a particular race, color, religion, sex, or national origin (**blockbusting**);
8) discrimination by a commercial lender in making a loan for buying, building, repairing, improving or maintaining a dwelling, or in the terms of such financing;
9) denying access to a multiple listing service or any similar real estate broker's organization, or discriminating in the terms or conditions for access to the organization;
10) coercing, intimidating, threatening or interfering with anyone on account of his or her enjoyment, attempt to enjoy, or encouragement or assistance to others in enjoying the rights granted by the Fair Housing Act.

Discrimination terminology. Three terms that frequently arise in discussions of fair housing and fair lending laws are:

- steering
- blockbusting, and
- redlining.

Steering: channeling prospective buyers or renters to or away from specific neighborhoods, based on race, ethnic background, etc.

Steering is the channeling of prospective buyers or renters, based on race or other prohibited class, to or away from specific neighborhoods. For instance, white customers might only be shown homes in white neighborhoods and black customers only shown homes in black neighborhoods.

Example: In some areas it was a widespread practice to code listing agreements with an "X" or some other mark to indicate that the home could be shown to black prospects.

In Minnesota, a real estate agent's good faith answer to a buyer's question about the neighborhood's composition (racial, ethnic, religious, etc.) would violate anti-discrimination laws even if there was no intent to discriminate. An agent cannot direct or advise a buyer to buy or not buy based on the racial or ethnic composition of the neighborhood.

Example: "You probably wouldn't be interested in looking at that house, it's in a Hispanic neighborhood."
> or

"You wouldn't want to buy in this area, it's a changing neighborhood."

Blockbusting, **or panic selling, is when someone (such as a real estate agent) predicts the entry of minorities into the neighborhood and forecasts lower property values, higher crime rates, a decline in schools, or some other undesirable consequence.**

Blockbusting (panic selling): predicting the entry of minorities into a neighborhood and forecasting social consequences affecting property values

The purpose is to induce property owners to list their property for sale, or to sell their property at a reduced price, so the agent can make a profit.

Many blockbusting "techniques" commonly practiced have been cited in various cases. Listed below are some particularly notorious examples. (Note that less obvious activities should not be condoned by a licensee either.)

- Passing out literature stating that a member of a minority group has purchased a home nearby.
- "Wrong number" phone calls where the callers indicate that they thought they were calling "the black family that just moved in".
- Obtaining numerous listings in the area and placing "For Sale" signs on the properties that are intended to frighten local residents into selling.

- Purchasing a home in the area and selling it on contract to a minority buyer.
- Telling owners that the influx of minorities will adversely affect the schools.
- Implying that homes in the neighborhood are being sold to minorities and that the police will no longer be able to effectively patrol the area.

Redlining: the refusal, for discriminatory reasons, to make loans on property located in a particular neighborhood

> **Redlining** is the refusal, for discriminatory reasons, to make loans on property located in a particular neighborhood.

Many lenders used to automatically assume that property values in any predominantly black or integrated neighborhood were declining. They would then refuse to make loans in those neighborhoods.

Frequently, this was a self-fulfilling prophecy. The inability to obtain purchase or renovation loans made it difficult to sell, maintain or improve homes in the neighborhood, causing values to decline.

Lenders may still refuse to make a loan secured by property in a neighborhood where values are declining. However, the refusal must be based on objective economic criteria concerning the condition and value of the property and surrounding neighborhood, without regard to the racial composition of the neighborhood. A lender may not simply equate a minority or integrated neighborhood with declining values.

Exemptions.

> Although the act covers most residential transactions, there are several exemptions. Congress decided that it was inappropriate to prohibit some forms of discrimination in certain circumstances.

For example, an elderly woman living alone may feel uncomfortable renting out a room in her home to a man. One of the exemptions in the Fair Housing Act allows her to rent only to women. Here are the details of the various exemptions. Please note, however, that these exemptions never allow discrimination based upon race or ancestry (see the discussion of the Civil Rights Act of 1866, above).

1) The Fair Housing Act doesn't apply to a single-family home sold or rented by a private individual owner, provided that:

- the owner owns no more than three such homes,
- no discriminatory advertising is used, and
- no real estate broker (or anyone else in the business of selling or renting homes) is employed.

If the owner isn't the occupant or most recent occupant, he or she may use this exemption only once every 24 months.

2) The law doesn't apply to the rental of a room or unit in a dwelling with up to four units, provided that:

- the owner occupies one unit as his or her residence,
- no discriminatory advertising is used, and
- no real estate broker is employed.

This is often called the "Mrs. Murphy exemption."

Exemptions from Fair Housing Act:
1. single-family house sold or rented by private party;
2. room rented in owner's home;
3. private religious organizations and clubs

U.S. Department of Housing and Urban Development

EQUAL HOUSING
OPPORTUNITY

EQUAL HOUSING
OPPORTUNITY

We Do Business in Accordance With the Federal Fair Housing Law

(The Fair Housing Amendments Act of 1988)

It Is Illegal To Discriminate Against Any Person Because of Race, Color, Religion, Sex, Handicap, Familial Status, or National Origin

- In the sale or rental of housing or residential lots
- In advertising the sale or rental of housing
- In the financing of housing

- In the provision of real estate brokerage services
- In the appraisal of housing
- Blockbusting is also illegal

Anyone who feels he or she has been discriminated against may file a complaint of housing discrimination with the:

U.S. Department of Housing and Urban Development, Assistant Secretary for Fair Housing and Equal Opportunity Washington, D.C. 20410

Previous editions are obsolete   form HUD-928.1 (3-89)

3) In dealing with their own property in noncommercial transactions, religious organizations or societies or affiliated nonprofit organizations may limit occupancy or give preference to their own members, provided membership isn't restricted on the basis of race, color, or national origin.

4) Private clubs with lodgings that aren't open to the public and that aren't operated for a commercial purpose may limit occupancy to or give preference to their own members.

5) The act's provisions regarding discrimination based on familial status generally do not apply to retirement communities.

No exceptions where real estate broker or discriminatory advertising is involved

These limited exemptions apply very rarely. Remember, the 1866 Civil Rights Act prohibits discrimination based on race or ancestry in any property transaction regardless of any exemptions available under the Fair Housing Act. Also, there is no exemption for any transaction involving a real estate licensee. In 1972, the Fair Housing Act was amended to require display of fair housing posters and use of the fair housing logo in advertising. If a real estate broker is investigated for alleged discriminatory acts, failure to display the poster and logo may be considered evidence of discrimination.

Enforcement and Penalties.

Fair Housing Act complaints go to HUD's Office of Equal Opportunity, or to state or federal court

> **An individual unlawfully discriminated against under the Fair Housing Act may file a complaint with the Office of Equal Opportunity (OEO) of the Department of Housing and Urban Development (HUD), or may file a lawsuit in federal or state court.**

HUD may also file a complaint on its own initiative. A complaint must be filed with HUD within 180 days of the discriminatory conduct; a lawsuit must be brought within two years.

If a complaint is filed with HUD, HUD will negotiate for "voluntary" compliance. If that is unsuccessful, the case will be decided by HUD or by a federal district court. Compensatory damages, injunctions and civil penalties ranging from a maximum of $10,000 for a first offense up to $50,000 for a third offense may be awarded.

In states such as Minnesota, where there are state or local fair housing laws similar to the federal law, HUD may refer complaints to the equivalent state or local agency (e.g., the Minnesota Human Rights Commission).

FEDERAL FAIR HOUSING ACT

Prohibits discrimination based on: **Race, Color, Religion, Sex, Handicap, National Origin, Familial Status**

Exemptions:

1. Single-family home sold/rented by owner if:
   a. owner owns no more than three homes
   b. no discriminatory advertising
   c. no real estate agent
   (If owner not most recent occupant, exemption can be used only once every 24 months)
2. Mrs. Murphy exemption
3. Religious groups preferring their own members
4. Private clubs preferring their own members
5. Retirement communities (familial status)

A suit may be filed in federal district court or in the state trial court having general jurisdiction. The court may grant:

- a temporary restraining order,
- a permanent injunction,
- actual damages,
- punitive damages, and
- attorney's fees.

The defendant may also be ordered to take certain steps to prevent future discrimination.

The U.S. Attorney General may bring a civil suit in federal district court if there is evidence of a pattern of discriminatory activities, or if there is a group of people who have been denied their rights in such a way as to raise an issue of public importance. The Attorney General may request temporary or permanent injunctions or other orders necessary to insure that everyone receives the rights granted under the act. The court may also impose civil penalties of up to $100,000.

FAIR LENDING LAWS. Real estate agents and sellers are not the only ones who must avoid discriminatory activities. There are federal laws and regulations designed to eliminate discrimination in lending. They include:

- the Federal Fair Housing Act (discussed above),
- the Equal Credit Opportunity Act,
- the Home Mortgage Disclosure Act, and
- regulations to implement and explain these statutes.

The Fair Housing Act prohibits discrimination in home loans and other aspects of residential financing. It does not apply to any other credit transactions.

Equal Credit Opportunity Act (ECOA): prohibits discrimination in all consumer credit transactions

The **Equal Credit Opportunity Act (ECOA)** applies to all consumer credit, including residential real estate loans. Consumer credit is credit extended to an individual (not a corporation or business) for personal, family or household purposes. The act prohibits lenders from discriminating based on **race, color, religion, national origin, sex, marital status, age** (as long as the applicant is of legal age), or because the applicant's income is derived partly or wholly from **public assistance**.

Home Mortgage Disclosure Act: facilitates the enforcement of federal laws against redlining

The **Home Mortgage Disclosure Act** is a way of learning whether lenders are fulfilling their obligation to serve the housing needs of the communities where they are located. The act facilitates the enforcement of federal laws against redlining.

Under the Home Mortgage Disclosure Act, institutional lenders in metropolitan areas with assets of over $10 million must make annual reports on residential mortgage loans (both purchase and improvement loans) that were originated or purchased during the fiscal year. The information is categorized as to number and dollar amount, type of loan (FHA, VA, FmHA, other), and geographic location by census tract or county (for small counties with no established census tracts). The reports disclose areas where few or no home loans have been made and alert investigators to possible redlining.

MINNESOTA HUMAN RIGHTS ACT

> **In addition to complying with federal laws, agents, sellers, and landlords must also comply with state laws prohibiting discrimination. The state law in Minnesota that prohibits discrimination is the Minnesota Human Rights Act.**

PROTECTED CLASSIFICATIONS. The Minnesota Human Rights Act states that it is an unfair discriminatory practice for anyone having the right to sell, rent or lease real property (or their agents), to refuse to sell, rent, or lease because of:

- race,
- creed,
- color,
- sex,
- national origin,
- marital status,
- familial status,
- disability, or
- status with regard to public assistance.

PROHIBITIONS. Under the Human Rights Act, it is unlawful to refuse to sell, rent, or lease based on any of the factors listed above. It is also unlawful to discriminate in the terms or conditions of a sale or lease, or in furnishing facilities or services. It is also illegal to express any discriminatory limitation or specification in advertising, or for banks or other financial institutions to discriminate in any lending practices.

Like the Federal Fair Housing Act, the Minnesota law also prohibits redlining and blockbusting. In addition, the Minnesota law has a section making it unlawful to deny a handicapped person with a service dog (such as a seeing eye dog) equal access to real property. The person may not be required to pay any extra compensation for the service dog, but is liable for damage done to the premises by the dog.

Minnesota Human Rights Act: prohibits discrimination on the basis of race, creed, color, sex, national origin, marital status, familial status, disability, or status with regard to public assistance in real property transactions

EXCEPTIONS. There are certain limited exceptions under the Minnesota Human Rights Act. It is not a violation of the act to discriminate against protected classifications in the following situations:

Exceptions to the Human Rights Act are limited to non-profit and private residences

1. Sex discrimination in non-profit residence homes.

   Example: The YWCA is a non-profit residence home for women. It is not a violation of the Minnesota Human Rights Act for the YWCA to refuse residence to males.

2. If the resident owner of a single-family home is renting a room within the home, it is not unlawful to discriminate based on sex, marital status, status with regard to public assistance, or disability.

   Example: The Carlsons have a large house and decide to rent out a basement room to make some extra money. The Carlsons refuse to rent the room to Smith because he does not have a job and is living on welfare.

3. Excluding children from buildings that have been exempted by the Commissioner of Human Rights.

   Example: The Broadmoor Arms is a retirement community that has been exempted by the Commissioner of Human Rights. The landlord can refuse to rent to someone who has small children.

It is important to note that none of these exceptions apply if a real estate agent's services are used.

ENFORCEMENT AND PENALTIES. A person claiming a violation of the Minnesota Human Rights Act may file a charge with the Department of Human Rights. The charge must be filed within 180 days of the discriminatory conduct. Once a charge is filed, the department investigates the claim to see if there is probable cause to support the charge. If probable cause is found, the Commissioner of Human Rights may attempt to have the parties reconcile their differences through negotiation, or a formal hearing may be ordered.

If a hearing is ordered, a hearing examiner will listen to testimony and receive evidence. The examiner will then make a decision on the claim. If a finding of unlawful discrimination is made, the examiner may order the payment of compensatory damages and may also impose punitive damages of up to $6,000. The hearing examiner could also issue an injunction prohibiting sale or lease of the property to anyone else, and order the sale or rental of the property to the complainant. No fines or imprisonment are authorized by the Minnesota Human Rights Act, however. The hearing examiner's decision is subject to review by a judge.

Violation of the Human Rights Act by a real estate broker may result in license suspension or revocation, censure, monetary damages, and injunction

If a real estate broker or salesperson is found to have participated in any unlawful discrimination, it could result in license suspension, revocation, or censure, in addition to the penalties described above.

CHAPTER SUMMARY

1. An agent is a person who is authorized to represent or act for someone else (the principal) in dealing with third parties. The agent's authorized actions are binding on the principal, and the principal can be held liable if the agent's actions cause harm to a third party.

2. Agency is a fiduciary relationship. The agent's fiduciary duties to the principal include the duty to use reasonable care and skill, and the duties of obedience, accountability, and loyalty (C.O.A.L.).

3. An agency relationship may be created by written agreement, oral agreement, or ratification. Depending on the degree of authority conferred by the principal, an agent may be a special agent, general agent, or universal agent. In most cases, a real estate broker is a client's special agent, while a salesperson is a broker's general agent.

4. A dual agent represents both the buyer and the seller at the same time. Dual agency is only allowed if both parties consent to the arrangement.

5. A listing agreement is an employment contract between a broker and a seller, appointing the broker as the seller's special agent. It must meet all the requirements for a valid contract. In Minnesota, a listing agreement must also be in writing, state the listing price and terms of sale, state the amount of or method of computing the commission, notify the seller that the commission is negotiable, and have a definite expiration date. Holdover clauses are illegal, and an override clause must not create a protection period that lasts for more than six months.

6. The three types of listing agreements are exclusive right to sell listings, exclusive agency listings, and open listings.

7. An agency relationship may be terminated by accomplishment of purpose, expiration of the term, operation of law, mutual agreement, or revocation.

8. A real estate broker has important financial responsibilities. Minnesota has specific rules for brokers regarding trust funds and closing statements. Closing costs are generally allocated according to custom or an agreement between the parties.

9. There are both state and federal civil rights and fair housing laws that prohibit discrimination. The earliest federal law is the Civil Rights Act of 1866, which prohibits discrimination based on race or ancestry in any property transaction.

10. The Federal Fair Housing Act of 1968 prohibits discrimination based on race, color, religion, sex, national origin, handicap or familial status. There are several exemptions from this act. But remember that there are no exemptions from the 1866 Act, so the Fair Housing exemptions do not apply to race or ancestry.

11. Three practices specifically prohibited under the Fair Housing Act are steering, redlining, and blockbusting. Steering is channeling buyers or renters to or away from specific neighborhoods based on race or another protected characteristic. Redlining is the refusal to make loans on property located in particular areas for discriminatory reasons. Blockbusting (panic selling) is attempting to obtain listings or arrange sales by predicting the entry of minority residents into a neighborhood and representing that this will cause a decline in the neighborhood.

12. There are also federal laws and regulations designed to eliminate discrimination in lending. These include the Federal Fair Housing Act, the Equal Credit Opportunity Act, and the Home Mortgage Disclosure Act.

13. Agents, sellers, and landlords must also comply with the Minnesota Human Rights Act. This act prohibits discrimination based on race, creed, color, sex, national origin, marital status, familial status, disability, or status with regard to public assistance. This statute also makes it unlawful to deny a handicapped person with a service dog equal access to real property. There are limited exceptions to the Minnesota Act. However, none of the exceptions apply if a real estate agent's services are used.

CHAPTER 9—GLOSSARY REVIEW

A. principal
B. agent
C. third party
D. broker
E. salesperson
F. buyer
G. seller
H. exclusive right to sell
I. exclusive agency
J. open
K. dual
L. multiple

M. negotiation
N. Board of Realtors
O. fiduciary
P. general
Q. trust
R. commingling
S. steering
T. blockbusting
U. redlining
V. override
W. holdover

1. One who employs an agent to act in his or her stead is a *principal*

2. The person employed by a principal to act on his or her behalf is an *agent*.

3. Commissions charged by brokers for their services are set by *negotiation*

4. A listing agreement in which the owner agrees to pay the agent a commission regardless of who sells the property during the listing period is known as an _____ listing. *exclusive right to sell*

5. A listing which appoints one broker as the sole agent for the sale of a property, but allows the owner to sell it himself without paying a commission is an _____ listing. *exclusive agency*

6. A listing that allows an owner to list concurrently with more than one broker is known as an *open* listing. *non-exclusive*

7. The relationship of a broker to his or her principal is known as a *fiduciary* relationship.

8. When a broker serves as agent for both purchaser and seller, it is known as a *dual* agency.

9. Earnest money must be deposited in the broker's *trust* account.

10. Depositing client's money with the broker's money (which is illegal) is called *commingling*

11. The illegal practice of inducing panic selling in a neighborhood for financial gain is known as *blockbusting*

12. A clause in a listing which calls for automatic renewal (which is illegal) is known as a _____ clause. *holdover*

CHAPTER 9—REVIEW EXAM

1. A listing broker is the:

   a) seller's agent.
   b) buyer's principal.
   c) seller's subagent.
   d) third party.

2. In an exclusive right to sell listing, the principal contracts:

   a) with several brokers, each of whom deals with only one third party.
   b) to pay the broker a commission regardless of who procures the buyer.
   c) with only one broker but reserves the right to sell the property himself without paying a commission.
   d) with several brokers.

3. All of the following are valid methods of terminating a listing EXCEPT:

   a) destruction of the property
   b) mutual agreement
   c) expiration
   d) the seller has a change of heart

4. If the seller agrees to allow the broker to keep all money above a certain predetermined amount as his commission, what kind of listing do they have?

   a) Open
   b) Net
   c) Multiple
   d) Exclusive

5. If the principal insists that she will not sell her house to members of a certain ethnic group, the broker must:

   a) obey her request according to the law of agency.
   b) report the seller to the police.
   c) ignore the request.
   d) refuse the listing.

6. Attempting to obtain listings in changing neighborhoods by playing on the fears and prejudices of owners is known as:

   a) steering.
   b) commingling.
   c) redlining.
   d) blockbusting.

7. The amount of commission paid to a broker is established by:

   a) state law.
   b) negotiation between broker and seller.
   c) local custom.
   d) real estate boards.

8. A listing in which the principal agrees to contract with only one broker but reserves the right to sell the property him or herself without paying a commission is a(n):

   a) exclusive agency listing.
   b) open listing.
   c) exclusive right to sell listing.
   d) net listing.

9. The listing broker is entitled to a commission according to the terms of an exclusive agency listing if the property is sold by any of the following EXCEPT:

    a) a salesperson employed by the listing broker
    b) a salesperson employed by a cooperating broker
    c) the listing broker
    d) the owner

10. The owner of a property has signed an exclusive right to sell listing contract. Which of the following is true?

    a) The owner has promised to accept a reasonable offer.
    b) The owner has promised to accept any offer identical to the listed price and terms.
    c) The owner has promised to pay a commission if the property is sold during the listing period.
    d) The broker has promised to find a buyer.

11. The clause in a listing agreement that protects the broker's commission if someone with whom the broker negotiated purchases the property after the expiration of the listing is known as:

    a) a protective clause.
    b) a holdover clause.
    c) a due-on-sale clause.
    d) an override clause.

12. Which of the following establishes the broker's power to act as an agent for the seller?

    a) Real estate commissioner
    b) Multiple listing service
    c) Listing agreement
    d) Real estate license

13. An open listing would best be described as:

    a) a unilateral contract.
    b) an option.
    c) a bilateral contract.
    d) a negotiable instrument.

14. At closing, all of the following would be debits to the seller EXCEPT:

    a) pay off of an existing mortgage
    b) abstract of title update
    c) contract for deed between seller and buyer
    d) earnest money

15. Grandma Jones would like to rent out rooms in her home. According to the Minnesota Human Rights Act, she may discriminate against all of the following EXCEPT:

    a) foreign students
    b) an unmarried couple
    c) a person in a wheelchair
    d) single males

16. A builder who agrees to pay a commission to the first broker who negotiates a sale would sign:

    (a) an open listing agreement.
    b) a multiple listing agreement.
    c) an option listing agreement.
    d) an implied listing agreement.

17. Which of the following is an example of commingling?

    a) The broker deposits earnest money in her trust account.
    (b) The broker deposits earnest money in her business account.
    c) The broker deposits commissions earned in her business account.
    d) The broker deposits earnest money in an interest-bearing account with the consent of both buyer and seller.

18. If all the brokers in a town agreed to charge the same commission rate it would be a violation of the:

    a) law of agency.
    (b) antitrust laws.
    c) statutes of limitation.
    d) usury laws.

19. If a broker and a seller have a fiduciary relationship, the broker could:

    a) inform a buyer that the seller will accept substantially less than the listed price.
    b) fail to tell the buyer about hidden structural problems in order to protect the seller.
    (c) disclose the buyer's financial qualifications.
    d) honor the seller's request to refuse to show the property to minorities.

20. Which of the following classifications is the only one protected by both the 1866 Civil Rights Act and the Federal Fair Housing Act of 1968?

    a) Religion
    (b) Race
    c) Sex
    d) National origin

21. The owners of a warehouse refuse to rent storage space to a Catholic school. Which of the following is true under the Federal Fair Housing Act?

    a) They cannot discriminate on the basis of religion.
    (b) Their actions are not prohibited.
    c) They cannot discriminate on the basis of occupation.
    d) Their actions are an example of steering.

22. Under the Minnesota Human Rights Act, which of the following is allowed?

    a) An owner selling his or her own home may refuse to sell to a minority.
    b) The owner-occupant of a duplex may refuse to rent the other unit to men.
    (c) The owner-occupant of a duplex may refuse to rent to anyone over age 65.
    d) An owner selling his or her home with the aid of a broker may refuse to sell to foreign nationals.

23. Which of the following is not required in a listing agreement?

   a) Negotiable commission clause
   b) Expiration date
   c) List price
   d) Estimated closing costs

24. When a lender refuses to make loans in a given neighborhood because most of its residents are members of a racial minority group, it is an example of:

   a) steering.
   b) blockbusting.
   c) credit deviation.
   d) redlining.

25. Which of the following would be a violation of the Federal Fair Housing Act?

   a) A property manager refuses to rent a one-bedroom house to a family of five.
   b) A salesperson refuses to show property to a buyer with poor credit.
   c) A salesperson refuses to show a listed property to a customer because the seller does not want to sell to anyone of a different religion.
   d) A lender refuses to make a loan to a real estate broker.

CHAPTER 9—GLOSSARY REVIEW KEY

1. A
2. B
3. M
4. H
5. I
6. J

7. O
8. K
9. Q
10. R
11. T
12. W

CHAPTER 9—REVIEW EXAM KEY

1. a) The listing broker is the agent for the seller.

2. b) Under the exclusive right to sell listing, the broker is paid regardless of who procured the buyer.

3. d) One party's change of heart does not terminate a listing, unless the other party is also willing to terminate it.

4. b) For a net listing, price minus net equals commission.

5. d) The broker must not discriminate.

6. d) Blockbusting (panic selling) is the prohibited practice of representing that bad things will happen due to an influx of residents of a certain race, creed, color, or national origin.

7. b) Commission rates are determined by negotiation.

8. a) Under the exclusive agency listing, the owner retains the right to sell without compensating the listing broker.

9. d) The owner may sell without paying a commission in an exclusive agency. If anyone else sells the property, the listing broker gets paid.

10. c) In the exclusive right to sell listing, the broker is paid if the property is sold during the listing period, regardless of who obtains the buyer.

11. d) The override clause protects the broker's commission for up to six months after the listing terminates.

12 c) The listing agreement is a contract by which the seller authorizes the broker to use his or her best efforts to find a ready, willing, and able buyer.

13. a) An open listing is considered to be a unilateral contract.

14. d) The earnest money would be a credit to the buyer.

15. a) Owner-occupants of a single-family home may discriminate in the rental of rooms based upon sex, marital status, disability, receipt of public assistance, or family status.

16. a) In an open listing, the owner agrees to pay the first broker who negotiates a sale.

17. b) Trust funds may not be placed in the broker's business account. (And a trust account may contain only "other people's money" held pending completion of a transaction.)

18. b) Antitrust laws prohibit price fixing.

19. c) As a fiduciary of the seller, the broker has the obligations of care, obedience, accountability, and loyalty (COAL). However, these fiduciary duties do not require or permit the broker to commit fraud or violate anti-discrimination laws.

20. b) In addition to race, the Federal Fair Housing Act also protects color, religion, sex, national origin, handicap, or familial status. The Civil Rights Act of 1866 only prohibits discrimination on the basis of race or ancestry.

21. b) The Federal Fair Housing Act only prohibits discrimination in housing.

22. c) Age is not a protected classification under the Minnesota Human Rights Act.

23. d) Closing costs must be estimated upon presentation of an offer, not in the listing agreement.

24. d) Redlining is the prohibited practice of refusing to give loans in certain neighborhoods because of the race or ethnic background of the residents.

25. c) This is an example of steering.

Chapter 10

Minnesota License Law

Outline

KEY TERMS

Department of Commerce	Commissioner of Commerce
real estate laws	real estate rules
Advisory Task Force	continuing education
loan broker	limited broker
disciplinary action	license revocation/suspension
misrepresentation	actual or constructive fraud
caveat emptor	unauthorized practice of law
conversion	REERRF
Subdivided Lands Act	statutory new home warranty
manufactured home	

CHAPTER OVERVIEW

The business practices of real estate licensees in Minnesota are governed by specific state statutes and regulations, commonly called the Minnesota license law.

> **The main purpose of the license law is to protect the public from unscrupulous, uninformed, or negligent real estate agents.**

The license law determines who must have a real estate license, and sets out the licensing requirements. It also establishes grounds for suspending or revoking a real estate license. Anyone who is involved in the real estate business should be very familiar with the license law.

LICENSING LEGISLATION AND ADMINISTRATION

In Minnesota, the Department of Commerce oversees the real estate industry. This department is headed by the Commissioner of Commerce, who is appointed by the governor. The Commissioner administers the real estate laws, which are the state statutes that control real estate licensing and business practices (Chapters 82 and 83 of the Minnesota Code). The Commissioner of Commerce also formulates and administers the real estate rules (Chapters 2800, 2805, 2810 of the Minnesota Rules), which are the regulations that implement the real estate laws. Together, the real estate laws and the real estate rules are often referred to as the license law.

The Commissioner has the authority to screen and qualify applicants for a real estate license, issue and renew licenses, investigate complaints against licensees, investigate people alleged to be acting as real estate agents without a license, and regulate some aspects of the sale of subdivision lots, nonexempt franchises, and real property securities.

The Commissioner also has the power to hold formal hearings to decide issues involving a licensee, license applicant, or subdivider. After holding a hearing, the Commissioner may suspend, revoke, or deny a license, or order sales in a subdivision to be stopped. The Commissioner can sue to obtain an injunction or restitution for members of the public who have been harmed by real estate agents violating the license law. He or she can also bring an action to prevent trust fund violations.

> **Note that the Commissioner does not arbitrate disputes between individual real estate agents (such as fee splitting disputes, or problems between a salesperson and a broker).**

ADVISORY TASK FORCE. The Commissioner of Commerce appoints a Real Estate Advisory Task Force. The task force advises the Commissioner on all major policy questions relating to the administration of the license law, particularly education and pre-license requirements. The task force is made up of five real estate brokers with at least five years' experience in Minnesota, and members of the general public.

Minnesota Department of Commerce: oversees real estate licensing and business practices

WHO MUST BE LICENSED

Who must be licensed: anyone who lists, sells, exchanges, manages, buys, or rents real estate, a business opportunity, or a business, when action is taken for someone else for a fee or commission

> **In Minnesota, anyone who lists, sells, exchanges, manages, buys, or rents real estate, a business opportunity, or a business (or the goodwill, inventory, or fixtures of a business) must have a real estate license, if the action is taken for someone else and for a fee or commission.**

Example: You don't have to have a real estate license to sell your own home or business, but you must have a license if you agree to sell someone else's home or business for them, for a commission.

EXCEPTIONS

There are some exceptions to the license requirements. The following people are not required to have a real estate license:

1. a licensed practicing attorney;
2. a receiver, trustee, administrator, guardian, executor, or anyone else acting under court order;
3. anyone owning and operating a cemetery and selling lots solely for use as burial plots;
4. the custodian, janitor, or employee of the owner or manager of a residential building who leases units in the building;
5. a bank, trust company, savings and loan association, industrial loan and thrift company, public utility, land mortgage, or farm loan association engaged in a business transaction within the scope of its powers as provided by law;
6. public officers while performing their official duties;
7. a bonded auctioneer engaged in the specific performance of duties as an auctioneer, under the direction and supervision of an attorney or broker;
8. someone who acquires real estate for constructing buildings for resale, if no more than 25 transactions occur in any 12-month period;
9. anyone who offers to sell real estate that is a security as an incident to the sale of securities;
10. anyone who offers to sell a registered franchise;
11. someone who contracts with a resident to provide care in a continuing care facility;

12. a broker-dealer when participating in the conveyance of a business or business opportunity (when the broker-dealer is licensed pursuant to Chapter 80A of the Minnesota Code);
13. an accountant acting as an incident to the practice of accounting.

LOAN BROKERS

Loan brokers negotiate loans secured by mortgages or contracts for deed. They arrange loans between borrowers and lenders, but usually do not lend money themselves.

> **Loan brokers are required to be licensed real estate brokers. However, the licensing requirement does not apply to banks, savings and loans, and other lending institutions, or to their employees who negotiate loans.**

Loan broker: must have a real estate license and follow certain standards of conduct

Although loan brokers have real estate licenses, they are treated as a separate category from regular real estate agents. An ordinary agent who helps a buyer obtain financing is not considered a loan broker, as long as the agent doesn't receive a separate commission or fee for the financing assistance.

The license law prescribes special standards of conduct for loan brokers. A loan broker must enter into a written contract with each customer, and give the customer a copy of the contract before receiving any payment for loan brokerage services. The contract has to include specific provisions and disclosures, such as a description of the services the loan broker will perform, the maximum interest rate to be charged on any loan obtained, and the customer's right to cancel the contract within three days after signing.

If the customer pays any fees to the loan broker before a loan is actually funded, the broker has to deposit them in an escrow account within 48 hours. The contract must set forth the circumstances under which the loan broker will be entitled to payment from the account. The loan broker is required to keep a separate record for each customer, showing all fees received and each disbursement from the escrow account. At least once a month, the loan broker must provide each customer with a detailed written accounting.

NONINSTITUTIONAL LENDERS

The real estate licensing requirements also extend to people who make loans secured by real estate: someone who makes five or more real estate loans during one year is required to have a real estate broker's license. This rule only applies to noninstitutional lenders, private parties who lend money. Again, lending institutions and their employees are not required to hold real estate licenses.

LIMITED BROKERS

Limited broker: owner selling own property if involved in five or more transactions in a year; may not act as a real estate agent for others

Generally, a property owner does not need a real estate license in order to sell his or her own property.

> **However, an owner who is involved in five or more transactions in one year either must be represented by a real estate agent or else must obtain a limited broker's license.**

Limited brokers are only licensed to sell their own property, not to act as real estate agents for other property owners or buyers. A limited broker also cannot be a real estate salesperson's primary broker; the salesperson must be licensed under a regular broker.

Builders who sell no more than 25 units per year are not required to have full broker's licenses. (That's number 8 on the list of licensing exceptions shown earlier in this chapter.) They also do not have to have limited brokers' licenses, as long as they stay below the 25-transaction limit.

RENTAL SERVICES

Rental service: required to have real estate broker's license

Rental services provide information about properties that are available for rent.

> **A rental service is required to have a real estate broker's license. Employees acting on behalf of a rental service must have a salesperson's license if they give out information about rental properties to the public.**

Before providing any information regarding a rental unit, a rental service has to obtain the permission of the property owner (the landlord). It's illegal for a rental service to represent that a unit is currently available unless its availability has been verified within the preceding 72 hours.

RESIDENTIAL CLOSING AGENTS

Residential closing agent: required to have special license

A residential closing agent is someone who provides closing services in residential real estate transactions. A closing agent doesn't have to have a real estate broker's or salesperson's license, but is required to obtain a closing agent's license from the Commissioner of Commerce. Although real estate brokers and salespersons often provide residential closing services, they aren't required to have a closing agent's license in addition to a broker's or salesperson's license. Lawyers and title insurance company employees are also allowed to perform residential closing services without a closing agent's license.

LICENSING REQUIREMENTS

SALESPERSON'S LICENSE

An applicant for a Minnesota real estate salesperson's license must:

1. be at least 18 years old;
2. complete three 30-hour real estate courses (Courses I, II, and III);
3. pass the salesperson's examination within one year after completing Course I;
4. submit an application (on a form provided by the Commissioner and signed by the employing broker) and pay the license fee, within one year after passing the exam.

Salesperson's license:
1. 18 years old;
2. three 30-hour courses;
3. examination; and
4. written application and fee

The license application must be sworn to and signed by the applicant; it must also be signed by a licensed real estate broker. A salesperson is licensed to act on behalf of a broker, and may not act as a real estate agent independently.

The broker that a salesperson is licensed under is referred to as the salesperson's primary broker. A salesperson may only work for one broker in Minnesota at a time. The salesperson's license is mailed to the primary broker, and must remain in the broker's possession until it is canceled or the salesperson leaves the broker's employment.

Note that Minnesota does not require an applicant for a salesperson's license to have a high school diploma or a college degree. There is also no state residency requirement.

BROKER'S LICENSE

A person who has at least two years' experience as a real estate salesperson may apply for a broker's license. The applicant must also have completed a 30-hour broker's course, passed the broker's examination, and paid the license fee. (An applicant for a limited broker's license is not required to have experience as a salesperson.)

Broker's license:
1. two years' experience as real estate salesperson;
2. broker's course;
3. examination; and
4. application and fee

CORPORATION OR PARTNERSHIP LICENSES

Sometimes a corporation or partnership is licensed as a real estate broker.

Corporation or partnership license: at least one officer or partner individually licensed as broker

> **A corporation or partnership applying for a license must have at least one officer or partner individually licensed to act as broker for the corporation or partnership.**

In addition, any other officer or partner who intends to act as a broker must also obtain a license. These licenses only authorize the officers or partners to act as brokers for the corporation or partnership, not to represent anyone else in real estate transactions.

Until recently, the licensed corporate officers or partners were required to have brokers' licenses, not salespersons' licenses. The Commissioner would not issue a salesperson's license to any officer or partner of a corporation or partnership that was licensed as a broker. This rule changed as of August, 1991. Now officers or partners *may* hold salespersons' licenses, as long as they do not operate in a management capacity.

The individual licenses of all salespersons acting on behalf of a corporation or partnership are automatically ineffective if the license of the partnership or corporation is suspended or revoked. On the other hand, the Commissioner may suspend or revoke the license of an officer or partner without suspending or revoking the license of the corporation or partnership.

LICENSING FEES

The following fees must be paid to the Commissioner. The amounts listed were current in 1991; however, fees are subject to change, so you should check with the Department of Commerce before making payment.

Initial salesperson's license	$25
Salesperson's annual renewal	$10
Initial individual broker's license	$50
Broker's annual renewal	$25
Corporate or partnership license	$50
Corporate or partnership renewal	$25
Transfer	$10
Corporation or partnership name change	$25
Agent name change	$ 5
License history	$10
Duplicate license	$ 5

CONTINUING EDUCATION

After becoming licensed, real estate salespersons and brokers are required to take continuing education classes. New salespersons must complete 30 hours of continuing education within one year after receiving their licenses. All salespersons and brokers must successfully complete 15 hours of real estate education each year thereafter. Continuing education must be reported on an annual basis. If more than 15 hours are earned in any one year, up to 15 hours may be carried forward to the next year.

Continuing education: new salespersons, 30 hours; each year thereafter, 15 hours

EXPIRATION AND RENEWAL

All real estate licenses expire on June 30. Applications for license renewal must be mailed by June 15 each year. Renewal applications are made on forms provided by the Commissioner. They must be accompanied by the renewal fee. If application for renewal is not made in a timely fashion (by June 15), the license will become ineffective on July 1 and remain so until a new license has been issued.

LICENSE TERMINATION AND TRANSFER

As you've seen, a salesperson must be licensed under a primary broker. When the salesperson stops working for that broker, the salesperson's license becomes ineffective.

> **Within ten days after the termination, the broker is required to return the salesperson's license to the Commissioner.**

The salesperson may apply to have the license transferred to another broker at any time before it expires. If the license expires before an application for transfer is made, the Commissioner will require the salesperson to apply for a new license.

Salesperson's license:
- only effective while working for broker
- may transfer to another broker before expiration

> **Example:** John is a real estate salesperson; his primary broker is Ellen. John decides he can't stand working for Ellen, so he quits on April 20, even though he hasn't made arrangements to work for a different broker. Ellen sends John's license back to the Commissioner within 10 days. The Commissioner will transfer John's license to a new broker if John requests the transfer before June 30 (the license expiration date). But if John does not find work with another broker until August, he will be required to file an application for a new license.

Automatic Transfer. When a salesperson quits working for one broker in order to begin working for another broker right away, an automatic transfer of the salesperson's license can be arranged.

To apply for an automatic transfer, the salesperson fills out and signs an automatic transfer form, then asks both the former broker and the new broker to sign the form. Both brokers must indicate on the form the date and time that they signed it. The former broker must sign before the new broker does, and must destroy the salesperson's license immediately after signing. The new broker must sign within five days after the former broker signed. The salesperson is considered unlicensed during the period between the time the former broker signs and the time the new broker signs. The application form and a $10 transfer fee must be sent to the Commissioner (either by certified mail or personal delivery) within 72 hours after the new broker signs the form. The transfer is effective as soon as the form is sent or delivered.

The automatic transfer procedure can also be used when someone who has a broker's license decides to stop acting as a broker, in order to go to work as a salesperson under another broker instead.

PENALTIES FOR LICENSE LAW VIOLATIONS

The Minnesota license law includes many rules about what a licensee must do and must not do in handling real estate transactions. Those rules, known as the Standards of Conduct, are reviewed later in this chapter. A real estate licensee's failure to comply with the Standards of Conduct is grounds for disciplinary action by the Commissioner. Depending on the nature of the misconduct, the Commissioner may decide to censure the licensee, suspend the licensee's license temporarily, or permanently revoke the license. (Misconduct can also lead the Commissioner to deny an initial license application or refuse to renew a license.)

Violation of real estate license law is a crime

> **Violation of any provision of the license law is a gross misdemeanor.**

So a licensee's misconduct can result in criminal prosecution in addition to disciplinary action by the Commissioner. It is unusual for criminal charges to be filed except in serious cases. However, real estate licensees are frequently subject to civil liability in addition to losing their licenses. If a client or customer files a civil lawsuit against a licensee for breach of fiduciary duties, negligence, or fraud, the licensee may be required to compensate the injured party. (See Chapter 9.)

NOTICE TO THE COMMISSIONER

A real estate licensee who gets into serious trouble is required to notify the Commissioner. The Commissioner must be notified in writing within ten days after any of the following events:

1. A court enters a civil judgment against the licensee for fraud, misrepresentation, or the conversion of funds.
2. The licensee has a real estate license or any other occupational license suspended or revoked by the licensing authority (in Minnesota or another jurisdiction).
3. A licensee is charged with, convicted of, or pleads guilty (or nolo contendere) to any felony, or a gross misdemeanor involving fraud, misrepresentation, conversion of funds, or a similar license law violation.

The Commissioner must also be notified in writing within ten days if the licensee changes his or her name, home address, or business address.

Licensee with legal problem must notify Commissioner within 10 days

DISCIPLINARY ACTION

After receiving a written complaint, the Commissioner is required to investigate the actions of a licensee. An investigation may also be started on the Commissioner's own motion, without waiting for a complaint from a member of the public. The Commissioner (or someone authorized by the Commissioner) may call an informal conference and ask everyone involved in the problem to attend. If the initial investigation indicates that the complaint is serious enough, a formal hearing will be held. In most circumstances, a formal hearing must be held before the Commissioner may deny, suspend, or revoke any license.

For the formal hearing, the Commissioner appoints a hearing officer to hear the case and make recommendations. The Commissioner takes the role of the complainant, bringing the charges against the licensee. (The person who brought the matter to the Commissioner's attention may appear as a witness at the hearing.) The licensee is given notice of the hearing, and may attend it with or without a lawyer. At the hearing, witnesses testify under oath and a written record of the proceedings is made.

The Commissioner can accept, reject, or modify the recommendations of the hearing officer. If the Commissioner decides to suspend or revoke the license, the licensee has the right to appeal the decision to the district court.

Commissioner:
1. *must investigate any written complaint against real estate agent;*
2. *may hold a hearing;*
3. *may suspend or revoke license*

STANDARDS OF CONDUCT

> **When the Commissioner issues a real estate license, he or she grants the licensee the right to represent others in real estate transactions. In exchange for that right, the licensee is required to fulfill specific responsibilities and to meet certain standards of conduct outlined in the Minnesota license law.**

In this section, we'll look first at the rules that apply only to brokers, and then at the rules that apply to all real estate licensees.

BROKER'S RESPONSIBILITIES

In addition to the duties that all real estate licensees are required to fulfill, brokers have a number of special responsibilities. These include supervising salespersons, handling trust funds, and record keeping.

Broker's responsibilities: supervise salespersons; investigate complaints; review documents; maintain trust accounts; keep transaction records for three years

SUPERVISION. A broker is responsible for everything that a salesperson does while acting as a real estate agent on the broker's behalf. If the salesperson's action causes harm to a member of the public and the Commissioner determines that the salesperson was not adequately supervised by his or her primary broker, the broker's license (as well as the salesperson's) can be suspended or revoked.

Copy of license law. A broker must keep a copy of the license law and the Subdivided Lands Act at each of his or her real estate offices (main office and branch offices) and make them available to the salespersons who work there.

Complaints. If a client or customer complains about a salesperson, the broker is expected to investigate the problem and try to resolve it. The license law requires a broker to maintain a complaint file for each salesperson, and keep all documents relating to any written complaint for at least three years.

Documents and copies. As part of their supervisory duties, brokers are expected to review all the listing agreements, purchase agreements, and other documents their salespersons and employees prepare. Even though the broker has delegated the preparation of agreements to a salesperson, the broker remains responsible for their accuracy.

In Minnesota, a broker or salesperson is permitted to fill out standard contract forms for the parties in a real estate transaction. However, real estate agents should never insert complicated provisions that require legal expertise, and should never draft a contract from scratch instead of using a standard form. Those actions could be considered the unauthorized practice of law.

The parties to a real estate transaction are legally entitled to a copy of any document that pertains to their interests. The broker or salesperson must provide copies when the parties sign the documents or when the documents become available.

Unlicensed staff. It's not necessary for all of a broker's employees to be licensed salespersons. However, the broker must make sure that unlicensed employees do not give out any information about listed property except its address and whether it is available for sale or lease. Unlicensed employees aren't allowed to discuss the condition of the property, the listing price, or any other specific information of that nature with members of the public.

TRUST ACCOUNTS. The license law requires every broker to maintain an interest-bearing trust account and keep detailed records of deposits and disbursements. (See Chapter 9.) This is one of a broker's most important responsibilities. If there are any changes in the status of a broker's trust account (if the broker opens a trust account at a new bank, for example), the broker is required to notify the Commissioner. A broker may not close a trust account without giving the Commissioner notice ten days in advance.

RECORD KEEPING. In addition to trust account records, a broker must keep copies of all documents related to real estate transactions (listings, purchase agreements, and so on) and the brokerage business in general.

> **All of a broker's records (including trust account records) have to be retained for at least three years.**

The three-year period is measured from the closing date, or if the transaction never closed, from the listing date.

FEE SPLITTING. A broker is not allowed to pay a finder's fee or share a real estate commission unless the payment is made to:

- one of the broker's own salespersons;
- a real estate broker licensed in Minnesota or another state;
- a corporation owned solely by a licensed broker or salesperson; or
- one of the parties to the real estate transaction.

So it's illegal for a broker to pay an unlicensed person a finder's fee, either for helping the broker obtain a listing or for locating a buyer. This rule applies to gifts as well as monetary payments.

RULES FOR ALL LICENSEES

The license law's standards of conduct can be grouped into two main categories: prohibited conduct (things that real estate licensees are required to avoid) and mandatory conduct (things that licensees are required to do). The most important provisions are summarized here.

PROHIBITED CONDUCT. Any of the following actions is grounds for suspension or revocation of a real estate license.

Prohibited conduct is grounds for license suspension or revocation

- **Lying to the Commissioner.** This includes material misstatements in a license application or any other information provided to the Commissioner's office.
- **Guaranteeing future profits.** It's illegal for a real estate licensee to guarantee a buyer or tenant future profits from a purchase or lease, unless the terms of the guarantee are spelled out in the purchase agreement, lease, or other contract.
- **Disclosing an offer.** Never disclose the terms of one prospective buyer's offer to another prospective buyer before presenting the offer to the seller.
- **Interfering with an exclusive agency.** When you are aware that an owner, buyer, or tenant has already signed an exclusive contract with another broker, do not try to deal directly with the principal.

> **All negotiations must be conducted through the exclusive licensee.**

You are also required to ask owners, buyers, or tenants whether they have signed an exclusive contract with another real estate broker (so ignorance is no excuse).

- **Encouraging breach of contract.** A real estate licensee must not try to convince any party to a contract to breach it. That includes persuading a seller who has listed with another broker to list with you instead, or telling one of your clients to back out of a purchase agreement in order to accept a better offer.
- **Discouraging use of an attorney.** A licensee should never do anything to prevent or discourage any of the parties to a transaction from consulting a lawyer. That's a violation of the license law, even if you honestly believe a lawyer's services are an unnecessary expense in a particular case.

- **Undisclosed dual agency.** A licensee may not act on behalf of both the buyer and the seller in a transaction unless both of the parties have consented to that arrangement. (See Chapter 9.)
- **Blind or misleading advertising.**

> When a real estate licensee advertises property without mentioning his or her licensed status in the ad, it's called a "blind ad".

Blind advertising is illegal. Even when a real estate licensee advertises his or her own property, the ad must indicate that a licensee is involved.

The license law also forbids a real estate licensee from advertising property or brokerage services in any way that is misleading or inaccurate.

- **Discrimination.** Violation of any state or federal anti-discrimination law intended to protect real estate buyers or tenants is also a violation of the license law. (See Chapter 9.)
- **Misrepresentation.** A real estate licensee must not make any material misrepresentations, and also must not allow anyone else (a client, for example) to misrepresent the facts. In addition to that general rule against misrepresentation, the license law specifically prohibits licensees from making (or allowing anyone else to make) false or misleading statements that are likely to induce someone to enter a real estate transaction.

Not only can misrepresentation lead to license suspension or revocation, the real estate licensee may also be sued for fraud.

> Misrepresentation is actionable (grounds for a lawsuit) if the licensee knew or should have known that his or her statement was false.

If the licensee knew the statement was false and intentionally misled the other party, that's known as actual fraud. If the misrepresentation was the result of carelessness (rather than an intention to mislead), it's called constructive fraud. In either case, if the other party relied on the misrepresentation and was harmed as a result, the licensee can be held liable and ordered to pay damages.

- **Acting without a signed listing.** The license law forbids a real estate licensee from advertising another person's property for sale (including placement of a 'for sale' sign on the property) unless the seller has signed a listing agreement. And without a signed listing, the licensee cannot sue for a commission. (In addition, a licensee who sues must be able to prove that he or she was licensed at the time the commission was earned.) It's also a license law violation to demand a commission when you know you are not entitled to payment.

- **Price fixing.**

> **When two or more real estate brokers who do not work for the same firm agree to charge a certain commission rate, that's price fixing.**

Price fixing is a violation of the antitrust laws (see Chapter 9). The Minnesota license law also prohibits real estate licensees from engaging in any anticompetitive activity.

- **Accepting undisclosed kickbacks.** When acting on behalf of a client, it's illegal for a real estate licensee to accept any gift or payment from a third party without telling the client.
- **Holdover clauses and excessive override clauses.** Including a holdover clause (an automatic renewal clause) in a listing agreement is grounds for license suspension or revocation. So is including an override clause that creates a protection period longer than six months. (See Chapter 9.)
- **Commingling.** Commingling trust funds with personal funds (see Chapter 9) is a violation of the license law. In fact, it's probably the most common reason for revocation of a real estate license. The Commissioner can take disciplinary action against a licensee for commingling even if the licensee had no intention of misusing the trust funds. (When a licensee does use trust funds for his or her own purposes, it's called conversion of funds. Conversion is a crime, as well as grounds for disciplinary action.)

MANDATORY CONDUCT. A real estate licensee's failure to fulfill any of the following duties in appropriate circumstances is grounds for license suspension or revocation.

- **Disclosure of personal interest and licensed status; use of trust account.** When selling your own property or buying property for yourself, you must let the other party know that you have a direct interest in the transaction and that you have a real estate license.

> **It's illegal to pretend that you are representing a third party rather than yourself, or to pretend that you aren't a real estate agent.**

These disclosures must be made before you begin negotiating with the other party.

If you receive any money in the transaction that would be considered trust funds if you were acting on behalf of a client, you must put the money in a trust account, unless the other party agrees in writing to have it handled differently.

> **Example:** You're selling your own house. A prospective buyer gives you a $2,000 check as earnest money along with her offer to purchase. You must deposit the check in a trust account by the next business day. If you would rather place the check in a personal account, you must obtain the buyer's written permission to do so.

- **Agency disclosure.**

> **When you act as an agent in a real estate transaction, you are required to disclose to all the parties, in writing, which party (or parties) you are representing: the seller, the buyer, or both.**

This disclosure should be made before an offer is made or accepted. An agency disclosure statement must be printed in boldface type on the purchase agreement form, and both the buyer and seller must sign the disclosure statement to acknowledge that they accept the agent's characterization of the agency relationship(s).

A real estate salesperson often spends a considerable amount of time with a prospective buyer, showing the buyer many of his or her primary broker's listings. By the time the buyer has decided to buy a particular property, the buyer may have the impression that the salesperson is representing his or her interests in the transaction. But in most cases, the salesperson is representing only the seller, not the buyer, since the salesperson's broker (the listing broker) is the seller's agent. The agency disclosure statement is intended to prevent misunderstandings.

In many exclusive listing agreements, the seller authorizes the listing broker to split the commission with other brokers who help bring about a sale. The listing broker often ends up sharing the commission with a broker who is representing the buyer. As long as the seller has agreed to this commission-splitting arrangement, it is legal. Even though the buyer's agent is, in effect, receiving payment from the seller (a share of the commission paid by the seller), that does not create an agency relationship between the buyer's agent and the seller.

- **Disclosure of material facts.** In the past, the rule of "caveat emp-tor" ("let the buyer beware") governed real estate transactions. The real estate agent (and the seller) had very few duties of disclosure to a prospective buyer. It was up to the buyer to inspect the proper-ty and ask questions about it. The agent and the seller were required to answer the buyer's questions truthfully, but did not have to disclose problems that the buyer failed to ask about.

  It no longer works that way in Minnesota (or most other states).

  > Now, if a real estate licensee is aware of any material facts about the property that might adversely affect the use or en-joyment of it, Minnesota's license law requires the licensee to disclose those facts to prospective buyers.

  In complying with this rule, the licensee is supposed to consider how an ordinary buyer would be likely to use the property, not every possible use. But if the licensee knows that a particular buyer in-tends to make some special use of the property, the licensee must be sure to reveal any facts that could interfere with that intended use.

  Fraud usually involves a false or misleading statement, but con-cealing or failing to disclose information that you have a legal duty to disclose can also constitute fraud. Active concealment or an in-tentional failure to disclose is actual fraud, and negligent failure to disclose is constructive fraud.
- **Presentation of all offers.**

  > Whenever a prospective buyer or tenant gives a real estate licensee a written offer to buy or lease, the licensee must sub-mit the offer to the property owner promptly.

  The licensee should never hold an offer back in the hope that someone else will make a better one. It's also illegal for a licensee to decide that a particular offer is so low it isn't even worth present-ing to the owner at all. The owner, not the real estate agent, decides which offer is acceptable.
- **Disclosure regarding closing costs.** Before an offer to purchase is signed by the prospective buyer or presented to the seller, a real estate licensee must warn each party that he or she may be required to pay certain closing costs. The listing broker also has to give each party a detailed closing statement at the time of closing. (See Chapter 9.) Failure to fulfill these duties is grounds for disciplinary action by the Commissioner.

• **Deposit of earnest money checks.**

> **When a real estate licensee receives an earnest money deposit from an offeror (a prospective buyer), it must be deposited in the listing broker's trust account no later than the next business day.**

A broker cannot hold an earnest money check without depositing it unless:

1. the check is not negotiable by the broker, or the offeror has given written instructions that the check is not to be cashed until the offer is accepted; AND
2. when presenting the offer, the broker informs the offeree (the seller) that the check is being held.

A broker can also hold or disburse earnest money if authorized to do so by a written agreement between the parties or a court order.

If an offer is rejected after the offeror has provided earnest money, the earnest money must be returned to the offeror by the next business day.

> **Anything non-depositable (such as a promissory note or a stock certificate) that a real estate licensee receives in lieu of cash as an offeror's deposit must be held by an authorized escrow agent.**

The escrow agent has to be authorized in writing by the offeror. If the broker is acting as escrow agent, both the offeror and the offeree must give written authorization.

• **Disclosure of nonperformance.** When one of the parties to a purchase agreement notifies a real estate licensee that he or she is not going to perform as agreed, the licensee has a duty to let the other party know that immediately. (If possible, you should first warn the party who is backing out that you are required to inform the other party.)

• **Protective lists.** To enforce an override clause in a listing agreement, a real estate broker must have given the seller a protective list within 72 hours after the listing expired (see Chapter 9).

Licensees must disclose:

- personal interest
- licensee status
- party representation
- material facts
- all offers
- closing costs
- nonperformance
- effect of override clause
- guaranteed sale terms

If a broker uses a listing form with an override clause that remains in effect even when the seller owes a commission to a new broker, the license law requires the former broker to include a special notice in the protective list. This notice warns the seller that he or she could become liable for two commissions.

- **Guaranteed sale disclosure.** In a guaranteed sale plan, a listing broker promises to buy the property if he or she fails to find another buyer within a specified period.

> Guaranteed sale plans are legal in Minnesota, but the broker must give the seller a written disclosure that explains under exactly what conditions the broker will be required to purchase the property.

The disclosure must also state what will be done with any profit the broker makes by reselling the property after buying it from the seller. The broker is required to give the seller the written disclosure before the seller signs the listing agreement.

REAL ESTATE EDUCATION, RESEARCH AND RECOVERY FUND

The Real Estate Education, Research and Recovery Fund (REERRF) is administered by the Commissioner of Commerce. The fund can be used to:

a. promote the advancement of education and research in the field of real estate,

b. underwrite educational seminars and other educational projects for licensees,

c. establish a real estate chair or courses at Minnesota state institutions of higher learning,

d. contract for a particular educational or research project in the field of real estate,

e. pay the costs of the Advisory Task Force,

f. pay any reasonable costs and disbursements incurred in defending actions against the fund, and

g. provide information to the public on housing issues, including environmental safety and housing affordability.

Money for this fund is provided by real estate licensees. In addition to the other required fees, anyone who is granted a real estate license must pay $40 which goes to the REERRF. When renewing a license, each real estate broker or salesperson must pay an additional fee of $5 to the fund.

RECOVERY FUND

A certain part of the REERRF, known as the recovery portion of the fund, is used to satisfy unpaid claims against real estate licensees.

> **The claimant has to have obtained a court judgment against the licensee for fraudulent, deceptive, or dishonest practices or conversion of trust funds. The claimant must also have tried unsuccessfully to collect the judgment from the licensee.**

Recovery fund: used to satisfy unpaid claims against licensees

Out of the REERRF's total balance, at least $400,000 must be available to satisfy all claims authorized for payment each year. At the end of each year, if the recovery portion of the fund is less than $400,000, every broker and salesperson renewing a license may be obligated to pay up to $50 (in addition to the annual renewal fee and $5 REERRF fee). This money is used to restore the balance in the fund.

CLAIMS PROCEDURE. Once a final judgment has been entered against a real estate licensee and there are no other proceedings pending (such as an appeal), the judgment creditor may make a claim for payment from the recovery portion of the REERRF. The claimant files a verified application for payment in the court in which judgment was entered, requesting an order directing payment out of the recovery fund.

> **The claim has to be filed within one year after the claimant's judgment became final or any appeal in the case was decided.**

The claimant must be able to prove that he or she has made a diligent effort to collect the judgment from the licensee, and that the licensee does not have assets that could be used in collecting the judgment.

Payment from the fund will cover the amount of direct out-of-pocket losses (actual damages) in the real estate transaction, but will not cover any attorney's fees or interest included in the claimant's judgment.

Recovery fund limits:
$150,000 for one
claimant; for claims
against one licensee,
$250,000 in one year

The fund will not pay a claim filed by the spouse of the judgment debtor (in other words, by the guilty licensee's husband or wife).

RECOVERY LIMITS. There are limits on how much claimants can recover from the fund. These limits have increased substantially in the past few years.

> **One claimant cannot be paid more than $150,000 out of the fund for a claim based on a single real estate transaction (no matter how much the licensee actually owes the claimant).**

> **Example:** Mr. Arkwright hired a real estate broker to help him sell some valuable commmercial property, and the broker ended up swindling him out of a great deal of money in the transaction. Arkwright sued and was awarded a judgment for $180,000 in actual damages plus $17,000 in attorney's fees. The broker didn't pay the judgment, and doesn't have any assets that Arkwright can levy against to collect the judgment.
>
> Arkwright applies to the recovery fund for payment of his claim. He is paid $150,000, the maximum for one claimant in one transaction, even though the broker owed him considerably more than that. (Note that Arkwright's attorney's fees could not be paid out of the fund, even if Arkwright's claim had not reached the $150,000 limit.)

> **Also, the fund cannot pay more than $250,000 in one year for claims against one licensee, no matter how many claims have been filed against the licensee.**

When that $250,000 is not enough to pay all the valid claims in full, the money is distributed among the claimants according to the ratio that each one's claim bears to the total of all the claims.

> **Example:** Bailey, a real estate broker, got into financial difficulties and tried to extricate herself by defrauding several of the clients she worked for. She was sued by six clients, based on six different real estate transactions, and six

judgments were entered against her. Adams was awarded $15,000 in actual damages; Brand, $21,000; Cellini, $75,000; Domenowski, $36,000; Enderland, $90,000; and Frankel, $63,000.

Altogether, the judgments add up to $300,000, but the recovery fund will only pay $250,000 for claims against one licensee. The claimants against Bailey will receive the following shares of the $250,000:

Adams.....................5% ($12,500)
Brand 7% ($17,500)
Cellini 25% ($62,500)
Domenowski...............12% ($30,000)
Enderland................30% ($75,000)
Frankel 21% ($52,500)

Payment out of the fund is limited to damages that resulted from activities for which a real estate license is required. If someone who happened to be a licensed real estate agent defrauded people in a way that had nothing to do with real estate transactions (a credit card scam, for example), the recovery fund could not be used to pay the fraud victims' claims.

EFFECT ON LICENSE.

> **When a claim is paid out of the recovery fund, the license of the broker or salesperson whose actions gave rise to the claim is suspended.**

If recovery fund covers a claim, the license is suspended

The license is automatically suspended on the effective date of the order for payment from the fund.

The suspended license will not be reinstated until the broker or salesperson has reimbursed the fund for the full amount paid out, plus 12% interest, and has obtained a $40,000 surety bond. The bond must remain in effect for as long as the real estate broker or salesperson is licensed. No further payment will be made from the recovery fund based on claims against any broker or salesperson who was reinstated under this rule.

Repaying the fund does not automatically reinstate the agent's license. If there are other independent grounds for the suspension, the license will remain suspended.

SUBDIVIDED LANDS ACT

Subdivided Lands Act: applies to transfers in subdivisions of more than ten parcels located outside of a municipality

Another Minnesota law that real estate agents need to be aware of is the Subdivided Lands Act. The act generally applies to any real estate divided for sale or lease, located outside of a Minnesota municipality, that is offered or sold in Minnesota. (In the wording of this law, "sale" refers to any transfer of an interest in real estate, including a lease.) Timeshare and cooperative housing transactions are covered by the act. It does not apply to subdivided lands that are registered as securities, however. Subdivisions with ten parcels or less and condominium sales (other than timeshares) are also exempt.

Real estate license and special license required

Property must be registered; a public offering statement must be filed; advertising must be approved

REQUIREMENTS. The Subdivided Lands Act requires everyone who offers or sells interests in subdivided lands to have a real estate broker's or salesperson's license. They must have an additional license (also issued by the Commissioner of Commerce) specifically for offering or selling subdivided lands. Before property covered by the Subdivided Lands Act can be offered for sale or sold, the following requirements have to be met:

- The property must be registered with the Commissioner.
- A public offering statement must be filed, and a copy must be given to each person to whom an offer is made (each prospective buyer). The public offering statement must disclose to prospective buyers all unusual and material circumstances or features affecting the property.
- Any advertising must be approved by the Commissioner. (Approval of the advertising does not mean that the Commissioner approves or recommends the property.)

For property covered by the Subdivided Lands Act, a buyer (or lessee) has a five-day right to rescind. That means the buyer can rescind or cancel the purchase agreement within five days after receiving a legible copy of it.

OTHER STATUTES

The Subdivided Lands Act is essentially a consumer protection law. Minnesota has some additional statutes that protect buyers of certain types of real estate. These include the Statutory New Home Warranty Law and the Manufactured Home Sales Law.

STATUTORY NEW HOME WARRANTY LAW

> **The Statutory New Home Warranty Law establishes that certain warranties are implied in every sale of a newly completed dwelling, and in every contract for the sale of a dwelling to be completed.**

Statutory New Home Warranty Law: establishes warranties for new dwellings

Under this statute, the builder warrants or promises that:

1. during the one-year period after the warranty date, the dwelling will be free from defects caused by faulty workmanship and defective materials due to noncompliance with building standards;

2. during the two-year period after the warranty date, the dwelling will be free from defects caused by faulty installation of plumbing, electrical, heating, and cooling systems; and

3. during the ten-year period after the warranty date, the dwelling will be free from major construction defects.

These statutory warranties survive the passing of title. In other words, if the original purchaser later sells to a second purchaser, the warranties still apply.

> **Example:** In 1984 Addington bought a new house. In 1987 he sold to Barton, and in 1990 Barton sold it to Carlyle. In 1992 Carlyle discovered cracks and buckling in the foundation, and learned that the foundation had not been adequately reinforced when the house was built. This would be considered a major construction defect. It would be covered by the statutory new home warranty, since it is less than ten years since the home was built.

Breach of any new home warranty gives the purchaser or current owner a right to sue the builder for damages or for specific performance. Damages are limited to the amount necessary to remedy the defect, or the difference between the value of the dwelling without the defect and its value with the defect. An order of specific performance would require that the defect actually be repaired for the owner.

MANUFACTURED HOME SALES LAW

The Manufactured Home Sales Law is intended to protect purchasers of manufactured homes (commonly called mobile homes).

Manufactured Home Sales Law: requires licenses for dealers, and provides warranties

> **A manufactured home is a structure that is transportable, is not affixed to real estate, is built on a permanent chassis, and is designed to be used as a dwelling with or without a permanent foundation.**

Under the Manufactured Home Sales Law, no one may act as a dealer in manufactured homes (new or used) without a manufactured home dealer's license. However, there is one exception to this rule: anyone who is already licensed as a real estate broker or salesperson is not required to obtain an additional license for the sale of *used* manufactured homes.

The law provides warranties for all manufactured home buyers. In every sale of a manufactured home, there is an implied warranty that the home conforms in all material respects to applicable federal or state laws and regulations establishing standards of safety or quality. There is also an implied warranty of merchantability and fitness for use as permanent housing in the climate of this state.

The implied warranties run for one year from the date the manufactured home is delivered to the buyer. To invoke the warranties, the buyer must notify the dealer and the manufacturer within a reasonable time after discovering the breach, and no later than 90 days after the expiration of the warranties.

CHAPTER SUMMARY

1. In Minnesota, the Commissioner of Commerce administers the real estate license law, formulates rules implementing the law, issues licenses, and takes disciplinary action against those who violate the law.

2. Anyone who lists, sells, exchanges, manages, buys, or rents real estate, or a business opportunity or a business (or a business's goodwill, inventory, or fixtures) must be licensed, if the action is taken for someone else and for a fee or commission. Loan brokers, certain noninstitutional lenders, and rental services are also required

to have a broker's license. A property owner involved in more than four transactions per year may be required to have a limited broker's license or be represented by a broker.

3. Every applicant for a Minnesota real estate salesperson's license must be at least 18 years old, complete three 30-hour real estate courses, pass the salesperson's examination, and pay the license fee. Each first-year salesperson must complete 30 hours of continuing education. All salespersons and brokers must complete 15 hours of continuing education each year thereafter.

4. A salesperson must be licensed under a primary broker. When a salesperson stops working for a broker, the salesperson's license is ineffective until it has been transferred to another broker.

5. A real estate licensee's failure to comply with the Commissioner's Standards of Conduct is grounds for license suspension or revocation. A disciplinary hearing will be held before the license is suspended or revoked.

6. A broker's special responsibilities include supervising his or her salespersons, maintaining a trust account, and keeping records for each real estate transaction.

7. The license law includes detailed Standards of Conduct that all real estate licensees are required to meet. Among many other provisions, there are prohibitions against guaranteeing future profits, interfering with an exclusive agency, misrepresentation, and acting without a signed listing. Licensees are required to make several disclosures, including an agency disclosure (to all parties) and a disclosure to the buyer of known material facts that might adversely affect the use or enjoyment of the property.

8. The Real Estate Education, Research and Recovery Fund promotes education and research in the real estate field. The recovery portion of the fund is used to compensate claimants who have obtained a judgment against a licensee based on fraud in a real estate transaction, but have been unable to collect the judgment from the licensee.

9. The Subdivided Lands Act, the Statutory New Home Warranty Law, and the Manufactured Home Sales Law are consumer protection statutes that apply to particular types of real estate sales.

CHAPTER 10—REVIEW EXAM

1. Salesperson Hayes works for Broker Jackson. Hayes takes earnest money given him by a buyer and puts it in his personal savings account. As a result, Broker Jackson's license is suspended. For which of the following reasons was Jackson's license suspended?

   a) Commingling
   b) Fraud
   c) Failure to supervise
   d) Depositing money in an interest-bearing account

2. To collect a commission from both the buyer and seller, a broker must:

   a) hold an exclusive right to sell listing.
   b) have the written consent of all parties to the transaction.
   c) have a signed purchase agreement.
   d) provide a payback agreement to both the buyer and the seller.

3. A prospective buyer makes an offer to purchase and gives the real estate salesperson an earnest money deposit. What should the salesperson do with the earnest money?

   a) Deliver it to her broker for deposit in the broker's trust account by the end of the next business day.
   b) Hold it until the closing.
   c) Give it to the seller when he accepts the buyer's offer.
   d) Keep it in a property file.

4. An unlicensed secretary may give a prospective buyer the address of a listed property, and is also allowed to state:

   a) whether the property has been sold.
   b) the price of the property.
   c) the square footage of the property.
   d) None of the above

5. All real estate licenses expire on:

   a) January 31.
   b) June 30.
   c) September 30.
   d) December 31.

6. A salesperson licensed in Minnesota:

   a) must be licensed to act on behalf of a Minnesota broker.
   b) must be a resident of Minnesota.
   c) may be licensed to act on behalf of a limited broker.
   d) may be licensed to act on behalf of two or more Minnesota brokers.

7. A salesperson may receive compensation for his or her services from:

   a) a seller.
   b) another salesperson.
   c) his or her broker.
   d) a cooperating broker.

8. Which of the following must be licensed under Chapter 82 of the Minnesota Code?

a) A cemetery owner
b) Someone who will manage three properties that she owns
c) Someone selling business opportunities
d) An auctioneer working for an attorney

9. Jake Peters is a professional investor who buys and sells at least 15 properties each year. Which of the following licenses should Jake have in Minnesota?

a) Limited salesperson's license
b) Investor's license
c) Limited broker's license
d) Securities license

10. The Real Estate Advisory Task Force must include:

a) two salespeople.
b) five brokers with five or more years of experience.
c) three legislators.
d) six members from local Boards of Realtors.

11. Harriet Hanson is one of the officers of a real estate company. She wants to take an active role in managing all aspects of the company. In order to do so, Hanson must:

a) surrender her real estate license to the Commissioner.
b) register all real estate transactions with the Commissioner.
c) have a salesperson's license.
d) have a broker's license.

12. In regard to the automatic transfer procedure, all of the following are true EXCEPT:

a) The licensee must send the completed form to the Commissioner within five days after obtaining the second broker's signature.
b) The form must contain three signatures.
c) The salesperson is unlicensed when the first broker signs the form.
d) The first broker must destroy the salesperson's license.

13. How long may a salesperson's license be held by the state without requiring re-examination of the licensee?

a) One year.
b) Two years.
c) Indefinitely, as long as the licensee meets the continuing education requirements.
d) Re-examination is always required when the state has been holding a salesperson's license.

14. In Minnesota, a licensed real estate broker who does not have a manufactured home dealer's license may sell manufactured homes only if they are:

a) used, not new.
b) less than one year old.
c) intended to be mounted on a permanent foundation.
d) covered by the Statutory New Home Warranty Law.

15. Under the Statutory New Home Warranty Law, the implied warranty against major construction defects is in effect for:

   a) one year.
   b) two years.
   c) five years.
   d) ten years.

16. Which of the following do not need to have a real estate license when working for another and for a fee?

   a) Property managers
   b) Attorneys doing work incidental to their law practice
   c) Loan brokers
   d) Brokers specializing in exchanges

17. When someone applies for a real estate salesperson's license, which of the following does not need to be part of the application?

   a) Certification that the applicant is a high school graduate
   b) Broker's signature
   c) Applicant's signature
   d) Date

18. George Morrison's former broker just signed the automatic transfer form. Morrison's new broker must also sign the form:

   a) the same day.
   b) within 72 hours.
   c) within five days.
   d) by December 31.

19. Which of the following is not a penalty for violation of the Standards of Conduct in Chapter 82 of the Minnesota Code?

   a) Censure
   b) Felony prosecution
   c) Prosecution for a gross misdemeanor
   d) License suspension

20. Excess funds from the Recovery Fund may be used for all of the following EXCEPT:

   a) Advisory Task Force
   b) Education
   c) Research
   d) Defense of real estate salespeople

21. If an award is made from the Recovery Fund as a result of a judgment against a broker:

   a) the broker will automatically be prosecuted.
   b) the Commissioner may elect to suspend the broker's license.
   c) the broker's license is automatically suspended.
   d) the broker's license is automatically permanently revoked.

22. Buyer A submits a written offer for one of Broker Smith's listings. Before Broker Smith has a chance to present A's offer, Buyer B writes an offer for the same listing. Broker Smith:

   a) must first present A's offer to the seller, and may present B's offer only if A's offer is rejected.
   b) may present both offers to the seller simultaneously.
   c) does not have to present A's offer if B's offer is higher.
   d) None of the above.

23. Broker Smith listed the Bakers' property. At the closing, the Bakers refused to pay Smith's commission. In order to successfully sue for the commission, Broker Smith must prove that:

   a) he was licensed at the time of the closing.
   b) he is licensed at the time he files the legal action.
   c) he has been licensed for at least two years.
   d) he was licensed at the time the Bakers' home was sold.

24. Which of the following must a licensee disclose to a buyer?

   a) Agency representation
   b) The amount of the commission the licensee will earn from the sale
   c) The amount of the commission a cooperating broker will earn
   d) The monthly balance of the licensee's trust account

25. Oscar Brown, a licensee, bought a home directly from a seller without informing the seller that he was a licensee. The seller may:

   a) sue Brown for fraud.
   b) file a complaint with the Commissioner, to get Brown's license suspended.
   c) Both a and b
   d) Neither a nor b

26. A broker must give notice to the Commissioner within ten days after he or she:

   a) sells more than $1 million in real estate.
   b) joins the National Association of Realtors.
   c) changes his or her name.
   d) lists his or her own home for sale.

27. The seller told Salesperson Greenfield about a water problem in the basement. Greenfield intentionally withheld this information from the buyer. Greenfield has:

   a) committed fraud.
   b) violated the statute of frauds.
   c) done nothing wrong, since she did not actually lie to the buyer.
   d) fulfilled her fiduciary duties to the seller by doing her best to get the property sold.

28. In order to sell timeshares, a licensee must hold a real estate license and:

   a) a securities license.
   b) a subdivided land license.
   c) an insurance license.
   d) a reciprocal license.

29. In order to advertise a listed property, a broker must:

   a) have a six-month listing on the property.
   b) obtain the seller's approval of the advertisement.
   c) include his or her name, as licensed, in the ad.
   d) None of the above.

CHAPTER 10—REVIEW EXAM KEY

1. c) The salesperson commingled; the broker failed to supervise.

2. b) This is a dual agency, which requires written consent of both principals.

3. a) Earnest money must be deposited in the listing broker's trust account by the next business day after receipt.

4. a) Only the Address and Availability of listed property may be disclosed by a broker's unlicensed employees.

5. b) Licenses are NOT good for one year; they all expire on June 30.

6. a) A salesperson may only be licensed to one Minnesota broker.

7. c) A salesperson may only be paid by his or her broker.

8. c) Cemetery owners selling burial plots, individuals managing or selling their own properties, and auctioneers under the direction of a broker or attorney are exempt from real estate licensing requirements.

9. c) An investor who is a principal in five or more transactions in a twelve-month period must obtain a salesperson's, broker's, or limited broker's license, or else be represented by a broker.

10. b) In addition to its public members, the task force includes five brokers, each with five or more years of experience.

11. d) An officer of a real estate company must have a broker's license if he or she acts in a managerial capacity.

12. a) The form must be sent within 72 hours after obtaining the second broker's signature.

13. b) Licenses may remain inactive for no more than two years.

14. a) A licensed broker without a manufactured home dealer's license is only allowed to sell used manufactured homes.

15. d) The implied warranty against major construction defects lasts for ten years.

16. b) Attorneys are exempt from real estate licensing laws when engaged in real estate activities incidental to their law practice.

17. a) High school graduation is not a licensing requirement.

18. c) The new broker must sign the automatic transfer form within five days after the former broker signs it.

19. b) If criminal charges are brought against a real estate licensee for violating Chapter 82, the violation is treated as a gross misdemeanor, not a felony.

20. d) Salespeople must defend themselves.

21. c) When a claim is paid out of the recovery fund, the licensee's license is automatically suspended. It cannot be reinstated until the licensee has reimbursed the fund and obtained a surety bond.

22. b) All written offers must be presented to the seller.

23. d) Brokers suing to collect a commission must prove (1) that they were licensed at the time of sale, and (2) that they had a signed listing agreement.

24. a) In Minnesota, a licensee must disclose to both the buyer and the seller which party or parties he or she is representing in the transaction.

25. c) A licensee may not be a principal in a real estate transaction without disclosing his or her licensed status to the other party. Failure to make this disclosure is a violation of the license law and may also constitute fraud.

26. c) A change in name, address, or business location requires written notice to the Commissioner within ten days.

27. a) Intentional deceit is fraud, even if it does not involve a false statement.

28. b) Timeshare sales are regulated by the Subdivided Lands Act, which requires a license under Chapter 82, plus an additional (subdivided land) license under Chapter 83.

29. c) The broker's name as licensed must appear in all ads for listed properties.

Glossary

Abandonment—Failure to occupy and use property; may result in loss of rights.

Abatement of Nuisance—The extinction, termination, removal, or destruction of a nuisance, either personally by the injured party or by a lawsuit instituted by him/her.

Absolute Fee—Fee simple absolute. Absolute or fee simple title is absolute and unqualified, unlimited in duration and unconditional. It is the highest, most complete, and best title one can have.

Abstract of Judgment—A summary of the essential provisions of a court judgment which, when recorded, creates a lien upon all the real property of the debtor within the county where recorded.

Abstract of Title—An abstract of title is a short account of what appears in the public records affecting the title of a particular parcel of real property. It should normally contain a chronological summary of all grants, conveyances, wills, transfers and judicial proceedings which in any way affected title, together with all liens and encumbrances of record, showing whether or not they have been released.

Abut—To touch, border on, end at, share a common boundary with.

Acceleration Clause—A clause in any loan agreement that calls for immediate payment of the entire debt if one or more of the provisions of the agreement is breached by the borrower.

Acceptance—Agreeing to the terms of an offer to enter into a contract, thereby making it a binding contract. Also, the act of accepting delivery of a deed.

Acceptance, Qualified—Where the offeree accepts certain provisions of an offer but rejects others. It is a counteroffer or, more accurately, a new offer.

Accession—The acquisition of title to additional real estate by its annexation to existing property. This can be caused by humans (e.g. through the addition of fixtures), or by nature (e.g. the alluvial deposits on the banks of a stream by accretion).

Accretion—The gradual increase of dry land by the forces of nature, as when water deposits sediment on waterfront property. The owner of that property becomes the owner of the new soil.

Acknowledgment—A formal declaration made before an authorized official, such as a notary public or county clerk, by a person who has signed a document, that he or she has done so as a willful act and deed. The official witnesses the signature as being the voluntary and genuine signature of the one signing. Acknowledgment is required before a document (such as a deed, mortgage, or land contract) will be accepted for recording.

Acquisition Cost—The sum required to obtain title to a piece of property. In addition to the selling price, such things as closing costs, appraisal fees, title insurance and legal fees would be included.

Acre—An area of land equal to 43,560 square feet, or 4,840 square yards, or 160 square rods. There are 640 acres in a section of land.

Actual Age—The age of the structure from a chronological standpoint—as opposed to its effective age. (Appraisers are concerned with effective age.)

Adaptation—Where an item has been specially designed for use in a particular building, or is essential to the use of the building, and therefore is a fixture.

Adjacent—Nearby, bordering, or neighboring; may or may not be in actual contact.

Administrator—A person appointed by the probate court to manage and distribute the estate of a deceased person when no executor is named in the will or there is no will.

Ad Valorem—Latin phrase meaning "according to value," used in connection with property taxation.

Adverse Possession—Acquiring title to real property owned by someone else, by means of open, notorious, and continuous possession of the property, under color of title, hostile to the title of the owner of record, for the statutory period.

Advisory Task Force—A group of appointed real estate brokers and members of the public, serving the Commissioner of Commerce by advising on all major policy questions relating to the administration of real estate licensing law, education, and pre-license requirements.

Affiant—The one who makes an affidavit.

Affidavit—Sworn statement made before a notary public, or other official authorized to administer an oath, and then reduced to writing.

Affirm—To confirm or ratify. Also, to make a solemn declaration instead of making a statement under oath.

Agency—A relationship of trust created when one person, the principal, delegates to another, the agent, the right to represent the principal in dealings with third parties.

Agency, Apparent—Agency which appears to exist because of the acts of the agent and/or the principal.

Agency, Dual—Representing both parties to a transaction, such as a broker representing both buyer and seller. This can result in loss of any commission and revocation of the broker's license, if both parties are not fully informed of the dual agency.

Agency, Exclusive—A written listing agreement giving one agent (broker) the right to sell a piece of property for a specified period of time, but allowing the owner to sell the property him or herself without having to pay a commission.

Agency, Ostensible—Refers to authority an agent appears to possess that, in fact, does not exist or is in excess of that granted by the principal. If through want of ordinary care the principal allows a third party to conclude that the apparent authority exists, the principal could be liable for damages to that third party.

Agency Coupled With an Interest—An agency where the agent has an interest in the subject of the agency.

Agent—In an agency relationship, the one who is authorized to represent another (the principal).

Agent, Actual Authority of—The authority which is given to an agent by a principal, either expressly or by implication.

Agent, General—An agent authorized to handle all the affairs of the principal in one area or in specified areas.

Agent, Gratuitous—An agent who does not have a valid employment contract and therefore has no right to compensation.

Agent, Implied Authority of—The authority of an agent which is implied as necessary to the performance of the express authority.

Agent, Special—An agent with limited authority to do a specific thing or conduct a specific transaction.

Agent, Universal—An agent authorized by the principal to do all things that can be lawfully delegated to a representative.

Agreement, Express—An agreement where the terms are expressed in writing.

Agreement, Mutual—An agreement where both of the parties reach a "meeting of the minds."

Air Lot—A parcel of property which does not contain any land, such as a condominium.

Air Rights—The right to undisturbed use and control of the airspace over a given parcel of land. Such rights may be acquired for construction of a building above the land or building of another, or for the protection of the light and air for structures on adjoining lands.

Alienation—The transfer of title, ownership, or an interest in property from one person to another.

Alienation, Involuntary—The involuntary transfer of real estate by operation of law (such as a mortgage foreclosure), natural processes or adverse possession.

Alienation, Voluntary—Voluntary transfer of real property from one person to another.

Alienation Clause—A provision in a promissory note or mortgage calling for immediate full payment of the debt if the mortgaged property is sold. Such a provision effectively prevents sale by assumption or land contract.

Alien Ownership Act—Provides that purchasers of Minnesota agricultural land must be U.S. citizens or permanent resident aliens.

Alluvion—The solid material added along the bank of a river or lake by accretion.

Alluvium—SEE: **Alluvion.**

Amenities—The intangible benefits that accompany ownership of a particular residence, such as proximity to public transportation, schools, or shopping, as well as panoramic views, architectural excellence, or the prestige that goes with living in a given community.

American Institute of Real Estate Appraisers—An association of real estate appraisers. Members are given the designation M.A.I. (Member Appraiser Institute).

Amortization—Gradual payment of a debt in installments that include principal and interest, over a set period of time.

Amortized Loan, Fully—A loan that is completely paid off, interest and principal, by equal (or nearly equal) installment payments.

Amortized Loan, Partially—A loan in which the principal balance is paid off by a large balloon payment, after the borrower has made installment payments of principal and interest over a relatively short period.

Annexation, Actual—Means by which personal property is converted to real property; involves a physical attachment of the property to land. SEE: **Fixture.**

Annexation, Constructive—Conversion of personal property to real property without physical attachment to land. SEE: **Fixture.**

Annual Percentage Rate (A.P.R.)—The annual percentage rate reflects all charges paid for the borrowed money, including the nominal interest rate (stated in the note) and all other discounts and finance charges.

Anticipation, Principle of—According to the principle of anticipation, value is created by the expectation of benefits to be received in the future.

Appeal—To present a case to a higher decision-making body for rehearing.

Appellant—The party appealing a decision or ruling.

Appellee—The party against whom a case is appealed. Also known as the respondent.

Apportionment—A division of property (as among tenants in common when the property is sold or partitioned) or liability (as between seller and buyer with closing costs) into proportionate, but not necessarily equal, parts.

Appraisal—An estimate or opinion of the value of a piece of property as of a certain date.

Appraiser—One who estimates the value of real or personal property, particularly one qualified by education, training and experience to do so.

Appreciation—Increase in value or worth. Opposite of depreciation.

Appropriation—Taking property or reducing property to personal possession to the exclusion of others.

Appropriation, Prior—Doctrine of water rights, wherein priority of right is determined by priority in time of use of water. COMPARE: **Riparian Rights.**

Appurtenance—Anything that is incident to, attached to, or pertains to the land and is transferred with it, but is not necessarily a part of it.

Appurtenances, Intangible—Rights which go with or pertain to real property and which do not involve ownership of physical objects; for example, easements or covenants.

Area—1. Locale or region. 2. The size of a surface in square units of measure, as in a house with 2,000 sq. ft. of floor, or a tract covering 10 sq. miles. 3. In residential design, the function of a spot or location, as in work area or recreation area.

Arm's Length Transaction—Transaction where there are no preexisting family or business relationships, both parties have an equal bargaining position, and each protects his or her own interests.

Artificial Person—A person created by law, with legal rights and responsibilities, such as a corporation, as distinguished from a natural person, a human being.

Assessment—1. The valuation of property for taxation. 2. A non-recurring specific charge against property for a definite purpose, such as curbs or sewers.

Assessor—Official who determines the value of property for taxation.

Assets, Liquid—Cash on hand or other assets that can readily be turned into cash. Real estate holdings are not considered very liquid.

Assign—To transfer a right, title, or interest in property to another.

Assignee—The one to whom a right, title or interest in property has been transferred.

Assignment—A transfer of contract rights from one person to another.

Assignment of Contract and Deed—The substitution of a new person for the original vendor in a contract for deed.

Assignor—One who transfers a right, title or interest in property.

Assume—To take upon oneself. Example: A buyer may assume the seller's loan and mortgage when purchasing a piece of property, thereby becoming personally liable for repayment.

Assumption Fee—A sum paid to the lender, usually by the purchaser, when a mortgage is assumed.

Attachment—Seizure of real or personal property of a defendant in a lawsuit, by court order, so that it will be available to satisfy a judgment.

Attachments, Man-Made—Personal property attached to land by human effort; fixtures.

Attachments, Natural—Things attached to land by nature, such as trees, shrubs or crops.

Attorney In Fact—One who has authority to act for another under a power of attorney. The power of attorney may be limited to a particular act or purpose, or it may be general. In real estate transactions, the power of attorney must be recorded.

Avulsion—Sudden loss of land due to the action of water, as when a river suddenly changes course.

Balance, Principle of—The maximum value of real estate is achieved when the agents in production—labor, coordination, capital, and land—are in proper balance with each other.

Balance Sheet—A financial statement showing personal or corporate assets, liabilities and net worth (the difference between assets and liabilities) as of a specific date.

Bank Insurance Fund (BIF)—A federal fund organized under the Deposit Insurance Fund to insure deposits in commercial banks and savings banks.

Bankrupt—1. When the liabilities of a person, firm or corporation exceed its assets. 2. One who has been determined bankrupt by a court of law.

Base Lines—East-west lines, parallel to the equator, from which township lines are established in government survey legal descriptions.

Basis—The figure on which profit from the sale of real estate is based for income tax purposes.

Basis, Adjusted—Initial basis in a property adjusted upward or downward to reflect expenditures for improvements minus any deductions taken or allowable.

Bench Mark—A mark made at a known elevation point on a permanent monument, used to calculate other elevations in a surveyed area.

Beneficiary—1. One for whom a trust is created and in whose favor the trust operates. 2. One entitled to receive the proceeds of a life insurance policy. 3. The lender on a note and deed of trust transaction.

Bequeath—To transfer personal property to another by a will.

Bequest—Personal property that is transferred by a will.

Betterment—An improvement to real property which is more extensive than ordinary repair or replacement and which increases the value of the property.

Bilateral Contract—A contract in which there has been an exchange of promises by all parties, and all parties are legally obligated to perform.

Bill of Sale—Document used to transfer title, ownership, or interest in personal property from one person to another.

Binder—1. An agreement to consider the deposit or earnest money as evidence of the potential purchaser's good faith when he or she makes an offer to buy a piece of real estate. 2. An instrument giving immediate insurance coverage to an insured person until the regular policy is issued.

Blighted Area—An area where real property has deteriorated in value.

Blind Ad—An advertisement of property by a real estate agent who fails to disclose his or her licensed status in the ad. Blind advertising is illegal and grounds for license suspension or revocation.

Block—A unit of land comprised of several lots, surrounded by streets or unimproved land.

Blockbusting ("panic selling")—An unethical and illegal act where one person induces another to sell property, possibly at a deflated price, by stating that a change in the neighborhood with respect to race, creed, color or national origin may occur and cause property values to decline. This practice violates both federal and state anti-discrimination laws.

Blue Laws—Statutes or ordinances restricting the transaction of business on Sundays and certain holidays.

Blue Sky Laws—Laws designed to protect the public from fraud in the promotion and sale of securities by regulating those practices.

Bona Fide—Acting in good faith, without fraud.

Bond—1. A written obligation, normally interest bearing, to pay a certain sum at a specified time. 2. A sum of money posted as a guarantee of performance, which is forfeited in the event of default.

Bookkeeping, Double Entry—An accounting technique used in settlement statements to show debits and credits for both the buyer and seller side by side.

Boot—A term used in connection with tax-free exchanges when the properties are not equal in value, to describe whatever is given (cash, services, etc.) to make up the difference in value.

Boundary—The perimeter or limit of a parcel of land; the border.

Bounds—Boundaries.

Branch Manager—An associate broker designated by the primary broker of the firm to manage the operations of a branch office.

Breach—Violation of an obligation, duty or law.

Broker—A licensed natural or artificial person who acts, for a fee, as an intermediary between parties to a real estate transaction.

Broker, Associate—One who has qualified as a real estate broker but who works for a principal broker.

Broker, Designated—A natural person, licensed as a broker, who is responsible for the brokerage activities of a partnership or corporation.

Brokerage—A broker's business. The compensation or commission charged for the broker's services is called a brokerage fee.

Building Code—Rules set up by local governments providing minimum construction standards.

Building Restrictions—Public or private limitations imposed on buildings with respect to the allowable size or type. Zoning is an example of a public restriction, while conditions or covenants in deeds are examples of private restrictions.

Bulk Transfer—This refers to the sale and transfer of all or a substantial part of the merchandise, equipment or other inventory of a business not in the ordinary course of that business.

Bulk Transfer Law—A law that requires sellers who negotiate bulk transfers (usually as a part of the sale of the business itself) to furnish buyers with a list of creditors and a schedule of the property being sold. The creditors must be notified of the impending sale.

Bundle of Rights—The theory that an undivided ownership of a parcel of real estate includes varied rights, such as the right to possess and use, sell, lease, and so on.

Business Opportunities—Any business which is for sale. A real estate salesperson's or broker's license authorizes its holder to engage in the sale of business opportunities, even if no real estate is involved in the transaction.

Bylaws—The rules and regulations that govern a corporation or condominium association.

Call—In a metes and bounds description of real estate, reference to a distance, course, or monument.

Cancellation—Termination of a contract without undoing acts which have already been performed under the contract.

Canons of Ethics—SEE: **Code of Ethics.**

Capacity—The legal ability or competency of a person to perform some act, such as enter into a contract or execute a deed or will. SEE: **Competent.**

Capital Improvement—Any improvement which is designed to become a permanent part of existing real property, or any improvement which will have the effect of substantially prolonging the life of the property, such as replacement of the roof or installation of new siding.

Capitalization—A method of appraising real property by converting into present value the anticipated future net income from the property. Also known as the income approach to appraisal.

Capitalization Rate—A rate used in the capitalization method or income approach to appraising property. It is the rate believed to represent the proper relationship between the value of real property and the income it produces, a reasonable rate of return on an investment or the yield rate necessary to attract investment capital.

Capitalize—1. To provide with cash, or capital. 2. To determine the present value of an asset by discounting expected future income into current value.

Capture, Rule of—Person who is first to extract a mineral gets rights of ownership; applies to oil and gas.

Carry-Over Clause—SEE: **Override Clause.**

Cash Flow—The net income after deducting from the gross income all operating and fixed expenses, including both interest and principal paid on loans.

Caveat Emptor—A Latin term meaning "let the buyer beware," expressing the common law rule that a buyer purchases "as is" and at his or her own risk. The buyer is expected to examine and evaluate the property carefully before buying. This rule has lost much of its earlier strength, particularly in residential leases and sales.

C. C. & R's—The abbreviation for covenants, conditions, and restrictions.

Certificate of Eligibility—A certificate issued by the Veterans Administration to a veteran as evidence of eligibility for a Veterans Administration loan.

Certificate of Occupancy—A statement issued by a local government verifying that a newly constructed building is in compliance with all codes and may be occupied.

Certificate of Reasonable Value—A document issued by the Veterans Administration setting forth the property's current market value, based on a VA approved appraisal.

Cesspool—Underground pit used to catch and temporarily hold sewage while it decomposes and leaches into the surrounding soil.

Change, Principle of—According to this principle, it is the future, not the past, that is of prime importance in estimating value, due to social and economic forces which continually modify the value of real property.

Charter—A written instrument showing a grant of power or right of a franchise.

Chattels—SEE: **Personal Property**.

Chattel Real—Personal property which is closely associated with real property, such as a lease.

Civil Law—The body of law concerned with the rights and liabilities of individuals (such as contracts), as distinguished from criminal law.

Civil Rights—Those rights guaranteed to a person by the law. The term is commonly used in reference to constitutional and statutory protection against discrimination based on race, color, religion, sex, national origin, handicap, or familial status.

Civil Rights Act of 1866—A federal law that prohibits discrimination on the basis of race or ancestry.

Civil Wrong—SEE: **Tort**.

Clean Air Act—A federal law requiring the control of the emission of air pollutants and establishing national standards for certain pollutants.

Clean Water Act—A federal law enacted to safeguard water and prevent water pollution.

Client—One who employs a broker, a lawyer, an appraiser or some other type of professional. A real estate broker's client can be the seller, the buyer, or both, but is usually the seller.

Close—To close means to complete a transaction. It may mean reaching an agreement or putting the agreement into effect. In real estate, closing is the final stage in the transaction, when the seller delivers the deed and the buyer pays the purchase price.

Closing Costs—The expenses incurred in the transfer of real estate in addition to the purchase price. A typical list might include: appraisal fee, title insurance premium, real estate commission, deed tax, etc.

Closing Date—Date on which the terms of a contract must be met, or else the contract is terminated.

Closing Statement—A financial account given to buyer and seller at completion of a real estate transaction showing their respective credits and debits and the sums received and expended by the escrow holder.

Cloud on the Title—Any claim, encumbrance or apparent defect which affects clear title to real property.

Code of Ethics—A system of standards of accepted conduct. In the real estate profession, the Code of Ethics of the National Association of Realtors expresses the high standard of conduct expected of Realtors. Sometimes called the Canons of Ethics.

Codicil—An addition or change to a will. It must be executed with the same formalities as a will.

Collateral—Anything of value given or pledged as security for a debt or obligation.

Collusion—An agreement between two or more persons to defraud another.

Color of Title—Title that appears to be good title, but which in fact is not.

Commercial Acre—The remainder of an acre of newly subdivided land after deducting the amount of land dedicated for trees or sidewalks.

Commercial Bank—A repository for demand and savings deposits, a large percentage of which are reinvested in a variety of commercial areas.

Commercial Paper—Negotiable instruments such as promissory notes, sold normally by business corporations to meet short-term capital needs.

Commercial Property—Income producing property zoned for income producing business purposes, such as warehouses, restaurants, hotels and office buildings. To be distinguished from residential, industrial or agricultural property.

Commingle—To mingle or mix. In real estate circles, it means to mix personal funds with money held in trust on behalf of a client. The law is clear in this regard: trust money and personal funds must be kept separate; failure to do so will likely result in the suspension or revocation of the offender's license. SEE: **Conversion.**

Commission—1. The compensation or fee paid a broker for services in connection with a real estate transaction. 2. A group of people organized for a particular purpose or function.

Commitment—A promise to do something in the future, such as a lending institution's promise or commitment to make a loan. The commitment may be "firm" or "conditional." A conditional commitment might be contingent on something such as a satisfactory credit report on the borrower.

Common Elements—The land and improvements in a condominium, planned unit development or cooperative housing project that are owned and used collectively by all the residents. Common elements usually include driveways, recreational facilities, stairwells, and other areas available for common use.

Common Law—The body of law based on the decisions of judges, developed in England and incorporated into the American system of justice in every state but Louisiana, which bases its laws on old French law.

Community Property—In certain states (not Minnesota), the property owned jointly by a married couple. Community property laws hold that any property acquired through labor or earnings of either spouse (but not through gift or inheritance) belongs to both of them equally.

Competent—Legally qualified to enter into contracts; of legal age and sound mind.

Competition, Principle of—According to this principle, profits tend to encourage competition, and excess profits tend to result in ruinous competition.

Compliance Inspection—An inspection of a building to determine, for the benefit of a real estate lender, whether such things as building codes, specifications or conditions established by a prior inspection have been met before a loan is made.

Comprehensive Plan—SEE: **Master Development Plan**.

Condemnation—1. The taking of private property for public use through the government's power of eminent domain, such as for streets, sewers, airports or railroads. 2. Declaration that a structure is unfit and must be closed or destroyed.

Condemnation Appraisal—An estimate of the value of condemned property to determine the just compensation to be paid the parties.

Condition—A provision in an agreement or contract, limiting or modifying the rights and obligations of the parties.

Conditional Commitment—An agreement (most often used in connection with FHA loans) to loan a definite amount of money on a particular piece of property, subject to approval of a credit rating of some future unknown buyer.

Conditional Fee—Ownership of land which may be terminated by the previous owner if certain conditions occur.

Conditional Use Permit—Permit which allows property to be used in a manner not normally allowed under the zoning laws; may be revoked if the property is used for any purpose not specified in the permit. Also called a special use permit or special exception permit.

Condominium—A type of ownership of real property consisting of a separate interest in an individual unit combined with an undivided interest in common areas (such as hallways, stairways, the land and so forth). A condominium can be commercial or industrial, as well as residential.

Condominium Association—An association made up of condominium unit owners, formed to manage, control, regulate, and maintain the common elements in the condominium.

Confirmation of Sale—Court approval of a sale by an executor, administrator or guardian.

Conformity, Principle of—According to this principle, the maximum value of property is realized when there is a reasonable degree of social and economic homogeneity in the neighborhood.

Consent—To agree, to give permission or assent.

Conservation—1. Regarding real estate, conservation means preservation of structures or neighborhoods in a sound and favorable condition. 2. Regarding natural resources, it is preserving and/or utilizing them in such a way as to provide the most long term benefit.

Conservator—A person appointed by a court to take care of the property of another who is incapable of taking care of his or her own property.

Consideration—Anything of value given to induce another to enter into a contract, such as money, services, goods or a promise.

Consideration, Valuable—Consideration that has monetary value; for example, a promise to pay money, convey property, deliver goods or services, or relinquish a legal right. The consideration required for a valid contract does not have to be valuable consideration; the law regards "love and affection" as good consideration, sufficient to support a contract, although it is not regarded as valuable consideration. SEE: **Love and Affection.**

Conspiracy—An agreement or plan between two or more persons to perform an unlawful act.

Consummate—To complete.

Contiguous—Physically adjoining, abutting or in close proximity, such as two parcels of real estate next to each other.

Contingency—A happening or event that must occur in order to make a contract binding.

Contour—The surface shape or configuration of land. A contour map depicts the topography by means of lines, called contour lines, which connect points of equal elevation.

Contract—An agreement, for consideration, between competent parties to do or not do a certain thing. It is an agreement enforceable at law and as a general rule may be written or oral.

Contract, Bilateral—A contract in which each party promises to do something in exchange for the other's promise.

Contract, Broker and Salesperson—A contract between a broker and a salesperson outlining their mutual obligations.

Contract, Conditional Sales—SEE: **Contract for Deed.**

Contract, Executory—A contract in which one or both parties have not yet completed performance. (As opposed to an executed contract, one in which both parties have completely performed their obligations under the contract.)

Contract, Implied—One deduced from or implied by the actions of the principals; contrasted with an express contract, where the words forming the agreement are stated, orally or in writing.

Contract, Installment Sales—SEE: **Contract for Deed.**

Contract, Oral—A verbal or spoken agreement.

Contract, Unenforceable—One that will not be enforced through the courts because its contents can't be proven (usually an oral contract), or because it is a type that is required to be in writing (like a real estate contract) but is not, or because it is voidable by the other party.

Contract, Unilateral—A contract which is accepted by performance. The offeror is not required to perform his or her part of the contract (a promise), until the offeree has performed.

Contract, Valid—A binding, legally enforceable contract.

Contract, Void—A "contract" which is really not a contract because it lacks some key element or is otherwise defective.

Contract, Voidable—A contract which may be terminated without liability by one or both of the parties.

Contract of Sale—SEE: **Purchase Agreement.**

Contract for Deed—A contract for the sale of property in which the buyer receives possession of the property upon signing the contract, but the seller retains title. When the full purchase price has been paid, the deed is delivered to the buyer and title is conveyed. This type of contract is also referred to as a conditional sales contract, installment sales contract, or land contract.

Contractor—One who contracts to deliver labor or materials, to construct a building, or to do other work for a certain price.

Contribution, Principle of—According to this principle, the value of real property reaches its maximum when the improvements on the property produce the highest return commensurate with the investment.

Conversion—1. Changing the use or character of a property from one thing to another. 2. Appropriating property belonging to another.

Conveyance—The transfer of title to real property from one person to another by means of a written document, such as a deed.

Co-operative Apartment or Building—In a co-operative, the individual owner purchases shares in the corporation that owns the building. The individual receives a proprietary lease on the individual unit and the right to use the common areas.

Co-ownership—Two or more people simultaneously share title to one piece of property.

Corner Influence—The increase in value of a piece of property due to its being on or near a corner.

Corporation—An artificial person, consisting of an association of individual natural persons, but regarded by the law as a single person, separate from the individuals.

Corporation, Foreign—A corporation doing business in one state, that was created or incorporated in another state.

Correction Lines—Adjustment lines used in the government survey system to compensate for curvature of the earth. They occur at 24 mile intervals, every fourth township line, where the distance between north and south range lines is corrected to 6 miles.

Correlation—In appraisals, correlation is the bringing together of the estimates obtained separately from three methods of appraisal (Market Data, Cost and Capitalization) to form a single final estimate of value.

Cost—The amount paid for anything in money, goods or services.

Cost Approach to Value—One of the three appraisal methods. A value estimate is arrived at by estimating the cost of replacement or reproduction of improvements on the property, then deducting from that the estimated accrued depreciation and adding the estimated market value of the land.

Cost Basis—SEE: **Basis.**

Co-Tenancy—A type of ownership where two or more persons own undivided interests in the same property at the same time. SEE: **Tenancy, Joint** and **Tenancy in Common.**

Counteroffer—A new offer made by the offeree in reply to an offer to enter into a contract. It constitutes a rejection of the first offer, and the roles of the two parties are now reversed. The original offeror is the offeree and can accept or reject the counteroffer. This situation commonly arises when the original offeree wants to make some change in the offer he or she has received. Any change, however slight, constitutes a rejection of the original offer.

County—A subdivision of the State created by the State and deriving all its powers from the State.

Courses—Directions in terms of compass bearings, used in metes and bounds descriptions.

Covenant—1. A written agreement or promise to do or not do something. 2. A stipulation that a property be used or not used for a particular purpose or purposes. 3. A guarantee that some state of facts exists (good title in a grantor of a deed). It occurs in such documents as leases, mortgages, land contracts and deeds.

Covenant, Restrictive—A promise not to do an act or use property for a specific purpose.

Covenant Against Encumbrances—A promise that a property is free from all unspecified encumbrances.

Covenant of Further Assurance—Makes the grantor responsible for any further acts necessary to clear title, such as a lawsuit.

Covenant of Quiet Enjoyment—A promise that the owner will not be disturbed in the use of the land by claims of other persons.

Covenant of Seizin—A promise that the grantor has good title and right to possession of land, and the right to convey title.

Covenant of Warranty Forever—A promise that the grantor will defend the grantee's title if it is challenged in court.

C.P.M. (Certified Property Manager)—A professional property manager who has satisfied the requirements to be designated a Certified Property Manager by the Institute of Real Estate Management of the National Association of Realtors.

C.R.E. (Counselor of Real Estate)—A member of the American Society of Real Estate Counselors.

Credit—A payment which is receivable, as opposed to a debit, which is a payment due.

Creditor, Secured—A creditor who has a lien on specific property, such as a mortgagee.

Cul-De-Sac—A dead end street, normally with a circular turnaround at the end.

Customer—In real estate, a customer is usually a prospective purchaser.

Damages—The amount of money one can recover as compensation for injury to his or her person or property resulting from an act or failure to act.

Damages, Compensatory—The amount of money awarded for injury or losses incurred.

Damages, Liquidated—A sum stipulated and agreed upon by the parties at the time of entering into a contract, as being payable as compensation for loss suffered in the event of a breach. The buyer's earnest money deposit is often retained by the seller as liquidated damages in the event of a breach of contract by the purchaser.

Datum—Reference point used by surveyors to determine elevation.

Dealer—One who regularly buys and sells property in the ordinary course of business.

Dealer Property—Property held for sale to customers rather than long-term investment.

Debit—A charge or a debt, listed on the left side of an accounting statement, showing a debt owing.

Debtor—One who owes something, normally money, to another.

Debt Service—The amount of money required to make the periodic payments of principal and interest on an amortized debt.

Decedent—A person who has died.

Declaration of Restrictions—A statement of all the conditions, covenants and restrictions affecting a piece of property.

Dedication—An express or implied grant of private property for public use; may be of the entire fee simple interest or just an easement, such as for sidewalks or streets.

Dedication, Common Law—Transfer of land from private to public ownership or use by virtue of acquiescence in public use of the land for an extended period of time.

Dedication, Statutory—Transfer of land from private to public ownership as required by law; for example, as a prerequisite to subdivision approval.

Deduction—An amount a taxpayer is allowed to subtract from his or her income before taxation, or from the value of a property before its value is taxed.

Deductions, Recovery—Deductions allowed businesses to enable them to recoup capital outlays for business property.

Deduction, Repair—A deduction allowed on most types of property (but not personal residences) for expenditures made to keep the property in ordinary, efficient operating condition.

Deed—A written instrument which, when properly executed and delivered, conveys title or ownership of real property from the owner to the grantee.

Deed, Administrator's—Form of deed used by the administrator of an estate to convey property owned by a deceased person.

Deed, Correction—A deed used to correct minor mistakes in an earlier deed, such as misspellings of names or errors in description of the parcel.

Deed, General Warranty—A deed containing warranties or guarantees of clear title and the right to convey, as well as the grantor's willingness to defend against claims that the title conveyed is not good. This is the type of deed most commonly used in Minnesota.

Deed, Gift—A deed freely given in which the consideration is love and affection, rather than valuable consideration, such as money, goods or services.

Deed, Limited Warranty—A deed in which the grantor warrants title only against defects arising during the time he or she owned the property and not against defects arising before that time; often used by executors and administrators of estates. Also called a special warranty deed.

Deed, Partial Reconveyance—The document used to release a portion of the secured property from the lien of a blanket deed of trust. SEE: **Mortgage, Blanket.**

Deed, Quitclaim—A deed which operates to convey and release any interest in a piece of real property which the grantor may have. It contains no warranties of any kind, but does transfer any right, title, or interest the grantor has at the time the deed is executed.

Deed, Sheriff's—A deed transferring title to a property to the successful bidder at a mortgage foreclosure sale.

Deed, Tax—The deed given to the successful bidder when property is sold to satisfy unpaid property taxes.

Deed, Wild—Deed which cannot be located under the grantor-grantee system of indexing.

Deed Executed Under Court Order—A deed, such as a sheriff's deed or tax deed, which is the result of a court action, such as foreclosure.

Deed in Lieu of Foreclosure—Deed given by a mortgagor to the mortgagee to satisfy the debt and avoid a foreclosure suit.

Deed of Partition—Deed used by co-owners, such as joint tenants or tenants in common, to divide up the co-owned property so that each can own a separate portion.

Deed of Release—Deed used to release property or part of it from a lien created by a land contract. Most often used when the contract covers more than one parcel of land.

Deed of Trust—SEE: **Trust Deed.**

Deed Restrictions—Limitations in a deed restricting the use of the property (such as "residential use only" or "no building over 35 feet in height").

Default—Failure to fulfill an obligation, duty or promise. The most common default is probably failure of a borrower or lessee to pay money when due.

Defeasance Clause—A clause in mortgages, deeds of trust and leases which cancels or defeats a certain right upon the occurrence of a certain event.

Defeasible Fee— SEE: **Fee Simple Defeasible.**

Deferred Maintenance—Repair or maintenance of property that should be done but is postponed, resulting in physical deterioration of the building; a cause of depreciation.

Deficiency Judgment—A personal judgment against a debtor in the event that the proceeds from the sale of the security, after default, are not enough to pay off the loan.

Degree—In surveying, a unit of circular measurement equal to 1/360th part of one complete rotation around a point in a plane.

Delivery—The legal transfer of an instrument evidencing title or ownership. A deed must be delivered and accepted to convey title.

Demand—The desire to buy something, coupled with the ability to buy it. One of the four elements of value. SEE: **Scarcity, Transferability,** and **Utility.**

Demise—A transfer of an estate or interest in real property to another for years, for life or at will.

Density—The term refers to the number of buildings per acre or the number of occupants per unit of land, square mile, acre, etc. Zoning ordinances are designed to control not only the manner in which the land is used (residential, industrial or agricultural), but also the number of buildings situated on the land and the number of people using it.

Department of Commerce—The department of the state government that oversees the real estate industry in Minnesota.

Deposit—Money offered as an indication of good faith for the future performance of a contract to purchase. Also called earnest money. SEE ALSO: **Security Deposit**.

Deposit Insurance Fund (DIF)—The federal deposit insurance system, under the control of the FDIC. Under DIF there are two insurance funds: BIF provides deposit insurance for commercial and savings banks, and SAIF provides deposit insurance for savings associations.

Deposit Receipt—SEE: **Purchase Agreement.**

Deposition—Formal out-of-court testimony of a witness in a lawsuit taken before trial, for possible use later in the trial. Testimony taken either for discovery, to determine the facts of the case, or when a witness will be unable to attend the trial, or both.

Depreciation— A loss in value. For appraisal, depreciation results from physical deterioration, such as cracks in the foundation, functional obsolescence, such as old fashioned plumbing or lighting fixtures, or economic obsolescence, such as changes in the neighborhood.

Depreciation, Curable—Physical deterioration and functional obsolescence which would ordinarily be repaired or replaced by a prudent owner.

Depreciation, Incurable—Physical deterioration, functional obsolescence or economic obsolescence that is physically impossible or not economically feasible to correct.

Depreciation, Straight Line—A method of calculating depreciation for appraisal purposes where an equal portion of a structure's value is deducted each year over the anticipated useful life. When the full value of the improvement has been depreciated, its economic life is exhausted.

Depth Table—Mathematical table used in real estate appraisal to estimate the differences in value between lots with different depths. Front footage has the greatest value and land at the rear of the lot has the least value.

Dereliction—SEE: **Reliction**.

Detached Residence—A home physically separated from and not connected to another by a common wall.

Developed Land—Land which has been improved by man-made additions, such as buildings, roads or sidewalks.

Developer—One who makes changes to bring land to its most profitable use by subdividing and/or improving it.

Devise—Gift of real property through a will. The donor is the testator and the recipient is the devisee.

Devisee—Recipient of real property under a will.

Disbursements—Term used in accounting to describe money paid out or expended.

Discount—1. The amount withheld from a loan amount at the time the loan was made. 2. To sell a note at a reduced value or less than face value.

Discount Points—A sum paid to a lender at the time a loan is made, to give the lender an additional yield above the nominal interest rate; one point is one percent of the loan amount. As a result of the payment of discount points, the lender is willing to make the loan at a lower interest rate than it otherwise would have.

Discount Rate—The interest rate charged by the Federal Reserve System for loans it makes to its member banks.

Discrimination—Unequal treatment, either favorable or unfavorable, based on a class, race or group to which a person or persons belong.

Disintegration—The declining period when property's present economic usefulness is near an end and constant upkeep is necessary.

Disintermediation—Withdrawal of savings deposits from an intermediary financial institution, such as a savings and loan association or a commercial bank, by its depositors, in favor of direct investment.

Domicile—The state where a person has his or her permanent home. To establish domicile, it is necessary to have both a physical presence in the state and the intent to make the state one's permanent residence.

Down Zoning—The act of rezoning land for a more limited use.

Drainage—A system which draws water off land, either artificially (as with pipes) or naturally (as by slope or natural watercourse).

Due on Sale Clause—A clause in a loan agreement which states that the entire amount of the loan shall be due and payable if the security property is sold.

Duplex—A single structure that contains two separate housing units, with separate entrances, living rooms, baths and kitchens.

Duress—Unlawful force, constraint, threats or actions used to compel someone to do something against his or her will.

Dwelling—A building or part of a building used or intended to be used as living quarters.

Earnest Money—A deposit made by the prospective purchaser of real estate as evidence of a good faith intention to complete the purchase.

Earnest Money Agreement—SEE: **Purchase Agreement.**

Easement—A right to use some part of the property of another for a particular purpose, such as for a driveway or for installing and maintaining a water line.

Easement Appurtenant—An easement for the benefit of a particular piece of property. COMPARE: **Easement in Gross.**

Easement by Express Grant—Easement given to another by means of a deed.

Easement by Express Reservation—Easement created by deed in favor of a landowner who transfers part of the property.

Easement by Implication—Unwritten easement, created when a parcel of land is divided.

Easement by Necessity—An easement implied by law because it is essential to the use of the property, as for example when a parcel of land is sold without any access to a road.

Easement by Prescription—One that is acquired by open, notorious, continuous, and uninterrupted use hostile to the will of the owner for the prescribed period of time. COMPARE: **Adverse Possession.**

Easement in Gross—An easement for the benefit of a person. COMPARE: **Easement Appurtenant.**

Economic Life—The period during which improved property will yield a return over and above the rent due to the land itself.

Economic Obsolescence—Loss in value caused by factors outside the property itself, such as zoning changes or deterioration of the neighborhood.

Economic Survey—Part of the land use planning process where an analysis is made of the present and anticipated future economic needs of an area.

Effective Age—The effective age of an improvement is determined by its condition, not the actual chronological age. Such things as good or poor maintenance may increase or decrease the effective age. A fifty-year-old home, well maintained, may have an effective age of ten or fifteen years; in terms of remaining usefulness, it is no older than a ten- or fifteen-year-old home.

Egress—A passageway leading from property; a means of exiting. It is the opposite of ingress. The terms ingress and egress are usually used in reference to easements.

Ejectment—Legal action to evict someone who is not legally entitled to possession of real property. SEE: **Eviction, Unlawful Detainer.**

Elements of Comparison—Elements used in the market data approach to appraisal: time, location, and physical characteristics.

Emblements—Crops which are produced annually through the labor of the cultivator, such as wheat.

Emblements, Doctrine of—Right of an agricultural tenant to enter land after termination of the lease for the purpose of harvesting crops.

Eminent Domain—The power of the government to take (condemn) private property for public use, upon payment of just compensation to the owner. The power may be delegated to public corporations, such as utilities, or to public service corporations, such as railroads.

Encroachment—Unlawful physical intrusion upon the property of another, usually the result of mistake.

Encumbrance—Any right or interest in a piece of property held by someone other than the owner.

Endorsement—A method of transferring ownership of a negotiable instrument, such as a promissory note, by signing on the back of the instrument.

Endorsement, Special—An endorsement to a specific transferee (new holder).

Endorsement "In Blank"—An endorsement where no transferee (new holder) is specified.

Enjoin—To prohibit by a court order, to forbid. A court can issue an injunction enjoining an individual from doing something, like behaving in a discriminatory manner. Enjoin can also mean to command performance of an act.

Environmental Impact Statement (EIS)— A document that contains detailed information about how a proposed project would affect the environment.

Equal Credit Opportunity Act (ECOA)— A federal law that applies to all consumer credit transactions and prohibits discrimination on the basis of race, color, religion, national origin, sex, marital status or age.

Equilibrium— A period of stability, during which property undergoes little, if any, change.

Equity— 1. The difference between the value of a piece of property and the charges against it. 2. In law, equity is a system that overrides the common and statutory law in order to bring about a fair and just result, particularly in those areas where the remedy at law (money damages) is inadequate. Specific performance of a contract ordered by the court is an equitable remedy.

Erosion— Gradual loss of soil due to the action of water or wind.

Escalator Clause— A clause in a contract or mortgage providing for the adjustment of payments or interest in the event of certain contingencies, such as changes in taxes or the prime interest rate.

Escape Clause —A clause in a sales contract allowing the buyer to terminate the contract if the appraised value is significantly below the purchase price. Required for FHA and VA loans where the applicant has signed the contract prior to receiving the appraisal.

Escheat— The reversion of property to the state when a person dies without leaving a will and without heirs entitled to the property.

Escrow— 1. The process in which something of value (such as money or documents) is held by a disinterested third party, a stakeholder called an escrow agent, until certain conditions contained in the escrow instructions have been complied with. 2. A deed or money or piece of property delivered into the keeping of a third party, called an escrow agent, pending compliance by all parties to the real estate agreement.

Estate— 1. An interest in real property that is, or may become, possessory. There are freehold estates (fee simple and life estates) and less-than-freehold estates (leasehold interests). 2. The property left by a decedent (someone who has died).

Estate, Less-Than-Freehold— A leasehold estate; an estate held by a tenant under a lease. The less-than-freehold estates include estates for years and estates at will.

Estate at Sufferance— A situation where a "tenant" originally took possession of property lawfully, but stays on without the owner's consent.

Estate at Will— A leasehold estate for an indefinite period, which continues until either the landlord or the tenant terminates it by giving notice of termination to the other party. Also called a month-to-month tenancy, periodic tenancy, or tenancy at will.

Estate for Life, or Life Estate—A freehold estate which is held for the life of its owner or for the life of some other person (the measuring life). The person holding this estate is called a "life tenant."

Estate for Years—An estate for a definite period of time, after which the estate automatically terminates.

Estate in Fee Simple—SEE: **Fee Simple.**

Estate in Remainder—SEE: **Remainder.**

Estate in Reversion—SEE: **Reversion.**

Estate of Inheritance—An estate which may descend to heirs, such as a fee simple estate.

Estoppel—A legal doctrine that prevents a person from asserting rights or facts that are inconsistent with a previous position or representation.

Estoppel Certificate—An instrument which itself prevents individuals from later asserting facts different from those contained in the document. Often used in assignments of mortgages. The lender signs the estoppel certificate, confirming the mortgage balance to be a given figure, and may not thereafter make any claim to the contrary. Also called a Certificate of No Defense or Declaration of No Set-Off.

Ethics—A system of accepted principles or standards of moral conduct and behavior. SEE: **Code of Ethics.**

Eviction—Dispossession, expulsion or ejection of someone from property. May be either actual, a physical removal from the premises, or constructive, a violation by the landlord of the covenant of quiet enjoyment (as by shutting off the water or electricity).

Eviction, Constructive—Any act by a landlord that so impairs the tenant's quiet enjoyment of the premises or makes the property unfit for its intended use that the tenant is forced to move out.

Exchange of Real Estate—SEE: **Tax-free Exchange.**

Exclusive Agency Listing—A written listing agreement giving one broker the right to negotiate the sale of a piece of property; the broker is entitled to a commission if the property is sold by anyone besides the seller.

Exclusive Right to Sell—Written listing agreement giving one agent (broker) the right to negotiate the sale of a piece of property during a specified period of time, and giving the broker the right to receive the commission if the property is sold during that time, regardless of who sells it.

Execute—To do, to perform or complete, as in executing a deed by signing and acknowledging it.

Execution—Legal process whereby the court orders an official, such as a sheriff, to seize and sell property of a judgment debtor to satisfy a judgment or other lien.

Executor—The person named in a will to carry out the provisions of the will. COMPARE: **Administrator.**

Executory Contract—A contract that has not yet been fully performed.

Exemption—In a statute or regulation, a provision establishing that the law or rule does not apply to certain groups; for example, someone who qualifies for a particular tax exemption is not required to pay that tax.

Express—Stated in spoken words or writing, as opposed to implied. An express contract is one entered into through oral or written agreement of the parties.

Extender Clause—SEE: **Override Clause.**

Failure of Purpose—Excuse for rescinding a contract; if the contract cannot achieve its intended purpose, the parties are released from their obligations.

"Fannie Mae"—A popular name for the Federal National Mortgage Association. Also called F.N.M.A.

Farmer's Home Administration (FmHA)—A federal agency of the Department of Agriculture that provides or assists in providing credit to farmers and others in rural areas, where reasonable financing from private sources is not readily available.

Feasibility Study—An analysis of the cost-benefit ratio of a proposed project, often required by lenders before giving a loan commitment.

Federal Deposit Insurance Corporation (F.D.I.C.)—A federal agency which controls the insurance funds for deposits in state and federally chartered banks and savings and loans.

Federal Fair Housing Act—A law enacted in 1968 which makes it illegal to sell or rent residential property or vacant land that will be used for residential construction on a discriminatory basis. It does not prohibit discriminatory practices related to business or industrial real estate transactions.

Federal Home Loan Bank System (F.H.L.B.)—A federal organization which provides reserve funds for federal savings and loan associations.

Federal Home Loan Mortgage Corporation (F.H.L.M.C.)—A federal agency that buys mortgages in the secondary market from banks and savings and loans. Also called "Freddie Mac."

Federal Housing Administration—A federal agency within the Department of Housing and Urban Development (HUD); its mortgage insurance programs encourage lenders to make loans to low- and middle-income buyers.

Federal Land Bank—One of twelve federal banks established to make mortgage loans to qualified borrowers for the purchase of farms, agricultural lands, livestock, farm machinery and the like.

Federal National Mortgage Association (F.N.M.A.)—A private corporation, originally a government agency, popularly known as "Fannie Mae," which supports a secondary mortgage market by buying and selling mortgage loans.

Federal Savings and Loan Insurance Corporation (F.S.L.I.C.)—A former federal agency which insured deposits in savings and loan associations. Under the Financial Institutions Reform, Recovery, and Enforcement Act of 1989 (FIRREA), the FSLIC was eliminated. Deposits in savings and loan associations are now insured by the Savings Association Insurance Fund (SAIF).

Federal Trade Commission (F.T.C.)—A federal agency responsible for investigating and eliminating unfair and deceptive business practices. It is also the agency charged with enforcing the Truth in Lending Act.

Fee—An estate of inheritance in real property.

Fee, Qualified—A fee simple estate which is conveyed subject to certain conditions or limitations. For example, the grantor may deliver title with a stipulation in the deed that the property being conveyed always be used as a single family residence. If the grantee violates this condition, title reverts to the grantor. Also called a fee simple defeasible or defeasible fee.

Fee Simple Absolute—The greatest estate one can have in real property; of indefinite duration; with no conditions or restrictions on the use of the land other than public ones, such as zoning regulations; freely transferable or inheritable. Also called the fee simple.

Fee Simple Defeasible—A fee estate in real property which is subject to being divested, or dispossessed, upon the happening of a certain occurrence or condition. Also called a qualified fee or defeasible fee.

Fee Simple Determinable—A defeasible fee which is terminated automatically if certain conditions occur.

Fee Simple Subject to a Condition Subsequent—A defeasible fee which may be terminated by re-entry of the grantor after breach of a condition in the grant.

F.H.A.—Abbreviation for Federal Housing Administration.

Fiduciary Relationship—A relationship of trust and confidence, often existing where one person is allowed to represent, transact business, or hold or manage property for another.

Finance Charges—All charges assessed a borrower, directly or indirectly, in connection with the credit extended.

Financing Statement—A brief instrument which, when recorded, perfects or gives notice of a creditor's security interest in an item of personal property.

Finder's Fee—A referral fee paid to someone for directing a buyer or seller to a real estate agent.

Firm Commitment—A definite agreement by a lender to make a loan to a particular borrower on a particular piece of property. Also, an agreement by the F.H.A. to insure a loan made to a specified borrower on a particular piece of property. SEE: **Conditional Commitment.**

Fiscal Year—Any twelve month period used as a business year for accounting, tax, and other financial purposes, as opposed to the calendar year.

Fixed Disbursement Plan—A type of construction financing which calls for a series of predetermined disbursements at various stages of construction.

Fixed Term—A period of time which has a definite beginning and ending.

Fixture—Personal property which has become so affixed to or associated with real property that it has become real property.

Foreclosure, Judicial—A sale of property by a court order to satisfy a lien.

Foreclosure by Advertisement—A non-judicial foreclosure under a power-of-sale clause in a mortgage, allowing property to be advertised and then sold at a public auction held by the sheriff.

Forfeiture—Loss of a right or something else of value as a result of failure to perform an obligation or condition.

Forbearance—An agreement wherein one of the parties agrees not to do something.

Franchise—A right or privilege granted by a government to conduct a certain business, or a right granted by a private business to use its trade name in conducting business.

Fraud—A misrepresentation or concealment of a material fact, either known to be false or without regard as to its truthfulness or falsity, which misrepresentation is relied upon by another to his/her damage.

Fraud, Actual—Intentional deceit or misrepresentation to cheat or mislead another.

Fraud, Constructive—Action which does not reach the degree of deceit or intentional misrepresentation which is required for actual fraud but still does not meet an accepted standard of behavior at law. Often it is a result of a misuse or breach of a fiduciary relationship.

Free and Clear—Title, or ownership, of real property that is completely free of encumbrances (such as mortgages, liens and so forth).

Freehold—An ownership estate in real property; can be either a fee simple or life estate. The holder of a freehold estate has title, as opposed to the holder of a less-than-freehold estate (leasehold estate), who is a tenant.

Frontage—The distance a piece of property extends along a street or body of water.

Front Foot—A measurement of property for sale or valuation, with each foot of frontage presumed to extend the entire depth of the lot.

Fructus Industriales—Those fruits of the land which are produced by the labor and industry of the occupant, such as crops.

Fructus Naturales—Those products which are produced by the powers of nature alone, such as trees, or wool on an animal.

Functional Obsolescence—An improvement's loss in value due to inadequate or outmoded equipment or as a result of either age or poor design.

Funding Fee—A fee charged in connection with VA loans; the funding fee can be financed along with the loan.

Gain—That portion of the proceeds from the sale of a capital asset, such as real estate, that the I.R.S. recognizes as taxable profit.

Good Faith—SEE: **Bona Fide.**

Good Will—An intangible asset of a business resulting from a good reputation with the public and an indication of future, return business.

Government Lots—In the government survey system, parcels of land that could not be divided into regular sections because of their location (for example, beside a body of water). They are given government lot numbers.

Government National Mortgage Association (G.N.M.A.)—A federal agency created when F.N.M.A. was divided into two corporations in 1968. Popularly known as "Ginnie Mae," it is one of the major secondary market agencies.

Government Survey—A system of land description in which the land is divided into squares each approximately six miles square (containing 36 square miles) called townships, which are divided into 36 sections, each approximately one mile square and containing approximately 640 acres. Also called Rectangular Survey or Township and Range System.

Graduated Payment Loan—A loan providing for lower payments at the beginning of the loan term; the payments increase gradually until they level off in five to seven years.

Grant—To transfer or convey real property or an interest therein.

Grantee—The one who receives a grant of real property, regardless of the type of deed used.

Granting Clause—Words in a deed which indicate an intent to make a transfer of an interest in land.

Grantor—The one who conveys or transfers real property or an interest therein.

Green Acres Act—A special state agricultural property tax statute designed to equalize the tax burden on certain agricultural property. Applies to real estate consisting of 10 acres or more, a nursery, or a greenhouse, if it's actively and exclusively devoted to agricultural use and is homestead property.

Gross Income Multiplier Method—A method of valuing residential property by reference to the rental value of the property; also called the gross rent multiplier method.

Gross Rent Multiplier—A figure which is multiplied by the gross income of a piece of property to arrive at an estimate of the property's market value. The multiplier is obtained by dividing the sales price by the rental income.

Guardian—One appointed by the court to care for or administer the affairs of another, called a ward, because of the ward's inability to conduct his or her own affairs due to age, infirmity or insanity.

Guide Meridians—North-south lines in the government survey, spaced 24 miles apart.

Habendum Clause—The clause in a deed beginning "to have and to hold" which follows the granting clause and describes how the estate will be held.

Heir—One entitled to inherit property under the laws of intestate succession.

Heirs and Assigns—Heirs are those who inherit property. Assigns are successors in interest to property, i.e., by deed.

Highest and Best Use—The use which at the time of appraisal is most likely to produce the greatest net return from the property over a given period of time.

Holder in Due Course—One who obtained a negotiable instrument in good faith and for value, before the instrument was due, and without knowledge of any defects or that the instrument had been dishonored previously.

Holdover Clause—A clause in a listing agreement that states that the listing will renew itself indefinitely unless cancelled by the seller; illegal in Minnesota.

Home Mortgage Disclosure Act—A federal law that facilitates the enforcement of laws against redlining by requiring reports on the geographic distribution of loans.

Homeowner's Association—A non-profit association comprised of homeowners within a subdivision, including planned unit developments and condominiums, which is charged with the responsibility of enforcing the subdivision's property restrictions. The association is usually created by the developer to ensure that the neighborhood will have a means of protecting itself against future depreciation after the lots are sold.

Homestead—A limited exemption against the claims of unsecured creditors for property used as the debtor's residence. A means of protecting the debtor's home from a forced sale to satisfy certain debts.

H.U.D.—Abbreviation and popular name for the Department of Housing and Urban Development.

Hypothecate—To give real or personal property as security for an obligation without giving up possession of it.

Improvements—Man-made additions to real property.

Improvements, Misplaced—Improvements on land which do not conform to the most profitable use of the site. A misplaced improvement can be an overimprovement or an underimprovement.

Income Approach to Value—A method of appraising property, basing the value upon the net income produced by the property. It is calculated by subtracting the expenses of the property from the total income to determine the net profit. Also known as the Capitalization Method or Investor's Method.

Income, Disposable—Income remaining after payment of income taxes.

Income, Effective Gross—A measure of the income-generating capacity of rental property, defined as the economic rent less the bad debt/vacancy factor.

Income, Gross—Total income before deductions for expenses, depreciation, taxes and so forth.

Income, Net—Income after deductions for expenses, depreciation, taxes, etc.

Income, Spendable—The money that remains after deducting operating expenses, principal and interest payments, and income tax from the gross income. Also called net spendable income or cash flow.

Incompetent—A person not legally qualified to reach proper decisions, such as a minor, insane person or one who is feeble minded.

Incorporeal Rights—Non-possessory (intangible) rights in real estate, such as a dominant tenant's right to use a servient tenant's land (easement). An easement appurtenant is an incorporeal hereditament (inheritable), and an easement in gross is an incorporeal right, but not inheritable.

Increasing and Diminishing Returns, Principle of—Holds that a point is reached where additional investments in land in the form of labor or capital will not be justified by the resulting increase in net income.

Independent Contractor—One who, exercising independence in the choice of work to be performed, contracts to do or perform certain work for another person according to the independent contractor's own means and methods, without being subject to the control of such other persons except as to the product or result of the work. Real estate brokers are usually independent contractors.

Indexing—Means of cataloging documents such as deeds in the recording office; deeds are indexed according to grantor and grantee, and sometimes according to location of the land.

Ingress—Refers to access to property by a dominant tenant while exercising his or her use right (easement). Sometimes refers to the access a tenant has to leased property. Opposite of egress.

Injunction—A court order prohibiting some act or compelling an act to be done.

Innocent Improver—One who makes an improvement on land in the mistaken belief that he or she owns the land.

Installment Sale—A sale in which less than 100% of the selling price is received in the year of sale. SEE: **Contract for Deed.**

Instrument—A written legal document, such as a contract, deed, mortgage, will or lease, that is used in the transaction of business.

Insurance, Casualty—Insurance against losses on property caused by fire, flood, theft or other disaster.

Insurance, Mutual Mortgage—The insurance provided by FHA to insure lenders against loss through foreclosure. The premium is paid by the borrower to the lender, who forwards it to the FHA.

Insurance, Private Mortgage—Insurance available to conventional lenders who are willing to make real estate loans exceeding the standard 80% loan-to-value ratio. The excess amount is insured by a private mortgage insurance company.

Insurance, Title—An insurance policy under which the insured is protected against any loss suffered because title to the property is not as represented in the policy.

Insurance, Title, Extended Coverage Policy—A form of title insurance that includes an inspection and survey of the insured land. Also called a mortgagee or lender's policy.

Insurance, Title, Standard Coverage—A form of title insurance that protects against title defects appearing in the chain of title, including such things as forgeries or deeds executed by incompetents, but does not protect against defects not appearing in the chain of title, such as the rights of parties in possession (i.e., adverse possessors) or unrecorded easements. Also called an owner's policy.

Integration—The beginning stage of the life cycle of a property. Integration is the development stage.

Interest—1. A charge for the use of another's money, sometimes referred to as rent for the use of money. 2. A right in or share of something. For example, a tenant under a lease and an easement holder each have an interest in real property.

Interest, Compound—Interest computed both on the principal and its accrued interest.

Interest, Prepaid—Interest on a loan which is paid at the time of closing or settlement; sometimes called interim interest.

Interest, Simple—Interest that is computed on the principal amount of the loan only. The type of interest charged in connection with real estate loans.

Interstate Land Sales Full Disclosure Act (ILSFDA)—Federal legislation designed to provide consumers with full and accurate information in regard to property which is sold or advertised across state lines.

Intestate—The characterization of a person who has died without leaving a valid will.

Intestate Succession—Transfer of property of a decedent who has not left a will; controlled by statutes.

Invalid—Unfounded in law; not of binding force; not valid.

Inventory—A detailed list of the stock-in-trade of a business.

Inverse Condemnation Action—A court action by a private landowner against the government, seeking compensation for damage to property as a result of government action.

Investment Property—Unimproved property that produces no income, but is held for capital growth through increases in price.

Inverted Pyramid—A way to envision ownership of land; theoretically, a person owns all the earth and sky which is enclosed by an inverted pyramid with its tip at the center of the earth and its base corresponding to the boundaries of the property and extending into the sky.

Joint Venture—Two or more individuals joining together for one specific project as partners. A joint venture is of limited duration; if the members of the venture undertake another project together, the association becomes a partnership.

Judgment—The final consideration and determination by a court as to the rights and responsibilities of the parties in dispute. If the court's finding includes an award of money as damages, it becomes a general lien on the debtor's property. The individual awarded damages is called the Judgment Creditor; the person who must pay is the Judgment Debtor.

Judgment Creditor—A person to whom money is owed by virtue of a judgment in a lawsuit.

Judgment Debtor—A person who owes money by virtue of a judgment in a lawsuit.

Just Compensation—SEE: **Eminent Domain.**

Land—In a legal sense, it is the solid part of the surface of the earth (as distinguished from water), everything affixed to it, by nature or by man, and anything on it or in it, such as minerals and water.

Landlocked—A parcel of land without access to any type of road or highway. The owner of landlocked land can obtain an easement by necessity from the court.

Landlord—A lessor; a landowner who has leased his or her property.

Landlord-Tenant Act—SEE: **Minnesota Landlord-Tenant Act.**

Landmark—A monument, natural or artificial, set up on the boundary line of two adjacent estates, to fix the boundary.

Latent Defects—Defects in property that are not visible or apparent.

Lateral Support—The right to support of soil in its natural state by land adjoining it. An owner is protected by law from excavation on neighboring property that would deny this support. COMPARE: **Subjacent Support.**

Lawful Objective—An objective or purpose of a contract that does not violate any law or public policy.

Lease—A contract for the possession and profits of real estate in return for rent. The property owner is the lessor, the tenant is the lessee.

Lease, Escalator—A lease in which the tenant pays a fixed rent plus any increases in operating expenses.

Lease, Fixed—SEE: **Lease, Gross.**

Lease, Flat—Also called a straight lease, it is one with regular, equal payments; one in which the amount and the time for payment remain constant throughout the term of the lease.

Lease, Graduated—A lease in which the payments begin at one rate but increase at agreed intervals over the time of the lease.

Lease, Gross—A lease where the lessee pays a fixed amount and the lessor pays the charges incurred through ownership of the property, such as taxes and insurance. Also called a fixed lease. COMPARE: **Lease, Net.**

Lease, Ground—A lease of the land only, normally for a long term, and sometimes secured by improvements placed on the land by the user.

Lease, Net—A lease requiring the tenant to pay all the costs of maintaining the building, such as taxes, utilities and insurance, in addition to the rental fee paid the landlord.

Lease, Percentage—A lease in which the rental is based on a percentage of the monthly or annual gross sales.

Lease, Sandwich—A leasehold interest lying between the primary lease and the operating lease, or the lease of the lessee in possession.

Lease, Straight—SEE: **Lease, Flat.**

Leaseback—SEE: **Sale-Leaseback.**

Leasehold Estate—A tenant's right to occupy real estate during the term of the lease.

Legacy—A gift of personal property by will; a bequest. The person receiving a legacy is a legatee.

Legal Description—A method of describing a parcel of real estate that is recognized by law. The most common methods of legal description are metes and bounds, government survey, and recorded plat.

Legal Person—A person created by law, possessing some of the powers and duties of a natural person; usually this is a corporation. Also called an artificial person.

Legatee—Recipient of personal property under a will.

Lenders, Institutional—Financial institutions (such as banks and savings and loans) that invest others' funds in mortgages and other loans; as distinguished from individual or private lenders who invest their own money.

Lessee—One who is leasing property from another; the party to a lease known as the tenant.

Lessor—One who has leased property to another; the party to a lease known as the landlord.

Leverage—The effective use of borrowed money to finance an investment such as real estate.

Liability, Joint and Several—A form of liability in which several persons are responsible for a debt both individually and as a group.

License—1. A special privilege, not a right common to all. The privilege conferred by a public body that allows a person to do something which he or she otherwise would not have the right to do. 2. The personal, revocable and non-assignable permission or authority to enter upon the land of another for a particular purpose.

Lien—A charge upon property for the payment or discharge of a debt or duty. The right which the law gives to have a debt satisfied out of a particular thing. A charge or claim upon property which encumbers it until the obligation is satisfied.

Lien, Attachment—A lien on property to prevent transfer of the property pending the outcome of litigation.

Lien, Equitable—A lien arising out of fairness. It can evolve from a written contract where intent to create a lien on a particular property is clearly indicated, or by court order in an effort to serve justice.

Lien, General—A lien against all the property of a debtor.

Lien, Involuntary—A lien placed against property by operation of law without consent of the owner. Mechanics' liens, judgment liens and I.R.S. liens are involuntary.

Lien, Judgment—A legal claim on all of the property of a judgment debtor, making it possible for the judgment creditor to have the property sold to satisfy the debt.

Lien, Materialman's—A type of mechanic's lien; specifically, a lien based on sums owed to a supplier for materials provided in connection with a construction project.

Lien, Mechanic's—A statutory lien against property claimed by those who have provided labor or materials for construction on that property and have not been paid.

Lien, Mortgage—A specific lien that attaches only to the particular piece of property offered as security for a loan.

Lien, Property Tax—A lien on property to secure payment of property taxes.

Lien, Specific—A lien which attaches only to a particular piece of property (as opposed to a general lien which attaches to all of the debtor's property).

Lien, Statutory—A lien created by law, rather than by contract, such as a tax lien.

Lien, Tax—A lien on property to secure the payment of taxes.

Lien, Voluntary—A lien placed on property with the consent of the owner.

Lien Notice—A written notice from a contractor or subcontractor informing a property owner that a lien could be enforced against the property if those who provided materials or labor are not paid. Must be given within 10 days of their agreement to perform the work.

Lien Priority—Among all the liens against a particular property, the order of precedence that determines the order in which they will be paid off in the event of a foreclosure. The lien with highest priority will be paid off first; the lien next in line will be paid off only if there are funds left over.

Lien Theory—The theory holds that upon giving a mortgage or deed of trust as security for a debt, the borrower does not give up any part of his or her title. The lender holds a lien during the period of indebtedness, but not title.

Limited Broker—A property owner who is licensed to participate as a seller in five or more real estate transactions per year, but is not allowed to represent others in real estate transactions.

Limited Common Element—Any common element or area of condominium property that is reserved for the exclusive use of certain units.

Liquidated Damages—An amount agreed to in advance by the parties to a contract that will serve as compensation in the event of default. In real estate transactions, the buyer's earnest money deposit is often treated as liquidated damages.

Listing—An employment contract between a real estate broker and a landowner authorizing the broker to find a ready, willing and able buyer to purchase the property. Must be in writing for broker to receive a commission. The three types are open, exclusive agency, and exclusive right to sell.

Listing, Net—A listing where the seller sets a minimum net amount he or she will accept for the property and permits the agent to collect as a commission the portion of the sales price exceeding that amount. Though legal, this type of listing is not favored by authorities because the manner in which the broker is compensated lends itself to fraud.

Listing, Open—A nonexclusive listing given by an owner to as many different brokers as desired. Only the broker who finds the buyer is entitled to a commission, and a sale automatically terminates all other open listings. Under an open listing the broker must be prepared to prove he or she was the procuring cause of the sale.

Littoral Land—Land which has as a boundary a body of standing water, such as an ocean or lake.

Littoral Owner—A landowner whose land borders on a lake.

Littoral Rights—The water rights of a littoral owner, including the right to make reasonable use of the water that is on or bordering his or her property.

Loan, Budget—A mortgage loan where the payments are set up to cover more than the principal and interests, normally for proportionate amounts of such things as property tax, fire insurance and special assessments.

Loan, Construction—A loan made to cover the cost of construction of buildings, usually with an agreement that the loan amount is advanced in installments as the work progresses.

Loan, Conventional—A real estate loan that is not insured or guaranteed by any government agency.

Loan, Interim—A temporary, short-term loan made to finance construction; usually paid off on completion of construction with the proceeds of a take-out loan.

Loan, Participation—A loan in which the lender receives some yield in addition to the specified interest rate, such as a percentage of income or profits, or some portion of ownership of the venture. Used primarily for large commercial projects.

Loan, Permanent—SEE: **Loan, Take-out.**

Loan, Seasoned—A loan with an established record of timely payment by the debtor.

Loan, Take-out—A long-term loan used to take over or pay off a short-term or interim loan.

Loan Assumption Fee—A fee charged to the buyer by the existing lender in return for permission to assume an existing loan.

Loan Broker—A licensed real estate agent who negotiates loans between borrowers and lenders, and for whom state law prescribes special standards of conduct.

Loan Correspondent—A representative who negotiates and services loans for other lenders. Loan correspondents are usually mortgage companies who sell loans to banks, savings and loans, and insurance companies at the secondary market level, while retaining the right to service the loan for a fee.

Loan Fee—A fee charged by lenders in return for the issuance of a loan; also called a loan origination fee.

Loan Origination Fee—SEE: **Loan Fee.**

Loan-to-value Ratio—This refers to the maximum loan the lender is willing to make in relation to the appraised value.

Lock-in Clause—A clause in a promissory note or contract for deed prohibiting full payment of the debt before the date set in the contract.

Lot—A parcel of land in a subdivision.

Lot, Block and Subdivision—A form of legal description; land is described by reference to a subdivision plat map recorded in the Office of the County Auditor or Recorder. Also called recorded plat or maps and plats description.

Love and Affection—The consideration often used when real estate is conveyed between family members with no money exchanged. The law recognizes love and affection as good consideration (as distinguished from valuable consideration, which is money, goods or services).

M.A.I.—Member of the Appraiser's Institute. The initials identify a member of the American Institute of Real Estate Appraisers of the National Association of Realtors.

Majority, Age of—Age at which persons become legally competent; in Minnesota, 18 years old.

Maker—A party to a promissory note; the borrower.

Manufactured Home—A structure that is transportable, is not affixed to real estate, is built on a permanent chassis, and is designed to be used as a dwelling with or without a permanent foundation.

Manufactured Home Sales Law—A state law requiring dealer licensing and providing warranties for buyers.

Maps and Plats—SEE: **Lot, Block and Subdivision.**

Market Data Approach—One of the three standard methods of appraisal; based on comparing similar properties. Also called the sales comparison or comparative analysis approach.

Market Price—The price actually paid for property. COMPARE: **Value, Market.**

Master Development Plan—An overall plan for the development of a city or county, which is used as a guide for the development of zoning regulations. Also called a comprehensive plan.

Material Fact—A material fact is one that the agent should realize would be likely to affect the principal's judgment in any decision relative to the subject of agency. Failure to disclose a material fact constitutes a violation of the agent's fiduciary duties.

Megalopolis—An extensive, heavily populated, continuously urban area, including any number of cities.

Merger—1. The union of two or more separate interests by the transfer of all the interests into one. 2. The acquisition by one owner of the title to adjacent parcels. If a dominant and servient tenement are merged under one ownership, the easement is no longer necessary and is terminated.

Meridians—Imaginary north-south lines which intersect base lines to form a starting point for the measurement of land in the government survey method of land description.

Metes—Measurements.

Metes and Bounds—A method of legal description. A metes and bounds description starts at an easily identifiable point of beginning, follows boundaries in specified directions for precise distances, and ultimately returns to the point of beginning.

Mill—One-tenth of one cent; the measure used to state the property tax rate. A tax rate of one mill on the dollar is the same as a rate of one-tenth of one percent of the assessed value of property.

Mineral Rights—Rights to subsurface lands and the profits from them. Mineral rights usually belong to the owner of the surface lands, unless reserved by a previous grantor or otherwise conveyed.

Minimum Property Requirements (MPR)—Requirements concerning the physical condition of a building; meeting the MPRs is a prerequisite to approval of financing from certain lenders.

Minnesota Human Rights Act—A state law that prohibits descrimination on the basis of race, color, religion, national origin, sex, marital status, status with regard to public assistance, disability or familial status in real property transactions.

Minnesota Landlord-Tenant Act—State law that sets out certain requirements that landlords and tenants must follow, such as rules concerning security deposits, required notice of termination, etc.

Minnesota Plain Language Act—State law requiring certain consumer contracts to be written in a clear and coherent manner, using words of common, everyday meaning.

Minor—A person who has not reached the age at which the law recognizes a general contractual capacity; in Minnesota, a person under 18.

Monument—A visible marker, natural or artificial, used to establish the lines and boundaries of a survey. Natural monuments can include boulders, marked trees, streams or rivers; artificial (man-made) monuments might take the form of stakes, wood or steel posts, or a cement slab.

Mortgage—A document that makes specified real property security for a loan. Parties to the agreement are the mortgagor (borrower) and mortgagee (lender).

Mortgage, Adjustable-Rate (ARM)—A mortgage with an interest rate that is adjusted at specific intervals.

Mortgage, Assumption of—Taking over the primary liability on an existing mortgage.

Mortgage, Balloon—A mortgage that provides for payments that do not fully amortize the loan by the loan's maturity date. The balance of the mortgage is then due in one lump sum (balloon payment) at the end of the term.

Mortgage, Blanket—A mortgage that covers more than one piece of real estate.

Mortgage, Budget—A mortgage with payments that include amounts for property taxes and insurance (in addition to principal and interest).

Mortgage, Chattel—A mortgage of personal property. It has been replaced in states which have adopted the Uniform Commercial Code by the security agreement.

Mortgage, First—The mortgage that is superior in right to any other on a property. Without a subordination agreement, this will normally be the one that is recorded first. COMPARE: **Mortgage, Junior.**

Mortgage, Hard Money—A mortgage given to a lender in exchange for cash, as opposed to credit.

Mortgage, Junior—A mortgage with lower lien priority than another mortgage on the same property; a second mortgage (or third, fourth, etc.). COMPARE: **Mortgage, First.** SEE: **Lien Priority.**

Mortgage, Open-end—A mortgage which permits the borrower to reborrow the money paid on the principal, usually up to the original amount, without rewriting the mortgage.

Mortgage, Package—A mortgage used in home financing that is secured by both the real property and certain items of personal property, such as appliances, drapes, carpeting, etc.

Mortgage, Purchase Money—1. A mortgage given by a buyer to a seller for part or all of the purchase price of the property. 2. Sometimes used more generally to refer to any mortgage given in exchange for a loan that is used to purchase the mortgaged property (as opposed to a mortgage given on property the borrower already owns).

Mortgage, Reverse Annuity—A mortgage where the lender pays the loan proceeds to the borrower in monthly payments.

Mortgage, Satisfaction of—The instrument given to the mortgagor by the mortgagee when the debt has been paid in full, acknowledging that the debt has been paid and consenting to discharge of the mortgage.

Mortgage, Senior—A mortgage which has a higher lien priority than other liens. COMPARE: **Mortgage, Junior.**

Mortgage, Wraparound—A mortgage which secures a loan that includes the amount of the balance due on an existing loan.

Mortgage Company—A loan correspondent that deals in real estate loans that are readily saleable in the secondary mortgage market.

Mortgagee—The receiver of the mortgage; the lender of the money secured by the mortgage.

Mortgaging Clause—The clause in a mortgage that describes the security interest which will be conveyed to the mortgagee.

Mortgagor—A person who mortgages his or her property to another; the maker of a mortgage.

Mutual Agreement—When all parties approve or assent to the terms of a contract freely. One of four essential elements to any valid contract; the others include capacity, lawful objective and consideration.

Mutuality—SEE: **Mutual Agreement.**

Multiple Listing Service—An organization of brokers who share their exclusive listings.

N.A.R.—National Association of Realtors.

Narrative Report—A thorough appraisal report in which the appraiser summarizes factual material, techniques and appraisal methods used, to convince the reader of the soundness of the estimate. It is a more comprehensive report than the form report or the estimate given in a simple letter or certificate.

National Environmental Policy Act (NEPA)—Federal legislation which regulates all development by governmental agencies and all private development that requires a governmental permit or approval.

Natural Person—An individual, a private person, as distinguished from an artificial person, such as a corporation.

Natural Servitude—A legal doctrine which states that a property owner is liable for any damages caused by diversion or channeling of flood waters from his or her property onto someone else's.

Negligence—A breach of duty caused by failure to exercise reasonable care.

Negotiable Instrument—An instrument containing an unconditional promise to pay a certain sum of money on demand or at a specified time, to order or to the bearer. It can be a check, promissory note, bond, draft or stock.

Net Proceeds—The actual amount of money a seller will receive from the sale after costs and expenses have been paid.

Nominal Interest Rate—The interest rate stated in a promissory note. SEE: **Annual Percentage Rate.**

Nonconforming Use—A property use that does not conform to current zoning requirements, but is allowed because the land was being used in that way before the present zoning ordinance was enacted.

Notary Public—An appointed officer whose primary function is to attest and certify the acknowledgment made by another when signing documents such as deeds and mortgages.

Note, Demand—A note that is due whenever the holder of the note demands payment.

Note, Installment—A promissory note that calls for periodic payments of principal and interest until the debt is fully paid.

Note, Joint—A note signed by two or more persons with joint and several liability for payment; that is, each can be required to pay the full amount, not merely his or her share.

Note, Promissory—A written promise to repay a debt.

Note, Straight—A promissory note in which only interest payments are made during the term of the note, and the entire principal is due in one lump sum at maturity.

Notice, Actual—Actual knowledge acquired when given express information of a fact.

Notice, Constructive—Knowledge of a fact implied by law, based on a presumption of notice because the fact could be discovered by reasonable diligence or inspection of public records. Also called notice to the world.

Notice of Default—A notice sent by a secured creditor to a debtor, informing the debtor of a breach of the loan agreement.

Notice of Non-responsibility—A notice which, if recorded and posted on the property in a timely manner, will protect a property owner from the effect of mechanics' liens filed for work which was not requested by the owner.

Notice of Sale—A notice sent to a defaulting borrower informing him or her that foreclosure proceedings have been started against the property.

Notice to Quit—A notice to a tenant, telling him or her to vacate rented property.

Novation—The substitution of a new party for one of the original parties to a contract, or substitution of a new obligation for an old one.

Obligatory Advances—Disbursements from construction loan funds that the lender is obligated to make (by prior agreement with the builder) when the builder has completed certain phases of construction.

Obsolescence—Any loss in value due to reduced desirability or usefulness. There is functional obsolescence (factors within the property itself) and economic obsolescence (factors outside the property).

Offer—The terms of a potential contract as communicated by one party to another, showing the willingness of the person making it to enter into a contract under the stated terms.

Offer, Illusory—An offer which requires something more than simple acceptance in order to create a contract, and therefore is not a valid offer in the eyes of the law.

Offeree—One to whom an offer is made.

Offeror—One who makes an offer.

Oil and Gas Rights—The ownership rights to all oil and gas produced from wells on a piece of property.

Option—A right, given for valuable consideration, to purchase or lease property at a future date for a specified price and on specified terms.

Optionee—The person to whom an option is given.

Optionor—The person who gives an option.

Orientation—The placement of a house on its lot with regard to its exposure to the sun and wind, privacy from the street, and protection from outside noise.

"Or More"—A provision in a promissory note which permits an early payoff of the debt.

Overimprovement—An improvement to land that is more expensive than necessary.

Override Clause—A clause in a listing agreement providing that the broker will still be entitled to the commission if the property is sold during a specified period of time after the listing terminates, if the buyer is someone the broker dealt with during the listing term. Also called an extender clause, safety clause or carryover clause.

Ownership—The rights of an owner. Title to property, dominion over property. The right of possession and control, including the right to protect and defend such possession against intrusion or trespass.

Ownership, Concurrent—Ownership by more than one person at the same time.

Ownership in Severalty—Ownership by an individual person or entity; sole ownership.

Par—The accepted standard of comparison; average; face value; equal. A mortgage sold at the secondary market level for 97% of par has been sold for 3% less than the face amount of the loan.

Parcel—A specified lot or tract of real estate, particularly a specified part of a larger tract.

Partial Performance—A remedy in contract law used when one party has not completely accomplished all of the terms of the agreement. The other party agrees to accept the incomplete performance and consider the contract discharged.

Partial Satisfaction Clause—A clause in a blanket mortgage which requires the lender to release certain parcels from the blanket lien when agreed portions of the overall debt have been paid; frequently used by subdivision developers. Also called a partial release clause.

Partition Action—A court action to divide property among co-owners (such as joint tenants or tenants in common), normally occurring when one owner wishes to divide and the others do not, or when the co-owners cannot come to agreement as to how the division should be made. If the court cannot practically divide the property physically, as in the case of one house owned by six co-owners, the court will order a sale and divide the proceeds.

Partner, General—A partner who has the authority to manage and contract for a general or limited partnership, and who is fully and personally liable for debts of the partnership.

Partnership—According to the Uniform Partnership Act, "an association of two or more persons to carry on, as co-owners, a business for profit." Although a partnership may be operated under an assumed name or under the surnames of the partners, it is regarded as a collection of individuals and, unlike a corporation, does not have a separate existence.

Partnership, General—A form of business organization in which each member has an equal right to manage the business and collect profits, as well as an equal responsibility for the debts of the business.

Partnership, Limited—A business arrangement which limits certain of the partners' liability to the amount they invested. Usually a limited partner is not permitted to have a voice in managing the company; his or her role is primarily that of an investor. The limited partnership must have at least one managing partner (general partner), and the partnership agreement must be recorded.

Party Wall—A wall located on the boundary line between two adjoining parcels of land which is used or intended to be used by the owners of both properties.

Patent—The instrument used to convey federal or state government land to a private individual.

Payee—A party to a promissory note; the lender.

Per Annum—Annual rate of an expense.

Percolation Test—A test to determine the ability of the ground to absorb or drain water; used to determine the suitability of the site for construction, particularly for installation of a septic tank system.

Per Diem—Daily rate of an expense.

Personal Property—Any property which is not real property; movable property not affixed to land; also called chattels or personalty.

Personalty—Personal property.

Physical Deterioration—Loss in value (depreciation) resulting from wear and tear, deferred maintenance, etc.

Physical Life—Estimated time a building will remain structurally sound and capable of being used.

Plain Language Act—SEE: **Minnesota Plain Language Act.**

Plaintiff—The party who brings or starts a lawsuit; the one who sues.

Planned Unit Development (PUD)—A development designed for intensive use of the land, combining a high density of dwellings with maximum utilization of open space.

Planning Commission—A local governmental agency created to direct and control the use and development of the land by recommending zoning ordinances, adopting a master development plan, etc.

Plat—A detailed map of a large tract (usually a subdivision), recorded in the county where the land is located.

Plat Book—A public book of maps of subdivided land, showing the blocks, lots and parcels.

Plot Plan—A plan showing lot dimensions and the layout of improvements (such as buildings and landscaping) on a property site.

Plottage—The consolidation of several parcels of land into one, resulting in greater utility and consequent higher value.

Point of Beginning—A landmark used as the initial reference point in a metes and bounds description.

Points—SEE: **Discount Points.**

Police Power—The power of the state and local governments to enact and enforce laws for the general welfare of the public. Since the exercise of the police power is merely regulating and not taking private property, no compensation is paid to the owner.

Possession—The holding and peaceful enjoyment of property. In the case of a lease, the tenant is in actual possession; the owner has constructive possession by right of title.

Possessory Rights—Rights to occupy and use land; not necessarily ownership of land.

Potable Water—Water that is safe to drink.

Power of Attorney—A written instrument authorizing one person (the attorney in fact) to act as another's agent to the extent stated in the instrument. If it authorizes action in a real estate transaction (such as signing a deed on behalf of the principal), the power of attorney must be recorded.

Power of Sale Clause—A clause in a mortgage that gives the mortgagee the right to foreclose by advertisement (rather than having to go to court for a judicial foreclosure).

Prepayment Penalty—The amount the debtor must pay the creditor as a penalty for paying off a debt before maturity. Not permitted in FHA or VA loans.

Prepayment Privilege—The right of a borrower to pay off a loan before it is due, in the absence of a prepayment penalty clause.

Prescription—A method of acquiring a right in real property (normally an intangible right such as an easement) by open, notorious, continuous, and uninterrupted use hostile to the will of the owner, for the prescribed period of time (in Minnesota, fifteen years). COMPARE: **Adverse Possession.**

Primary Mortgage Market—The market where loan transactions are arranged directly between lenders and borrowers. COMPARE: **Secondary Mortgage Market.**

Prime Rate—The interest rate a bank charges its largest and most desirable customers.

Principal—1. One of the parties to a transaction, such as the buyer or seller of a home. 2. One who employs an agent in a principal-agent relationship. 3. The basic amount of a debt, as opposed to the interest.

Principal Meridian—In the government survey system, an area's principal or prime meridian is the north-south line used as a reference line for numbering ranges in that area.

Principal Residence Property—Any real estate an owner actually lives in as his or her principal dwelling. A person can only have one principal residence at any one time.

Private Restrictions—Restrictions on the use of land which are contained in private deeds or contracts; the restrictions apply only to the parties to the particular agreement and their successors in interest.

Privity—A relationship between people having simultaneous or successive interests in a right or property. For example, the dominant and servient tenants in an easement agreement are in privity to one another; so are the seller and buyer of a property.

Probate—A judicial proceeding to determine the validity of a will and to distribute the assets of a decedent. An estate is still subject to a probate action to satisfy any creditors' claims and to distribute assets, even if the decedent dies without a will.

Probate Court—The court which oversees the distribution of property under a will or intestate succession.

Procuring Cause—In a real estate transaction, the broker who produces a ready, willing, and able buyer at the agreed price and terms. A broker must be prepared to show he or she was the "procuring cause" of the sale if the listing agreement was non-exclusive.

Progression, Principle of—An appraisal principle which holds that a piece of property of lesser value tends to increase in value when placed in an area with properties of greater value. The opposite is the principle of regression.

Promissory Note—SEE: **Note, Promissory.**

Property—The rights of ownership in an object, such as the rights to use, possess, transfer or encumber the object. Property also refers to the object itself, the parcel of land or the automobile or whatever. Property is divided into two main classes, real and personal.

Property Held for Production of Income—Income-producing property, such as apartments and commercial buildings.

Property Manager—A person hired by a property owner to administer, merchandise, and maintain property, especially rental property.

Property Used in a Trade or Business—Property such as business sites and factories used in one's trade or business.

Proprietary Lease—In the cooperative form of ownership, the right of a stockholder/resident to occupy a particular unit.

Proprietorship, Individual or Sole—A business owned and operated by a single person.

Proration—The process of dividing or distributing proportionately.

Public Restriction—A law or governmental regulation limiting or restricting the use of real property.

Puffing—Superlative statements about the quality of a property that do not amount to factual representations. "The best buy in town," or "it's a fabulous location," are examples of puffing. Representations of this type, however inaccurate, are not actionable; that is, the person who said them cannot be sued for fraud, because the person who heard them should have been able to evaluate the accuracy of the statements.

Purchase Agreement—A contract for the purchase and sale of real property, in which the buyer promises to purchase and the seller promises to convey title. Upon signing the purchase agreement, the buyer usually makes an earnest money deposit as evidence of a good faith intention to go through with the purchase. Also called a contract of sale, deposit receipt, or earnest money agreement.

Quantity Survey Method—In appraisal, a method of estimating the replacement cost of a structure. It involves a detailed estimate of the quantities and grades of material used and their cost (i.e. 1,500 bricks at $0.12 each), the labor hours required and their cost, and overhead expenses such as insurance and contractor's profit. It is the most time-consuming of the three methods of replacement cost estimation. The other two methods are Unit-in-Place and Square Foot.

Quiet Enjoyment—The right of an owner or lessee legally in possession of property to the use and possession of the property without interference.

Quiet Title Action—A lawsuit to establish clear title to a piece of property or to remove a cloud on the title.

Range—In the Government Survey System, a strip of land six miles wide, running north and south.

Range Line—One of the north-south lines located six miles apart, used in the Government Survey System for the location and description of townships. They are meridians or longitude lines.

Ratification—The later confirmation or affirmation of an act that was not authorized when it was performed.

Real Estate—Land and all things affixed or appurtenant to land, including the improvements on the land and the rights that go with ownership of the land. Also called real property or realty. COMPARE: **Personal Property.**

Real Estate Education, Research and Recovery Fund (REERRF)—A fund made up of fees paid by real estate licensees and administered by the Commissioner of Commerce, which is used for education of the public and licensees, research, the Advisory Task Force, and other related purposes. The fund is also used to satisfy unpaid claims against licensees.

Real Estate Investment Trust—An unincorporated business association, with a minimum of 100 investors, which (if it meets certain requirements) is allowed to pass profits through to investors without paying corporate tax. The investors have limited liability.

Real Property—SEE: **Real Estate.**

Realtor—A broker or salesperson who is an active member of a state or local real estate board which is affiliated with the National Association of Realtors.

Realty—SEE: **Real Estate.**

Reasonable Use Doctrine—A limitation of riparian and littoral water rights which states that there is no right to waste water.

Recapture—1. Recovery by the investor of money invested in real estate. 2. Recapture clauses are of two types. One type, often found in percentage leases, especially shopping center leases, allows the lessor to terminate the lease and regain the premises if a certain minimum volume of business is not maintained. The second type, found in ground leases, allows the lessee to purchase the property after a specified period of time.

Reconciliation—The bringing together of the estimates obtained separately from three methods of appraisal to form a single final estimate of value.

Recording—Placing a document affecting the title to real property, such as a deed or mortgage, on file in the book of public records in the Office of the County Auditor or County Recorder for the county where the property is located. Placing such an instrument on file in the public records gives constructive notice (notice to all the world) of the existence of the instrument and its contents.

Rectangular Survey—Another name for the Government Survey System of land description. Sometimes called the Township and Range System.

Redemption, Equitable Right of—The right of a borrower to redeem property prior to the foreclosure sale, by paying the delinquent amount, together with interest and costs.

Redemption, Post-sale—SEE: **Redemption, Statutory.**

Redemption, Statutory—A borrower's right to redeem the property after the foreclosure sale, within the period set by statute (in Minnesota, six or twelve months).

Redlining—The refusal, for discriminatory reasons, to make loans on property located in a particular neighborhood.

Regression, Principle of—An appraisal principle that holds that a piece of property of greater value tends to lose value when placed in an area with properties of lesser value. Opposite of principle of progression.

Regulation Z—SEE: **Truth in Lending Act.**

Reinstate—To prevent a forced sale of security property by curing the default which is the basis for the foreclosure.

Release—The act or means of giving up a legal right.

Release Clause—1. A clause in a blanket mortgage or deed of trust which allows the borrower to get certain parcels of land released from the lien upon payment of a specific sum or a specific portion of the loan. 2. A clause in a real estate contract providing for a deed to a portion of the land to be delivered upon fulfillment of a certain segment of the contract. Also known as a deed release provision.

Reliction—The gradual withdrawal or recession of water, exposing land that was previously under water. The newly exposed land belongs to the riparian or littoral owner. Also called dereliction.

Remainderman—The holder of a future possessory interest in property, who will take possession and title upon the termination of a life estate.

Remise—To give up; a term used in quitclaim deeds.

Rent—Compensation paid by the tenant or occupant of real property to the owner in exchange for the use and possession of the property.

Rent, Contract—The actual rent that is currently being paid for a piece of property, in contrast to the economic rent.

Rent, Economic—The rent which a piece of property would bring on the open market at a given time, as contrasted with the actual rent being received (contract rent).

Rent, Ground—The earnings of improved property which are credited to the land itself after allowance is made for the earnings of the improvements.

Replacement Cost—In appraisal, the amount of money that would be needed (on the basis of current prices) to replace a structure with one having the same utility, but constructed with modern materials, design, etc. COMPARE: **Reproduction Cost.**

Reproduction Cost—The amount of money that would be needed (on the basis of current prices) to duplicate the structure being appraised, using the same or similar materials, design, quality of workmanship, layout, etc. COMPARE: **Replacement Cost.**

Rescission—In contract law, the remedy of abrogating, annulling, or terminating a contract and restoring the parties, as nearly as possible, to the positions they were in before entering the contract.

Reservation—A right retained by the grantor when conveying property; for example, mineral rights, an easement, or a life estate can be reserved in the deed.

Reserve Account—Money deposited with a lender for the purpose of paying property taxes and insurance premiums on land financed by the lender; also called an escrow account.

Resident Manager—A salaried manager of a single apartment building or complex who lives on the premises. A resident manager, unlike a property manager, is not required to have a real estate license.

Residual—1. A property's remaining value after the economic life of the improvements has been exhausted. 2. Commissions in the form of delayed payments (when a part of the commission is paid with each installment on a contract for deed, for example) are referred to as residuals.

R.E.S.P.A.—The Real Estate Settlement Procedures Act, a federal law that governs real estate closings.

Respondeat Superior, Doctrine of—A master (employer) is liable for the torts (civil wrongs) committed by a servant (employee) within the scope of his/her employment.

Restriction—A limitation on the use of real property. Restrictions may be private, such as restrictive covenants dealing with setbacks, or public, such as zoning ordinances.

Restrictive Covenant—Similar to a condition imposed in a deed, the restrictive covenant is a private agreement between the grantor and all subsequent grantees restricting the use or occupancy of the property being conveyed. Violations of covenants are stopped by court injunctions, but no reversion of title occurs.

Reversion—1. A future estate held by a grantor (or the grantor's heirs or assigns). 2. A transfer which takes effect immediately following the preceding estate.

Reverter—The person who holds an estate in reversion.

Revocation—The unilateral termination of an agency relationship by the principal. Can be held to be a breach of contract.

Rezone—SEE: **Zoning Amendment.**

Right of Rescission—A buyer's right to rescind after signing any contract to buy or lease a lot covered by ILSFDA.

Right of Way—A public or private easement giving the holder the right to pass over the land of another.

Riparian Land—Land that is bordered or crossed by a river, a stream, or other flowing surface waters. COMPARE: **Littoral Land.**

Riparian Owner—A person who owns riparian land.

Riparian Rights—The water rights of a riparian owner, including the right to make reasonable use of the water that flows past or across his or her property.

Running with the Land—Rights, restrictions, or covenants which affect successive owners of a parcel of land are said to run with the land.

Sale-Leaseback—A form of real estate financing in which the owner of industrial or commercial property sells the property and leases it back from the buyer, normally under a net lease in which the seller/lessee pays taxes, insurance, etc. In addition to certain tax advantages, the seller/lessee obtains more cash through the sale than would normally be possible by borrowing and mortgaging the property, since lenders will not often lend 100% of the value.

Savings and Loan Association—A type of depository financial institution whose main form of investment has traditionally been residential mortgage lending.

Savings Association Insurance Fund (SAIF)—A new federal agency which replaced the Federal Savings and Loan Insurance Corporation (FSLIC). SAIF insures deposits in savings and loan associations.

Scarcity—A limited or inadequate supply of something. Scarcity is one of the four elements of value. SEE: **Demand, Transferability,** and **Utility.**

Secondary Financing—A loan from any source used to make the required downpayment and/or pay closing costs in connection with a primary loan. A personal loan from a bank to pay the finance charges connected with a conventional home loan would be an example of secondary financing.

Secondary Mortgage Market—The process of buying and selling existing mortgages and trust deeds. Also known as the secondary money market.

Section—In the government survey system, a section is one mile square and contains 640 acres. There are 36 sections in a township.

Security Agreement—A document which creates a lien upon personal property being used to secure a loan.

Security Deposit—Defined in Minnesota as any deposit of money, the function of which is to secure the performance of a residential rental agreement. Most often required by landlords to insure payment of rent and protect the property against damage. Does not include a deposit that is exclusively an advance payment of rent.

Security Interest—The interest a secured creditor has in the personal property of a debtor. The interest created by a security agreement.

Seizin—Actual possession of real estate by one so entitled. Also called seizen and seisin.

SEPA—State Environmental Policy Act (similar to the NEPA) requiring the issuance of an environmental impact statement for all acts of local and state agencies that may have a significant impact on the environment. Applies to both private and government developments.

Separate Property—In a community property state, property belonging to a married person which is not community property; includes property acquired before marriage or by gift or devise after marriage.

Servant—An employee. SEE: **Master/servant relationship.**

Setback Ordinance—A local law prohibiting improvements from being erected within a certain distance from the property line.

Settlement—The fulfillment of promises made by the buyer and seller in the purchase agreement. Also called closing.

Settlement Statement—A document prepared by an escrow agent, which sets forth the financial details of a real estate transaction.

Severalty Ownership—Ownership by one person only, severed from anyone else.

Sheriff's Sale—A foreclosure sale.

Short Plat—The subdivision of a parcel of land into four or fewer lots is called short platting.

Soldier's and Sailor's Civil Relief Act—A federal law which protects persons in military service against foreclosure of property mortgaged before they entered the military, if their ability to repay the loan has been materially affected by their military service.

Special Assessment—A tax against certain parcels of land which have benefitted from a public improvement (such as a road, sewer, or street light), levied to cover the cost of the improvement. Also called an improvement tax.

Special Exception Permit—SEE: **Conditional Use Permit.**

Special Use Permit— SEE: **Conditional Use Permit.**

Specific Performance—A legal remedy in which a party to a contract is ordered by the court to actually perform the contract as agreed, or as nearly so as possible, rather than simply paying monetary damages.

Spot Zoning—A rezone of one property or a small area within a neighborhood.

Square Foot Method—In appraisal, a method of estimating the replacement cost of a structure; it involves multiplying the cost per square foot of a recently built comparable structure by the number of square feet in the subject structure.

S.R.A.—A member of the Society of Real Estate Appraisers.

S.R.E.A.—The Society of Real Estate Appraisers.

Statute—A written law of the federal government or of a state government.

Statute of Frauds—A law which requires certain types of contracts to be in writing in order to be enforceable.

Statute of Limitations—A law requiring certain legal actions to be brought within a specified time limit.

Statutory New Home Warranty Law—A state law that establishes that certain warranties are implied in every sale of a newly completed dwelling, and in every contract for the sale of a dwelling to be completed.

Steering—The channeling of prospective buyers or renters, based on race or other prohibited class, to or away from specific neighborhoods.

Subagent—An agent of an agent.

Subcontractor—A contractor who, at the request of the general contractor, provides a specific service, such as plumbing or drywalling, in connection with the overall construction project.

Subdivided Lands Act—A state law applying to subdivisions of ten or more parcels located outside a municipality and requiring that all prospective purchasers be given a public offering statement, and that interests be registered with the Commissioner of Commerce.

Subdivision—A piece of land divided into two or more parcels.

Subdivision Plat—SEE: **Plat.**

Subdivision Regulations—Local laws and regulations which must be complied with before land can be subdivided.

Subjacent Support—The support which the surface of land receives from the subsurface soil. COMPARE: **Lateral Support.**

Subject to—When a purchaser takes property subject to a trust deed or mortgage, he or she is not personally liable for paying off the loan; in case of default, however, the property can still be foreclosed on.

Sublease—A lease given by a lessee where he or she retains some portion of or interest in the leasehold, as opposed to an assignment of the entire leasehold interest.

Subordination Clause—A clause in a mortgage which permits a subsequent mortgage to take priority. Often found in instruments that secure land acquisition loans, in order to make it possible to secure construction financing with a first lien position.

Subrogation—The substitution of one person in the place of another with reference to a lawful claim or right. For instance, a title company that pays a claim on behalf of its insured, the property owner, is subrogated to any claim the owner successfully undertakes against the former owner.

Substitution, Principle of—This is a principle of appraisal stating that the maximum value of a piece of property is limited by the cost required to obtain another piece of property that is equally desirable and valuable, assuming there are no lengthy delays or costly incidental expenses involved in obtaining the substitute property.

Substitution of Liability—A buyer wishing to assume an existing loan may apply for lender approval to do so. Once approved, the buyer assumes liability for repayment of the loan, and the original borrower is released from liability.

Succession—Acquiring property through descent, by will or inheritance.

Sufferance—Acquiescence, implied permission, or passive consent through a failure to act, as opposed to express permission.

Supply and Demand, Principle of—This economic principle holds that value varies directly with demand and inversely with supply; that is, the greater the demand the greater the value, and the greater the supply the smaller the value.

Support Rights—The right to the support of land that is furnished by adjacent (lateral) or underlying (subjacent) land.

Surplus Productivity, Principle of— According to this principle, the net income from a property which remains after paying the costs of labor, organization, and capital is credited to the land and tends to set its value.

Surrender—Yielding or giving up an estate, such as a life estate or leasehold, before its expiration.

Survey—The process of locating and measuring the boundaries and determining the area of a parcel of land.

Survivorship, Right of—The right of surviving joint tenants to automatically acquire the interest of a deceased joint tenant. A distinguishing characteristic of joint tenancy.

Syndicate—An association of two or more people formed to make and operate an investment. This can be a corporation, real estate investment trust, or partnership. A limited partnership is the most common type of syndicate.

Tacking—The process whereby the period of use required for adverse possession is satisfied by two or more adverse possessors in succession.

Tax, Conveyance—An ad valorem tax which is charged when property is transferred from one owner to another; also called an excise tax. Minnesota's state deed tax is an example of a conveyance tax.

Tax, Excise—A tax on the production, sale, or consumption of certain commodities.

Tax, General Real Estate—Property taxes which apply to all land on an ad valorem basis.

Tax, Improvement—SEE: **Special Assessment.**

Tax, Mortgage Registration—A Minnesota tax charged on all new mortgages of real property. Currently 23 cents on each $100 of debt.

Tax, Property—An ad valorem tax levied on real or personal property.

Tax, State Deed—A Minnesota tax charged on the difference between the purchase price and the assumed mortgage when real estate is sold. If no mortgage is assumed, the tax is based on the total purchase price. Currently $1.65 per $500.

Tax Foreclosure—Foreclosure by a government agency to obtain payment of delinquent taxes.

Tax-free Exchange—A transaction in which one piece of real estate is traded for another in compliance with certain rules, which allows one or both of the property owners to defer payment of some or all of the federal income tax that would otherwise be owed on any gain from the transaction. The real estate exchanged must be income-producing or investment property.

Tax Sale—Sale of property under a tax foreclosure.

Tenancy—Possession of land under right or title. The possessor is the tenant.

Tenancy, Joint—A form of concurrent ownership of property by two or more people, with the distinctive characteristic of right of survivorship. Joint tenants each hold an equal interest.

Tenancy, Month-to-Month—SEE: **Estate at Will.**

Tenancy, Periodic—SEE: **Estate at Will**

Tenancy at Sufferance—SEE: **Estate at Sufferance.**

Tenancy at Will—SEE: **Estate at Will.**

Tenancy by the Entirety—A special form of joint tenancy used for married couples. Not used in Minnesota.

Tenancy in Common—The most basic form of co-ownership of real property. There are no restrictions on the division of ownership, and there is no right of survivorship. All owners are necessary to transfer a complete parcel.

Tenant, Dominant—The owner of a dominant tenement.

Tenant, Servient—The owner of a servient tenement.

Tender—An unconditional offer of performance by one of the parties to a contract, as when the buyer under a purchase agreement offers to pay the purchase price, usually by depositing it in escrow. Failure of the seller to accept the money and perform the contractual obligation would place the seller in default.

Tenements—All the rights of a permanent nature associated with the land which pass with the land, such as buildings or air rights.

Tenement, Dominant—Also called a dominant estate, it is property that receives benefits from a servient tenement (estate) by means of an easement appurtenant.

Tenement, Servient—Land burdened by an easement in favor of another property (the dominant tenement).

Tenure—The period of time during which a person holds certain rights with respect to real property.

Term—A prescribed period of time. A loan that is to be paid back over thirty years has a thirty-year term.

Testament—A will.

Testate—The condition of leaving a will upon death. The person leaving the will is the testator.

Testator—A person who makes a will.

Tier—SEE: **Township Tier.**

Tight Money Market—A time when there is low availability of loan funds, resulting in high interest rates and discount profits.

Time is of the Essence—A clause in a contract which means that performance on the exact dates specified is an essential element of the contract; failure to perform on time is a material breach.

Timeshare—A method of ownership in which co-owners each have an exclusive right to possess the property for a specified time period each year.

Title—Lawful ownership of or right to land. Also, the document that evidences that ownership (such as a deed).

Title, After-Acquired—When a grantor attempts to convey property he or she does not have title to, but later obtains title, it is called after-acquired title. If the attempted conveyance was by a deed which warranted good title, such as a general warranty deed or a limited special warranty deed, the title acquired by the grantor passes automatically to the grantee.

Title, Chain of—The history of ownership, conveyances and encumbrances that have affected title to a particular parcel of real estate.

Title, Clear—A good title to property, free from encumbrances or defects; a merchantable or marketable title.

Title, Equitable—The vendee's interest in property under a contract for deed. Also called equitable interest.

Title, Imperfect—Defective or incomplete title. An adverse possessor has imperfect title until he or she obtains a quitclaim deed from the owner of the land adversely possessed, or prevails in a quiet title action confirming that the requirements for acquiring title by continuous use have been met.

Title, Marketable—Title free and clear of objectionable liens or encumbrances, so that a reasonably prudent person with full knowledge of the facts would not hesitate to purchase the property. Also called merchantable title.

Title Opinion—An attorney's professional opinion of the current condition of a title.

Title Plant—A collection of duplicates (usually microfilmed) of all instruments of public record affecting real estate in the county, maintained by a title company in each county in which the title company operates.

Title Report—A report issued by a title company which discloses the condition of the title to a specific parcel of land.

Title Report, Preliminary—A title report issued early in the transaction for the purpose of revealing all matters that presently affect the title. It differs from an abstract in that the latter will show all incidents related to the title from the original grant to the present.

Title Search—An inspection of the public record to determine all rights to and encumbrances on a piece of property.

Title Theory—This theory states that the lender is considered to hold legal title to the mortgaged property while the debt is being repaid. In most states, lien theory is followed instead.

Topography—The contour of the surface of the land, such as level or hilly.

Torrens System—A system for the registration of land used in Minnesota and some other states to verify title without the necessity of a title search. It is an alternative to title insurance, since title to the land is free of all encumbrances or claims not registered with the title registrar.

Tort—A civil wrong (other than breach of contract) for which there is a remedy at law.

Township—In the government survey system, a parcel of land six miles square containing 36 sections.

Township Lines—East-west lines, spaced six miles apart, used to describe land in the government survey system.

Township Tier—An east-west strip of land, six miles wide and bounded on the north and south by township lines.

Tract—1. A parcel of land of undefined size. 2. In the government survey system, an area comprised of 16 townships; 24 miles by 24 miles.

Trade Fixtures—Articles of personal property annexed to real property by a tenant that are necessary for his or her trade or business; the tenant is allowed to remove them at the end of the lease.

Transferability—An object is transferable if ownership and possession of it can be conveyed from one person to another. Transferability is one of the four elements of value. SEE: **Utility, Scarcity,** and **Demand.**

Trespass—An unlawful physical invasion of property owned by another.

Trust Account—A bank account in which a broker deposits trust funds, to keep them segregated from the broker's own money.

Trust Deed (or Deed of Trust)—A document used in some states (not Minnesota) in financing the purchase of real estate, similar to a mortgage. Under the trust deed, power to sell the secured property on behalf of the beneficiary (lender) in the event of default by the trustor (borrower) is given to an independent third party, the trustee. A trust deed can be foreclosed at a trustee's sale. Judicial intervention is not required, and there is no period of redemption following the trustee's sale. A trustee's deed is issued after the sale.

Trust Funds—Money or things of value received by a real estate agent on behalf of a principal or another in the performance of any acts for which a real estate license is required, and not belonging to the agent but being held for the benefit of others.

Trustee—SEE: **Trust Deed.**

Trustee in Bankruptcy—An individual appointed by the court to handle the assets of a person in bankruptcy.

Trustee's Sale—SEE: **Trust Deed.**

Trustor—SEE: **Trust Deed.**

Truth in Lending Act—A federal law, implemented by the Federal Reserve Board's Regulation Z, which requires lenders to disclose certain information to consumer credit borrowers. The most important required disclosures are the total finance charge and the annual percentage rate.

Underimprovement—An improvement which, because of its deficiency in cost or size, is not the most profitable use of the land and is therefore not the highest and best use. Opposite of overimprovement. Both are misplaced improvements.

Underwriting—In real estate lending, the lender's analysis of risk to determine the probability that the borrower will repay the loan as agreed, matching the risk to an appropriate term and rate of return.

Undivided Interest (UDI)—A co-tenant's right to possession of the whole property, rather than to any particular part. Co-tenants' financial interests may be equal, as in a joint tenancy, or unequal, as in many tenancies in common, but they still have equal rights to possess and use the whole property.

Undue Influence—Exerting excessive pressure on someone so as to overpower the person's free will and prevent him or her from acting according to rational decision. A contract entered into as a result of undue influence is voidable by the victim.

Uniform Commercial Code—A body of law adopted in slightly varying versions in most states, which attempts to standardize commercial law dealing with such things as promissory notes and sales or mortgages of personal property. Its main applications to real estate law concern security interests in fixtures and bulk transfers.

Uniform Vendor and Purchaser Risk Act— A law that applies to purchase agreements in Minnesota. Under the act, if there is a material destruction of the property, and the buyer has not taken possession and title has not passed, the seller cannot enforce the contract.

Unilateral Contract—A contract that binds only one party and is accepted by performance. An option agreement is an example of a unilateral contract.

Unit-In-Place Method—In appraisal, a method of computing the replacement cost of an improvement by estimating the cost of each component (foundation, chimney, roof, etc.) and then adding the costs of all components to determine the total replacement cost. The estimated cost of each component includes material, labor and overhead.

Unjust Enrichment—An undeserved benefit. A court of equity will not allow a remedy (such as forfeiture of a contract for deed) if the remedy will result in unjust enrichment of one of the parties.

Unlawful Detainer—A summary legal action to regain possession of real property, normally from a tenant who is in default under the lease; an eviction lawsuit.

Useful Life—The period over which a property is economically useful to the owner. Also called economic life.

Usury—Charging an interest rate higher than permitted by law.

Utility—The ability of an object to satisfy some need and/or arouse a desire for possession. One of the four elements of value. SEE: **Demand, Scarcity,** and **Transferability.**

V.A.—Veteran's Administration.

Vacancy Factor—An allowance for anticipated vacancies in a rental project, such as an apartment house. It is usually a percentage of the potential gross income.

Valid—The legal classification of a contract that is binding and enforceable in a court of law.

Valuation—The act or process of estimating value; essentially synonymous with appraisal.

Value—Generally, how much something is worth. There are many different kinds of value (see below); in real estate, the term is most often used to refer to market value.

Value, Assessed—The value placed on property by the taxing authority (County Assessor) for the purposes of taxation.

Value, Book—The amount at which an asset is carried on the owner's accounting books, equal to the cost, plus improvements and additions, less accrued depreciation. It is normally the adjusted book value or adjusted cost basis.

Value, Face—The value of an instrument, such as a bond, note or security, which is indicated on the face of the instrument itself.

Value, Market—The amount of money that a piece of property would bring if placed on the open market for a reasonable period of time, with a buyer willing but not forced to buy, and a selling willing but not forced to sell, and both buyer and seller fully informed as to the possible uses of the property. Also called value in exchange or objective value.

Value, Objective—SEE: **Value, Market.**

Value, Salvage—The estimated amount for which a structure can be sold at the end of its economic or useful life.

Value, Subjective—The value of a product in the eyes of a particular person.

Value, Utility—The value to an owner or user; a type of subjective value. Also called value in use.

Value in Exchange—SEE: **Value, Market.**

Value in Use—SEE: **Value, Utility.**

Variable Interest Rate—An interest rate on a loan that is periodically adjusted.

Variance—Permission obtained from the zoning authority to use or build on land in a manner contrary to existing zoning ordinances.

Vendee—The buyer or purchaser, particularly someone buying property under a contract for deed.

Vendor—The seller, particularly someone selling property under a contract for deed.

Vested—An immediate fixed right, interest or title in real property, even though the right to possession might not occur until some time in the future.

Void—Having no legal force or effect.

Voidable—That which can be nullified or adjudged void (particularly a contract) but which is valid until some action is taken to void it. A voidable contract must be disaffirmed by the innocent party if he or she wishes to avoid performance. Inaction can result in ratification of the contract.

Waiver—The voluntary relinquishment or surrender of a right.

Warranty, Implied—In the sale of property, a warranty created by operation of law irrespective of any intention of the seller to create it.

Warranty Forever—A promise that the grantor is responsible and will bear the expense of defending the title if anyone asserts a claim against it.

Warranty of Habitability—A promise implied in every residential lease that the landlord will keep the premises in habitable condition: safe, functional, and reasonably sanitary.

Waste—The destruction, damage, or material alteration of property by one in possession of the land who holds less than a fee estate, such as a life tenant or lessee.

Water Rights—The right to use water from a source such as a river or lake. Water rights appurtenant to real estate are riparian rights or littoral rights.

Water Table—The level at which water may be found, either at the surface or below.

Will—The written declaration of an individual that stipulates how his or her estate will be disposed of after death. Also called a testament.

Will, Holographic—A will written, dated and signed entirely in the testator's handwriting, which was not witnessed. Not recognized in Minnesota.

Will, Nuncupative—An oral will made in contemplation of death, often by soldiers on the field of battle. Cannot be used to transfer real property.

Will, Written—A will which meets the statutory requirements for a valid will; must be signed by witnesses.

Without Recourse—A qualified or conditional endorsement on a negotiable instrument which removes the endorser from liability on the instrument.

Words of Conveyance (Granting Clause)—The portion of a deed containing the words that actually convey the property to the new owner.

Writ of Execution—A court order directing a public officer, normally the sheriff, to seize and sell property to satisfy a debt.

Yield—The return of profit to an investor on an investment, stated as a percentage of the amount invested.

Zone—An area of land set off for a particular use or uses, subject to certain restrictions.

Zoning—Government regulation, through zoning ordinances and regulations, of the uses of property within specified areas.

Zoning Amendment—A change in the zoning law of a community, requiring the approval of the local legislative body. Also called a rezone.

INDEX

(continued)